Franklin Education Foundation
Journal of Quantitative and Qualitative Research

Contents:

ANALYSES OF ASIAN-AMERICAN AND ASIAN DIABETIC PATIENTS: GENDER, AGE, MEDICAL PROCEDURES, AND MEDICATIONS 4

ANALYSES OF FACTORS THAT ARE RELATED TO THE JUDGEMENT OF NOVELS 10

ANALYSES OF HOW READERS EVALUATE SPECULATIVE AND LITERARY FICTION: MAJOR THEMES AND GENERAL PRINCIPLES ...15

ANALYSES ON THE MENTAL-HEALTH ISSUES OF HIGH-SCHOOL STUDENTS: TYPES, SOURCES, AND VIEWS 22

COFFEE-EFFICIENT COEFFICIENT FOR ENVIRONMENTAL PROTECTION: THE CORRELATIONS BETWEEN GROSS DOMESTIC PRODUCT AND WASTE FOR COFFEE-PRODUCING AND COFFEE-CONSUMING COUNTRIES 30

COMPARING MACHINE LEARNING ALGORITHMS FOR TEMPERATURE PREDICTION WITH FUEL PRODUCTION AND CONSUMPTION 35

DRAGON REBORN: COGNITIVE IMPACT OF USER INTERFACE AND AESTHETICS ON PLAYER ENGAGEMENT 43

FACTORS THAT INFLUENCE STUDENT BEHAVIOR REGARDING ACADEMIC INTEGRITY 55

FROM FOOD WASTE TO FOOD GUARD: CREATING A NOVEL CHITOSAN BIOPLASTIC WITH NANOPARTICLE COATING AND ITS UNIQUE EFFECT ON WATER RESISTANCE AND FOOD PRESERVATION 74

GENDER, FASHION, INCOME, AND BRAND IMAGE...83

HIDDEN CONNECTIONS: THE FACTORS THAT ARE ASSOCIATED WITH PUBLIC FAMILIARITY AND OPINIONS OF EMERGING, PROMINENT MEDICAL TECHNOLOGIES 90

KNOW KETO OR NO KETO? A META-ANALYSIS OF THE KETOGENIC DIET...116

LIBRARY LIABILITY: ANALYSES ON AGE, GENDER, BOOK CONTENT, AND OPINIONS OF CENSORSHIP 126

ON WIND ENERGY CIRCUITS: PERFORMANCE COMPARISON AND ENHANCEMENT...137

POSSIBLE SOLUTIONS TO HOMELESSNESS FOR CALIFORNIANS WITH MENTAL HEALTH ISSUES................................144

RECOMMENDATION ALGORITHMS: PROCESS OF IMPLEMENTATION AND ACCURACY 149

THE EFFECTIVENESS OF MOTORSPORTS ADVERTISEMENTS ON CURRENT ADOLESCENT RACE FANS COMPARED TO NEW ADOLESCENT FANS...154

USING SVM ANALYSIS TO COMPARE THE RELATIVE IMPORTANCE OF UNEMPLOYMENT ON TECHNOLOGY STOCKS AND RETAIL STOCKS...166

Franklin Education Foundation
Journal of Quantitative and Qualitative Research

Research has become all the more important for tackling the multifaced new challenges and exploring exciting opportunities in our increasingly fast changing world. It has been a vital part of the mission of higher education in the United States. In institutions of higher education, especially top universities, research is becoming an integral part of the educational experience of undergraduate students. At the University of California, Irvine, for example, a majority of students participate in a wide range of research programs and activities.

The 2021 Franklin summer internship and research program offered high school students a precious educational opportunity to gain valuable research experience through their own exciting research projects. Having attended numerous activities of the program from its beginning to its conclusion, I think it was a big success.

It was a well-designed program, covering foundational research issues, such as methodology and ethics and introducing important skills in areas like software programming, writing, data collection, and critical thinking. The program was not just focused on STEM fields but also made a fruitful effort to expose students to research in the Humanities and Social Sciences. This is significant because many of the challenges we face in our life and society cannot be solved with science and technology alone but require interdisciplinary approaches and solutions.

The success of the program was also because of the dedication and professionalism of the teachers. Teaching students understand fundamental issues in research, they also introduced primary sources like databases in areas like medicine/health to students and helped them from the design of their individual project to its implementation. In addition, the summer program recruited outside experts from research organizations such as the UCLA and UC San Diego gave students access to professional expertise.

Finally, the summer internship and research program's success reflected the diligent and fruitful efforts of students. In their research projects, students asked and explored important topics different fields, ranging from self-driving cars to programs in public schools, using refreshing they collected and analysed themselves. The student research papers I have read are remarkably well-written and thoughtful and would earn a good grade in college classes.

I am glad that the Franklin Education Foundation will publish student papers. The collection of these papers will illustrate the fruit of the extraordinary work of students and serve as a source of inspiration for other students in the future.

Professor Yong Chen
Franklin Research Internship Program Mentor

The high school experience has a great influence on a person's life – in terms of career choices, personal passions, and even the direction of one's lifelong journey. Take my own experience, for example, of coming across a small book during high school, describing medicine, molecules that can treat diseases. The book illustrated the chemical composition as well as the structure of the molecules. It ushered me into a new world of structures and functions. As a result, I developed a lifelong passion in associating chemical structures and how they treat diseases, and in turn, improving patients' lives.

The Franklin Research Internship Program (FRIP), similarly, provides this kind of opportunity to high school students. Motivated students can seek and find their own passions in humanities, science, technology, and mathematics. Students have gained hands-on research experience on trendy topics in a myriad of fields, including artificial neural network, aerodynamic engineering, molecular biology, human psychology, and physics.

I feel so honored to meet some of these wonderful students in person. Each of them exhibits a unique set of talents. Some were able to grasp psychological ideas better than those in a college class; others were able to author articles with writing skills on par with a postdoctoral fellow; and still others were able to design artificial neural networks and train them for solving real-life problems.

Assembled in this journal is the resulting papers of the projects completed by some of these talented students. I sincerely hope that this publication provides a sound platform for the career development of these students and foreshadows a bright future for their scientific research pursuits. With this, I wish the best of success for all students who have already participated in FRIP and others who will join us in this program in the future.

Dr. Ge Peng
Franklin Research Internship Program Mentor

Analyses of Asian-American and Asian Diabetic Patients: Gender, Age, Medical Procedures, and Medications

Ariel Zhou

1. Introduction

In a world where diabetes prevalence is reaching epidemic proportions, understanding its multifaceted impact on global health becomes imperative. Diabetes mellitus, commonly referred to as diabetes, is a group of metabolic disorders characterized by chronic high blood sugar levels resulting from issues with insulin secretion, action, or both. This leads to abnormal metabolic processes involving carbohydrates, lipids, and proteins. Insufficient insulin levels or insulin resistance in target tissues, such as muscles, fat, and the liver, contribute to these abnormalities (Darwish & Kharroubi, 2015).

Diabetes involves various pathogenic processes, ranging from autoimmune destruction of pancreatic β-cells leading to insulin deficiency, to abnormalities causing resistance to insulin action. These abnormalities affect carbohydrate, fat, and protein metabolism, primarily due to insufficient insulin action on target tissues. This deficiency arises from inadequate insulin secretion and/or reduced tissue responsiveness to insulin along the complex hormonal pathways. Often, patients exhibit impaired insulin secretion and defects in insulin action simultaneously, making it challenging to determine the primary cause of hyperglycemia (Kuzuya, Nakagawa, Satoh, Kanazawa, Iwamoto, Kobayashi, Nanjo, Sasaki, Seino, Ito, Shima, Nonaka, & Kadowaki, 2022; American Diabetes Association, 2014). Excess fructose consumption is linked to diabetes and cardiovascular disease risk as well. High fructose intake can cause hyperglycemia, dyslipidemia, atherosclerosis, and sometimes hypertension (Delbridge, Benson, Ritchie, & Mellor, 2016).

Diabetes mellitus, often undetected, is associated with poor health care, leaving 46.5% of those affected unaware of their condition. Alarmingly, current projections indicate that 10% of the global population already lives with diabetes, and by 2025, an estimated 300 million people will be affected. About 75% of people with diabetes are from developing countries, as a 170% increase in new cases is estimated for these countries, while an increase of 42% is expected for people in developed countries (Silva, Souza, Böschemeier, Costa, Bezerra, & Feitosa, 2018).

Diabetes is a complex condition with multiple types. Type 1 Diabetes Mellitus (T1DM) stems from the immune-mediated destruction of insulin-producing cells, often starting in childhood. Genetic factors play a role, and they can trigger infections that lead to its development. Type 2 diabetes (T2DM) is the most common form, marked by insulin deficiency and resistance. Obesity and inflammation contribute to T2DM, affecting glucose and lipid metabolism. Gut microbiome changes also impact T2DM by affecting short-chain fatty acid production, bile acid signaling, and insulin sensitivity (Sakran, Graham, Pintar, Yang, Kassir, Willigendael, Singhal, Kooreman, Ramnarain, Mahawar, Parmar, Madhok, & Pouwels, 2022).

Carbohydrate-restricted diets have effectively treated obesity and T2DM for a century by lowering glucose and insulin levels. Improvements in hyperglycemia and hyperinsulinemia result from these diets, supporting treatments aiming to enhance glycemic control and reduce insulin levels in T2DM (Westman, 2021). Ultimately, both T1DM and T2DM can result in high blood sugar levels, leading to complications. The current study examines the medical conditions of diabetes patients as well as how they respond to medications.

2. Methods

The current project applies the method of medical archival research, and statistical tests are conducted to analyze data. The findings can help medical professionals and researchers understand more about patients. The data about diabetic patients were collected for close to ten years (1999-2008) from 130 hospitals, clinics, and health centers across the United States (Strack, DeShazo, Gennings, Olmo, Ventura, Cios, & Clore, 2014). These patients stayed in the hospitals, clinics, or health centers between 1 to 14 days, and laboratory tests were performed on them. The data collected included patients' gender, age, ethnic background, the number of lab tests performed, medications, and glycated-hemoglobin (HbA1c) test results (Strack et al., 2014).

Glycated hemoglobin (HbA1c) is a type of hemoglobin (Hb) bound to a sugar (Chandalia & Krishnaswamy, 2002). Many monosaccharides can bind with hemoglobin in the bloodstream. However, glucose is the main source of fuel in the human body, and it is less likely to bind to hemoglobin as compared to other monosaccharides. Consequently, the presence of HbA1c is typically indicative of excessive (i.e., high-level) sugars in the blood, and HbA1c levels greater than 6.4% or 6.5% signal the likelihood of diabetes mellitus (Huisa, Roy, Kawano, & Schrader, 2013; Chandalia & Krishnaswamy, 2002). HbA1c is measured as the three-month average of blood sugar levels. Higher amounts of glycated hemoglobin have been linked to cardiovascular disease, nephropathy, neuropathy, and retinopathy (Teliti, Cogni, Sacchi, Dagliati, Marini, Tibollo, De Cata, Bellazzi, & Chiovato, 2018).

The current project analyzed more than 101,000 people from various backgrounds. However, the specific focus was on Asian-American and Asian diabetic patients; there were 641 individuals in this sample. The factors analyzed included ethnic background, gender, age, treatment, and medication. The factor of weight was not included in the current study because less than five percent of the Asian-American and Asian patients reported their weight. Among those who reported their weight, about 89% of them were between 50-75 kg (or approximately 110-165 pounds), and about 11% of them were between 75-100 kg (or approximately 165-220 pounds).

3. Results

There was a significant difference in the distribution of genders among the ethnic groups, X^2 (5, N=101763) = 517.89, $p < 0.05$. For African Americans and Whites/Caucasians, significantly more females were hospitalized than males. However, there were no such significant differences among patients of other ethnic backgrounds. While the gender difference for Whites/Caucasians was smaller, the gender difference for African Americans was much larger than the rest of the groups. Figure 1 shows the percentages of patients grouped by ethnicity and gender.

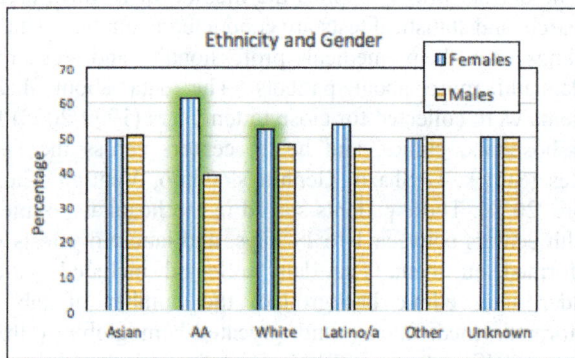

Figure 1: The Percentage of Patients Grouped by Ethnicity and Gender.

Figure 2 shows the percentages of ethnic backgrounds for patients in the sample as well as for those of the general US population (United States Census Bureau, https://www.census.gov/). African Americans and Whites/Caucasians were more likely to be hospitalized. In contrast, Asians, Latinos/Latinas, and other groups were less likely to be hospitalized. Or, perhaps they were less likely to seek hospitalization.

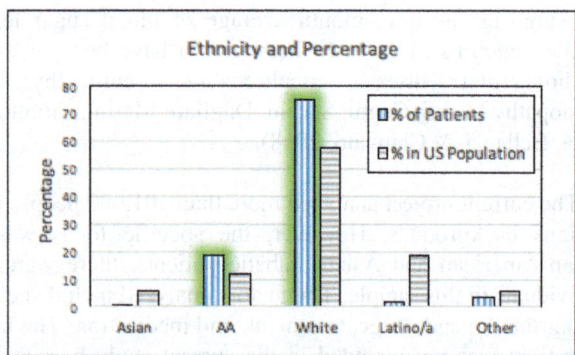

Figure 2: Percentage of Ethnicity for Patients in the Sample and for the US Population.

For Asian Americans and Asians, the number of female and male patients differed depending on the age groups, X^2 (6, N=641) = 26.27, $p < 0.05$. Specifically, while there were more male patients in the 50-60 age group, there were more female patients in the 80-90 age group. Figure 3 shows the number of Asian patients grouped by age and gender.

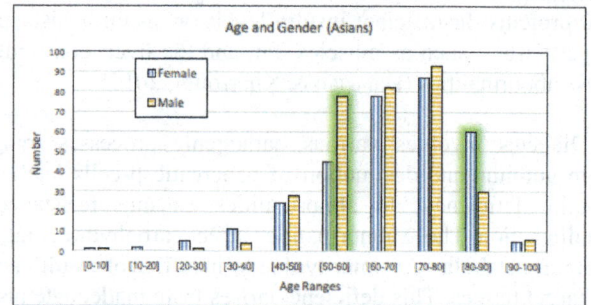

Figure 3: The Number of Asian-American/Asian Patients Grouped by Age and Gender.

For the Asian-American and Asian patients, there were no significant gender differences in terms of the time spent in the hospital, the number of laboratory procedures, the number of medications, and the number of previous diagnoses. However, there was a significant difference in the number of medical procedures between the females and the males, t(639) = -2.21, $p < 0.05$. Specifically, the female patients (M = 1.21, SD = 1.44) had less medical procedures than the male patients did (M = 1.48, SD = 1.67). Figure 4 shows the average number of procedures for Asian females and Asian males.

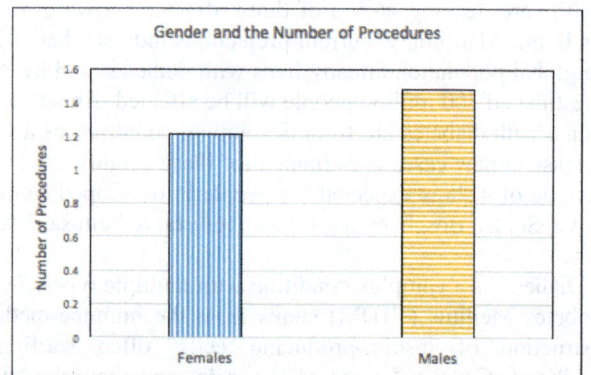

Figure 4: The Number of Medical Procedures for Asian Females and Asian Males.

Figure 5 shows the number of medical procedures across age for Asian-American and Asian patients; its pattern followed an approximately normal distribution, with the peak at the age 60-70 group. The lowest number of medical procedures were found for people before age 20 and after age 90. On the other hand, the number of medications generally increased across age for these patients. Figure 6 shows this pattern.

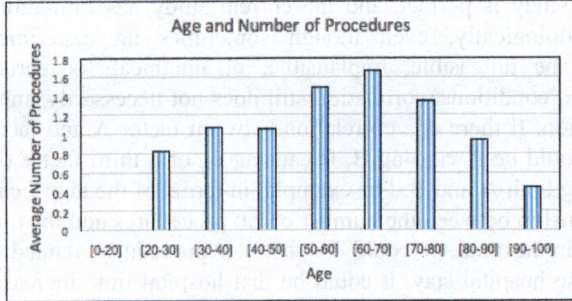

Figure 5: Age and the Number of Procedures for Asian Patients.

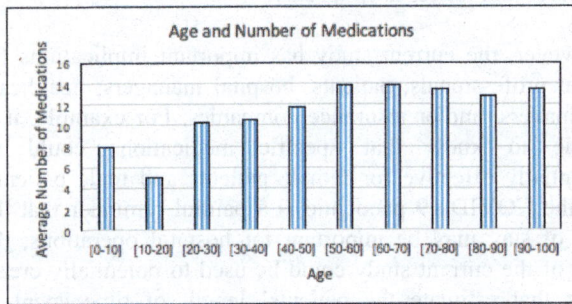

Figure 6: Age and the Number of Medications for Asian Patients.

For Asian-American and Asian patients, there was a weak positive correlation (r = 0.30) between the number of diagnoses and the number of medications; the slope of the best-fit regression line was significantly greater than zero, t(640) = 8.06, p < 0.01. Generally, those who had more diagnoses also had more medications. Figure 7 shows this relationship.

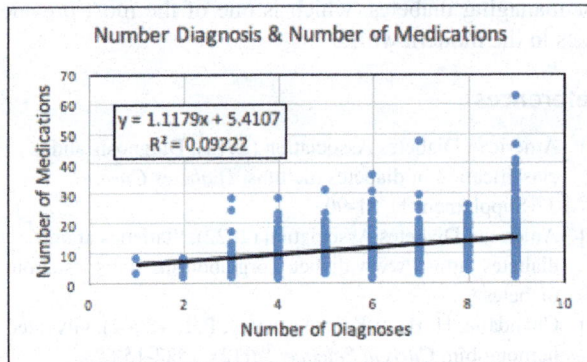

Figure 7: The Number of Diagnoses and the Number of Medications for Asian Patients.

Moreover, there was a moderately positive correlation (r = 0.40) between the number of laboratory procedures and the time spent in the hospitals; the slope of the best-fit regression line was significantly greater than zero, t(640) = 11.14, p < 0.01. Generally, those who had more lab procedures also spent longer times in hospitals. Figure 8 shows this relationship.

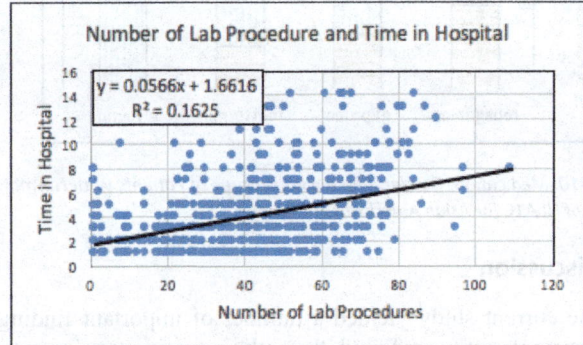

Figure 8: The Number of Lab Procedures and the Time in Hospital for Asian Patients.

Furthermore, there was a moderately-strong positive correlation (r = 0.51) between the number of medications and the time spent in the hospitals; the slope of the best-fit regression line was significantly greater than zero, t(640) = 15.18, p < 0.01. Generally, those who had more medications also spent longer times in hospitals. Figure 9 shows this relationship.

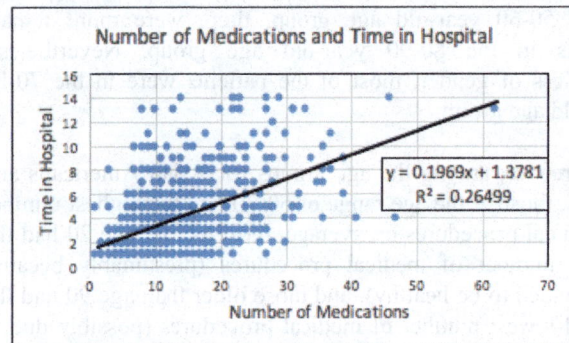

Figure 9: The Number of Medications and the Time in Hospital for Asian Patients.

Finally, various types of medications could be differentially effective for females and males. Figure 10 shows the percentages of Asian-American/Asian diabetic patients who had normal HbA1C levels while taking repaglinide, glipizide, metformin, and glyburide. As can be seen in the figure, glyburide seemed to be relatively more effective for Asian-American/Asian females, while repaglinide seemed to be relatively more effective for Asian-American/Asian males.

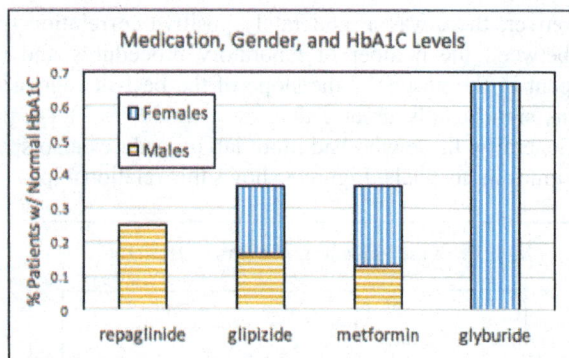

Figure 10: Medication, Gender, and the Percentage of Patients With Normal Levels of HbA1C for Asian Americans and Asians.

4. Discussion

The current study yielded a number of important findings. For example, it was found that ethnicity was an important factor in the hospitalization of diabetic patients. While African Americans and Whites/Caucasians were more likely to be hospitalized (especially for African-Americans and Whites/Caucasian females), Asians and Latinos/Latinas were less likely to be hospitalized or less likely to seek hospitalization in the first place.

For Asian Americans and Asians, specific medications could be differentially effective for females and males. Also, the female patients had less medical procedures than the male patients did. In addition, while there were more male patients in the 50-60 year-old age group, there were more female patients in the 80-90 year-old age group. Nevertheless, regardless of gender, most of the patients were in the 70-80 year-old age group.

Moreover, among the age groups for Asian Americans and Asians, those at the age range of 60-70 had the highest number of medical procedures on average, those before age 20 had the lowest number of medical procedures (presumably because they tended to be healthy), and those older than age 90 had the second-lowest number of medical procedures (possibly due to higher death rates and/or being too "old" for certain operations). On the contrary, the number of medications generally increased across age, presumably because medications tended to be less invasive. The medications for patients before the age of 20 might have been for diseases that were at least partly inherited or partly genetic (such as type-1 diabetes).

Why was the correlation between the number of medications and time spent in hospital (Figure 9) stronger than the correlation between the number of laboratory procedures and time spent in hospital (Figure 8)? Perhaps medications were more indicative of disease in patients, while lab procedures

could include tests that might be negative. This interpretation seemed consistent with the correlation between the number of diagnoses and the number of medications (Figure 7).

5. Conclusion

No study is perfect, and the current study has limitations. Methodologically, even though sometimes an experiment would be unfeasible, implausible, or unethical for certain medical conditions, correlation still does not necessarily imply causation. If there is a correlation between factor A and factor B, it could be A causing B, B causing A, or a third factor (C) causing both A and B. For example, in terms of the significant relationship between the number of lab procedures and the time spent in hospital, it could be that lab procedures tended to increase hospital stay, it could be that hospital time increased the chances of conducting lab procedures, or it could be that underlying medical condition(s) caused both more lab procedures and longer hospital stay.

However, the current study has important implications for medical professionals, patients, hospital managers, healthcare policymakers, and/or insurance companies. For example, it is valuable to know that specific medications could be differentially effective for female patients and male patients. Also, the COVID-19 pandemic is a painful reminder that the length of stay may be important for hospital operations; the results of the current study could be used to potentially create models that estimate the patients' length of time spent in hospitals, increase efficiency, lower costs, and improve patient outcomes.

Finally, possible future directions can analyze other factors that could be related to diabetes (e.g., weight, dietary habit, or medical conditions), study other populations (i.e., non-Asians), and examine the effectiveness of other medications. After all, the more researchers understand diabetic patients, the more effective medical professionals can be in preventing, treating, and/or managing diabetes, which is one of the most prevalent diseases in the modern world.

6. References

[1] American Diabetes Association (2014). Diagnosis and classification of diabetes mellitus. *Diabetes Care, 37*(Supplement 1), 81-90.

[2] American Diabetes Association (2022). Statistics about diabetes. https://www.diabetes.org/about-us/statistics/about-diabetes

[3] Chandalia, H. B., & Krishnaswamy, P. R. (2002). Glycated hemoglobin. *Current Science, 83*(12), 1522-1532.

[4] Delbridge, L. M. D., Benson, V. L., Ritchie, R. H., & Mellor, K. M. (2016). Diabetic cardiomyopathy: The case for a role of fructose in disease etiology. *Diabetes, 65*(12), 3521-3528.

Franklin Education Foundation   Analyses of Asian-American and Asian Diabetic Patients: Gender, Age, Medical Procedures, and Medications

Journal of Quantitative and Qualitative Research   Ariel Zhou

[5] Huisa, B. N., Roy, G., Kawano, J., & Schrader, R. (2013). Glycosylated hemoglobin for diagnosis of prediabetes in acute ischemic stroke patients. *Journal of Stroke and Cerebrovascular Diseases, 22*(8), 564-567.

[6] Kharroubi, A. T., & Darwish, H. M. (2015). Diabetes mellitus: The epidemic of the century. *World Journal of Diabetes, 6*(6), 850-867.

[7] Kuzuya, T., Nakagawa, S., Satoh, J., Kanazawa, Y., Iwamoto, Y., Kobayashi, M., Nanjo, K., Sasaki, A., Seino, Y., Ito, C., Shima, K., Nonaka, K., & Kadowaki, T. (2022). Report of the committee on the classification and diagnostic criteria of diabetes mellitus. *Diabetes Research and Clinical Practice, 55*(1), 65-85.

[8] Sakran, N., Graham, Y., Pintar, T., Yang, W., Kassir, R., Willigendael, E. M., Singhal, R., Kooreman, Z. E., Ramnarain, D., Mahawar, K., Parmar, C., Madhok, B., & Pouwels, S. (2022). The many faces of diabetes. Is there a need for re-classification? A narrative review. *BMC Endocrine Disorders, 22*(1), 9. https://pubmed.ncbi.nlm.nih.gov/34991585/

[9] Silva, J. A., Souza, E. C. F., Böschemeier, A. G. E., Costa, C. C. M., Bezerra, H. S., & Feitosa, E. E. L. C. (2018). Diagnosis of diabetes mellitus and living with a chronic condition: participatory study. *BMC Public Health, 18*, 699. https://doi.org/10.1186/s12889-018-5637-9

[10] Strack, B., DeShazo, J. P., Gennings, C., Olmo, J. L., Ventura, S., Cios, K. J., & Clore, J. N. (2014). Impact of HbA1c measurement on hospital readmission rates: Analysis of 70,000 clinical database patient records. *BioMed Research International, 2014*, 1-11 (Article ID 781670).

[11] Teliti, M., Cogni, G., Sacchi, L., Dagliati, A., Marini, S., Tibollo, V., De Cata, P., Bellazzi, R., & Chiovato, L. (2018). Risk factors for the development of micro-vascular complications of type 2 diabetes in a single-centre cohort of patients. *Diabetes & Vascular Disease Research, 15*(5), 424-432.

United States Census Bureau (2020). 2020 census results. https://www.census.gov/

[12] Westman, E. C. (2021). Type 2 diabetes mellitus: A pathophysiologic perspective. *Frontiers in Nutrition, 10*(8), 707371. https://www.ncbi.nlm.nih.gov/pmc/articles/PMC8384107/

Analyses of Factors that are Related to the Judgement of Novels

Yufei Wang

1. Introduction

In many countries, novels are influential components of popular culture. For instance, many authors in the United States write novels that are later made into films, and a lot of these fictional stories revolve around coming-of-age themes (Ziewacz, 2001). Famous examples of novels/fictions (and/or characters in those novels) that have inspired movies include Harry Potter (1997-2007), Sense and Sensibility (1811), Canon of Sherlock Holmes (1887-1927), The Lord of the Rings (1954-1955), and many others. Through the fame of Hollywood as well as the process of globalization, plenty of novel-based films and movies have gained international influences, becoming popular across cultures and even around the world.

In the Sinosphere, especially in regions that have a lot of Chinese speakers and Vietnamese speakers, Chinese novels/fictions, TV drama series, and films have been popular throughout the 1970s, 1980s, 1990s, and 2000s. In those places, there were fewer TV stations at that time; most people in those regions watched TV regularly, and there were not a lot of competing sources of media during that era. Therefore, this phenomenon helped make Chinese novel-based TV series/films very popular, and they have had high levels of influence in a number of Asian cultures.

For example, writer Jin Yong's wuxia (martial-art adventure) novels inspired many wuxia-themed movies and TV series. In one of his most famous works, Xiao Ao Jiang Hu ("the Smiling, Proud Wanderer"), there is a transgender or gender-bending character called Dongfang Bubai ("The Invincible East"), and this character has become a LGBTQ+ symbol/icon in Chinese culture (Cai, 2005). Also, author Chen Che (more well-known for her pen name Chiung/Qiong Yao) has been considered as one of the most popular writers of Chinese romance novels (Lang, 2003; Ying, 2010); she has written more than 60 novels, which have been made into more than 100 films and TV drama-series. Her novels inspired films such as The Young Ones, The Heart with a Million Knots, and The Autumn Love Song; these works not only portrayed love stories but also helped encourage upward social mobility for working-class Asian women (Lin, 2010).

In the Chinese-speaking world, Hong Kong was a major producer of movies during that era. Perhaps one of the most famous examples is the movie "A Chinese Ghost Story" (1987), which is based on Pu Songling's fiction "Strange Stories from a Chinese Studio" (Liaozhai zhiyi, 1740) originally written during the Qing dynasty. This fiction has become one of the most popular ghost-stories in Chinese literature (Hui, 2019), and its most famous film-adaptation,

A Chinese Ghost Story, has generated cult followings throughout the Chinese-speaking world (Wang, 2018). Outside of Hong Kong, this film also became very popular in several Asian countries, especially in South Korea and Japan. Through this movie, its leading actress (Joey Wong) would become famous in Korea, and its leading male actor (Leslie Cheung) would become popular in Japan.

Indeed, the impacts of novels can transcend across long ranges of times and cultures. Among classic Chinese novels, four of them (known as the "Four Great Classic Novels") have had especially wide-spread influences in the world: "Journey to the West," "Dream of the Red Chamber," "Romance of the Three Kingdoms," and "Water Margin" (or "Outlaws of the Marsh") (Shen Yun, n.d.). Considered to be among the most popular East-Asian novels of all time, these literary works were translated into many languages and adapted for various countries. Moreover, thanks to technology and widespread literacy in the modern age, they have inspired numerous mangas, animes, plays, artworks, songs, films, and video games (Nishijima, 2022; No Sweat Shakespeare, n.d.; KBS World, 2021; Havis, 2021).

Given the powerful cultural influences of popular novels, it is important to understand how readers evaluate them. The current research project examines the possible factors that may play a role in the ratings of modern novels.

2. Method

For the current project, information about modern or newer novels in China and their ratings were collected from a popular website (https://www.jjwxc.net/topten.php?orderstr=20) in October and November of 2022. The data were collected and transferred to Excel spreadsheets. They included information such as the novel names, their authors, the average rankings, the types of content (i.e., categorized into wuxia/martial-arts or legendary content, mystery or suspense, love, drama, derivative, light-hearted, etc.), the style of the novels (i.e., mainstream, comedy, and light-hearted styles), the setting of the novels (i.e., past, modern, and future or futuristic), their popularity, their rating scores, their word lengths, etc. Note that the "derivative" type means that it is loosely based on or inspired by other stories or story-lines. Also, the "mainstream" style means that its story or story-line is usually considered as "regular," "uncontroversial," "standard," and "logical"; it is considered as neither "overly happy" nor "tragic." The top-200 novels (i.e., the rankings were based on ratings from readers) were chosen for quantitative analyses.

3. Results

3.1 Novel Length, Popularity, Style, and Type

There was a small but positive correlation (r = 0.14) between the word count of the novels and their ratings; the slope of the best-fit regression line was significantly greater than zero, t(199) = 2.02, p < 0.05. Generally, novels with more content had higher ratings. Figure 1 shows this relationship.

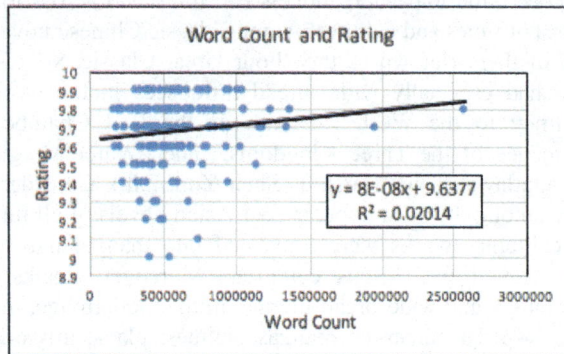

Figure 1: The Word Count of the Novels and Their Ratings.

There was also a small but positive correlation (r = 0.21) between the ratings of novels and the novels' popularity; the slope of the best-fit regression line was significantly greater than zero, t(199) = 3.04, p < 0.01. Generally, novels that were more popular had higher ratings. Figure 2 shows this relationship.

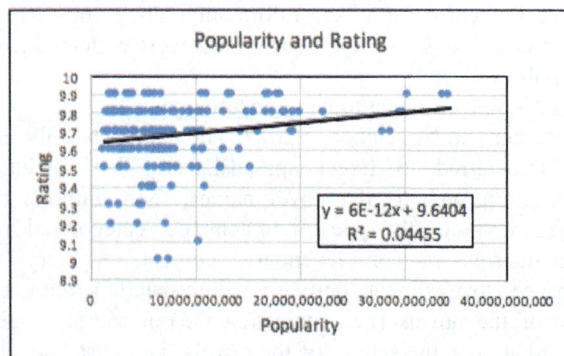

Figure 2: Novel Ratings and Popularity.

In terms of the styles of the novels, an analysis of variance (ANOVA) found that the three types of novels (i.e., mainstream, comedy, and light-hearted styles) had significantly different ratings, F(2, 197) = 6.97, p < 0.01. There was no significant difference in the overall ratings between novels of the light-hearted style (mean = 9.66, SD = 0.18) and novels of the comedy style (mean = 9.63, SD = 0.15), t(137) = 0.34, p = 0.37. However, novels of the mainstream style (mean = 9.75, SD = 0.12) had significantly

higher rating scores than both novels of the light-hearted style, t(194) = 3.66, p < 0.01, and those of the comedy style, t(63) = 2.06, p < 0.05. Figure 3 shows the ratings for the three types of novels.

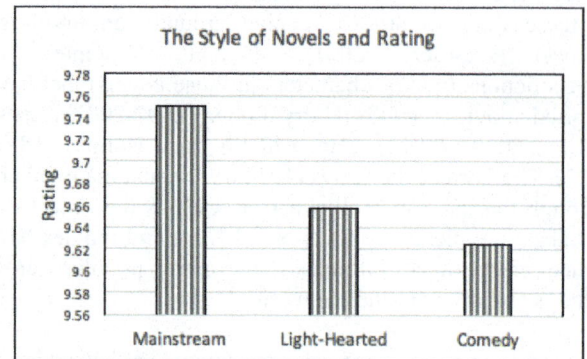

Figure 3: The Styles of Novels and Their Ratings.

In terms of the type of novel content, there were differences in ratings between the various content types, and Figure 4 shows their ratings. Specifically, novels with "wuxia and/or legendary" content (i.e., a genre of fiction involving the adventures of martial-art superheroes or mythological characters) (mean = 9.73, SD = 0.08) had significantly higher ratings than novels with "light" content (mean = 9.57, SD = 0.16), t(16) = 2.98, p < 0.01. Also, novels with love-related content (mean = 9.69, SD = 0.16) had significantly higher ratings than novels with "light" content, t(151) = 1.86, p < 0.05.

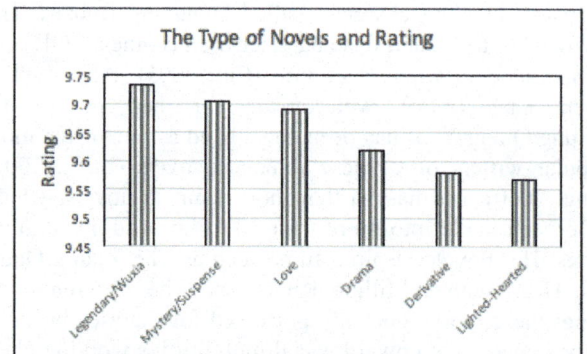

Figure 4: The Types of Novel Content and Their Ratings.

3.2 Novels with Love-Related Content

Given that most of the novels analyzed in the current study were novels primarily with love-related content, it is interesting to compare the types of love-related content. Figure 5 shows novels with various types of love-related content and their ratings. An ANOVA found that the overall difference in ratings of among the various types of love

12

content in the novels (i.e., no love/couple, male-male, male-female love, and female-female love) were approaching statistical significance, F(3, 196) = 2.50, p = 0.06. Specifically, novels with love content involving females (mean = 9.85, SD = 0.06) had significantly higher rating scores than novels with no love content or no couple-based love content (mean = 9.56, SD = 0.30), t(7) = 1.85, p = 0.05.

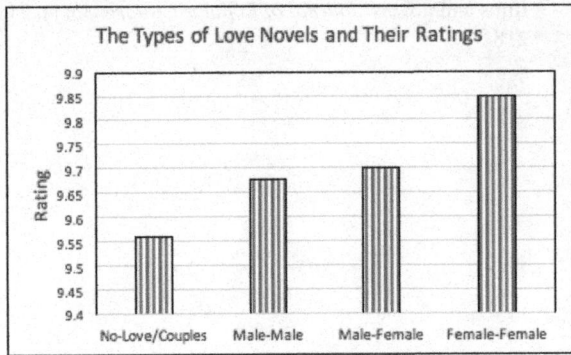

Figure 5: The Types of Love-Related Content in Novels and Their Ratings.

In terms of the setting of love novels, the love novels with past or future settings (mean = 9.72, SD = 0.11) had significantly higher rating scores than the love novels with current or modern settings (mean = 9.66, SD = 0.17), t(94) = 1.62, p = 0.05. Figure 6 shows these ratings.

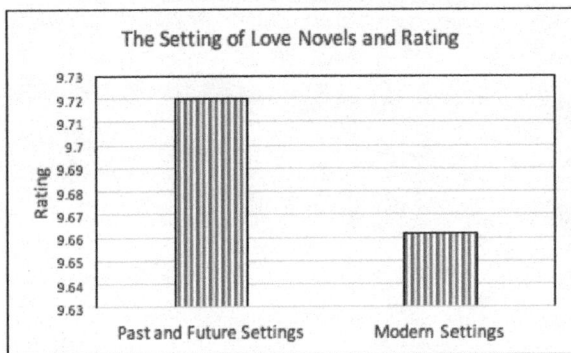

Figure 6: The Settings of Love Novels and Their Ratings.

4. Discussion

Many of the current results have practical importance. These results can help researchers and writers understand more about modern Chinese readers in general. For example, the results showed that both novels with more or longer content and popular novels had higher ratings. Furthermore, novels of the mainstream style as well as novels that had "wuxia/legendary" content, mystery/suspense content, and love content tended to have higher ratings. It also seemed

harder for novels of the light-hearted style and novels of the comedy style to have contents as long as those of the other (mainstream) styles. Regarding the specific love content, novels with love content involving females had higher rating scores than those with no love content or no couple-based love content. Through examining the factors that may play a role in the ratings of modern novels, the current research project has successfully reached its goal.

Another interesting result was the finding that the love novels with past or future settings had higher rating scores than the love novels with current or modern settings. It may be possible that many past settings and future settings can render more creative possibilities for love stories than modern settings can. For example, the modern time can seem relatively more "uneventful," "stable," or "peaceful" compared to other times. On the other hand, certain past historical eras may seem more "unstable" or tumultuous, setting-up more dramatic twists and turns for love stories that may be harder to create in the modern times. After all, many of the famous novels by Chiung/Qiong Yao (Chen Che) and Jin Yong are portrayed in the past setting. Also, the future times can be designed to set-up situations for love stories that are not possible in the modern times. In this sense, the past setting and the future setting appeared to leave more room for imagination.

5. Conclusion

No single study is perfect, so the current project has limitations. In terms of methodology, correlation does not necessarily imply causation. For example, regarding the significant relationship between the popularity of the novels and the ratings, it could be that more popular novels caused higher ratings, or it could be that higher ratings increased the novels' popularity, or it could be that another factor (such as the depth of the content) caused both high popularity and high ratings. Another limitation is sampling. The current study applied convenient sampling, and the generalizability is limited. It remains to be seen whether the findings can be generalized to non-Chinese novels or non-Chinese readers.

Nevertheless, the findings of the current study have a number of implications. For example, the results have implications for researchers, scholars, and writers; they increase the understanding of how readers assess stories. Also, bookstores or book sellers can use the findings to promote certain novels. For film-makers and directors who make movies that are based on or inspired by novels, the findings can help them preserve certain parts of the novel style, content, and/or setting in their movies that may please the audience members, especially fans of the corresponding novels. As for educators and teachers, perhaps language classes that discuss certain types of novel content/style might garner more interest from students who are enthusiastic about reading.

Finally, future directions include various lines of research. For example, qualitative studies have the potential to help researchers know more about why novels with wuxia, mystery/suspense, and/or love-related contents tended to have higher ratings than novels with other types of content. Moreover, other studies can examine the judgments of novels in other languages or other cultures and compare the findings to those of the current study. In particular, it would be interesting to assess whether judgments of different types of love content/relationship differ across languages, cultures, and/or backgrounds. In addition, the current findings can be compared to studies that assess the perception of other creative story-telling arts (such as films, poetry, music, documentary, etc.). In this field of inquiry, while we appreciate how novels entertain us or touch our hearts, we also gain a deeper understanding of human nature.

6. REFERENCES

[1] Cai, R. (2005). Gender imaginations in Crouching Tiger, Hidden Dragon and the wuxia world. *Positions: East Asia Cultures Critique, 13*(2), 441-471.

[2] Havis, R. J. (2021, September 19). *What martial arts storytelling owes to The Water Margin, wuxia novel from 14th century adapted for Japanese TV and by Chang Cheh for cinema, and how its themes and style still resonate.* South China Morning Post. https://www.scmp.com/lifestyle/entertainment/article/3149074/what-wuxia-storytelling-owes-water-margin-martial-arts.

[3] Hui, L. (2019). Mastering a minor tradition: Pu Songling and the Chinese Ghost Tale. https://doi.org/10.1002/9781118635193.ctwl0132.

[4] Lang, M. (2003). San Mao and Qiong Yao, a "popular" pair. *Modern Chinese Literature and Culture*, 15(2), 76-120.

[5] Lin, W. (2010). More than escapist romantic fantasies: Revisiting Qiong Yao films of the 1970s. *Journal of Chinese Cinemas, 4*(1), 45-50.

[6] Nishijima, C. (2022, March 1). *Dragon Ball was inspired by this piece of classic Chinese literature.* Comic Book Resources. https://www.cbr.com/dragon-ball-journey-to-the-west-inspiration/.

[7] Shen Yun Performing Arts. https://www.shenyunperformingarts.org/.

[8] Songs inspired by Romance of The Three Kingdoms (2021, August 25). KBS World. https://world.kbs.co.kr/service/contents_view.htm?lang=e&menu_cate=culture&id=&board_seq=409521.

[9] The Dream of the Red Chamber: An Overview (n.d.). No Sweat Shakespeare. https://nosweatshakespeare.com/literature/most-influential-fiction/dream-red-chamber/.

[10] Wang, H. (2018). A Chinese Ghost Story: A Hong Kong comedy film's cult following in Mainland China. *Journal of Chinese Cinemas, 12*(2), 142-157.

[11] Ying, L. (2010). *Historical Dictionary of Modern Chinese Literature.* The Scarecrow Press.

[12] Ziewacz, L. E. (2001). Holden Caulfield, Alex Portnoy, and Good Will Hunting: Coming of age in American films and novels. *Journal of Popular Culture, 35*(1), 211-218.

Analyses of How Readers Evaluate Speculative and Literary Fiction: Major Themes and General Principles

Caroline J. Li

Abstract

Because of the cultural, economic, social, and educational significance of fiction, it is important to understand how readers psychologically evaluate novels. The current study conducted qualitative and quantitative analyses on the reviews, evaluations, and critiques of six novels from two styles (i.e., speculative fiction and literary fiction). The results showed that the content could be described by five major themes (each with its own subcategories): Writing/tone, narrative/story, author/reader analysis, character analysis, and depth of the novel. Generally, regardless of the type of fiction or the specific novels, comments about the narrative/story had the highest percentage, comments about the depth of novels had the lowest percentage, and comments about the other three themes (i.e., authors/author's work, characters, and writing/tone) had percentages that were somewhere in between. Possible explanations are proposed, and future directions are discussed. The findings have implications and applications for writers, educators, readers, filmmakers, and researchers (especially in psychology and linguistics).

Franklin Education Foundation   Analyses of How Readers Evaluate Speculative and Literary Fiction: Major Themes and General Principles

Journal of Quantitative and Qualitative Research   Caroline Li

1. Introduction

As the ultimate consummation of form and content, the novel has become a staple of English and philosophy courses alike; in fact, its significance reaches beyond the classroom and into the domains of entertainment, politics, art, and daily life. So powerful a cultural force is the novel that several of the most famous have been subject to harsh censorship for their subversive topics (e.g. *Lord of the Flies*, *1984*, and *The Bluest Eye*), establishing the medium as a symbol of intellectual freedom, cultural development, and social mobility.

Take, for instance, Dr. Henry Lee, a forensic scientist famous for his seemingly preternatural deductive skills and extensive experience in the field. Despite the recent charges he has been found liable of (Eaton-Robb, 2023), Lee's career is evidence of the power dormant in fiction, drawing from the method and mind of Sir Arthur Conan Doyle's timeless Sherlock Holmes series (Pbs Publicity, 2013) and featuring in some of the most infamous trials of the century. Lee himself has often been referred to as "the modern Sherlock Holmes" (CGTN, 2017; Audacy, 2023).

Economically speaking, the technological awareness ushered in by the pandemic popularized ebooks, audiobooks, and book review sites such as Goodreads (Harris, 2020). Accounting for 65% of all book sales in 2021, the audiobook industry has grown to be such a significant marketplace that, in an act of advocacy, world-renowned fantasy author Brandon Sanderson refused to sell his future books on Amazon's audiobook service, Audible, because of the predatorily low rates it pays smaller authors (Roman, 2022). In a similar vein, thousands of readers came together to support underpaid HarperCollins workers in the 2023 HarperCollins strike, illustrating the significant economic role novels play in workers' rights within the publishing industry itself. Novels, with their in-depth explorations of humanity and sharp critiques of social phenomena, compel readers to take actual action to bring changes to their society.

From a social and educational standpoint, novels contribute to a sense of community (by providing commonalities through book clubs, social media, and online discussion) and equip students with the historical knowledge, compositional skills, and analytical background to thrive in a variety of fields. With the growing representation of diverse experiences and backgrounds in popular media, novels do their part in accurately representing cultures different to one's own and spotlighting minority voices in a historically majority-white industry (So & Wezerek, 2020). Not only does this cultural exchange provide a significant source of social interaction and fulfillment, it also encourages more nuanced academic discussions about current/historical events, promotes intercultural solidarity, and fosters a powerful collective voice that can advocate for justice, as exhibited by the HarperCollins strike.

Given the cultural, economic, social, and educational significance of novels, it is important for researchers to understand how readers psychologically evaluate them. The current project aims to conduct qualitative analyses on the critiques of novels from reviewers; the goal is to identify common themes or factors discussed across different novels. It is hypothesized that reviews of speculative fiction will show an emphasis on the narrative, while reviews of literary fiction will show an emphasis on character, depth, and writing.

2. Method

Six novels were selected from two styles – speculative fiction and literary fiction. Speculative fiction refers to stories that can deviate away from reality-based storytelling and the rules of physics; they can include sci-fi stories, magical worlds, supernatural legends, fairy tales, fantasy adventures, superhero characters, and people with superpowers, etc. (Manusos, 2020). On the other hand, literary fiction refers to stories that are typically based on the real world and the rules of physics; they tend to be more focused on characters and various aspects of the human experience (Woodson, 2023).

Three of the selected novels were speculative fiction: *Klara and the Sun* (Ishiguro, 2021), *The Way of Kings* (Sanderson, 2010), and *Babel,* which is also called *Babel: Or the Necessity of Violence: An Arcane History of the Oxford Translators' Revolution* (Kuang, 2022). The other three selected novels were literary fiction: *The Secret History* (Tartt, 1992), *A Man Called Ove* (Backman, 2014, translated by Koch), and *Yellowface* (Kuang, 2023).

Among the three speculative novels, one was chosen because it is currently "popular" (*Babel*), one was chosen because it was written by a "famous" author (the author of *Klara and the Sun* is Kazuo Ishiguro, who won the 2017 Nobel Prize in Literature), and one was chosen because it is considered to be a strong example of the speculative style (*The Way of Kings*).

In a similar manner, among the three literary novels, one was chosen because it is currently "popular" (*Yellowface*), one was chosen because it was written by a "famous" author (the author of *The Secret History* is Donna Tartt, who won the 2014 Pulitzer Prize for Fiction), and one was chosen because it is considered to be a strong example of the literary style (*A Man Called Ove*).

For each of the novels, the top three most popular reviews, evaluations, or critiques (as of June 18, 2023) were collected from the Goodreads (https://www.goodreads.com/) website. Then, thematic analyses were carried out to examine the specific contents of these reviews, evaluations, or critiques; this qualitative method is used to effectively analyze words. In addition, inter-rater reliability was established by having two raters who reached an agreement on the rules for all of the themes and categories. While the reviewers were those who wrote the reviews, evaluations, or the critiques regarding the novels, the raters were those who conducted the thematic analysis.

3. Results

Thematic analyses for each of the reviews, evaluations, or critiques were analyzed independently. Next, the results for the three reviewers or critics of each novel were combined for the six novels. Thematic analyses of the reviews, evaluations, and critiques for all of the six novels revealed five major themes or categories, and each of the major themes/categories was further divided into subcategories. These five major themes captured, summarized, and categorized all of the contents from the reviews, evaluations, and critiques. Table 1 lists the five major themes/categories with their subcategories.

Theme/Category	Subcategories
Writing/Tone	- Tone of the novel. - Quality/Technical skill of writing. - Style or structure. - Readability or re-readability. - Ease of comprehension. - Subtlety.
Narrative/Story	- Addresses or relates to real-life issues. - Specific theme or storyline (sci-fi, coming of age, etc.). - Originality/creativity/variety (or the lack of). - Pacing, eventfulness, length, tension, or intention. - Plot-twist reaction, climax, or emotional impact. - Setting, immersiveness, realism, detail. - Ending or the anticipation of conclusion.
Author/Reader Analysis	- Opinions and views. - Reputation. - Comparisons to other authors' works. - Expectations or curiosity. - Comparisons to the same author's other works. - Humor. - Other readers' review of the novel.
Character Analysis	- Representation/Diversity. - Complexity or Development - Voice - Comparisons to other characters. - Character interactions or relationships. - Likability or relatability. - Personality or emotional content.
Depth of the Novel	- General. - Self-exploration or philosophical content. - Well-researched. - Significance or importance. - Cover art.

Table 1: The Thematic Analyses for the Contents of Reviews, Evaluations, and Critiques Regarding the Novels.

The theme/category called "writing or tone" refers to comments about a novel's quality of writing, tone, style, structure, readability, re-readability, ease of comprehension, and subtlety, etc. Its subcategory of re-readability represents comments regarding the evaluation of whether a novel could be read over and over again. The theme/category of "narrative/story" refers to comments about various aspects of a novel's storyline, such as its relatability to real-life issues, originality/creativity, pacing, plot-twist, emotional impact, and ending, etc.

The theme/category called "author/reader analysis" refers to comments about the author or the reader, including the authors' opinions/views, reputation, and sense of humor as well as the reader's comparisons to the same author's other works, other authors' works, or even other readers' reviews. The theme/category of "character analysis" refers to comments about characters in a novel, including their representation or diversity, complexity, character development, interactions, relationships, likability, relatability, personality, and emotional content. The theme/category called "depth of the novel" refers to comments about deeper issues or philosophical content related to a novel, such as topics related to self-exploration or the significance of an underlying issue discussed in a story.

The percentages of comments representing the five major themes/categories were calculated for the reviews/critiques of the six novels. Figure 1 shows the percentage of comments representing the five major themes/categories for the reviews/critiques of the novel *Klara and the Sun*. Comments about its narrative/story had the highest percentage (46.7%), while comments about its depth had the lowest percentage (6.7%).

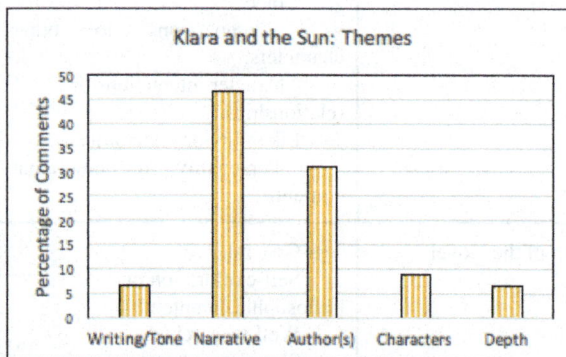

Figure 1: The Percentages and the Types of Comments for the Reviews/Critiques of the Novel Klara and the Sun.

Figure 2 shows the percentage of comments representing the five major themes/categories for the reviews/critiques of the novel *The Way of Kings*. A similar pattern emerged: Comments about the narrative/story of the novel had the highest percentage (47.4%), while comments about the depth of the novel had the lowest percentage (5.3%).

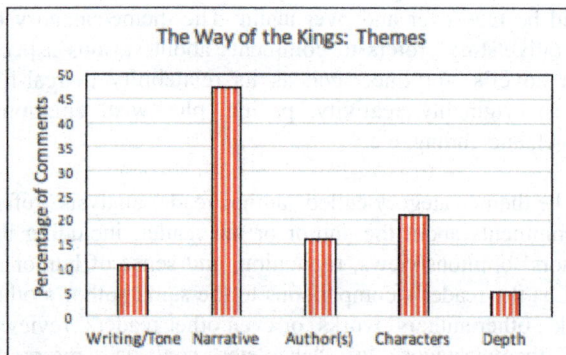

Figure 2: The Percentages and the Types of Comments for the Reviews/Critiques of the Novel The Way of Kings.

Figure 3 shows the percentage of comments representing the five major themes/categories for the reviews/critiques of the novel *Babel*. Again, another similar pattern emerged:

Comments about the narrative/story of the novel had the highest percentage (35.3%), while comments about the depth of the novel had the lowest percentage (14.0%).

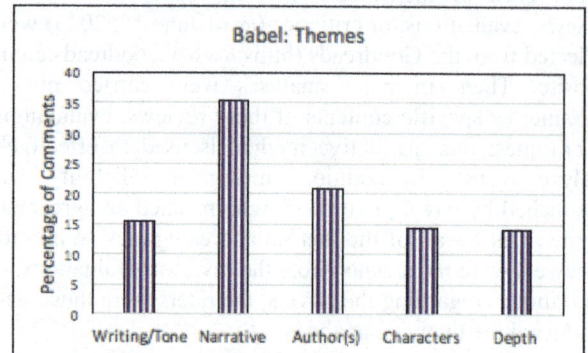

Figure 3: The Percentages and the Types of Comments for the Reviews/Critiques of the Novel Babel.

Figure 4 shows the percentage of comments representing the five major themes/categories for the reviews/critiques of the novel *The Secret History*. Still, the similar pattern emerged yet again: Comments about the narrative/story of the novel had the highest percentage (44.7%), while comments about the depth of the novel had the lowest percentage (10.6%).

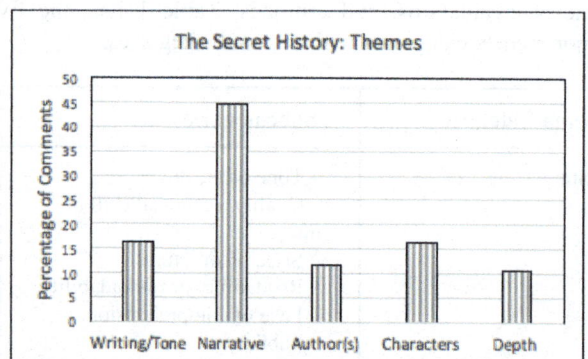

Figure 4: The Percentages and the Types of Comments for the Reviews/Critiques of the Novel The Secret History.

Figure 5 shows the percentage of comments representing the five major themes/categories for the reviews/critiques of the novel *A Man Called Ove*. This time, the pattern of results is slightly different: Comments about the narrative/story of the novel (31.6%) and its characters (31.6%) both had the highest percentage, while comments about the depth of the novel (9.2%) and its author (9.2%) both had the lowest percentage. However, even in this case, no theme had a higher percentage of comments than that of the narrative/storyline, and no theme had a lower percentage of comments than that of the depth.

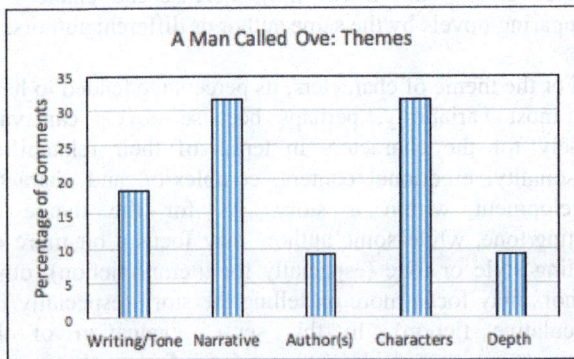

Figure 5: The Percentages and the Types of Comments for the Reviews/Critiques of the Novel A Man Called Ove.

Figure 6 shows the percentage of comments representing the five major themes/categories for the reviews/critiques of the novel *Yellowface*. Similar to most of the previous figures, the familiar pattern of results is observed again: Comments about the narrative/story of the novel had the highest percentage (34.2%), while comments about the depth of the novel had the lowest percentage (11.9%).

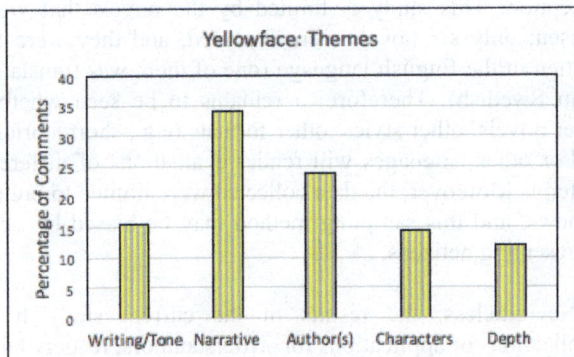

Figure 6: The Percentages and the Types of Comments for the Reviews/Critiques of the Novel Yellowface.

Given that the patterns of results for the novels were mostly similar to each other, the comments were combined for speculative fiction and literary fiction. Figure 7 shows the percentage of comments representing the five major themes/categories for the reviews/critiques of all three speculative novels. The overall pattern is the same: Comments about the narrative/story of the novel had the highest percentage (40.9%), while comments about depth of the novel had the lowest percentage (10.1%).

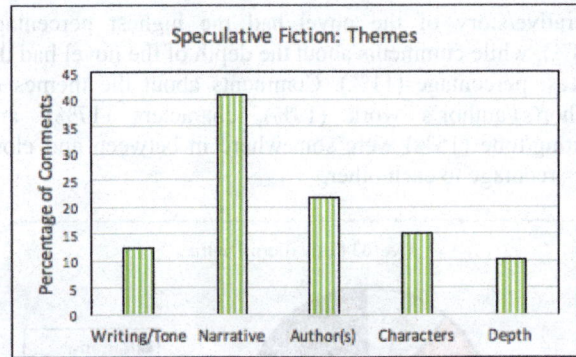

Figure 7: The Percentages and the Types of Comments for the Reviews/Critiques of the Combined Speculative Fiction.

Figure 8 shows the percentage of comments representing the five major themes/categories for the reviews/critiques of all three literary novels. Again, the overall pattern is roughly the same: Comments about the narrative/story of the novel had the highest percentage (36.2%), while comments about the depth of the novel had the lowest percentage (11.0%).

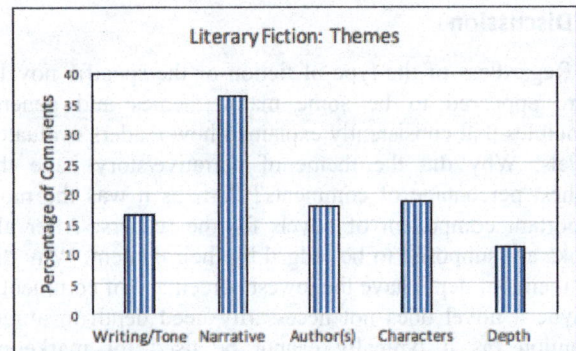

Figure 8: The Percentages and the Types of Comments for the Reviews/Critiques of the Combined Literary Fiction.

Consistent with what one might expect regarding the different styles of novels, speculative fiction generated slightly more comments about the themes of narrative/storyline and author(s)/author's work, while literary fiction generated slightly more comments about novels' characters, depth, and writing/tone. However, a chi-square test found that the overall patterns of results for speculative fiction and literary fiction were not significantly different from each other, X^2 (4, N = 567) = 4.45, p > 0.05. In other words, regardless of the style of the fiction, the pattern of results remained roughly similar across novels.

Figure 9 shows the overall percentage of comments representing the five major themes/categories for all of the novels combined. Regardless of the specific novels, this pattern seemed roughly "universal": Comments about the narrative/story of the novel had the highest percentage (38%), while comments about the depth of the novel had the lowest percentage (11%). Comments about the themes of author(s)/author's work (19%), characters (17%), and writing/tone (15%) were somewhere in between and close in percentage to each other.

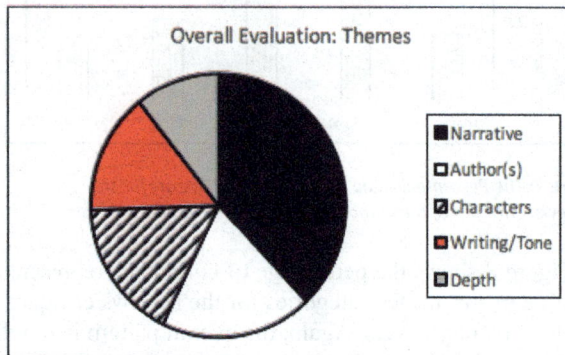

Figure 9: The Overall Percentages and the Types of Comments for the Reviews/Critiques of All Novels Combined.

4. Discussion

Regardless of the type of fiction or the specific novels, there appeared to be some major themes and general principles that consistently explained how readers evaluated novels. Why did the theme of narrative/story have the highest percentage of comments? Perhaps it was the most important component of novels for the readers. After all, books are supposed to be judged by their content. Why did the theme of depth have the lowest percentage of comments? Maybe a novel does not necessarily need depth to attract attention (as it typically cannot be used for marketing purposes). Even if there is content of depth, it may be too "deep" for some readers to notice or appreciate. Apparently, it takes a good reader as well as more time or effort to identify, re-read, understand, evaluate, and write about a novel's depth.

What about the other three themes in between? Their percentages of comments were close to each other, together totaling to approximately half of all comments. For the theme of author(s)/author's work, perhaps it consisted of about one-fifth of all comments because not all readers knew very much about the author's other work or other authors' comparable work. On the other hand, for reviewers who read a lot and for readers who like a novel by a particular author, they may be more likely to read other novels written by the same author because of the mere exposure effect (Bornstein, 1989; Zajonc, 2001). Then, once readers and/or reviewers form a "schema" about an author, the cognitive processes of accommodation and assimilation

(Myers & DeWall, 2018) may increase the chances of comparing novels by the same author or different authors.

For the theme of characters, its percentage tended to have the most variability, perhaps because novels can vary widely for the characters in terms of their relatability, personality, emotional content, complexity, and character development within a story. As for the theme of writing/tone, while some authors may focus a bit more on writing style or tone (especially for literary fiction), other authors may focus more on telling the story (especially for speculative fiction). In this sense, evaluation of the writing/tone seemed like a "secondary" feature that took a backseat to the storyline, analogous to "sauce" on food. A sauce or condiment can make something better or worse, but it typically does not get more attention than the main item of food. When the writing/tone is good, it may also accentuate the overall story, so even if it gets noticed, it is still unlikely to be a bigger component than the narrative/story.

5. Conclusion

No single study is perfect, and the current one is no exception. This study is limited by the novels that were chosen; only six novels were analyzed, and they were all written in the English language (one of them was translated from Swedish). Therefore, it remains to be seen whether other novels, other styles, other formats (e.g., short stories), and/or other languages will render evaluations of different patterns. Moreover, the data collected were limited to online reviews, and this sampling method may be biased by only representing netizens.

Nevertheless, the results of the current study have implications or applications for writers/authors, readers/fans, educators, filmmakers, and researchers (especially in psychology and linguistics). Specifically, the findings are useful for writers/authors to understand more about how novels are evaluated, for readers/fans to improve their ability in evaluation, for educators to teach students on novel analysis, for filmmakers to create better films that are based on novels, and for researchers to further examine the psychology of judging stories or interpreting language.

Finally, there are a number of possible future directions. For example, further research can assess how people evaluate novels of the past, present, and future as well as compare readers of different generations in their evaluations of novels. Specifically, it may be possible that younger reviewers perceive the depth of novels differently than older reviewers, or it may be possible that certain subcategories of a theme can vary across the different types of novels (as comments about or "immersiveness/realism" may be more prevalent for literary novels and less prevalent for speculative novels). Of course, it will be interesting to test whether the same set of major themes and general principles from the current study can be used to adequately explain the evaluations of fiction from other cultures and languages.

Transcendent across space and time, great novels throughout history have instilled a sense of wonder, inspired people, and changed the world. Hopefully, the current line of research can lead scholars down a path that will be just as inspiring, thought-provoking, adventurous, and meaningful.

6. References

[1] Audacy (2023, January 31). Henry C. Lee: A master class - the Pocahontas case. *Audacy.com*. https://www.audacy.com/podcast/crime-waves-78663/episodes/henry-c-lee-a-master-class-the-pocahontas-case-26a5c

[2] Audiobooks Market Size, Share & Trends Report (n.d.). *Grand View Research*. https://www.grandviewresearch.com/industry-analysis/audiobooks-market

[3] Backman, F. (2014). *A Man Called Ove* (H. Koch Trans.). New York City, NY: Atria Books (original work published in 2012).

[4] Bornstein, R. F. (1989). Exposure and affect: Overview and meta-analysis of research, 1968-1987. *Psychological Bulletin, 106*(2), 265-289.

[5] CGTN (2017, November 7). World's first forensic science museum named after Henry Lee opens. *CGTN News*. https://news.cgtn.com/news/7755544e34597a6333566d54/share_p.html

[6] Eaton-Robb, P. (2023, July 26). Forensic scientist Henry Lee defends work after being found liable for falsifying evidence. *The Associated Press*. https://apnews.com/article/forensic-scientist-henry-lee-evidence-blood-1cb5af3fbeca94dc45465d874063cfa4

[7] Golding, W. (1954). *Lord of the Flies*. London, England: Faber and Faber.

[8] Harris, E. A. (2020, December 29). Surprise Ending for Publishers: In 2020, Business Was Good. *The New York Times*. https://www.nytimes.com/2020/12/29/books/book-publishing-2020.html

[9] Ishiguro, K. (2021). *Klara and the Sun*. London, England: Faber and Faber.

[10] Kuang, R. F. (2022). *Babel: Or the Necessity of Violence: An Arcane History of the Oxford Translators' Revolution*. New York City, NY: Harper Voyager.

[11] Kuang, R. F. (2023). *Yellowface*. New York City, NY: William Morrow and Company.

[12] Manusos, L. (2020, January 24). What is speculative fiction? *Book Riot*. https://bookriot.com/what-is-speculative-fiction/

[13] Morrison, T. (1970). *The Bluest Eye*. New York: Holt, Rinehart and Winston.

[14] Myers, D. G., & DeWall, N. C. (2018). *Myers' psychology for the AP® course, third edition*. New York, NY: BFW/Worth Publishers.

[15] Orwell, G. (1949). *Nineteen Eighty-Four*. London, England: Secker & Warburg.

[16] Pbs Publicity (2013, January 14). How Sherlock Changed the World explores the impact of the legendary detective on criminal investigation. *Public Broadcasting Service*. https://www.pbs.org/about/about-pbs/blogs/news/how-sherlock-changed-the-world-explores-the-impact-of-the-legendary-detective-on-criminal-investigation/

[17] Roman, D. (2022, December 30). Brandon Sanderson takes stand against Audible for "unconscionable" indie author pay rates. *Winteriscoming.net*. https://winteriscoming.net/2022/12/30/brandon-sanderson-blasts-audible-unconscionable-indie-author-pay-rates/

[18] Sanderson, B. (2010). *The Way of Kings*. New York City, NY: Tor Books.

[19] So, R. J., & Wezerek, G. (2020) Just how white is the publishing industry? *The New York Times*. https://www.nytimes.com/interactive/2020/12/11/opinion/culture/diversity-publishing-industry.html

[20] Tartt, D. (1992). *The Secret History*. New York City, NY: Alfred A. Knopf, Inc.

[21] Woodson, M. (2023, March 17). What is literary fiction? *Writer's Digest*. https://www.writersdigest.com/write-better-fiction/what-is-literary-fiction

[22] Zajonc, R. B. (2001). Mere exposure: A gateway to the subliminal. *Current Directions in Psychological Science, 10*(6), 224-228.

Analyses on the Mental-Health Issues of High-School Students: Types, Sources, and Views

Munan Cheng

1. Introduction

Mental-health issues are widespread around the globe. For example, it has been estimated that one in every eight humans live with mental-health problems (WHO, 2022), and behavioral or psychological disorders have been found in (at least) more than one-half of a billion people throughout the world (Myers & DeWall, 2018). For teenagers and young adults, suicide is the fourth leading cause of death (WHO, 2022).

Moreover, mental-health problems may have been even more prevalent during the COVID-19 pandemic (Wu, Jia, Shi, Niu, Yin, Xie, & Wang, 2021). For instance, healthcare professionals showed higher rates of insomnia. Also, people who suffered from chronic diseases, patients who have been infected by the COVID-19 virus (SARS-CoV-2), and those who were suspected to have the COVID-19 disease all showed higher rates of depression and anxiety than the general population (Wu et al., 2021).

To understand the field of mental health, it helps to examine some of the related factors. One such factor is gender. Specifically, the types of mental disorders, the prevention strategies, and how people seek help can differ between genders (Afifi, 2007). For example, adolescent girls showed higher rates of depression as well as eating disorders, and women were more likely to suffer from affective disorders. On the other hand, males were more likely to suffer from substance-use disorder and antisocial personality disorder. These differences may be linked to how females and males are typically socialized to cope with stressors in their lives (Afifi, 2007).

Another factor is cultural or ethnic background. Even though Asian Americans are among the fastest-growing populations in the USA, not much research has been done on the mental-health issues in Asian-American communities. Upon experiencing psychological or behavioral problems, Asian Americans were less likely to use mental-health services for help. Then, when they did seek professional help, Asian-American patients tended to focus more on physical problems and less on emotional symptoms, and there were frequent cases of misdiagnosis (Lin & Cheung, 1999).

Indeed, an important consideration for mental health is the stigma that surrounds it. One main problem for teens is the unfulfilled mental-health needs. The expectation that they would receive negative responses from their peers, family, administrators, and teachers is a key negative contributing factor to teens' unwillingness to address and present their mental-health concerns (Chandra & Minkovitz,

2007). And yet, seeking and receiving help or support is critical for the positive mental-health experience and attitudes in teens.

In addition, the level of performance of students is also an important factor for mental health. Higher-achieving students have been found to have higher levels of stress than their peers (Suldo, Shaunessy, & Hardesty, 2008). Finally, schools can play a role in helping young people deal with mental disorders. If schools provide mental-health resources (especially the ones related to early identification), then adolescents with mild or moderate psychological/behavioral disorders may be more likely to use mental-health services (Green, McLaughlin, Alegría, Costello, Gruber, Hoagwood, Leaf, Olin, Sampson, & Kessler, 2013). Therefore, inspired by the need to understand and address the mental-health issues of adolescents, the current study aims to assess the psychological well-being of students as well as the possible roles of parents and schools.

2. Method

The goal of the current project is to collect information about high-school students' mental-health status, the sources of their stress, their opinions on the level of support from parents, and their thoughts regarding mental-health support from the school. The online survey method is used because it allows the participants to express themselves honestly and anonymously. It is impossible, unethical, and/or impractical to manipulate or control many of the variables measured in the current study (such as mental health, parenting, and educational environment), so experiments are not feasible in this situation.

First, to collect students' background information, the mental-health questionnaire asked them about their gender, grade level, and ethnic background. Then, to assess the students' mental health, the questionnaire asked them whether they have ever (at some point in their lives) dealt with depression, anxiety, self-harm, suicidal thoughts, eating disorder, mental/physical abuse, and/or other issues. Also, they were asked the following two questions: "How often during the school year per week do you feel down, sad, or depressed?" and "How often during the school year per week do you feel extremely anxious, stressed, or panicked?". They picked from one of the four choices – very often, often, not very often, or almost not at all.

Next, to assess the nature of the students' stress, participants were asked to indicate the source of the pressure that brings them the most stress in their lives (i.e., teachers/administrators, parents, themselves, peers, social media / Internet, or others) as well as what kind of stress it is (i.e., expectation to look, dress, or act a certain way, expectation to excel in school / academics / extracurriculars, both, or others).

Then, to assess the participants' opinions about the support from their parents, they were asked whether they feel comfortable talking to their parents about their mental health and their mental-health needs (i.e., yes, no, somewhat, or other), what their parents do (if anything) that makes them comfortable talking to the parents, what factors (if any) prevent them from talking with their parents, whether they wish their parents supported them more, and if so, what they wish they your parents did that would support them more.

Finally, to assess students' thoughts about mental-health support from the school, they were asked about whether they feel that the school is doing enough to assist students with their mental health (i.e., yes, no, or maybe), what the school is doing that is supportive or effective, what the school is doing that is ineffective, and what they think the school can do to improve their mental health (activities, education, etc.). Both quantitative and qualitative data were collected from 38 participants, and the results were subsequently analyzed.

3. Result

3.1 Gender and the Types of Stress Experiences

Figure 1 shows the percentages of females who have ever experienced or dealt with each of the stress types, and Figure 2 shows these percentages for males. Figure 3 shows the percentages of gender-fluid and agender individuals who have experienced or dealt with each of the stress types. In all of the above cases (i.e., female, male, gender-fluid, and agender individuals), anxiety, depression, and suicidal thoughts were the top-three most widely experienced types of stress. There were only one gender-fluid participant and one agender participant in the current sample, so the small sample size did not allow for more accurate assessments. If more gender-fluid and agender individuals were included in the sample, then the study likely would find that they also have experienced other types of stress as well.

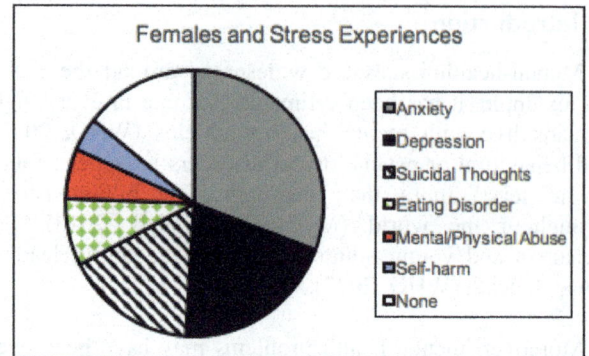

Figure 1: The Percentages of Females that Have Experienced Each of the Stress Types.

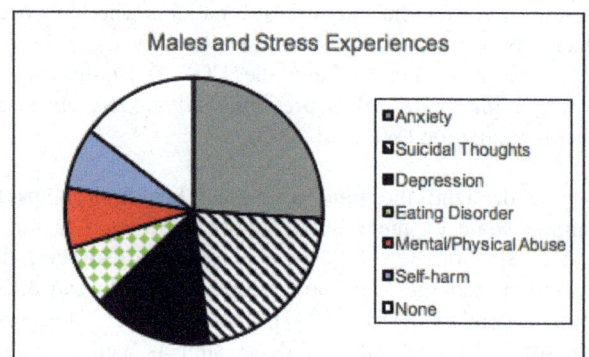

Figure 2: The Percentages of Males that Have Experienced Each of the Stress Types.

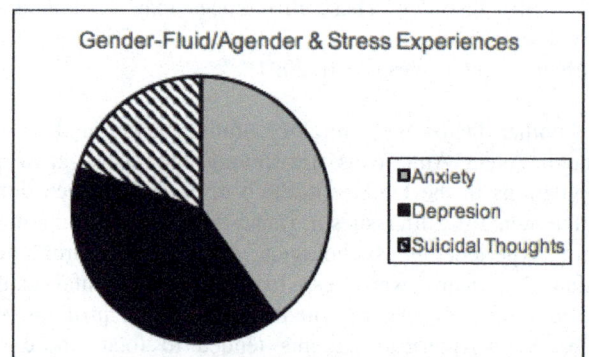

Figure 3: The Percentages of Gender-Fluid and Agender Individuals Who Have Experienced Each of the Stress Types.

Figure 4 compares females and males in the distribution of people who have ever experienced the top-three most common types of stress: anxiety, depression, and suicidal thoughts. As can be seen in this figure, anxiety was the most prevalent type of stress for both genders. However, females were more likely to have experienced anxiety and depression, while males were more likely to have experienced suicidal thoughts.

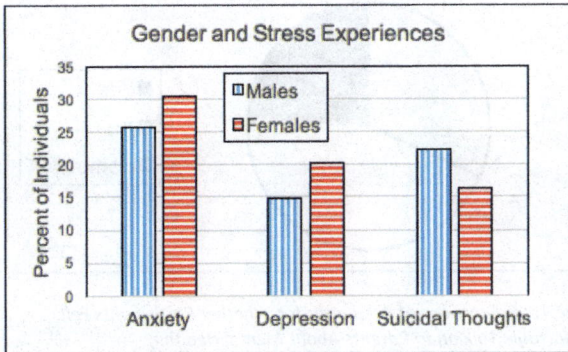

Figure 4: The Percentages of Females and Males Who Have Experienced Anxiety, Depression, and Suicidal Thoughts.

Given that the females in the current study were more likely to have experienced anxiety and depression than the males, it is important to further assess the severity or the frequency of these two mental-health issues. Figure 5 shows the percentage of individuals who felt anxious during the school year, and Figure 6 shows the percentage of individuals who felt sad/depressed during the school year. As can be seen in these figures, females experienced anxiety and depression more frequently than males.

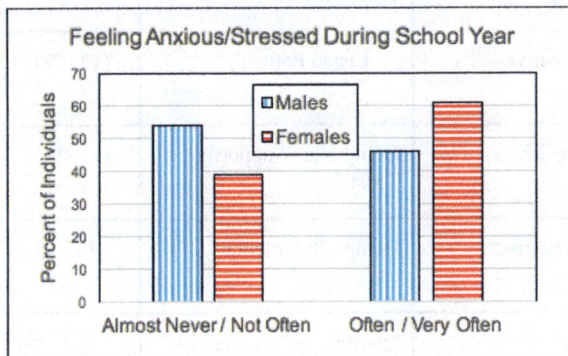

Figure 5: Percentage of Individuals Who Felt Anxious During the School Year.

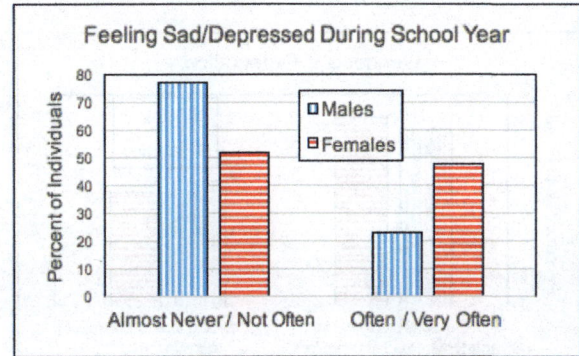

Figure 6: Percentage of Individuals Who Felt Sad/Depressed During the School Year.

3.2 Gender and the Source of Stress/Pressure

Figure 7 graphs the perceived sources of stress for the participants. In terms of the source that pressured participants the most and/or brought the most stress in their lives, most of the females (51.9%) indicated that this source of stress was from themselves, and relatively fewer females indicated other sources of stress, such as parents, peers, social media (SM) or Internet, and teachers/administrators. On the other hand, most of the males indicated that this source of stress was from teachers/administrators (35.7%) or from parents (28.6%). While females were more likely to put pressure on themselves, males were more likely to perceive stress from other people.

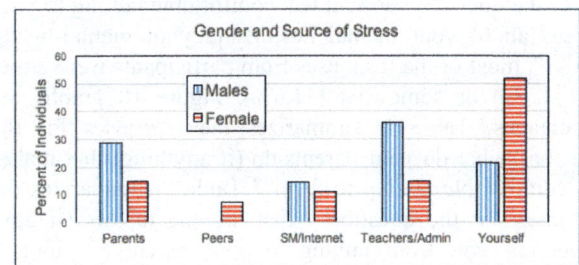

Figure 7: The Sources of Stress/Pressure Grouped by the Gender of the Participants.

Figure 8 graphs the percentage of females and males who faced expectations regarding stress, while Figure 9 graphs the percentage of participants who experienced one or both of the expectations. Both males and females were more likely to be expected to excel in academic or extracurricular activities and less likely to be expected to look, dress, or act in certain ways. However, a higher proportion of females felt the expectation to both excel in academic or extracurricular activities as well as to look/dress/act in certain ways.

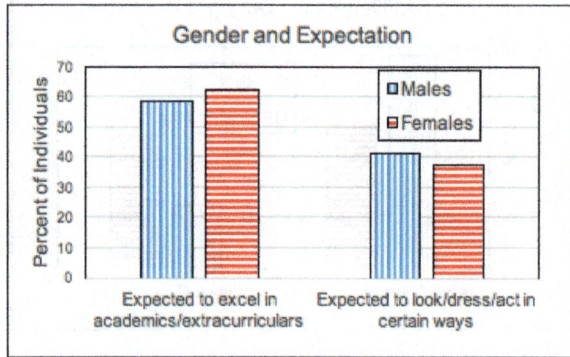

Figure 8: The Expectations Faced by Female and Male Participants.

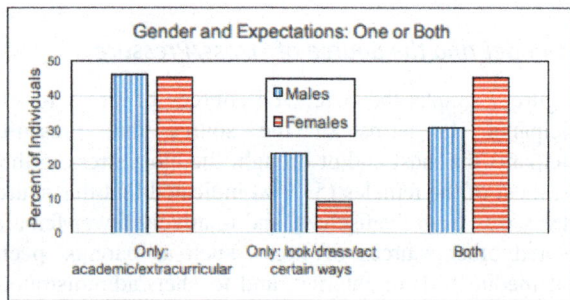

Figure 9: The Percentage of Females and Males Who Faced One or Both Expectations.

3.3 Views Regarding Parents and Mental Health

For the question "do you feel comfortable talking to your parents about your mental health and your mental-health needs?", most of the responses from participants were either no (44.7%) or somewhat (31.6%). Figure 10 graphs the percentages. Table 1 summarizes the responses for the question "what do your parents do (if anything) that makes you comfortable talking to them?" Table 2 summarizes the responses for the question "what are the factors (if any) preventing you from talking to your parents?" Table 3 summarizes the responses for the question "do you wish your parents supported you more? If so, what do you wish that your parents did that would support you more?"

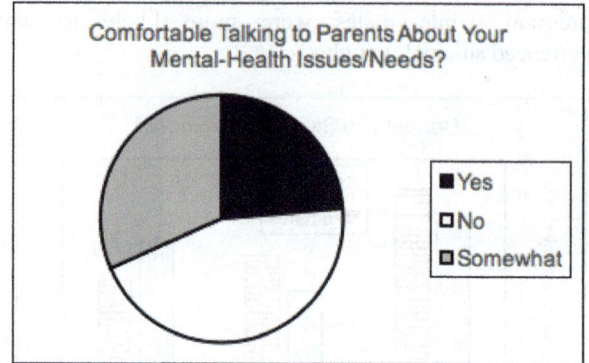

Figure 10: Proportions of Responses for Whether Participants Felt Comfortable Talking to Parents About Mental Health.

Response Type	Response Examples	Number (%)
Neutral	Nothing; Not Much; N/A; Don't Know	13 (29.5%)
Positive	Open for Communication; Open-Minded; Understanding	10 (22.7%)
Positive	Encourage; Reassure; Offer Advice	7 (15.9%)
Positive	Listen Patiently	6 (13.6%)
Positive	Being Nice/Supportive; Trust	5 (11.4%)
Negative	Being "Judgmental"	1 (2.3%)
Negative	"Pretend to care then use it against me"	1 (2.3%)
Negative	"Scorn me for not performing well"	1 (2.3%)

Table 1: What Teenagers Thought That Parents Could Do to Make It More Comfortable to Talk.

Source	Factors	Number (%)

Parents	Don't understand, pay attention, or care (9).	9 (19.1 %)
Parents	Being judgmental, annoying, and/or easily annoyed (8).	8 (17.0 %)
Parents	Being strict/stubborn and/or setting high expectations (5).	5 (10.6 %)
Parents	Not open about certain topics; Don't accept teen's gender identity (3).	3 (6.4 %)
Parents	General: The way they react/respond, generational differences, etc.	3 (6.4 %)
Teens	Do not want the parents to worry (3).	3 (6.4 %)
Teens	Scared to take up the parents' time (1); Don't feel comfortable (1).	2 (4.3 %)
Teens	School and pressure (1).	1 (2.1 %)
Other	None or N/A (9); Fear (3); Don't know (1).	13 (27.7 %)

Table 2: Factors That Teenagers Thought Prevented Them From Talking to Their Parents.

Type	Response	Number (%)
Less	Less pressure (5); Less unrealistic expectations (2); Less judgmental (2)	9 (45%)
More	More listening, acceptance, and/or support (4)	4 (20%)
More	More understanding of the student or his/her actions (3)	3 (15%)
More	More mental-health considerations in general (2)	2 (10%)

More	More open about LGBTQ+ issues (2)	2 (10%)

Table 3: What Teenagers Wished That Their Parents Did to Support Them More.

3.4 Views Regarding School and Mental Health

For the question "do you feel that the school is doing enough to assist students with their mental health?", most of the responses were either no (39.5%) or maybe (44.7%). Figure 11 graphs the percentages. Table 4 summarizes the responses for the question "what is the school doing that is supportive/effective?" Table 5 summarizes the responses for the question "what is the school doing that is ineffective?" Table 6 summarizes the responses for the question "what do you think the school can do to improve your mental health?".

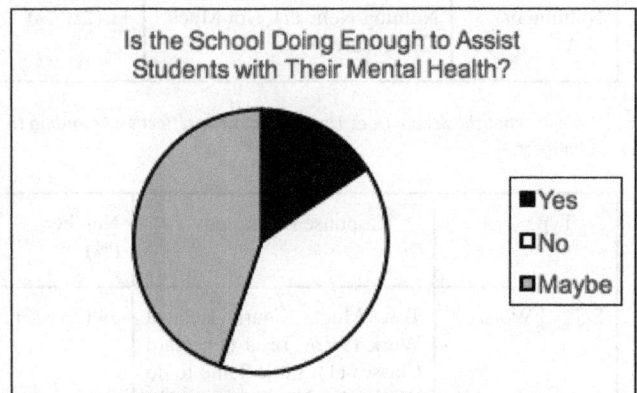

Figure 11: Proportions of Responses for Whether Participants Felt that the School is Doing Enough to Assist Students with Mental Health.

Type	Response Examples	Number (%)
Mental-Health (MH) Counseling	Having Available/Supportive/Helpful Counselor(s) (7) or MH Specialist (1); Hope Squad Positivity Group (1)	9 (18.4%)
Mental-Health (MH) Facility	Wellness/Health Center(s) (5); MH "Homeroom" or Lunch Classrooms (2); "Safe Space" to Talk (1)	8 (16.3%)
Mental-Health (MH) Activities	MH Breaks or Break Days (2); MH Awareness Week (1); MH Course (1); Reach-	6 (12.2%)

	Out Effort (2)	
Dog(s)	Therapy or Emotional-Support Dogs (3); Dog/Puppy (3)	6 (12.2%)
People or Resources	Willing to Change or be Flexible (2); Care About Students (1); Playing with Friends (1); Providing Resources (1)	5 (10.2%)
Teachers	Teachers are Nice/Understanding/Perceptive (3); Educating Teachers on the Issue (1)	4 (8.2%)
Nothing or N/A	Nothing/None (7); Not Much (2); Unsure (2)	11 (22.5%)

Table 4: What the School Does That Is Supportive/Effective According to Teenagers.

Type	Response Examples	Number (%)
School Work	Too Much Course-Related Work (9) or Tests (1); Hard Classes (1); Little Time to do Work (1); Not Setting (AP) Class Limits/Boundaries for Students (1).	13 (28.3%)
Counseling or Mental Health	Ineffective/Inaccessible Counseling (6); Telling Parents (1); Lack Mental-Health Resources (1), Group Counseling (1), or Individual Attention (1); Christian Mental Health (2).	12 (26.1%)
Environment (General)	Weak Support Systems (3); Everything (2); Lack Resources (1); Empty Talk Without Doing Much (1); Dining Hall: Long Waiting Time, Not Enough Time to Eat/Socialize (1).	8 (17.4%)

Teachers	Teachers' Empty Talk (1); Students Don't Feel Confident Enough to Open Up to Teachers (1).	2 (4.3%)
Unsure or N/A	N/A (5); Unsure (3) or Don't Know (2); Nothing (1).	11 (23.9%)

Table 5: What the School Does That Is Ineffective According to Teenagers.

Type	Response Examples	Number (%)
Mental-Health (MH) Related	More MH Awareness/Knowledge (5), Resources (3), Services/Counseling (2), Options (2), or Clubs/Groups (1); Wellness Center (1); Surveys to Check and Reach Out (1).	15 (23.1%)
Free Time or Rest	More Breaks (6), Free Time (3), Naptime (1), Rest Days (2), Holidays (1), or Resting Spaces (1).	14 (21.5%)
Academics or Class	Less Homework/Coursework (5); More Options/Learning (4), School Activities (3), or Teacher-Student Understanding (1).	13 (20.0%)
System-Related	Change System (1); Make It Easier to Get Into School (1); AP Caps (1); Allocate Resources (1); More Helpful/Friendly for Students (2), Newcomers (1), or LGBTQ people (1).	8 (12.3%)
Extracurricular	More Fun/Outside Activities (3), Social Gathering (2), Sports/Exercise (2), or Relaxation Programs (1).	8 (12.3%)
N/A or Unsure	N/A (3); Nothing (2); Not Sure (2).	7 (10.8%)

Table 6: What Teenagers Thought That the School Can Do to Improve Students' Mental Health.

4. Discussion

The current quantitative results are important because they identified the types and the sources of mental-health issues for adolescents. In terms of the types of stress, it was found that anxiety, depression, and suicidal thoughts were the most widely experienced types of stress. However, females were more likely to have experienced anxiety and depression, while males were more likely to have experienced suicidal thoughts. In terms of the sources of stress, males were more likely to perceive stress from teachers/administrators or parents. On the other hand, females were more likely to perceive stress from themselves, and females were more likely to be expected to excel in both academics or extracurricular activities as well as to look, dress, or act in certain ways.

The current qualitative results are important in identifying teenagers' views on their parents and schools regarding mental-health issues. Most of the participants were not very comfortable with talking to their parents about mental health. The most frequent reasons were the perceptions of their parents as being disinterested in mental health, judgmental, impatient, strict, demanding, and close minded. To make it more comfortable to talk, they thought that their parents could be more open for communication, more open minded, more understanding, and more encouraging. Also, they wished that their parents could be less strict, less demanding, and less judgmental. Regarding school and mental health, many participants thought that their school was not doing enough for the students' mental health. Even though most of them approved counselors, mental-health specialists, support groups, facilities, and therapy dogs, students thought that the mental-health support system could be improved and that having too much coursework or exams was stressful. Specifically, they believed that the school should provide more mental-health awareness, knowledge, resources, services, and support. Also, they thought that there should be more free time and rest time as well as more fun, outside, and social activities.

5. Conclusion

Although the current study generated many important results, no single study is perfect, so there are some limitations. For instance, the current study used convenient sampling, which limits the representativeness of samples and the generalizability of the findings. Moreover, there were only one gender-fluid participant and one agender participant in the current samples. Future research can include participants from the LGBTQ+ populations and those from other diverse groups. Also, further studies can examine people from different ages, different ethnic backgrounds, different religious beliefs, and different types of schools (e.g., private schools vs. public schools, high

schools vs. colleges or universities, etc.). In addition, it would be interesting to assess the views of parents or educators regarding mental-health issues and compare them to the views of students.

Despite the limitations of the current study, its findings do have applications or implications for parents, students, school administrators, teachers, researchers, counselors, and therapists. For example, parents can adjust how they interact with their children, schools can promote mental health according to students' perspectives, and counselors can use the findings to help identify the potential or possible mental-health issues of students. Finally, administrators may take heed to some of the specific qualitative comments from the participants regarding what schools can do to help. For example, it might be helpful for schools to conduct surveys to check-on the mental health of students (and reach-out to them), encourage less competitive or stressful academic environments (e.g., setting limits for AP courses), and develop programs that offer mental-health support (e.g., for newcomers and marginalized groups). After all, no one doubts that most parents and schools do what they can to provide good educational experiences, but the students' voices should be heard as well. Just as athletics pursuits should not result in detriments to physical health, intellectual pursuits should not result in detriments to mental health.

6. References

[1] Afifi, M. (2007). Gender differences in mental health. *Singapore Medical Journal, 48*(5), 385-391.

[2] Chandra, A., & Minkovitz, C. S. (2007). Factors that influence mental health stigma among 8th grade adolescents. *Journal of Youth and Adolescence, 36,* 763-774.

[3] Green, J. G., McLaughlin, K. A., Alegría, M., Costello, E. J., Gruber, M. J., Hoagwood, K., Leaf, P. J., Olin, S., Sampson, N. A., & Kessler, R. C. (2013). School mental health resources and adolescent mental health service use. *Journal of the American Academy of Child & Adolescent Psychiatry, 52*(5), 501-510.

[4] Lin, K.-M., & Cheung, F. (1999). Mental health issues for Asian Americans. *Psychiatric Services, 50*(6), 774-780.

[5] Myers, D. G., & DeWall, N. C. (2018). *Myer' Psychology for the AP Course* (Third Edition). BFW/Worth Publishers: New York, NY.

[6] Suldo, S. M., Shaunessy, E., & Hardesty, R. (2008). Relationships among stress, coping, and mental health in high-achieving high school students. P*sychology in the Schools, 45*(4), 273-290.

[7] WHO. (2022). Mental Disorders. World Health Organization.

Retrieved from https://www.who.int/news-room/fact-sheets/detail/mental-disorders

[8] Wu, T., Jia, X., Shi, H., Niu, J., Yin, X., Xie, J., & Wang, X. (2021). Prevalence of mental health problems during the COVID-19 pandemic: A systematic review and meta-analysis. *Journal of Affective Disorders, 281*, 91-98.

Franklin Education Foundation
Journal of Quantitative and Qualitative Research

Coffee-Efficient Coefficient for Environmental Protection: The Correlations Between
Gross Domestic Product and Waste for Coffee-Producing and Coffee-Consuming Countries
Zhixuan Yin

Coffee-Efficient Coefficient for Environmental Protection: The Correlations Between Gross Domestic Product and Waste for Coffee-Producing and Coffee-Consuming Countries

Zhixuan Yin

Franklin Education Foundation

Journal of Quantitative and Qualitative Research

Coffee-Efficient Coefficient for Environmental Protection: The Correlations Between
Gross Domestic Product and Waste for Coffee-Producing and Coffee-Consuming Countries

Zhixuan Yin

1. Introduction

Coffee, a globally cherished commodity, traces its roots back to the ancient forests in Ethiopia. According to legend, a 9th-century goat herder discovered coffee when he noticed how energetic his goats became after eating the beans from a coffee tree. From humble beginnings, coffee spread to the Arabian Peninsula, then to Europe, and it eventually evolved into a vital driver of the global economy (National Coffee Association USA, n.d.).

Historically, coffee has been instrumental in the global trade dynamics, playing the role of a catalyst for cultural exchange and economic success. For instance, the "Coffee Houses" in Europe during the 17th century were significant hubs of social interaction, intellectual discourse, and business transactions. As time went on, coffee transformed from a luxurious, expensive product into one which most people can afford, due to innovations in transportation and improved production technologies (National Coffee Association USA, n.d.; Avey, 2013).

From an economic perspective, the coffee industry has significant implications on both the macro and the micro scale. On the macro level, coffee is a significant part of the global agricultural economy, especially to developing nations. Countries such as Brazil, Colombia, and Vietnam heavily rely on coffee exports for their economic stability. The global coffee market is projected to reach 134.25 billion (in US dollars) by 2024, creating a larger economic impact (Global Coffee Market, 2020). At the micro level, coffee plays an important role for small farmers by offering employment opportunities and acting as a major source of income. It is estimated that over 125 million people worldwide depend on coffee for their livelihoods (The Fairtrade Foundation, n.d.).

Furthermore, the applications of agricultural technologies have increased the economic efficiency and the productivity of coffee. For example, ecological agricultural techniques were able to improve the soil quality of coffee plantations through increasing phosphorus, carbon, phosphate solubilizers, and cellulolytic fungi (Pinzon, Vargas, & Avellaneda-Torres, 2022). Also, the use of fertilization technologies has led to more nitrogen for Coffee arabica plants and coffee products, resulting in more efficient nitrogen fertilization (de Souza, de Oliveira, Santos, Reis, Cabral, Resende, Fernandes, de Souza, Builes, & Guelfi, 2023).

In addition, agricultural technologies could decrease environmental emissions, though there is room for improvement. For instance, it was found that some coffee farms were better than others in producing more yields, less emissions, and more jobs, suggesting that it is possible to produce coffee efficiently while generating less pollution (Skevas & Martinez-Palomares, 2023). Moreover, analytics and technologies (such as wireless sensor networks, cloud computing, neural networks, remote sensing, etc.) could be implemented to improve the effectiveness of the entire supply chain for coffee. Specifically, they can help reduce cost, decrease time, improve services, and ensure sustainable growth of the industry (Kittichotsatsawat, Jangkrajarng, & Tippayawong, 2021).

Given that coffee is a global business worldwide, it is important to learn more about its economic aspects as well as how it can be related to environmental sustainability. Therefore, the current project aims to analyze the relationship between economic development and environmental pollution for coffee-producing and coffee-consuming countries or regions.

2. Methods

Data collection and archival research were carried out to gather information regarding more than 200 countries and regions. The information collected included each country's or each region's gross domestic product (GDP), total tons of solid waste generated per year, estimated total number of people in the population, estimated coffee production per year, and estimated coffee consumption per year. For each of the measures, the newest (i.e., for the most recent year) collected numbers or statistics were used.

Data were taken from various sources, including WorldAtlas.com, U-Earth.eu, WorldPopulationReview.com, Statistica.com, etc. Whenever possible, the particular measures were compared and/or calculated from multiple sources to cross-check and verify. If the reports from various sources regarding a particular measure were close to each other, then they were averaged for the purpose of statistical analyses. After the data were collected, they were compiled in Microsoft Excel and analyzed using Excel's statistical software.

The method is appropriate because it allows the researcher to assess the relationship between variables on a large scale. Besides, an experiment is not possible in this case, because it is unfeasible for the researcher to independently manipulate and control a country's or a region's GDP, waste generated, population, coffee production, and coffee consumption; doing so would require high levels of coordinated effort among governments and various institutions.

Franklin Education Foundation

Journal of Quantitative and Qualitative Research

Coffee-Efficient Coefficient for Environmental Protection: The Correlations Between
Gross Domestic Product and Waste for Coffee-Producing and Coffee-Consuming Countries

Zhixuan Yin

Not all measures were able to be collected for all of the countries and regions; although efforts were taken to collect as much data as possible, if a particular number could not be found for a certain country or region, then it was excluded from statistical analysis. For the data on coffee production and coffee consumption (i.e., in 60 kg bags, 60-lb bags, metric tons, and/or pounds), they were only collected for the top 50 coffee-producing countries/regions and the top 50 coffee-consuming countries/regions.

3. Results

For the top coffee-producing countries (i.e., the 50 countries that produced the most amounts of coffee), there was a very strong positive correlation ($r = 0.73$) between their gross domestic product (GDP) per capita and their waste (i.e., the total tons of municipal solid waste generated per year) per capita; the slope of the best-fit regression line was significantly greater than zero, $t(49) = 7.51$, $p < 0.01$. Figure 1 shows this relationship. Generally, countries that produced higher levels of GDP also generated more waste.

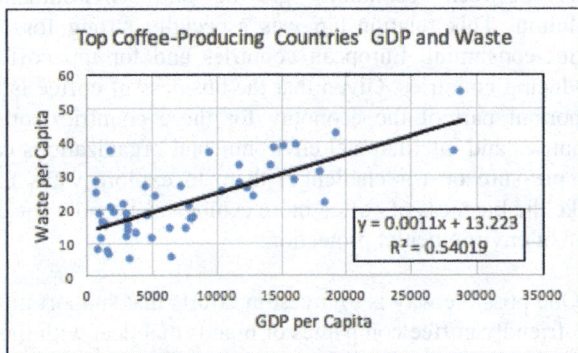

Figure 1: The Top Coffee-Producing Countries' Gross Domestic Product Per Capita and Tons of Waste Per Capita.

However, for the other countries (i.e., those that were not the top coffee-producing countries), the relationship between gross domestic product (GDP) per capita and waste produced per capita was weaker. For the other countries, there was a moderately strong positive correlation ($r = 0.62$) between their GDP per capita and their generated waste per capita; the slope of the best-fit regression line was significantly greater than zero, $t(164) = 9.99$, $p < 0.01$. Figure 2 shows this relationship. Generally, although countries that produced higher levels of GDP also generated more waste, this trend was less pronounced for the other countries.

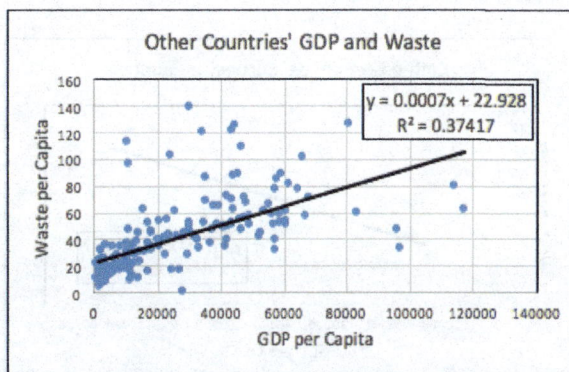

Figure 2: The Other Countries' (i.e., Non-Top Coffee-Producing Countries') Gross Domestic Product Per Capita and Tons of Waste Per Capita.

As for the top coffee-consuming countries (i.e., the countries that consumed the most amounts of coffee other than the top coffee-producing countries), there was a moderate positive correlation ($r = 0.58$) between their GDP per capita and their generated waste per capita; the slope of the best-fit regression line was significantly greater than zero, $t(38) = 4.31$, $p < 0.01$. Figure 3 shows this relationship. Again, although countries that produced higher levels of GDP also generated more waste, this trend was less pronounced for the top coffee-consuming countries.

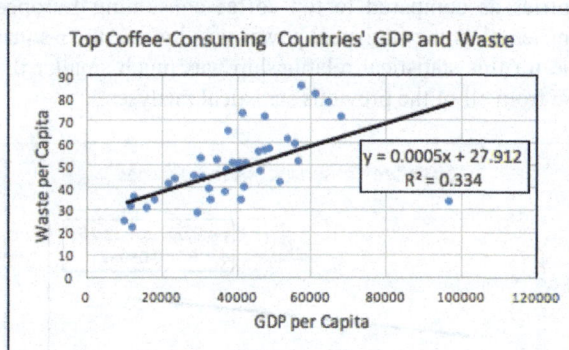

Figure 3: The Top Coffee-Consuming Countries' Gross Domestic Product Per Capita and Tons of Waste Per Capita.

Nevertheless, when those top coffee-consuming countries were analyzed separately by their geographic regions, different patterns of results emerged. Specifically, for the top coffee-consuming European countries, there was a very strong positive correlation ($r = 0.83$) between their GDP per capita and their generated waste per capita; the slope of the best-fit regression line was significantly greater than zero, $t(27) = 7.54$, $p < 0.01$. Figure 4 shows this relationship. The relationship between GDP and waste was especially pronounced for the top coffee-consuming European countries.

Franklin Education Foundation

Journal of Quantitative and Qualitative Research

Coffee-Efficient Coefficient for Environmental Protection: The Correlations Between
Gross Domestic Product and Waste for Coffee-Producing and Coffee-Consuming Countries

Zhixuan Yin

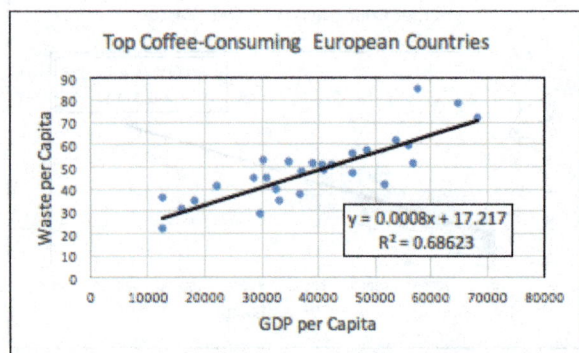

Figure 4: The Top Coffee-Consuming European Countries' Gross Domestic Product Per Capita and Tons of Waste Per Capita.

On the other hand, for the top coffee-consuming Asian (i.e., East-Asian and Southeast-Asian) countries, there was only a weak positive correlation (r = 0.30) between their GDP per capita and their generated waste per capita; the slope of the best-fit regression line was not significantly greater than zero, $t(6) = 0.70$, $p = 0.51$. Figure 5 shows this relationship. The relationship between GDP and waste was weak (at best) or almost non-existent for the top coffee-consuming East-Asian and Southeast-Asian countries. Even though there were fewer top coffee-consuming Asian countries as compared to top coffee-consuming European countries (thus the statistical power was lower), the r-square value for this statistical relationship was much smaller than those from all of the previous statistical analyses.

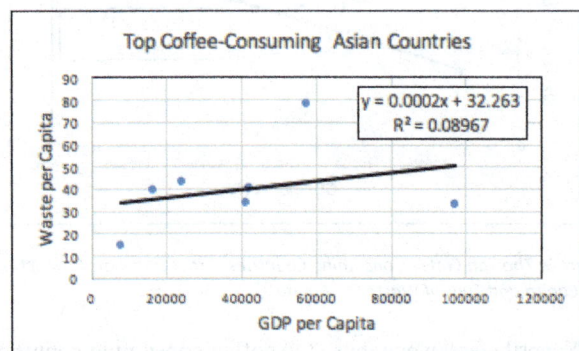

Figure 5: The Top Coffee-Consuming Asian Countries' Gross Domestic Product Per Capita and Tons of Waste Per Capita.

Figure 6 shows the "coffee-nation correlation coefficient" or the "coffee coefficient" regarding the correlations between GDP and waste for the various groups of top coffee-producing countries, top coffee-consuming countries, and other countries (i.e., non-top coffee-producing countries). As can be seen in this figure, the

relationship between GDP and waste was strongest for top coffee-consuming European countries and for top coffee-producing countries.

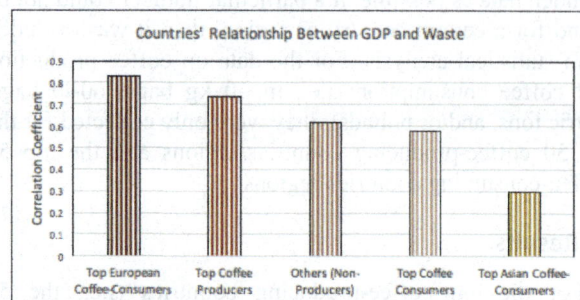

Figure 6: The Correlation Coefficients Between Gross Domestic Product and Waste for the Various Groups of Top Coffee-Producing Countries, Top Coffee-Consuming Countries, and Other Countries.

4. Discussion

The current study yielded a number of important findings. For example, the results suggest that there are significant links between economic growth and environmental pollution. This relationship was especially strong for top coffee-consuming European countries and for top coffee-producing countries. Given that the business of coffee is an important part of the economy for these countries, other countries and international environmental organizations can put pressure on (or challenge) them to explore ways that make the business of coffee more ecological-friendly for the sake of environmental protection.

One possible way is to invest in efforts that support more eco-friendly coffee companies or brands that deal with these countries. Most coffee consumers probably already know about the famous coffee companies/brands such as Starbucks, McCafé, Costa Coffee, Nestlé, and Peet's Coffee; efforts can be devoted to promoting more sustainable coffee companies or brands, such as Larry's Coffee, Ethical Bean, and Higher Ground Roasters (Matthews, 2023).

Another possibility is to adopt more sustainable farming practices in coffee plantations as well as to improve the process of importing and exporting coffee. Nab and Maslin (2020) examined the carbon footprint of Arabica coffee that was exported to the United Kingdom from the producers of Brazil and Vietnam. Sustainable coffee growing methods (e.g., optimal use of agricultural chemicals) resulted in less average carbon footprint than conventional coffee growing methods, and exporting coffee beans via ships instead of airplanes could reduce the carbon footprint by more than 70% (Nab & Maslin, 2020). These promising practices should be

Franklin Education Foundation
Journal of Quantitative and Qualitative Research

Coffee-Efficient Coefficient for Environmental Protection: The Correlations Between
Gross Domestic Product and Waste for Coffee-Producing and Coffee-Consuming Countries
Zhixuan Yin

adopted by more top coffee-producing countries and top European coffee-consuming countries.

5. Conclusion

No single study is ever perfect, so the current study has its limitations. Methodologically, even though an experiment that manipulates GDP, waste, or the business of coffee would be unfeasible and impractical for the researcher, it should be noted that correlation still does not necessarily imply causation. For example, in the case of a correlation between the GDP per capita and the generated waste per capita, it does not necessarily mean that an increase in GDP caused an increase in waste. Theoretically, it could be that (A) an increase in GDP (which supposedly reflects economic performance) caused an increase in waste, or it could be that (B) an increase in waste caused an increase in GDP (e.g., by hypothetically creating financial opportunities that led to economic growth), or it could be that (C) a third factor (such as business development of a region) caused both an increase in GDP and an increase in waste simultaneously. However, the aforementioned possibilities of A and/or C seemed to be much more likely than the possibility of B.

Nevertheless, the findings of the current study have important implications. Specifically, the correlations between economic development and environment pollution provide measures to monitor, assess, and compare countries or regions, quantifying the amount of their potential to become more "coffee-efficient." Finally, possible future research can examine specific coffee companies' wastes, compare the environmental impacts of coffee to those of other beverages (such as tea), and explore how the business of coffee can be improved for conservation. After all, it is important to decrease the association between GDP and waste. When these correlation coefficients turn into "coffee-efficient" coefficients, then hopefully the top-producing countries and the top-consuming countries can grow their economy without significant increases in pollution, and the people can be awakened by environmentalism as much as they are awakened by coffee.

6. References

[1] Avey, T. (2013, April 8). The caffeinated history of coffee. *PBS.* https://www.pbs.org/food/the-history-kitchen/history-coffee/

[2] de Souza, T. L., de Oliveira, D. P., Santos, C. F., Reis, T. H. P., Cabral, J. P. C., Resende, E. R. S., Fernandes, T. J., de Souza, T. R., Builes, V. R., Guelfi, D. (2023). Nitrogen fertilizer technologies: Opportunities to improve nutrient use efficiency towards sustainable coffee production systems. *Agriculture, Ecosystems & Environment, 345*(1), 108317. https://www.sciencedirect.com/science/article/abs/pii/S0167880922004662

[3] Global Coffee Market (2020, May 13). *Businesswire.com.* https://www.businesswire.com/news/home/20200513005323/en/Global-Coffee-Market-2020-to-2024---Insights-Forecast-with-Potential-Impact-of-COVID-19---ResearchAndMarkets.com

[4] Kittichotsatsawat, Y., Jangkrajarng, V., & Tippayawong, K. Y. (2021). Enhancing coffee supply chain towards sustainable growth with big data and modern agricultural technologies. *Sustainability, 13*(8), 4593. https://doi.org/10.3390/su13084593

[5] Matthews, L. (2023, January 12). The 12 best ethical & sustainable coffee brands for 2023. *LeafScore.* https://www.leafscore.com/eco-friendly-kitchen-products/best-sustainable-coffee-brands/

[6] Nab, C., & Maslin, M. (2020). Life cycle assessment synthesis of the carbon footprint of Arabica coffee: Case study of Brazil and Vietnam conventional and sustainable coffee production and export to the United Kingdom. Geo: *Geography and Environment, 7*(2), e00096. https://rgs-ibg.onlinelibrary.wiley.com/doi/10.1002/geo2.96

[7] National Coffee Association USA (n.d.). The History of Coffee. https://www.ncausa.org/about-coffee/history-of-coffee (accessed on 7/12/2023).

[8] Pinzon, P. D. G., Vargas, L. K. A., & Avellaneda-Torres, L. M. (2022). Changes in soil quality associated with the implementation of ecological agriculture techniques in coffee plants under different coverings. *Colombia Forestal, 25*(1), 5-20.

[9] Skevas, T., & Martinez-Palomares, J. C. (2023). Technology heterogeneity and sustainability efficiency: Empirical evidence from Peruvian coffee production. *European Journal of Operational Research, 310*(3), 1192-1200.

[10] The Fairtrade Foundation (n.d.). Coffee farmers. https://www.fairtrade.org.uk/farmers-and-workers/coffee/#:~:text=Around%20125%20million%20people%20worldwide,from%20the%20coffee%20they%20produce.

[11] The World's Most and Least Polluted Countries (2022, August 22). *U-Earth.eu.* https://www.u-earth.eu/post/world-most-least-polluted-countries

[12] Top Coffee Producing Countries (n.d.). *WorldAtlas.com.* https://www.worldatlas.com/articles/top-coffee-producing-countries.html

Comparing Machine Learning Algorithms for Temperature Prediction With Fuel Production and Consumption

Sophia Tang

1. Introduction

Most scientists have agreed that global warming is a disastrous problem, one that humans started and exacerbated in the past few decades. The Industrial Revolution was the start of this issue because it instigated the widespread use of fossil fuels, as before this time period, it was very difficult for humans to harvest energy. The discovery of how to use these fossil fuels led humans to realize that they were cheap, efficient, and readily available. However, despite the many advantages of these fossil fuels, the glaring downside is that the production and consumption warms the Earth by trapping in greenhouse gases. Burning nonrenewable resources releases greenhouse gases that trap in the sun's heat and heat up the planet. Activities like driving gasoline-powered cars, using coal to warm a house, and deforesting land are some examples of how carbon dioxide and methane, the most prevalent greenhouse gases, are emitted. If the temperature of the Earth continues to rise, severe weather will be more common, humans will encounter dire health problems, and biodiversity will drastically diminish. Since the late 1800s, about when the industrial revolution ended, the Earth has become approximately 1.1 degrees Celsius warmer. The Paris Agreement's agreed consensus is to curb temperatures below 2 degrees Celsius by 2050, preferably by 1.5 degrees Celsius, but based on current predictions, the Earth will be about 3.2C warmer by the year 2100 (*What Is Climate Change? | United Nations*, n.d.).

The 2021 Production Gap Report reveals that governments plan to manufacture double the amount of fossil fuels that the Paris Agreement calls for (*2021 Report - Production Gap*, 2021). This practice is opposite of the goal, because to avoid the worst consequences of climate change, the world must cut greenhouse gas emissions by 6% per year (*Cut the Coal | United Nations*, n.d.).

This research paper focuses on the production and consumption of three main fossil fuels: natural gas, coal, and crude oil. Their impacts on the globe's temperature are examined with two different machine learning algorithms. But before that, we need to understand why these three fossil fuels are so harmful to the environment. Note that natural gas is referred to as gas and crude oil is referred to as oil in this paper.

Gas production is completed by drilling wells. If the pressure difference between underground and above the well is great enough, the gas flows up easily, but oftentimes, hydraulic fracking is necessary if the gas is trapped in the sedimentary rock formation. Fracking is done by creating a high pressure well, and then forcing fluids down to crack the rock and release the gas (*Natural Gas Explained - U.S. Energy Information Administration*, 2021).

When natural gas is burned, it produces less air contaminants than when coal and oil is burned, but gas leaks cause methane, one of the most detrimental greenhouse gases, to be released. The fracking process also disturbs wildlife, biodiversity, and environment resources because it requires drilling and clearing the area (*Natural Gas and the Environment - U.S. Energy Information Administration*, 2021).

There are two methods used in the production of coal. Surface mining is performed if the coal is less than 200 feet below ground, while underground mining is performed when the coal is further down (*Coal Mining and Transportation - U.S. Energy Information Administration*, 2021). When coal is burned to transfer it into consumable energy, emissions such as sulfur dioxide, nitrogen oxides, particulates, and carbon dioxide are emitted (*Coal and the Environment - U.S. Energy Information Administration*, 2021). One research paper analyzed the effects of coal on climate change. Coal is one of the most used energy resources by humans as well as the most carbon intensive. To meet the Paris Agreement goal, only one-fifth of coal reserves should be consumed by the year 2050, compared to the two thirds of oil reserves and half of gas reserves that can be consumed (Edwards, 2019, 1).

Oil drilling is the process to extract and produce oil. When performed underwater, it can harm the marine ecosystem, but drilling on land also harms the wildlife because it is usually necessary to clear the land first. Oil production can be achieved with hydraulic fracking to extract oil from tight geological places, which requires intensive resources, such as water. Earthquakes are another repercussion of oil production, as large amounts of chemical-filled wastewater are often injected into deep wells (*Oil and Petroleum Products Explained Oil and the Environment*, 2022).

There are numerous previous studies related to predicting weather, such as predicting snowfall and rainfall, with various machine learning algorithms, such as Support Vector Regression, Random Forest, and Multi-Layer Perceptron. Much of these temperature prediction studies use weather patterns as the independent variables. One such study used features like location, elevation, and average temperature to predict monthly air temperature in Australia and New Zealand with Support Vector Regression and Multi-Layer Perceptron (Salcedo-Sanz et al., 2015, 3). Minimal studies have used fuel production and consumption to predict temperature, which is the aim of this paper. Fuel production and consumption is a huge issue because it is one of the main contributors to greenhouse gases. In 2020, 73% of the United States' total greenhouse gas emissions resulted from burning fossil fuels, such as natural gas, coal, and oil (*Where Greenhouse Gases Come From - U.S. Energy Information Administration*, 2022).

Understanding the link and correlation between these fuels and temperature is imperative, so countries can acknowledge the impact of their fuel production and consumption, and thus realize the importance of transitioning into renewable energy.

The subsequent sections follow the following format: the Methods section details my approach to the experiment and the different algorithms I employed. The Experiment section presents all my results and the accuracy of the machine learning models, as well as the environment in which the experiment took place in. Discussion interprets the significance of my results and discusses some potential applications. The Conclusion section finally wraps up the paper by summarizing the findings, applying the results to real-world situations, explaining the limitations and problems, and also giving some potential future research directions.

2. Methods

2.1 Datasets

The two datasets I used were Daily Temperature of Major Cities and Fuel Production and Consumption, both of which I downloaded from Kaggle. The former dataset is sourced from the University of Dayton, and it started with 2906327 rows and 8 columns before cleaning. The columns consisted of Region, Country, State, City, Month, Day, Year, and Average Temperature (F). The latter dataset is sourced from the US Energy Information Analysis (EIA), and it started with 9237 rows and 14 columns before cleaning. The columns consisted of Year, Country, Gas Production (m3), Gas Consumption (m3), Coal Production (ton), Coal Consumption, Oil Production (m3), Oil Consumption (m3), and all of the consumption and production columns per capita, as well as Population.

Formatting and cleaning datasets before analysis is necessary because discontinuities, null values, incorrect values, and zero values often occur. These small errors can consequently confound the genuine long term trend.

My goal for the Daily Temperature dataset was to average the temperature of each country by year, instead of by city and day. I first removed all the rows with an Average Temperature of -99 because they were considered null. I also removed all rows with the year 2020 because in the dataset, the year 2020 only included up until April at maximum. If I kept the year 2020, it would skew the average temperature for 2020 because it only included four months, which is not a good representative of the whole year. I then removed any years with less than six recorded months of temperature data for a similar reason. Another problem I detected was that for some countries, there were multiple cities, but the cities' years span were

different. Using all of the cities for these countries would significantly skew data, especially if one city was notably colder or hotter than the other, so I removed any city data that had less years than the maximum year span for a city in the same country. As a result, every country's cities would have the same year span, thus resulting in a more consistent mean because for my next step, I averaged the temperature by year and country. The resulting columns were Country, Year, and Average Temperature, with a total of 2929 rows.

To format the fuel dataset, I first dropped the population column and all of the "per capita" columns. From there, I separated this dataset into three individual datasets of gas, coal, and oil. For each individual dataset, I dropped rows with null values as well as rows with a zero because that would significantly skew my data and predictions. The gas dataset ended up with 1702 rows, the coal dataset 1252 rows, and the oil dataset 1700 rows.

For a third dataset, I merged the average temperature dataset with the three fuel datasets, only merging if all four datasets had a specific country. This dataset has 1043 rows.

2.2 Data Analysis

There is a clear upward trend in gas, coal, and oil production as well as consumption (Figures 1-6). Figures 1-6 illustrate the top 10 countries that produced or consumed the most gas, coal, or oil in the year 2019 and their production or consumption of these fuels from 1995 to 2019. Common top contenders that consistently produce and consume the most fuel include China, United States, Russia, India, and Germany. Future graphs and tables for this research paper will also primarily show these five countries because they are among the world's top emitters of carbon dioxide (Blokhin, 2022).

In the past few decades, the average temperatures of most countries have also been steadily increasing, most likely due to the sharp increase of greenhouse gas emissions, such as those emitted during the production and consumption of gas, coal, and oil (Figures 7-11). Figures 7-11 show a scatterplot of average temperatures from 1995 to 2019 of the previously mentioned five countries. The graphs also show the line of best fit, and the slope of the lines of these five countries are all greater than 0, proving that since 1995, the average temperature of these five countries has increased. Out of the 125 countries in the temperature dataset, 99 had a slope greater than 0, which amounts to 79.2% of the countries analyzed. This means a majority of the world's countries are increasing in temperature.

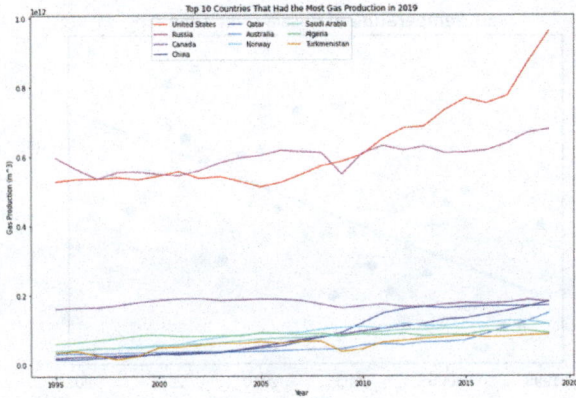

Figure 1 Countries With Most Gas Production

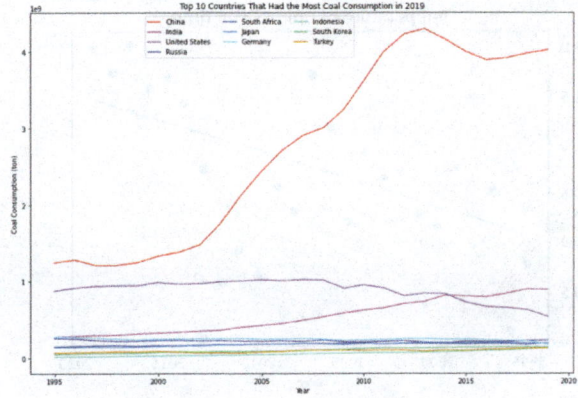

Figure 2 Countries With Most Gas Consumption

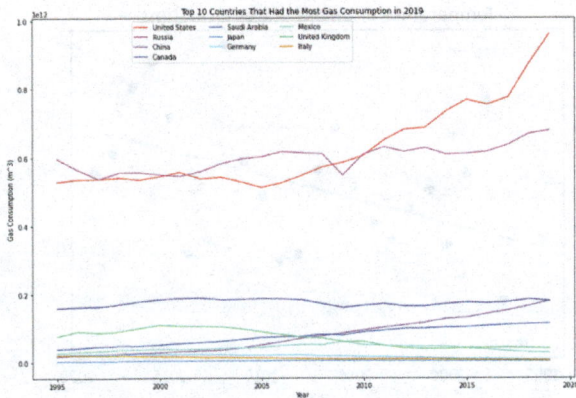

Figure 3 Countries With Most Coal Production

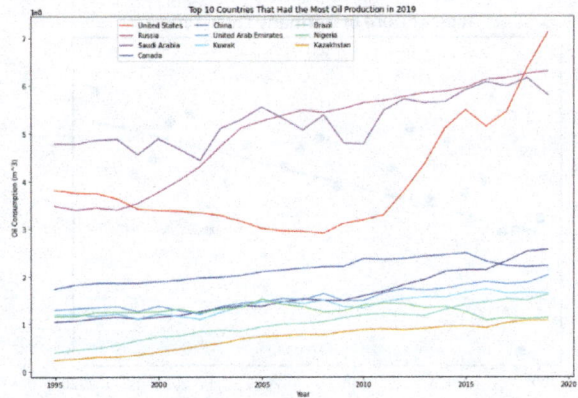

Figure 4 Countries With Most Coal Consumption

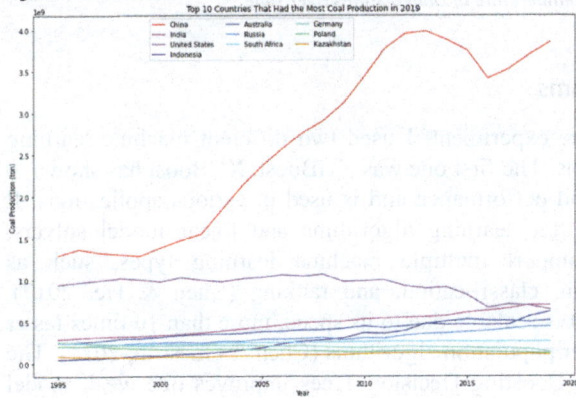

Figure 5 Countries With Most Oil Production

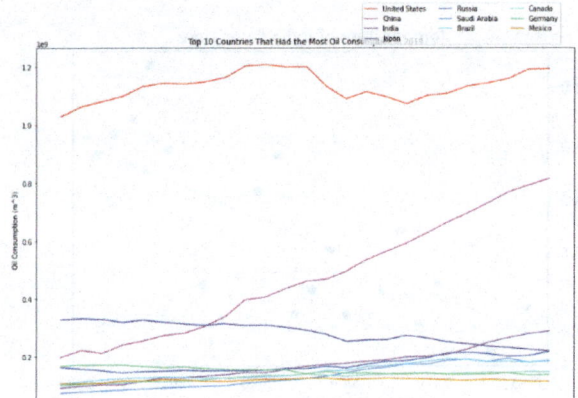

Figure 6 Countries With Most Oil Consumption

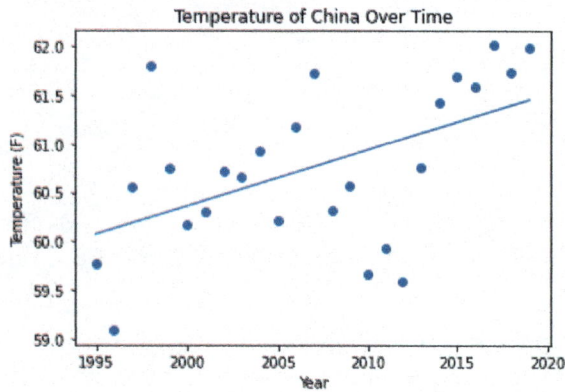

Figure 7 Temperature of China Over Time

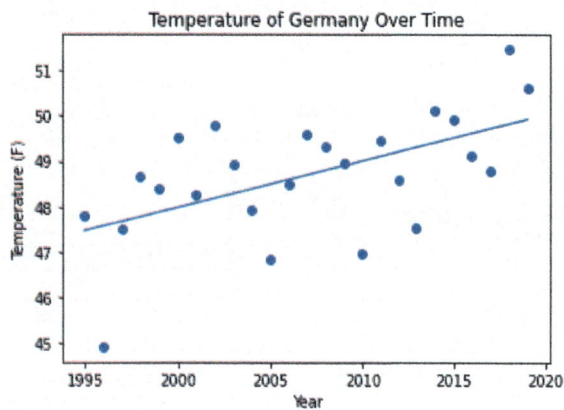

Figure 8 Temperature of Germany Over Time

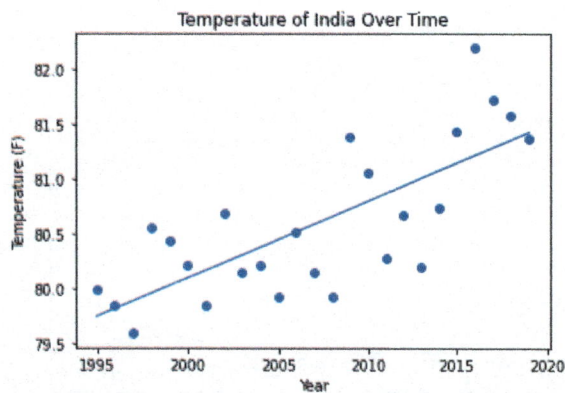

Figure 9 Temperature of India Over Time

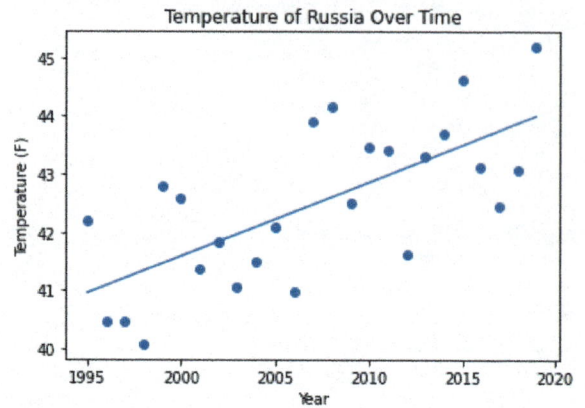

Figure 10 Temperature of Russia Over Time

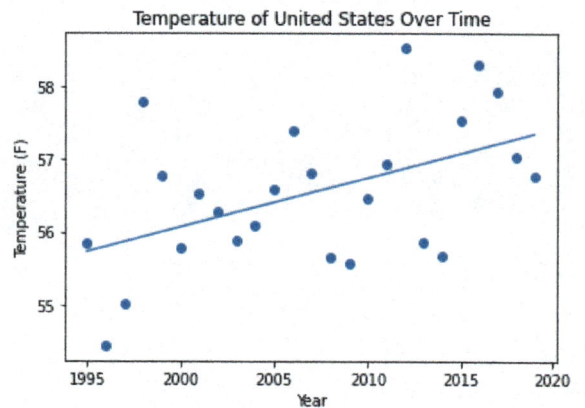

Figure 11 Temperature of United States Over Time

Algorithms

For the experiment, I used two different machine learning algorithms. The first one was XGBoost. XGBoost has shown to have good performance and is used in various applications. It includes tree learning algorithms and linear model solvers, which support multiple machine learning types, such as regression, classification, and ranking (Chen & He, 2017). XGBoost is scalable due to its speed, more than 10 times faster than other population algorithms (Chen & Guestrin, 2021). The Gradient Boosting Decision Trees improves one weak model by amalgamating it with other weak models to create a stronger model. Gradient boosting is more than just boosting because the process of continually creating weak models is made into a gradient descent algorithm over an objective function. It produces targeted outcomes for the next model to attempt to minimize errors, and these are based on the gradient of the error (*What Is XGBoost? | Data Science | NVIDIA Glossary*, n.d.).

Franklin Education Foundation   Comparing Machine Learning Algorithms for Temperature Prediction With Fuel Production and Consumption

Journal of Quantitative and Qualitative Research   Sophia Tang

The second machine learning algorithm I used was the random forest method. The random forest method combines a series of tree classifiers. Each tree casts one vote to another class and the combination of these gets the final result (Liu et al., 2012, 2). These features are all applicable to regression. Both of my models use regression because it evaluates the relationship between the dependent variables and the independent variable in a continuous state instead of categories.

2.3 Factors

Several factors were used in my machine learning models (Table 1). Units of variables are shown in parentheses. The range of most data spanned from 1995-2019, with some countries having a smaller time range.

Input Variables	Output Variables
Gas Production (m3), Gas Consumption (m3), Coal Production (ton), Coal Consumption (ton), Oil Production (m3), Oil Consumption (m3)	Average Temperature of Countries by Year (F)

Table 1 Features and Label of the Machine Learning Models

3. Results

The trend of gas, coal, and oil production and consumption was analyzed, and two machine learning algorithms were used to predict average temperature. Each country was analyzed separately because geospatial data was not included, and thus the algorithm would not account for temperature differences due to latitude, longitude, and altitude.

For both the XGBoost and Random Forest models, I separated the data for each country into two sections: training and validation data, 70% and 30% of the total data for that country respectively. The initial dataset was randomized to create these two separate datasets, which ensure the measure of model accuracy to be correct.

Model accuracy was measured by the mean absolute error of temperature in Fahrenheit. The closer the mean absolute error (MAE) is to zero, the more precise the model is. The mean absolute error was only calculated from the validation data, not including the training data. This is to acquire a true measurement of how well the model performs on data it has not seen before.

Table 2 shows the MAEs of the five countries mentioned previously for both machine learning methods. The last row displays the mean MAE for all countries. Overall, the XGBoost model did better with predicting average temperatures than the random forest model. India had consistent low MAEs with both

models, while Russia and Germany had relatively higher MAEs. The MAEs were relatively low because as temperature increases, a difference of one degree Fahrenheit translates to a lesser difference in degrees Celsius.

Country	XGB MAE (F)	RF MAE (F)
India	0.271304	0.249518
China	0.558778	0.610133
United States	0.603880	0.570686
Germany	0.954414	1.004690
Russia	1.166362	0.873582
Average for all countries	0.980233	1.027774

Table 2 Mean Absolute Error of XGBoost and Random Forest Machine Learning Algorithms

Table 3 consists of graphs for the five countries and both machine learning algorithms. Each graph shows the actual average temperature in blue and the predicted average temperature in red for each year. Both the training and validation data was utilized to generate these graphs. As shown by the difference between the red and blue lines, the models were not 100% accurate, but they predicted the overall trend relatively well, given the fuel production and consumption training data.

Country	XGB Graph	RF Graph
India		
China		

United States		
Germany		
Russia		

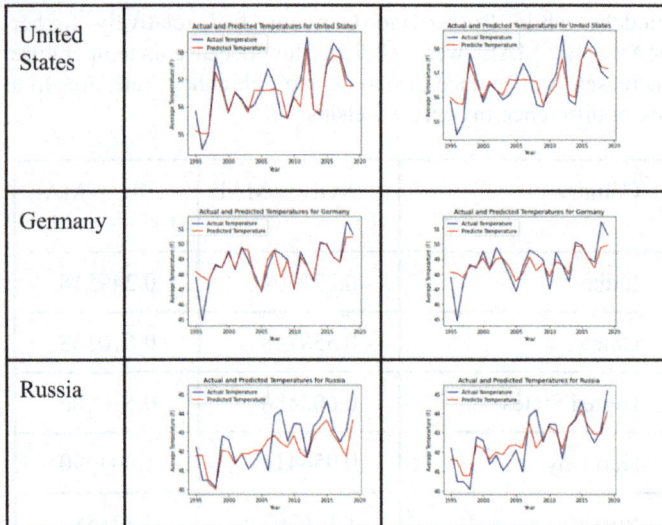

Table 3 Actual and Predicted Temperatures of Countries with XGBoost and Random Forest

All the code in the experiment was written and ran through Google Colaboratory, with a RAM of 12 GB and a disk space of 358.27 GB.

4. Discussion

In this study, the production and consumption of natural gas, coal, and crude oil were analyzed, and the two machine learning algorithms, XGBoost and Random Forest, were utilized to predict the average temperature of a country.

The results demonstrate that fuel production and consumption are devastating to the globe's temperature. This model can assist temperature predictions and to visualize the preferred 1.5C Paris Agreement. Inputs can be the anticipated or current fuel production and consumption, and the model can generate predicted temperatures. This can help countries decide how much to curb their fuel production and consumption to slow global warming and keep within the Paris Agreement limit.

5. Conclusion

The temperature prediction model was developed using the following steps. Independent variables were the production and consumption of the three types of fuel, while the dependent variable was average temperature of country by year. The next step was data pre-processing, and then the data was analyzed using two regression algorithms: XGBoost and Random Forest. Accuracy of the models were determined with mean absolute error. It was discovered that the XGBoost model produced the best results.

One area for further exploration is to use other types of machine learning algorithms and evaluate their MAEs, additionally, other metrics for calculating accuracy, such as mean squared error, root mean square deviation, and r squared. A second area for further exploration is to include green energy and study the differences of environmental impacts of green energy, such as solar and wind power, versus non-renewable energy.

Additionally, I generated a different model for each country because of the geographic differences and thus they would have temperature differences, for example countries closer to the equator are generally warmer. Future research could include latitude, longitude, and altitude in the dataset. In this way, one model can be generated for the entire dataset instead of for separate countries.

Instead of using gas production, coal production, and oil production and their own units, CO_2 emissions could have been used to have the same metric across all fuels, allowing comparisons of amounts of these fuels generated as well as analyses on how severe each one of them is, by analyzing the correlation to temperature.

Analysis of fuel is important because global warming is one of the most pressing issues in today's world. Imminent transition to green energy or reducing environmental impacts of current fuel production and consumption is extremely significant to our globe's future.

6. References

[1] Blokhin, A. (2022, July 2). *5 Countries Producing the Most Carbon Dioxide (CO2)*. Investopedia. Retrieved August 4, 2022, from https://www.investopedia.com/articles/investing/092915/5-countries-produce-most-carbon-dioxide-co2.asp

[2] Chen, T., & Guestrin, C. (2021, April 19). *XGBoost: A Scalable Tree Boosting System*. ACM. Retrieved August 4, 2022, from https://dl.acm.org/doi/pdf/10.1145/2939672.2939785

[3] Chen, T., & He, T. (2017, January 4). *xgboost: eXtreme Gradient Boosting*. Microsoft. Retrieved August 4, 2022, from https://cran.microsoft.com/snapshot/2017-12-11/web/packages/xgboost/vignettes/xgboost.pdf

[4] *Coal and the environment - U.S. Energy Information Administration*. (2021, December 2). EIA. Retrieved August 4, 2022, from https://www.eia.gov/energyexplained/coal/coal-and-the-environment.php

[5] *Coal mining and transportation - U.S. Energy Information Administration*. (2021, February 15). EIA. Retrieved August 4, 2022, from

Franklin Education Foundation   Comparing Machine Learning Algorithms for Temperature Prediction With Fuel Production and Consumption

Journal of Quantitative and Qualitative Research   Sophia Tang

https://www.eia.gov/energyexplained/coal/mining-and-transportation.php

[6] *Cut the Coal | United Nations*. (n.d.). United Nations. Retrieved August 4, 2022, from https://www.un.org/en/climate-action/cut-coal

[7] Edwards, G. A. S. (2019, August 15). Coal and climate change. *Wiley Interdisciplinary Reviews*, *10*(5).

[8] Liu, Y., Wang, Y., & Zhang, J. (2012). New Machine Learning Algorithm: Random Forest. *Springer Link*, *7473*. https://doi.org/10.1007/978-3-642-34062-8_32

[9] *Natural gas and the environment - U.S. Energy Information Administration*. (2021, December 8). EIA. Retrieved August 4, 2022, from https://www.eia.gov/energyexplained/natural-gas/natural-gas-and-the-environment.php

[10] *Natural gas explained - U.S. Energy Information Administration*. (2021, December 2). EIA. Retrieved August 4, 2022, from https://www.eia.gov/energyexplained/natural-gas/

[11] *Oil and petroleum products explained Oil and the environment*. (2022, August 1). EIA. Retrieved August 4, 2022, from https://www.eia.gov/energyexplained/oil-and-petroleum-products/oil-and-the-environment.php

[12] Salcedo-Sanz, S., Deo, R.C., & Carro-Calvo, L. (2015, May 10). Monthly prediction of air temperature in Australia and New Zealand with machine learning algorithms. *Springer Link*. https://doi.org/10.1007/s00704-015-1480-4

[13] *2021 Report - Production Gap*. (2021, October 21). Production Gap Report. Retrieved August 4, 2022, from https://productiongap.org/2021report/#R2

[14] *What Is Climate Change? | United Nations*. (n.d.). United Nations. Retrieved August 4, 2022, from https://www.un.org/en/climatechange/what-is-climate-change

[15] *What is XGBoost? | Data Science | NVIDIA Glossary*. (n.d.). Nvidia. Retrieved August 4, 2022, from https://www.nvidia.com/en-us/glossary/data-science/xgboost/

[16] *Where greenhouse gases come from - U.S. Energy Information Administration*. (2022, June 24). EIA. Retrieved August 4, 2022, from https://www.eia.gov/energyexplained/energy-and-the-environment/where-greenhouse-gases-come-from.php

Dragon Reborn: Cognitive Impact of User Interface and Aesthetics on Player Engagement

Maxwell Zhang

Abstract

In the burgeoning technology sector, the gaming industry is seeing exponential growth in popularity. While computer games have become increasingly popular, arcade games, which were pioneers in the gaming industry and once popular in the late 1970s, are falling behind computer games in terms of relative popularity. However, the predominantly wrist-operated joystick controllers were inherited and adapted to PC gaming products, making them a competitor of finger-actuated keyboards. One of the key differences between these two user interfaces is the rotational function of the joystick. Keyboards require multiple fingers to press keys, while joystick controllers rely on wrist rotation. Since speed and accuracy are key parameters in game design, researchers in neurology and computer science have closely examined the differential muscle response speed between the wrist and finger. Yet, the results have varied and do not seem to draw a clear conclusion. In my study, a 2D PC version of the game *Centipede* developed on a Unity platform based on a wizard theme, is used to examine the response time of joystick and keyboard interfaces for two age groups: adolescents and adults. The results indicated that the keyboard is a better choice for a faster response, especially for the adolescent group. Furthermore, I tested adolescent and adult preferences for the joystick and keyboard and found that the adolescents preferred the keyboard while the adults preferred the joystick. In addition, the enhanced gameplay entertainment features, such as graphics, background music, sound effects, storyline, and frame rate, were also evaluated and demonstrated to be attractive and captivating for both age groups, especially the visual representation of graphics.

Keywords: joysticks, keyboards, differential muscle response speed, wrist, finger, preferences, gameplay entertainment features

1. Dragon Reborn: Cognitive Impact of User Interface and Aesthetics on Player Engagement

Why do people love games? Games provide a source of amusement and enjoyment, as they offer a series of interesting choices that engage players. It is a great way to relax after a stressful workday for adults. In addition to their entertaining qualities, games foster a competitive environment, which drives individuals, especially teenage groups, to strive for optimal performance in competition. Game designers leverage principles of behavioral psychology to enhance the appeal and engagement of their products. Such efforts are evident in the ever-expanding game industry. The gaming computer market has experienced explosive growth in recent years, with a value of $40.13 billion in 2020 (Ruchal & Vineet, 2021). This market is projected to continue expanding, with estimates predicting it will reach a staggering $145.93 billion by 2030. This represents an impressive compound annual growth rate (CAGR) of 15.3% from 2021 to 2030.

Facing such an astonishing proliferation rate of PC video games, many researchers, such as neurologists, computational scientists, and myologists (a specialist in the study of muscles), conducted their studies on the impact of those games on cognitive abilities. Numerous experiments have been carried out to understand the connection to human well-being biologically and psychologically. Many game designers and scientists have launched a product called brain games (BG), a video game hypothesized to maintain the brain functioning of adults at the beneficial levels of adolescent minds. It branches out to the sub-cognitive games focusing on key features such as memory training (Clemenson et al., 2020), reducing the risk of dementia or Alzheimer's (Doraiswamy & Agronin, 2009), improving attention span (Alsaad et al., 2022), promoting mental agility (Lewis, 2013), or reducing reaction time with timed challenges (Dye et al., 2009). While the majority of games are cashed in for their entertainment value, the brain game market value is not insignificant, along with reflex and reaction games, a category of cognitive-motor games. The brain game industry reached a $6.5 billion market size in 2021 and is forecasted to have a market size of $44.4 billion by 2030 with a CAGR of 24.2% (Insightace Analytic Pvt. Ltd., 2022).

Looking back, Computer Space marked the beginning of the rich history of the video game industry with the invention of the first-ever computer arcade machine in 1971 (Kicks, 2023). Remarkably, the release one year later of the commercially successful game *Pong* truly kickstarted the sector. In the early 1980s, arcade machines were everywhere and enjoyed by people of all ages. The industry hit a major slump in the mid-1990s and, with the rise of PC gaming in the mid-2000s, never regained its original popularity of the 1980s. Despite its decreasing relative popularity, the arcade market, nevertheless, has a monetary increase of $1.98 billion and a CAGR of 1.99% predicted during the 2022-2027 period (Technavio, 2023). To provide familiarity to the adult test subjects, aged 45-60 and who grew up during the arcade's popular period, while also appealing to adolescents 15-18 years old, I adopted the concept of the popular arcade game *Centipede* and created my revamped PC version of the game *Dragon Reborn*. I inherited the joystick controller from the arcade machine for this study and compared it with keyboard operation and constructed specific movement functions to test the wrist and finger. *Dragon Reborn* is designed to examine human muscle responses when playing the game with two different user interfaces such that muscle reaction time can be collected when using a joystick or keyboard. Unlike the complex computational models and calculations used for similar studies, *Dragon Reborn* can directly gather experimental data.

2. Literature Review

No doubt, video games have become a powerful research tool for many neurophysiologists, computational researchers, and psychological professionals. The communication and connections of the human mind, nerve, and muscle to and from the central control system of the brain is a complex and intricate research topic. Marc Palaus, from the Cognitive Neurolab at Universitat Oberta de Catalunya, and colleagues provided a systematic review of a total of 116 articles and indicated that it has been possible to establish a series of links between the neural and cognitive aspects, including attention, cognitive control, and cognitive workload (Palaus et al., 2017). The authors concluded that "the lack of standardization in the different aspects of video game related research … could contribute to discrepancies in many related studies." Therefore, more research needs to be carried out to provide answers to these missing pieces.

Reaction time is one of the most critical parameters for evaluating human central nervous processing speed. According to Grrishma Balakrishnan, a professor at the Department of Physiology at Yenepoya Medical College, "It [Reaction time] reflects the speed of the flow of neurophysiological, cognitive, and information processes" (Balakrishnan et al., 2014). Typically, the faster the reaction time, the healthier the brain, and the better the memory and thinking skills. Reaction time is also an important parameter in many different fields. It plays an essential role in experimental cognitive psychology. Dr. Samantha Richerson from Penn State Health tried to build a correlation between the reaction time of people with type II diabetes and healthy adults. Part of the results indicated that the reaction time for diabetic adults is slower than for healthy adults. Richerson explained that diabetes affects peripheral nerves, which "slows psychomotor responses, and has cognitive effects on those individuals without proper metabolic control, all of which may affect reaction times" (Richerson et al., 2005). Furthermore, reaction time has been documented and examined in patients with multiple sclerosis (MS), a disease of the brain and central nervous system, in a study of 40 MS patients and 40 healthy controls conducted by researcher Douglas R. Denney from the University of Kansas. Data showed that the reaction time of MS patients is about 140 ms slower than healthy adults. The results indicated a strong correlation of reaction time to neural dysfunction in MS disease (Denney et al., 2011). This discussion is significant in that it serves as a variable between diseased and relatively healthy minds.

In the area of neuropsychology, reaction time is well studied as a natural kind of data to investigate cognitive ability. Yet, remarkably, few research studies on reaction time from the lower arm exist. Human-computer interaction research scientist Shumin Zhai and colleagues designed a 6-degree-of-freedom Glove and FingerBall to test reaction time. "The Glove design resembles many of the common virtual reality input devices" (Zhai et al., 1996). When using the Glove, most of the rotational operations are carried out by the wrist. The researchers found that users' task completion times were significantly shorter with an input system that utilized the fingers since the fingers have a pronounced representation in the human motor cortex, giving them more bandwidth relative to other human limbs. It has led to hypotheses that utilizing the fingers in the control of computer pointing devices will result in more effective input control. However, the above conclusions are quite the opposite of Professor Ravin Balakrishnan and Professor I. Scott MacKenzie, both at the Department of Computer Science at the University of Toronto. He argues that other research work comparing input devices, including 6-degree-of-freedom, operated by different parts of the lower arm was not as conclusive. "We conducted an experiment to determine the relative bandwidths of the fingers, wrist, and forearm and found that the fingers do not necessarily outperform the other limb segments" (Balakrishnan & MacKenzie, 1997). *Dragon Reborn* is designed to collect experimental data from players when they hit the keyboard or rotate the joystick in order to determine a relationship between reaction time and the behavior of the wrist and finger. Additionally, my study provides a better understanding of the reaction time of the lower arm in the field of neurology and myology. My

results can be used to address current limited and controversial research outcomes.

Today, research on reaction time in PC video games for different age groups is limited. Yet, great opportunities now exist to research brain functionality and muscle response when subjects play cognitive-motor games. Joseph J. Thompson and coauthors tested 3,305 participants between the ages of 16-44 and found that the reaction times for test subjects playing StarCraft 2 began to decline after the age of 24 (Thompson et al., 2014). Additionally, Carol Li and her colleagues from the Johns Hopkins University School of Medicine found a decline in the vestibulo-ocular reflex function of individuals over the age of 80 (Li et al., 2015). These articles support the notion of motor function degradation as a function of age. Clearly, there are a lot of missing pieces and a lack of research on a direct comparison between the reaction time of the wrist and finger, especially for adolescents, aged 15-18, and adults, aged 45-60. The intention of my study is to test the reaction time of adolescents and adults in a complex but controlled video game setting. Based on this gap in the past literature, I added a feature to *Dragon Reborn* that enables the direct collection of muscle reaction time to a flashing light integrated into a moving dragon in the game.

What is really happening in the brain when you play cognitive-motor games? It is not only a question for cognitive psychologists and neuroscientists but also an incentive for cognitive game designers to develop their games and one of the crucial reasons that I designed *Dragon Reborn*. Although the reaction time is connected to the hand-motor reflex, it is well connected to the primary motor cortex in the brain through nerve and muscle activities. The critical brain region responsible for controlling voluntary movements of the body is the primary motor cortex, playing a central role in the execution and coordination of motor skills. In fact, the motor cortex controls disparate finger movement, and neurons related to different finger movements are dispersed throughout the hand area of the motor cortex (Georgopoulos et al., 1999). In 1870, German anatomist Gustav Theodor Fritsch and neuropsychiatrist Eduard Hitzig discovered that by electrically stimulating various parts of a dog's motor cortex, different parts of the body would contract. They also found that if they destroyed an area of the motor cortex, the corresponding part of the body would become paralyzed. Surprisingly, Fritsch and Hitzig also found that parts of the body that can make the finest movements, such as fingers, take up much more space in the motor cortex than others (Hagner, 2012). Therefore, my study on the reaction time of the wrist and finger for adolescents and adults will add value to existing research in the cognitive, psychological, and neuroscientific fields and will provide a better understanding of the difference between the reaction time of the wrist and finger.

Since the visual stimulus is a sensory part of the brain-hands circuit, aesthetical appearances should be part of a successful cognitive game design. The game aesthetics, including graphics, sound effects, background music, etc., will bring entertainment value to the game and make it more effective. To build a cognitive and enjoyable game, it is critical to integrate the graphical entertainment elements with the cognitive concepts during game design, as advocated by Polona Caserman and colleagues. However, many cognitive game designers are not adequately considering the simultaneous achievement of intended cognitive effects and entertainment parts of the game (Caserman et al., 2020). My design will focus on achieving the fundamental goals of scientific study while also enhancing the existing recreational characteristics of entertainment game design. This includes improving graphics, background music, sound effects, storyline, and frame rate to create a game that is both effective and attractive. Using the results from these experiments, I can provide recommendations to improve the development of future games targeted at different age groups to further grow the cognitive gaming industry.

Overall, by designing a cognitive-motor game specifically for two different types of user interfaces (keyboard versus joystick) that would provide direct experimental data to address the reaction time difference between the wrist and finger in a controlled setting for two different age groups (adolescents and adults), my objective is to provide insight for cognitive psychology and the neuroscience community with a new understanding on the difference in reaction time between the wrist and finger as well as adolescents and adults. Ultimately my experimental approach can provide a clear answer to the research question: to what extent can the user interface of PC video games affect the motor response of adolescents and adults, and how does the muscle reaction time differ for the wrist and finger?

3. Method

This investigation's methodology consists of two parts: 1. developing a game and 2. collecting the relevant data. I created a revamped version of the classic *Centipede* and used it to collect data in three experiments.

3.1 Justification

I am inspired by the work conducted by the Dutch ophthalmologist and physiology professor Franciscus Donders, who was a leading figure in the area of reaction time study. In 1868, he conducted one of the first experiments in cognitive psychology, collecting reaction time to determine the duration it takes to make a decision through thinking and brain activity (Goldstein, 2011, 6). This experiment is used as a benchmark for many researchers studying in the field of cognitive psychology. In this experiment, Prof. Donders measured reaction time to an illuminated light. There were two types of reaction time tasks, simple reaction time and choice reaction time, and there was only one location for the light for simple reaction time, while the light could appear on the left or right for choice reaction time. The users would respond by pressing a button when they saw a light. I adapted the flashing light idea and designed it onto the head of the dragon in *Dragon Reborn*. Participants will either hit any of the "WASD" keys on the keyboard or rotate the joystick controller. The setup is straightforward and aims to collect direct responses from users.

Since my study evaluates the effects of different user interfaces, I chose to evaluate the joystick versus the keyboard since they represent gaming devices from two eras. *Centipede* was a hugely successful arcade game in 1982, created by Dona Bailey from the company Atari. It is known for its remarkable visual characteristics and complex structure (Perry, 1982). This makes *Centipede* a perfect candidate to use as a template and build a new game on top of it.

My recreation of *Centipede*, called *Dragon Reborn*, uses the following systems: Unity game engine for game functionality; Adobe Photoshop for all the art assets; and Reaper sound engine for the sound effects and background music. The general theme of the game revolves around wizardry, with inspiration from traditional Eastern culture. Over 500 art assets and 50 sound files were imported into the game to account for the various scenes and animations. Some examples of the art assets implemented into *Dragon Reborn* can be found in Appendix F.

Dragon Reborn has multiple scenes, with an opening cutscene that provides a background story, a menu screen, an instruction screen, and an in-game screen, as shown in Appendices A, B, C, and D, respectively. Users employ either a joystick or keyboard ("WASD") to play the game, and the objective is to kill the dragon as many times as possible before the player is killed. As a revamped version of *Centipede*, I specifically included improved graphics, background music, sound effects, storyline, and frame rate.

The graphics of *Centipede* included highly pixelated assets on a black backdrop. Intentionally, *Dragon Reborn* contained higher-resolution art assets and detailed pixel backgrounds for every game screen. The background music and sound effects for *Centipede* were created with 8-bit sound waves, whereas *Dragon Reborn* used standard Eastern instruments, such as the Erhu, as found in the Reaper sound engine library. *Centipede* did not include a storyline in its debut in the gaming market, but *Dragon Reborn* contains a cutscene with ten different shots, which highlight the background of the game. Finally, *Centipede* had a framerate nowhere close to that of *Dragon Reborn*, likely due to the vast new capabilities of contemporary computers.

I tested two age categories: adolescents, aged 15-18, and adults, aged 45-60. Test subjects in both age categories participated in the same series of three experiments on evaluating reaction time, user interface preference, and various game aesthetics. For purposes of testing motor response, I added a flashing light to the front of the dragon to test reaction time on different UI. The light would randomly blink, and the response time of the users would be recorded.

3.2 Data Collection

Data was collected through one-on-one sessions in a private conference room at a local library. The first experiment aimed to compare the effectiveness of different interfaces in a visual-motor task. In an experiment conducted with 36 adolescents and 34 adults in the game *Dragon Reborn*, the flashing light attached to the dragon was set to flash at an irregular frequency. Participants were asked to interact with the interface, using either a joystick (rotating the wrist) or keyboard (pressing "WASD"), when the light flashed. The game logged the time difference between the appearance of the light and the user response, and it calculated the averages of the response times. Each participant spent 20 minutes using each interface, and the average response time was recorded.

The second experiment aimed to evaluate the user experience of a joystick and keyboard and gather data on how age may affect the subjective experience of using them. In an experiment conducted with the same 36 adolescents and 34 adults, participants were asked to rate their experience playing *Dragon Reborn* using a joystick and keyboard, each independently. Each participant spent 20 minutes using each interface and then rated their experience on each using a scale from 1 to 10, with 1 being the worst and 10 being the best. This allowed a comparison of the preference for different control methods and an understanding of the impact the physical interface has on a user's enjoyment of the game.

The last experiment evaluated the impact of these various improvements on the player's enjoyment of the game and gathered data on how different age groups responded to these improvements. *Dragon Reborn*, which included improved graphics, background music, sound effects, frame rate, and storyline, was put to the test against the original version of *Centipede*. An experiment was conducted with the same 36 adolescents and 34 adults, who were asked to play both the original and updated versions of the game on a standard computer monitor using only the keyboard. Each participant spent 20 minutes playing each version of the game and then rated the impact of each improvement on their enjoyment of the game on a scale from 1 to 20, where 1 represents an extremely negative and 20 represents an extremely positive impact. Polling results identified which improvements had the most positive impact on a user's enjoyment of the game.

In the end, 6 adolescent and 4 adult trials were removed. This was due to either a misunderstanding of instructions or disinterest in the middle of their testing phase. Ultimately, 30 adolescent and 30 adult trials were used in the data analysis.

4. Results

4.1 Experiment 1: Reaction Time

For experiment 1, to analyze the effect of user interface on reaction time, I graphed the data in 4 separate box-and-whisker plots for each category of data (Figure 1). The reaction time was converted to milliseconds for better visualization of data. I evaluated the data by graphing 4 box-and-whisker plots for response time for each group. Adolescents were found to respond 16% faster on a keyboard than on a joystick. Using the two-sample t-test, I found that there were significant differences in the reaction time between adolescents and adults for both interfaces, with the adolescents' reaction time being much faster (Table 1 & Table 2). I also concluded that there is a statistically significant difference between the reaction time of the wrist and finger for adolescents. On the other hand, analysis indicates no significant reaction time difference for both user interfaces for adults. I concluded from the gathered data that teens generally have faster response times than adults. These findings support the notion that aging decreases the motor cortex size, which thus decreases the reaction speed. However, the restrictions of conclusions drawn from age-based comparisons will be discussed in the limitations.

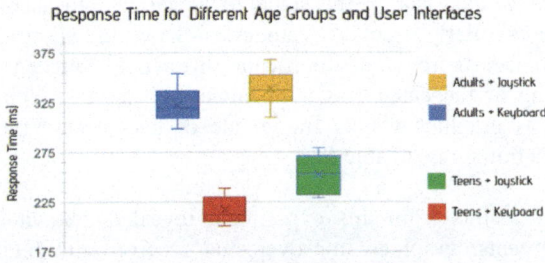

Figure 1. Box-and-whisker plot for response times

For experiment 2, to analyze the test subject preference for user interfaces, I used a two-sample t-test for means, as provided by Microsoft Excel, to find the mean and standard deviation, which were used to determine the significance of the data. I found that the adults rated the joystick an 8.5 and the keyboard a 3.5 (Figure 2). I also found that adolescents rated the joystick a 3.9 and the keyboard a 6.3 (Figure 3).

It was found that adults generally preferred the joystick, while teens preferred the keyboard. This conclusion was determined to be significant based on a 2 sample t-test, which showed that the preferences of these two age groups were significantly different (Table 3 & Table 4). These findings suggest that age may play a role in determining which computer interfaces individuals prefer to use and may have implications for the design and development of user interfaces in the future, as I will discuss later. However, similar to the last experiment, conclusions that involve age comparisons have their constraints, which will be discussed in the limitations.

t-Test: Paired Two Sample for Means (Joystick)		
	Average Reaction Time in ms (Adults)	Average Reaction Time in ms (Adolescents)
Mean	338.7	252.71
Variance	294.98	342.55
Std Dev	17.17	18.51
Lower Bound	321.53	234.2
Upper Bound	355.87	271.21
Observations	30	
df	29	
t Stat	20.8	

Table 1. Two sample t-test for joystick reaction time

t-Test: Paired Two Sample for Means (Keyboard)		
	Average Reaction Time in ms (Adults)	Average Reaction Time in ms (Adolescents)
Mean	322.37	217.87
Variance	278.86	163.71
Std Dev	16.70	12.79
Lower Bound	305.67	205.07
Upper Bound	339.07	230.66
Observations	30	30
df	29	
t Stat	27.03	

Table 2. Two sample t-test for keyboard reaction time

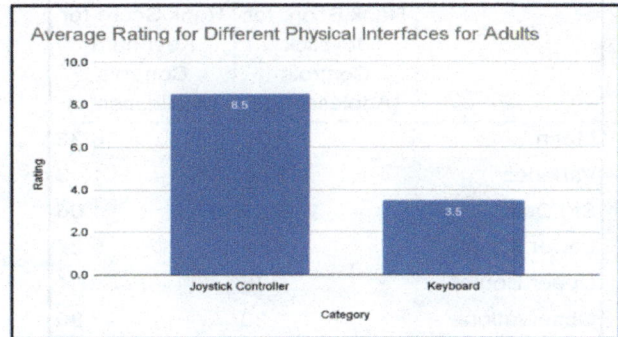

Figure 2. Bar chat containing average user interface rating for adults

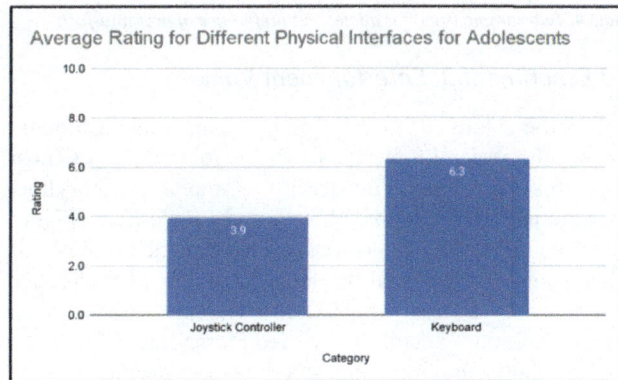

Figure 3. Bar chat containing average user interface rating for adolescents

4.2 Experiment 2: User Interface Preference

t-Test: Paired Two Sample for Means		
	Rank Score for Joystick Controls (Adults)	Rank Score for Keyboard Controls (Adults)
Mean	8.5	3.53
Variance	1.03	1.43
Std Dev	1.02	1.2
Lower Bound	7.48	2.34
Upper Bound	9.52	4.73
Observations	30	30
df	29	
t Stat	17.33	

Table 3. Two sample t-test for adult preference of user interface

t-Test: Paired Two Sample for Means		
	Rank Score for Joystick Controls (Adolescents)	Rank Score for Keyboard Controls (Adolescents)
Mean	3.93	6.33
Variance	1.51	1.13
Std Dev	1.23	1.06
Lower Bound	2.7	5.27
Upper Bound	5.16	7.4
Observations	30	30
df	29	
t Stat	8.09	

Table 4. Two sample t-test for adolescent preference of user interface

4.3 Experiment 3: Entertainment Value

For the adults, I found that by comparing arithmetic means, the order of preference is as follows (from most impactful to least impactful): Graphics, Storyline, Background Music, Sound Effects, and Frame Rate (Figure 4). Conversely, when comparing arithmetic means for adolescents, I discovered the following order of preference (from most to least impactful): Graphics, Background Music, Storyline, Sound Effects, and Frame Rate (Figure 5).

For adults, graphics and storyline improvements were rated the highest, while sound effects and background music were rated moderately. The improvement with the lowest rating was the frame rate. These findings suggest that graphics and storyline improvements have a greater impact on player enjoyment than sound effects, background music,

or frame rate. Taking the standard deviation into account, while similarly ranked categories had no significant difference, there is a significant difference between the ranking of the categories with higher and lower rankings, such as graphics versus frame rate or background music versus frame rate (Table 5).

My results from this experiment revealed that, among adolescents, graphics improvements received the highest rating, followed by moderate ratings for sound effects, background music, and storyline. The frame rate was rated the lowest. These findings suggest that graphics improvements have a greater impact on player enjoyment compared to the storyline, sound effects, background music, or frame rate. When considering the standard deviation, there was no significant difference among similarly ranked categories. However, there was a significant difference between the rankings of higher and lower-ranked categories, such as background music versus frame rate or graphics versus storyline (Table 6). Overall, some significant conclusions can be drawn based on these category ratings, which can inform the development of future updates to the game and potentially improve its overall popularity and success.

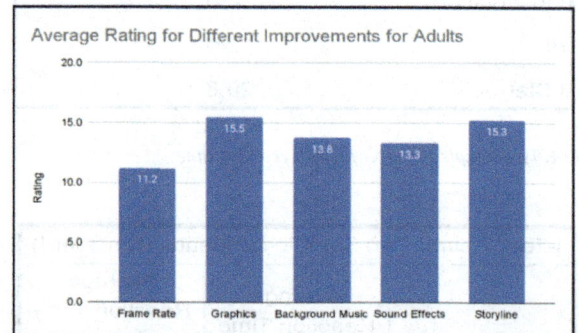

Figure 4. Bar chat containing average aesthetic rating for adults

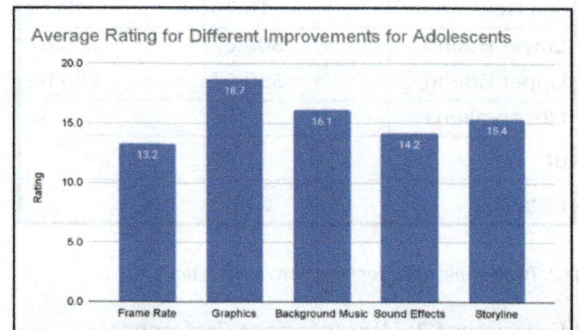

Figure 4. Bar chat containing average aesthetic rating for adolescents

	Frame Rate Score (Adults)	Graphics Score (Adults)	Background Music Score (Adults)	Sound Effects Score (Adults)	Storyline Score (Adults)
Mean	11.23	15.50	13.77	13.33	15.27
Variance	2.12	2.41	1.12	1.63	1.91
Std Dev	1.46	1.55	1.06	1.28	1.38
Lower Bound	9.78	13.95	12.71	12.06	13.88
Upper Bound	12.69	17.05	14.83	14.61	16.65
Observations	30	30	30	30	30
df	29	29	29	29	29

Table 5. Statistical analysis for adult aesthetic rating

	Frame Rate Score (Adolescents)	Graphics Score (Adolescents)	Background Music Score (Adolescents)	Sound Effects Score (Adolescents)	Storyline Score (Adolescents)
Mean	13.23	18.73	16.13	14.17	15.37
Variance	2.01	1.52	1.13	1.37	2.42
Std Dev	1.42	1.23	1.06	1.17	1.56
Lower Bound	11.82	17.50	15.07	13.00	13.81
Upper Bound	14.65	19.97	17.20	15.34	16.92
Observations	30	30	30	30	30
df	29	29	29	29	29

Table 6. Statistical analysis for adolescent aesthetic rating

5. Discussion

The evaluation metrics of the successful cognitive-motor game consist of three key elements: 1. demonstration of significance for cognitive-motor functionality, 2. capability to identify user preference with a high confidence level, and 3. ability to improve the existing game for its entertainment value. The evaluation of the three experiments discussed below reveals the significance of the impact of reaction time and user preference on player engagement.

To test cognitive-motor functionality for reaction time on a flashing light, the game is specifically designed as described in the method such that fingers are assigned to the keyboard while the wrist is deployed for the joystick. In order to evaluate the significance of the reaction time data collected for different age groups with different user interfaces, several statistical analyses are used for evaluation, cross reference, and verification. The box-and-whisker plot shows that the reaction time of adolescents is 16% faster when using the finger than the wrist with no overlap of the lower and upper quartile between these two groups. By the 2-sample t-test, the difference in the reaction times of the adults and adolescents was significant, and the difference between the joystick and keyboard for the adolescent was significant. Overall, the reaction time difference in age could add value to further understanding their connection to the human brain in the neuroscience world. Furthermore, the faster reaction time for fingers, especially in the teenage group, might shed some light on the contradictory research done on the reaction time of the lower arm.

Aesthetical appearance is not only for enhancing visual enjoyment but also to stimulate a sensory part of the brain-hands circuit, especially for cognitive-motor games. The improvements of *Dragon Reborn* are confirmed by both adolescents and adults as a reference to the PC version of the classic *Centipede*. For adolescents, only graphics design showed significantly higher polling results than other categories, and all other categories had overlapping significance bounds, showing that their results were insignificant. The ratings for key modifications (described in the method) are more positive than neutral. It indicates that cognitive-motor games can potentially morph existing recreational games. Indeed, the integrated aesthetics made cognitive games more attractive and effective, and a strong storyline development that includes more stimulating visuals and sound effects certainly will enhance audience engagement.

6. Conclusion

6.1 Limitations

The preference for the joystick was found to be the overwhelming choice for the majority of adults in the user interface experiment. However, it is important to note that this preference may not be applicable to all types of games. Certain genres or types of games may be better suited to a different type of controller. For instance, games that are designed to be played on a computer, such as first-person shooters, may be less enjoyable when played with a joystick. Moreover, certain sets of movements or inputs can favor one user interface over the other. For example, having the ability to have analog inputs for games such as racing games is much more favorable than a digital input. Analog input offers players greater control and precision, whereas digital input provides only binary commands, limiting the player's control over actions performed in the game. Therefore, it is crucial to consider the specific characteristics of a game when determining the best controller to use. Additionally, the conclusions drawn from the user interface experiment cannot be generalized to all games available today. Increasing the sample size may help to improve statistical analysis and provide more comprehensive findings.

Furthermore, conclusions made about differences in behavior caused by age can have some flaws. These differences could be caused by unaccounted factors, such as those that fall under the cohort effect. The term cohort effect describes variations in the characteristics of an area of study over time among individuals who are defined by some shared temporal or common life experience. For example, adult test subjects who grew up during the arcade's popular period might be more attached to the joystick, which might even produce a user bias for the group, as found in the second experiment on user interface preference for adolescents and adults. Therefore, the conclusions drawn regarding the limitations of the impact of age differences possess certain restrictions.

6.2 Implications

The gaming industry may benefit from the findings of my study that suggests joysticks may be a preferable option for adult users. My study highlighted the keyboard as a preferable choice for adolescents in terms of the user interface. These findings could indicate a potential market for joystick controllers in modern games targeted at adult players. Additionally, my study's aesthetic evaluation can help inform game design by identifying important parameters. In addition, the results I found can help further the study of the human wrist and finger and further the investigation of the connection between the decay of the motor cortex and the lower arm senses. In addition, my study highlights the difference in preferences of user interfaces for different age groups: adolescents prefer a keyboard, and adults prefer a joystick. As younger generations slowly replace the older, the shift of preference toward keyboard controls will likely continue to escalate, while the preference for the joystick will likely diminish. This demonstrates how the differing preferences of various age groups could potentially render the joystick an obsolete user interface in the future.

6.3 Future Research

More research can be done to understand the biological and neurological differences between the wrist and finger, as well as the stimulation of the brain and its relation to the motor cortex, which is crucial for developing effective treatments for motor control impairments. Further research into age-related preferences can provide valuable insights for developing therapies and assistive technologies that meet the unique needs of different age groups. In addition, similar studies can be performed using other common devices, such as mobile devices. The majority of individuals using technology have mobile devices. In 2018, over 4 billion mobile devices, which include tablets and phones, were in use, and many people reported having more than one device (Moser, 2019). Upwards of 96% of people live within the range of a mobile network, and 50% of people have access to the internet. Furthermore, mobile devices are seeing most of their popularity in the younger community. Individuals belonging to the Gen Z category, aged 16-24, devote 20% additional time on their phones compared to other age groups and interact with their applications around 30% more than others. The massive popularity of mobile

devices shows the significance of pursuing similar research on mobile devices and how it can be more applicable to future studies, especially among adolescents and young adults.

7. References

[1] Alsaad, F., Binkhamis, L., Alsalman, A., Alabdulqader, N., Alamer, M., Abualait, T., Khalil, M. S., & Al Ghamdi, K. S. (2022, January 14). *Impact of Action Video Gaming Behavior on Attention, Anxiety, and Sleep Among University Students*. NCBI. Retrieved May 1, 2023, from https://www.ncbi.nlm.nih.gov/pmc/articles/PMC8765604/

[2] Balakrishnan, G., Uppinakudru, G., Singh, G. G., Bangera, S., Raghavendra, A. D., & Thangavel, D. (2014, December 16). *A Comparative Study on Visual Choice Reaction Time for Different Colors in Females*. NCBI. Retrieved May 1, 2023, from https://www.ncbi.nlm.nih.gov/pmc/articles/PMC4280496/

[3] Balakrishnan, R., & MacKenzie, I. S. (1997, March 27). *Ethernet: distributed packet switching for local computer networks: Communications of the ACM: Vol 19, No 7*. ACM Digital Library. Retrieved May 1, 2023, from https://dl.acm.org/doi/10.1145/258549.258764

[4] Caserman, P., Hoffmann, K., Müller, P., Schaub, M., Straßburg, K., Wiemeyer, J., Bruder, R., & Göbel, S. (2020, July 24). *Quality Criteria for Serious Games: Serious Part, Game Part, and Balance*. PubMed. Retrieved May 1, 2023, from https://pubmed.ncbi.nlm.nih.gov/32706669/

[5] Clemenson, G. D., Stark, S. M., Rutledge, S. M., & Stark, C. E. (2020, July 15). *Enriching hippocampal memory function in older adults through video games*. PubMed. Retrieved May 1, 2023, from https://pubmed.ncbi.nlm.nih.gov/32439346/

[6] Denney, D. R., Gallagher, K. S., & Lynch, S. G. (2011, January 6). *Deficits in Processing Speed in Patients with Multiple Sclerosis: Evidence from Explicit and Covert Measures*. Archives of Clinical Neuropsychology. Retrieved May 1, 2023, from https://academic.oup.com/acn/article/26/2/110/4787

[7] Doraiswamy, P. M., & Agronin, M. E. (2009, April 28). *Brain Games: Do They Really Work?* Scientific American. Retrieved May 1, 2023, from https://www.scientificamerican.com/article/brain-games-do-they-really/

[8] Dye, M. W., Green, C. S., & Bavelier, D. (2009). *Increasing Speed of Processing With Action Video Games*. NCBI. Retrieved May 1, 2023, from https://www.ncbi.nlm.nih.gov/pmc/articles/PMC2871325/

[9] Georgopoulos, A. P., Pellizzer, G., Poliakov, A. V., & Schieber, M. H. (1999, June). *Neural coding of finger and wrist movements*. PubMed. Retrieved May 1, 2023, from https://pubmed.ncbi.nlm.nih.gov/10406138/

[10] Goldstein, E. B. (2011). *Cognitive Psychology: Connecting Mind, Research, and Everyday Experience* (3rd ed.). Cengage Learning.

[11] Hagner, M. (2012, July). *The electrical excitability of the brain: toward the emergence of an experiment*. PubMed. Retrieved May 1, 2023, from https://pubmed.ncbi.nlm.nih.gov/22724486/

[12] Insightace Analytic Pvt. Ltd. (2022, August 29). *Global Brain Training Apps Market worth $ 44.43 Billion by 2030 - Exclusive Report by InsightAce Analytic*. EIN News. Retrieved May 1, 2023, from https://www.einnews.com/pr_news/588252392/global-brain-training-apps-market-worth-44-43-billion-by-2030-exclusive-report-by-insightace-analytic

[13] Kicks, O. (2023, February 14). *The History & Evolution of Video Games*. Concept Ventures. Retrieved May 1, 2023, from https://www.conceptventures.vc/news/the-history-evolution-of-video-games

[14] Lewis, R. C. (2013, May 1). *Want to slow mental decay? Play a video game*. Iowa Now. Retrieved May 1, 2023, from https://now.uiowa.edu/2013/05/want-slow-mental-decay-play-video-game

[15] Li, C., Layman, A. J., Geary, R., Anson, E., Carey, J. P., Ferrucci, L., & Agrawal, Y. (2015, February). *Epidemiology of Vestibulo-Ocular Reflex Function: Data from the Baltimore Longitudinal Study of Aging*. NCBI. Retrieved May 1, 2023, from https://www.ncbi.nlm.nih.gov/pmc/articles/PMC4297246/

[16] Moser, C. A. (2019, November 19). *News & Views – The Popularity of Mobile Devices: Why It Matters and What Practices Can Do*. Children's Hospital of Philadelphia. Retrieved May 1, 2023, from https://www.chop.edu/news/news-views-popularity-mobile-devices-why-it-matters-and-what-practices-can-do

[17] Palaus, M., Marron, E. M., Viejo-Sobera, R., & Redolar-Ripoll, D. (2017, May 22). *Neural Basis of Video Gaming: A Systematic Review*. Frontiers. Retrieved May 1, 2023, from https://www.frontiersin.org/articles/10.3389/fnhum.2017.00248/full

[18] Perry, T. S. (1982, Dec 1). *The Creation of the Arcade Game Centipede*. IEEE Spectrum. Retrieved May 1, 2023, from https://spectrum.ieee.org/centipede-game

[19] Richerson, S. J., Robinson, C. J., & Shum, J. (2005, February 21). *A comparative study of reaction times between type II diabetics and non-diabetics*. NCBI. Retrieved May 1, 2023, from https://www.ncbi.nlm.nih.gov/pmc/articles/PMC555589/

[20] Ruchal, H., & Vineet, K. (2021, August). *Gaming Computer Market Size, Share and Analysis | 2030*. Allied Market Research. Retrieved May 1, 2023, from https://www.alliedmarketresearch.com/gaming-computer-market-A13073

[21] Technavio. (2023, February). *Arcade Gaming Market by End-user, Genre, and Geography - Forecast and Analysis 2023-2027*. Technavio. Retrieved May 1, 2023, from https://www.technavio.com/report/arcade-gaming-market-size-industry-analysis

[22] Thompson, J. J., Blair, M. R., & Henrey, A. J. (2014, April 9). *Over the Hill at 24: Persistent Age-Related Cognitive-Motor Decline in Reaction Times in an Ecologically Valid Video Game Task Begins in Early Adulthood*. PLOS. Retrieved May 1, 2023, from https://journals.plos.org/plosone/article?id=10.1371/journal.pone.0094215

[23] Zhai, S., Milgram, P., & Buxton, W. (1996). *The Influence of Muscle Groups on Performance of Multiple Degree-of-Freedom Input*. ACM Digital Library. Retrieved May 1, 2023, from https://dl.acm.org/doi/fullHtml/10.1145/238386.238534

Appendix A

Cutscene for *Dragon Reborn*

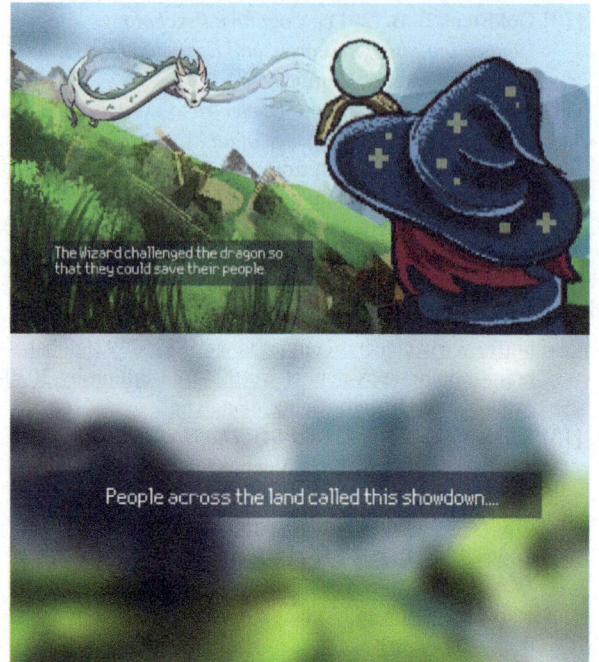

Appendix B

Menu scene in *Dragon Reborn*

Appendix C

How-to-play scene in *Dragon Reborn*

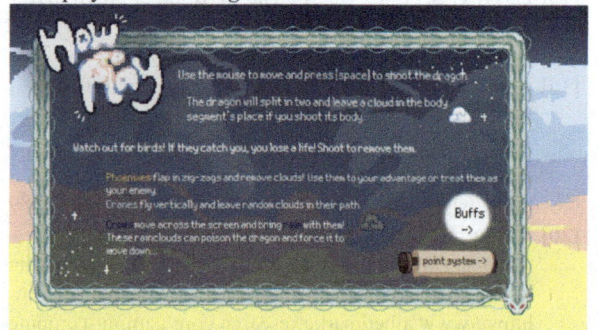

Appendix D

In-game scene in Dragon Reborn

Dragon Components:

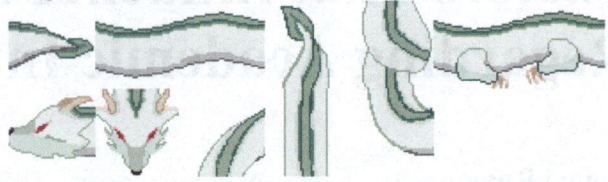

Appendix E

Example assets in *Dragon Reborn*

Phoenix

Death:

Idle:

Crow

Death:

Idle:

Crane

Death:

Idle:

Raincloud

Idle:

Factors That Influence Student Behavior Regarding Academic Integrity

Fengyi Ruan

1. Introduction

Academic dishonesty is a highly prevalent occurrence of which 95% of high school students have admitted to participating in (McCabe, n.d.). Cheating comes in many forms, but for this paper, it is best defined as "a transgression against academic integrity which entails taking an unfair advantage that results in a misrepresentation of a student's ability and grasp of knowledge" (King et al., 2008). Ranging from sharing test answers to copying homework, cheating has become a rapidly normalized exploit. After surveying 70,000 high school students from 2002-2015, Dr. Donald McCabe and the International Center for Academic Inquiry found that 64% of students have cheated on a test and 58% have plagiarized work.

2. Literature Review

Many students believe that cheating is neither consequential nor unethical. Others believe it is wrong, but set certain lines they will not cross to rationalize their actions. To illustrate, many students will copy homework, but not cheat on tests. They justify this cheating through rationalizations such as the need to attain a certain grade or the lack of value in certain assignments (Simmons, 2018). Thus, splitting the grounds for cheating into two fronts. Academic expectations and under-engaging work. The majority of students admit to cheating due to their competitive environments (Yee, 2012). Portrayed perfectly in the infamous Stuyvesant High School scandal, students were pushed to cheat mainly due to the pressure to maintain high grades vital for college admissions (Dorn & Edelman, 2018). On the other hand, as already mentioned, students cheated so they would not have to complete work they viewed as tedious or uninteresting (Stephens, Gehlback, 2007).

Homework, a target of this study, is one of the most excusable offenses in the eyes of students. In most schools, the expectation is that students should go home each day with homework (Kohn, 2006). The convention is not without merit. Homework is valuable practice for concepts learned in school and provides the repetition needed for students to better understand the material. It has been shown to cause improved results in exams and there is a positive correlation between the amount of homework done and outcomes in tests (Cooper et al., 2006). However, between 2008 and 2017, the percentage of college students who reported not benefiting from correctly answering homework questions went from 14% to 55% (Glass & Kang, 2020). This is not a novel issue. Many have criticized the quantity and low quality of homework often assigned without purpose. (Marzano & Pickering, 2007).

This combination of factors has fostered a climate that undervalues academic integrity, encourages academic dishonesty, and warps students' perception of cheating. After witnessing classmates cheat, students become desensitized to the behavior and are more likely to partake in the same action (Carrell et al., 2007). Thus making it a more acceptable and less reprehensible decision (O'Rourke et al., 2010). Such conduct is particularly well highlighted through the rates of academic dishonesty during online learning due to COVID-19. College students cheated more during remote learning than during in-person learning (Janke et al., 2021). This was due to a variety of factors, the most prominent one being how online learning helped facilitate cheating. Students could easily ask their friends through social media or search up the answers while taking a test. (Adzima, 2021). A student's perception of cheating is vital to understanding the reasoning behind their actions.

To explain human behavior, psychologists have proposed a number of different perspectives including psychodynamic, behavioral, cognitive, biological, evolutionary, socio-cultural, and humanistic. Each perspective provides a unique interpretation and framework for understanding the factors that shape our thoughts and actions. In this paper, the most important perspectives are behavioral and cognitive.

First, to analyze students' motivations to cheat from the behavioral perspective, it is necessary to analyze the relationships between environmental factors and their behavior. One method to do so is through the theory of operant conditioning. Operant conditioning is defined as "a process by which humans and animals learn to behave in such a way as to obtain rewards and avoid punishments" (Staddon & Niv, 2008). Coined by psychologist B.F. Skinner and further elaborated on by Edward Thorndike, Ivan Pavlov, and Albert Bandura, this framework explains how the environment affects behavior. Thorndike's law of effect states that "a behavior followed by a satisfactory result was most likely to become an established response to a particular stimulus" (Britannica, n.d.). Although established through experiments on animals, when translated to human behavior it emphasizes the relationship and reinforcement of cheating and obtaining a higher grade. In operant conditioning, reinforcement increases the likelihood of future behavior and punishment decreases. Positive means to add and negative means to subtract. Thus putting these meanings together, there are the four response consequences. Positive punishment means adding something to decrease behavior. Negative punishment means subtracting something to decrease behavior. Positive reinforcement means adding something to increase behavior.

And finally, negative reinforcement means subtracting something to increase behavior. For example, for positive punishment, a parent gives their child a higher allowance for playing fewer video games. It is positive, adding something, the money for the allowance. And its punishment, decreasing the likelihood of playing video games. Thus, viewing behavioral change through operant conditioning makes it possible to find the environmental pushes behind behavioral change. The behavioral change in this case being academic integrity and the pushes being what this study will explore.

On the other hand, the cognitive psychological perspective emphasizes mental processes as the drivers of behavior. Two critical aspects of this perspective in relation to academic integrity are cognitive load theory and cognitive dissonance. Cognitive load theory explains that if the mental effort required to perform a task exceeds the capacity of a person it will affect their learning abilities (Chandler & Sweller 2009, Sweller 1988). Students under high cognitive load may be more likely to engage in cheating behaviors (Anderman & Murdock, 2007) Furthermore, the theory of cognitive dissonance explains that when a person has two or more conflicting beliefs they are, "psychologically uncomfortable" which "motivates the person to reduce the dissonance and leads to avoidance of information likely to increase the dissonance" (Jones & Mills 2019). To reduce dissonance regarding behavior the person often either stops the behavior or rationalizes it (Festinger, 1957). For example, they say the cheating was justified because the test was too difficult, or that everyone else was also cheating. Therefore, in addition to understanding the environment that facilitates cheating, understanding cognitive rationalizations is also important.

In summary, academic pressure and under-engaging work have contributed to the normalization of academic dishonesty. Factors studied that promote cheating includes homework, a beneficial yet often tedious task, and desensitization, which warps students' perception of its acceptability. In addition, the behavioral and cognitive perspectives offer further explanations of student behavior. Operant conditioning explains the reinforcement of behavior through rewards and punishments and cognitive load theory and cognitive dissonance explain the catalysts of such behavior. Thus it is clear that the study of academic integrity must be multifaceted.

2.1 Gap in Research

One gap in current research is the lack of emphasis on multiple environmental factors that may influence students' actions. While many studies have focused on individual factors such as homework, academic pressure, intrinsic vs extrinsic motivation, etc. there is a lack of research on how these factors are related and influence behavior as a collective. As such, this paper attempts to take a more holistic approach in examining multiple factors from one population sample and how they affect each other and contribute as a whole to academic dishonesty.

2.2 Research Question

How do factors such as educational environment, relevance of class material to grades and lives, and content of tests, quizzes, classwork, and homework affect students' perceptions and choices regarding academic integrity?

3. Method

An online survey was created to measure students' behavior, beliefs, and opinions regarding various topics in the field of education. This method was chosen because anonymous questionnaires allow students to be fully honest with their answers. A survey was also the best option because it was neither possible nor practical to carry out experiments that controlled students' classes, teachers, time spent on homework, or other specific environmental conditions in school. A major part of this study is focused on examining students' opinions and beliefs, so a survey was the most appropriate method.

3.1 The questionnaire contained six sections. (in the Appendix)

In the first section of the questionnaire, the participants were asked questions about their background information, such as their age, gender, ethnic/cultural background, grade, where they have completed the majority of their education, unweighted GPA, weighted GPA, and their general opinion about school. Nonetheless, a key component of the survey was its anonymity so no identifying information such as name or contact information was collected.

This was followed by questions to assess their general opinions about studying and grades: "How many hours per day do you spend on homework?", and "How important are your grades to you?" The latter was answered on a scale of zero to ten. 0 being not important at all and ten being very important. They then could choose from a variety of reasons to explain why their grades were or were not important. If none of the options applied they would provide another explanation.

In order to delve deeper into their specific actions in regard to academic integrity, the third section was designed to measure the participants' behavior and habits. They were asked to rate the following questions on a scale of 0 (never) to 10 (always): "How often do you google answers for classwork or homework?", "How often do you ask your friends for answers to classwork or homework?", "How often do you ask friends for hints of what kinds/types of questions will be on a test or quiz?" (questions about test format do not count), and "How often do you cheat on tests?". Hints would include anything from tips for content on tests to questions to watch out for. They were also asked to explain their answers for each of these questions.

Subsequently, participants were randomly divided into two groups by picking a random number. Those who chose one were directed into section 5 and those who chose two were placed into section 6. There was a 50/50 split between those who chose the 2 options. The fifth and sixth sections had identical questions, however, they were shown different independent variables. To address factors relating to student interest in a subject this study was able to manipulate an independent variable, which was the type/content of the online worksheet shown to the students (i.e., math vs. biology).

Group 1 (Section 5) viewed a math worksheet, while Group 2 (Section 6) viewed a biology worksheet (in the Appendix). This manipulation provided an opportunity to assess whether the type/content of the worksheet has an effect on students' opinions. After viewing the worksheet they were asked about their reactions to the worksheet which they answered on a scale of 0 (not excited) to 10 (very excited). Then, given a hypothetical scenario where the answers to the worksheet could be found online with no consequences to searching it up, they were asked what their reaction would be. Would they search or not search for the answers? And then to qualify that question they were asked if they believed searching or not searching up the answers would have a drastic impact on their grades. Again, they were asked to explain their answers to each of these questions.

Finally, in addition to asking participants about their opinions on the overall workload of honors or AP classes, the last (seventh) section was about "busy work". For the purposes of this study, busy work is any assignment that has no perceived value in aiding the student's understanding of the topic the class is meant to teach. The questions in this section were: How often they had to do busy work, how likely they would search up the answers, how often they found that their work did not provide value to understanding the subject, and whether they believed that some homework or review was useful to gain an understanding of a subject.

The data was collected from 54 high-school students at X High School who agreed to take part in the study. The data is representative of the gender breakdown at the school. 46.3% self-reported as male, 46.3% as female, 5.5% as nonbinary, and one participant preferred not to disclose. It is also representative of the grade level breakdown at X High School as there were 13 participants each in 9th and 12th grade respectively and 14 participants each in 10th and 11th grade respectively.

4. Results

4.1 Quantitative Analysis: Basic Data of Students

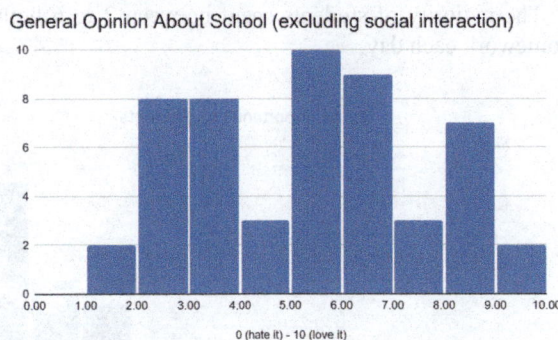

Figure 1: Students' General Opinions About School

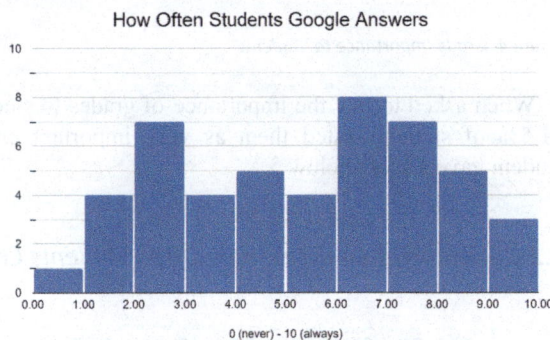

Figure 2: How Often Students Google Answers

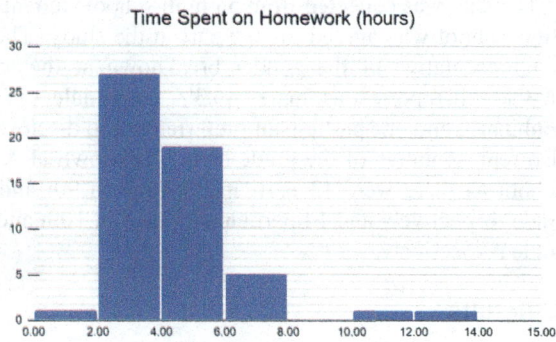

Figure 3: How Much Time Students Spent on Homework

The majority of students spent between 2 to 6 hours on homework each day.

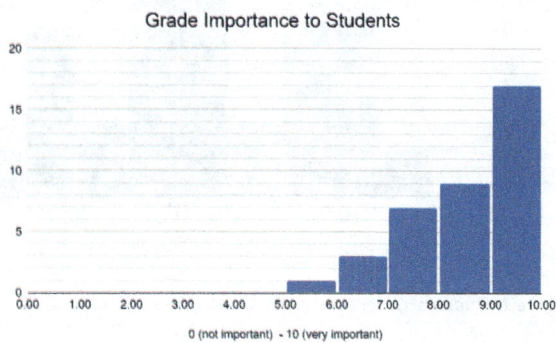

Figure 4: Grade Importance to Students

When asked to rate the importance of grades to students, 31.5% of students rated them as very important and no student gave a score below 5.

4.2 Quantitative Analyses: How Often Students Cheat

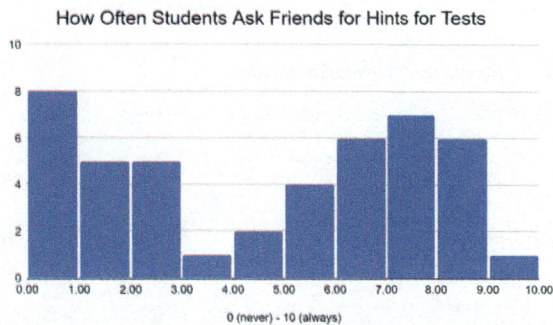

Figure 5: How Often Students Ask Friends for Hints for Tests

Many students consistently ask friends for hints on tests. Only 8 students answered that they have never asked friends for hints.

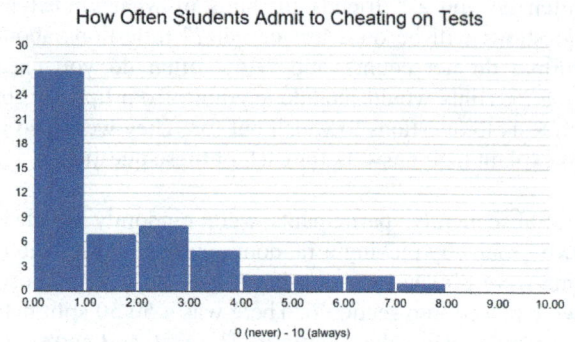

Figure 6: How Often Students Admit to Cheating on Tests

This is the graph of students rating how much they cheat on a scale of 0 (never) - 10 (always). Here, 27 students claim that they have never cheated on tests.

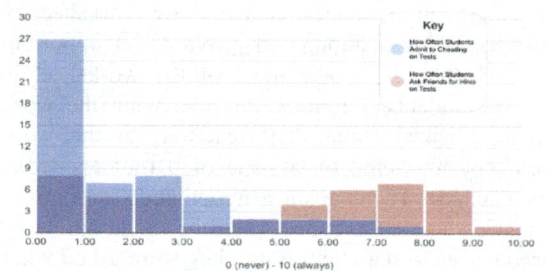

Figure 7: How Often Students Admit to Cheating on Tests vs How Often Students Ask Friends for Hints on Tests

Figure 7 compares the two graphs of how often students admit to cheating on tests versus how often students ask friends for hints on tests. This gives insight into what students believe is cheating. At many schools in the United States, cheating is defined as any academic dishonesty which includes telling classmates or asking friends for hints on tests. Even if the person does not reveal any specific information, speaking about the general topics on the test is still not allowed. This relates back to how students justify academic dishonesty.

4.3 Qualitative Analysis: How Often Students Cheat

When elaborating on their responses as to how much they cheat and how often they ask friends for hints on tests, students often cited a difference in the gravity of the two situations. For example, one student writes, "This isn't cheating this is strategizing- everyone does it; it helps you be just a bit more prepared".

Many students also qualified their answers by stating that there was a large difference between the amount they cheated during online learning vs in-school learning. Many responses stated, "I did during online schooling a lot", "6-7 during covid, 0 during in-person", or "During covid, I definitely searched some answers up. During in-person school, I have never cheated on an exam". However, this is not the case for all students, many also state they have never and will never cheat regarding homework, quizzes, or tests. Their responses in other categories also reflected these sentiments.

4.4 Quantitative Analyses: The Importance of Grades

The perceived importance of grades was positively associated with both the unweighted GPA ($r = 0.343$) and the weighted GPA ($r = 0.349$) of students. The slopes of the regression lines were significantly greater than zero in both of these cases [For grade importance and unweighted GPA, $t(51) = 2.58$, $p < 0.05$; for grade importance and weighted GPA, $t(47) = 2.53$, $p < 0.05$]. Putting more importance on grades was linked to higher grades (and vice versa). Figure 8 and Figure 9 show these relationships.

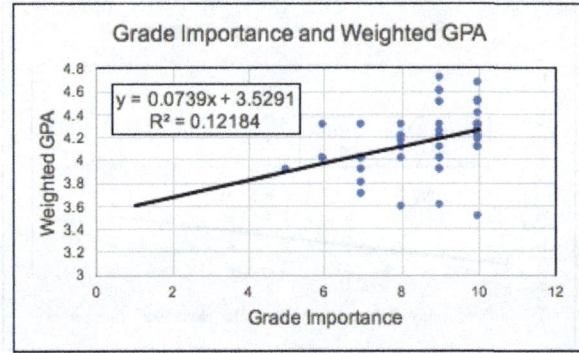

Figure 8: Ratings of Grade Importance and Unweighted GPA.

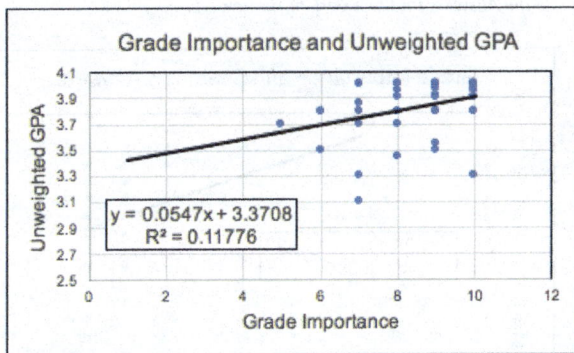

Figure 9: Ratings of Grade Importance and Weighted GPA.

4.5 Quantitative Analyses: The Frequency of Cheating for Students

Students' frequency of asking for hints about questions on a test/quiz was positively associated with their frequency of cheating ($r = 0.386$); the slope of the regression line was significantly greater than zero, $t(53) = 3.02$, $p < 0.01$. Asking friends for hints about tests was associated with more cheating on tests (and vice versa). Figure 10 shows this relationship.

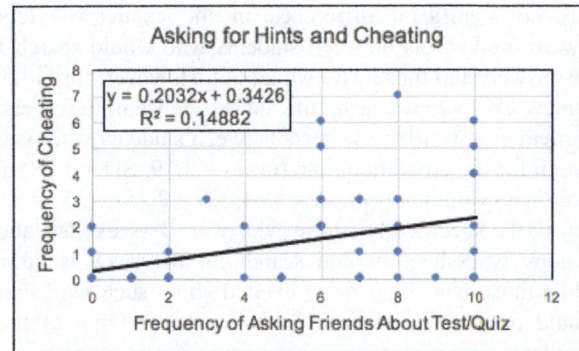

Figure 10: Asking Friends for Hints About Test/Quiz and Cheating on Test/Quiz

Furthermore, how often students googled answers for classwork or homework was positively associated with how often they cheated on tests ($r = 0.291$); the slope of the regression line was significantly greater than zero, $t(53) = 2.19$, $p < 0.05$. As the frequency of googling for answers increased, so did the frequency of cheating (and vice versa). Figure 11 shows this relationship.

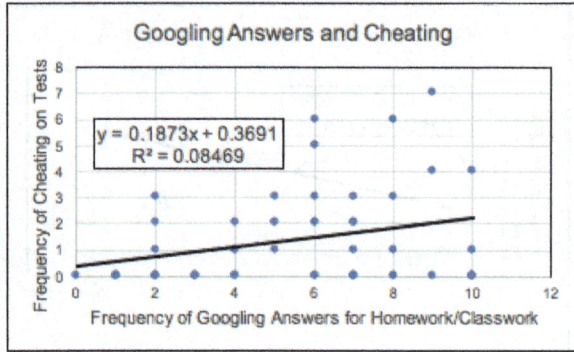

Figure 11: How Often Students Googled Answers for Classwork/Homework and How Often Students Cheated on Tests

4.6 Quantitative Analyses: Reactions to Online Homework/Worksheet

Overall, there was a significant difference in the excitement levels between those who would search up the answers (mean = 1.57, SD = 1.82) online and those who would not (mean = 3.53, SD = 2.58), $t(52)$ = 3.22, $p < 0.01$. However, the findings differed based on the type of homework/worksheet shown. For the math homework, there was no significant difference in the excitement levels toward worksheets between students who would search for the answers and those who would not. However, for biology homework, there was a significant difference in the levels of excitement toward worksheets between students who would search for the answers online (mean = 1.19, SD = 1.28) and those who would not (mean = 4.64, SD = 2.25), $t(25)$ = 5.08, $p < 0.01$. Specifically, those who were less excited about biology worksheets would search for the answers online, while those who were more excited about such worksheets would not do so. Figure 12 shows the patterns of these results.

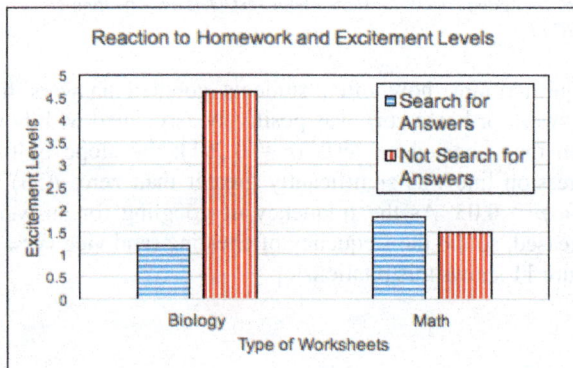

Figure 12: Reaction to Online Homework and Excitement Levels

Interestingly, the perceived importance of grades was somewhat related to the likelihood of people looking up the answers for classwork/homework. First, the negative relationship (r = -0.243) between ratings of grade importance and how often people would google answers was approaching significance, $t(53)$ = -1.81, p = 0.08. Figure 13 shows this relationship. Second, there was a negative correlation (r = -0.300) between the ratings of grade importance and the ratings of how likely students would search up the answers for when faced with busy work; the slope of this regression line was significantly less than zero, $t(53)$ = -2.27, $p < 0.05$. Figure 14 shows this relationship. Taken together, these results suggested that the more important grades were perceived to be for a student, the less likely she or he would just search up the answers online.

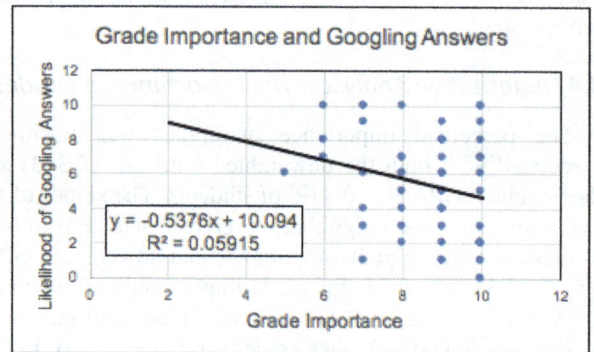

Figure 13: Ratings of Grade Importance and How Often Students Would Google the Answers for Classwork or Homework.

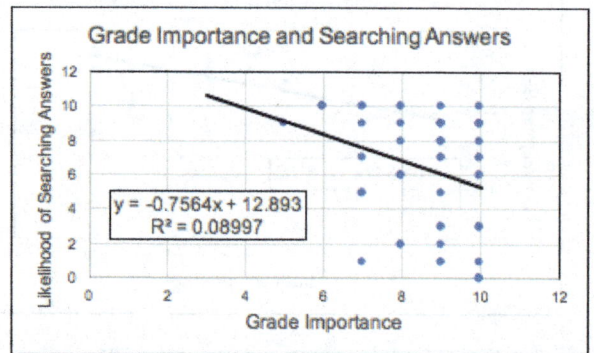

Figure 14: Ratings of Grade Importance and How Likely Students Would Search Up the Answers When Faced With Busy Work.

4.7 Quantitative Analyses: Students' Behavior Regarding Searching Up Answers vs. Googling Answers for Classwork/Homework

There was a significant difference in the frequency of googling answers (for homework or classwork) between those who would search up the answers (mean = 6.19, SD = 2.42) for worksheets online and those who would not (mean = 3.82, SD = 3.21), $t(52) = 3.00$, $p < 0.01$. There was also a significant difference in the frequency of googling answers between those who thought that searching or not searching the answers will have a significant impact on grades (mean = 4.27, SD = 3.09) and those who did not believe so (mean = 6.25, SD = 2.48), $t(52) = 2.61$, $p < 0.01$. Figure 15 shows these patterns of results. Taken together, these results suggest that students who googled answers for classwork or homework more often were more likely to be those who would search up answers for online worksheets as well as those who thought that this action would not impact their grades.

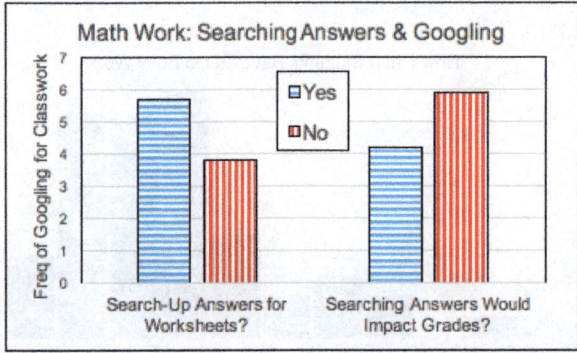

Figure 15: Students' Behavior/Opinions Regarding Searching-Up Answers Worksheets and Their Frequency of Googling Answers for Classwork/Homework.

These differences did not depend on whether the given assignment was mathematics or biology. When the data were split into two groups (i.e., participants who received the mathematics worksheet and participants who received the biology worksheet), both groups showed similar patterns, and all of the differences were either significant or approaching significant.

For the math group, there was an approaching-significant difference in the frequency of googling answers (for homework or classwork) between those who would search up the answers (mean = 5.71, SD = 2.26) for worksheets online and those who would not (mean = 3.83, SD = 4.12), $t(25) = 1.49$, $p = 0.07$. There was also an approaching-significant difference in the frequency of googling answers between those who thought that searching or not searching the answers will have a significant impact on grades (mean = 4.20, SD = 3.08) and those who did not believe so (mean = 5.94, SD = 2.49), $t(25) = 1.61$, $p = 0.06$. Figure 16 shows the patterns of results.

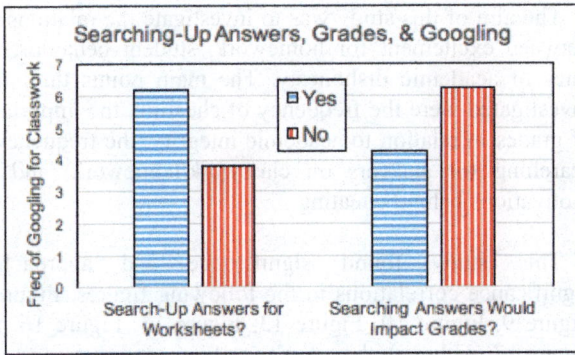

Figure 16: Students' Behavior/Opinions Regarding Searching-Up Answers for Online Math Worksheets and Their Frequency of Googling Answers for Classwork/Homework.

For the biology group, there was a significant difference in the frequency of googling answers (for homework or classwork) between those who would search up the answers (mean = 6.81, SD = 2.56) for worksheets online and those who would not (mean = 3.82, SD = 2.82), $t(25) = 2.86$, $p < 0.01$. There was also a significant difference in the frequency of googling answers between those who thought that searching or not searching the answers will have a significant impact on grades (mean = 4.33, SD = 3.23) and those who did not believe so (mean = 6.60, SD = 2.50), $t(25) = 2.06$, $p < 0.05$. Figure 17 shows these patterns of results.

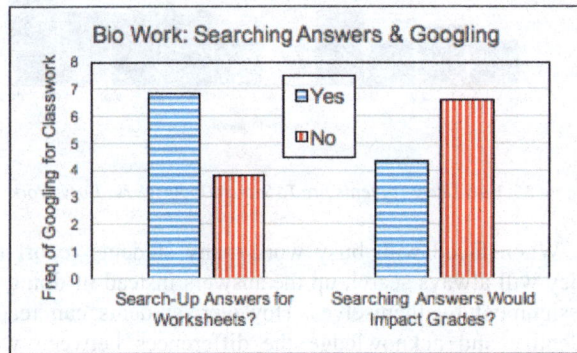

Figure 17: Students' Behavior/Opinions Regarding Searching-Up Answers for Online Biology Worksheets and Their Frequency of Googling Answers for Classwork/Homework.

4.8 Qualitative/Quantitative Analyses: Why Search Up Answers?

By using long and short answers, students were asked to explain their reasons for cheating or copying homework. Many cited the repetitive, dull, or unhelpful traits of the work they were assigned to complete. Thus questions were asked regarding the quantity and quality of the homework or classwork students were often assigned. This was in the 7th section titled "busy work".

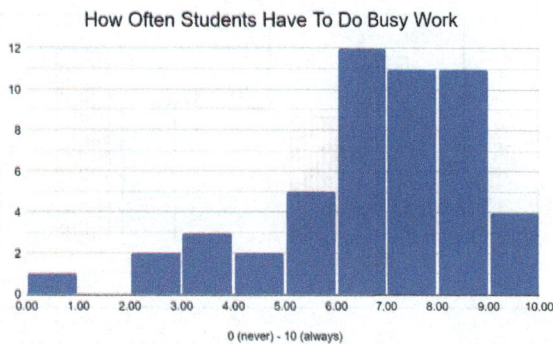

Figure 18: How Often Students Have To Do Busy Work

The majority of students, 79.6%, report that on a scale of 0 (never) to 10 (always) that they often have to complete busy work.

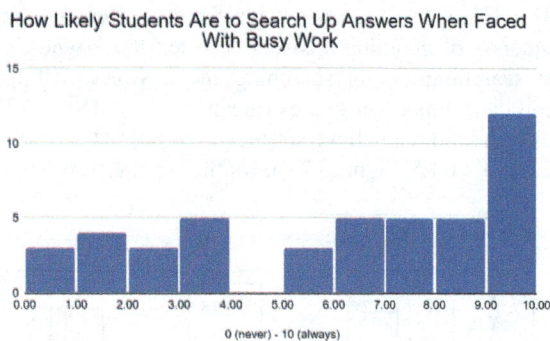

Figure 19: How Likely Students Are To Search Up Answers - Busy Work

When faced with busy work many students report that they will always search up the answers instead of doing the assignment by themselves. However, students can readily identify and acknowledge the differences between work they believe is useful and work that they categorize as busy work. This can be shown in the differences between Figures 18 and 19.

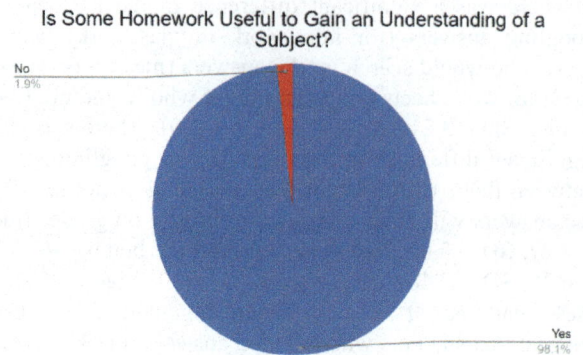

Figure 20: Is Homework Still Useful?

5. Discussion

The aim of this study was to investigate the relationships between excitement for homework, student behavior, and rates of academic dishonesty. The main points this study investigated were the frequency of cheating, the importance of grades in relation to academic integrity, the frequency of searching for answers on classwork/homework, and the motivations behind cheating.

This study found significance and approaching significance correlations in the following figures: Figure 8, Figure 9, Figure 10, Figure 13, Figure 15, Figure 16, and Figure 17. Although they don't verify nor indicate causation, there is a significant correlation between the aforementioned categories. One important note for this study is that in many graphs regarding cheating or rates of searching up answers, there are roughly symmetrical or roughly normal distributions which may imply no particular significance. However, in an ideal world with no academic dishonesty, there should only be one answer, the answer being that no one cheats at all.

Returning to operant conditioning from the behaviorist perspective, changes in behavior regarding academic integrity can be explained through environmental pushes. As previously explained in the introduction, operant conditioning is defined as, "a process by which humans and animals learn to behave in such a way as to obtain rewards and avoid punishments" (Staddon & Niv, 2008). In this case, the reward is to complete homework faster through means such as cheating. Possible punishments may include tedious hours of doing homework, lower grades, parental disapproval, etc. For example, potential decisions may be impacted by a variety of these rewards and punishments. A hypothetical student may be deciding whether to search up answers to a problem and from past experience of searching up answers with no consequences followed by a reward of more free time to pursue hobbies, they choose to cheat. This is an example of negative reinforcement. Something is taken away to increase behavior. In this case, the time needed to complete homework was removed thus reinforcing the behavior of cheating. This could also be viewed as positive reinforcement depending on what is being looked at. Positive reinforcement is the addition of something to increase behavior. The addition would be the homework answers and the increase in behavior would still be to cheat more.

Interestingly, the data when comparing biology and math was different. Such differences are best illustrated in Figures 15 and 16. There are many potential explanations, but looking through the student's elaborative statements, there is a clear pattern. The students who were placed into the math group were much more likely to want to search up the answers compared to the biology group. 77.8% of the math group would search up the answers and only 37% of the math group believed searching up answers would impact their grades. In comparison to the biology group, where 59.3% would search up the answers and 44.4% believed not doing the worksheet would impact their grade in the class. Here there is a clear distinction between how much value the students placed on the math worksheet versus the biology worksheet. In the elaborative statements, the student sentiment reflected this explanation with more of them reporting that they believe the biology worksheet would be useful in furthering their understanding of the subject. This is an example of students rationalizing their actions to decrease cognitive dissonance, as previously explained from the cognitive perspective.

In summary, this study focused on the frequency and causes of academic dishonesty primarily in regard to doing classwork/homework. The study results found significant correlations between users' excitement, opinions of cheating, and how often they would cheat. With these results in mind, it can be speculated that a lack of excitement towards the subject along with previous experience regarding tedious work results in a higher likelihood of searching up answers for classwork/homework.

6. Conclusion

6.1 Limitations:

No single project is perfect and the current study has its limitations. A convenient sample was used and the data was collected from a survey thus making it reliant on those who wished to respond. Thus, although the results are representative of X high school they may not be generalizable to the overall larger population of the United States or even all American high school students.

This concentrated sample can show potential bias within the results derived from the demographics surveyed. Moreover, correlation does not imply causation. Variables can be related, but it does not mean that one necessarily causes the other. Another critical difference is the average amount of time students who answered this survey spent on homework. In a survey by Challenge Success surveyed 50,000 high school students between 2012 and 2020, the United States national average is approximately 2.7 hours a night (Challenge Success, 2020). In this survey, students reported an average of 3.8 hours of homework each day. The range extended from 1 - 12 hours with a median of 3 hours. That means students who answered this survey normally spend 1.1 hours longer each day on homework compared to the national average.

Furthermore, there is the possibility of social desirability bias as some students may still have had the tendency to answer questions about academic dishonesty with answers viewed more favorably by others. However, as the study was anonymous, it has attempted to mitigate most of the potential bias. Finally, the data was collected through a survey in which students had to subjectively rate their answers to questions such as "How often do you cheat on tests/quizzes?" Although everyone understood that 0 meant never and 10 meant always, the values 6 and 7 may carry slightly different meanings depending on the person answering the survey causing minor inconsistencies.

6.2 Implications/Future Directions:

Academic integrity is one of the most important foundations of education and academia, especially in the modern world. There are many more questions that can be answered in relation to the broader opinions and correlations of the US student population. For instance, studies that examine at what grades or ages do students begin cheating. It can investigate the general mentality of students dependent on age, better highlighting the catalyst behind cheating so educators can rearrange the environment to promote academic integrity.

In addition, another interesting continuation of this project is potentially applying mathematical modeling and artificial intelligence that takes into account the factors identified in the current study to predict the probability of academic cheating. Furthermore, studies similar to this one that analyzes the factors that play into a student's desire to cheat could be supplemented with interviews and observations giving a more well-rounded and accurate data set that is not self-reported.

Furthermore, studies that take cross-sectional or longitudinal approaches that continually monitor and study various student populations over the course of their academic careers can bring better insight into overall opinions and actions regarding academic dishonesty. Thus giving further insight into students' perceptions of academic integrity.

7. References

[1] Adzima, Kerry. "Examining Online Cheating in Higher Education Using Traditional Classroom Cheating as a Guide." *EJEL*, 15 Mar. 2021, https://www.academic-publishing.org/index.php/ejel/article/view/1927.

[2] Anderman, Eric, and Tamera Murdock. "The Psychology of Academic Cheating." The Psychology of Academic Cheating - ScienceDirect, 28 Sept. 2007, https://doi.org/10.1016/B978-012372541-7/50002-4.

[3] Carrell, Scott E. *Peer Effects in Academic Cheating.* 1 Jan. 2008, jhr.uwpress.org/content/43/1/173.short.

[4] Chandler, Paul, and John Sweller. "Cognitive Load Theory and the Format of Instruction." Research Online, 14 Dec. 2009, ro.uow.edu.au/edupapers/128.

[5] Cooper, Harris, et al. "Does Homework Improve Academic Achievement? A Synthesis of Research, 1987–2003." *Sage Journals*, 1 Mar. 2006, https://journals.sagepub.com/doi/abs/10.3102/003465430 76001001.

[6] Desilver, Drew. "U.S. Students' Academic Achievement Still Lags That of Their Peers in Many Other Countries." *Pew Research Center*, 15 Feb. 2017, https://www.pewresearch.org/fact-tank/2017/02/15/u-s-students-internationally-math-science/.

[7] Edelman, Susan. "The Disgraceful Cheating Scandal at One of America's Best High Schools." *New York Post*, edited by Sara Dorn, 27 Jan. 2018, https://nypost.com/2018/01/27/cheating-still-rampant-at-disgraced-stuyvesant-school/.

[8] Festinger, Leon. A Theory of Cognitive Dissonance. 1957. Bowker, https://doi.org/10.1604/9780804709118.

[9] Glass, Arnold L. "Fewer Students Are Benefiting from Doing Their Homework: An Eleven-Year Study." *Taylor & Francis*, 12 Aug. 2020, tandfonline.com/doi/abs/10.1080/01443410.2020.180264 5.

[10] Janke, Stefan, et al. "Cheating in the Wake of COVID-19: How Dangerous Is Ad-Hoc Online Testing for Academic Integrity?" *Science Direct*, Dec. 2021, https://www.sciencedirect.com/science/article/pii/S26665 57321000264.

[11] Jong, Ton de. "Cognitive Load Theory, Educational Research, and Instructional Design: Some Food for Thought - Instructional Science." SpringerLink, 27 Aug. 2009, https://doi.org/10.1007/s11251-009-9110-0.

[12] Kauffman, Douglas F. "Can Online Academic Integrity Instruction Affect University Students' Perceptions of and Engagement in Academic Dishonesty? Results From a Natural Experiment in New Zealand." *Frontiers*, 3 June 2020, frontiersin.org/articles/10.3389/fpsyg.2021.569133/full.

[13] Marzano, Robert J., and Deborah J. Pickering. "Special Topic / The Case For and Against Homework." *ASCD*, 1 Mar. 2007, https://www.ascd.org/el/articles/the-case-for-and-against-homework.

[14] McCabe, Donald. "Facts and Statistics." *International Center for Academic Integrity*, https://academicintegrity.org/resources/facts-and-statistics.

[15] Murdock, Tamera B., et al. "Effects of Classroom Context Variables on High School Students' Judgments of the Acceptability and Likelihood of Cheating." *APA PsycNet*, psycnet.apa.org/record/2004-21454-015.

[16] O'Rourke, Jillian, et al. "Imitation Is the Sincerest Form of Cheating: The Influence of Direct Knowledge and Attitudes on Academic Dishonesty." *Taylor & Francis Online*, 10 Jan. 2010, tandfonline.com/doi/abs/10.1080/10508420903482616.

[17] Simmons, Andrew. "Why Students Cheat—and What to Do About It." *Edutopia*, 28 Apr. 2018, edutopia.org/article/why-students-cheat-and-what-do-about-it.

[18] Staddon, DrR., et al. *Operant Conditioning - Scholarpedia.* 1 May 2022, scholarpedia.org/article/Operant_conditioning#:~:text=Op erant%20conditioning%20.---. *Operant Conditioning - Scholarpedia.* 1 May 2022, scholarpedia.org/article/Operant_conditioning#:~:text=Op erant%20conditioning%20.

[19] Stephens, Jason M., and Hunter Gehlbach. "Under Pressure and Underengaged: Motivational Profiles and Academic Cheating in High School." *Science Direct*, 2007, https://www.sciencedirect.com/science/article/pii/B97801 23725417500097.

[20] Strom, Paris S., and Robert D. Strom. "Cheating in Middle School and High School." *Taylor & Francis Online*, 30 Jan. 2008, tandfonline.com/doi/abs/10.1080/00131720708984924. *View of Examining Online Cheating in Higher Education Using Traditional Classroom Cheating as a Guide.* academic-publishing.org/index.php/ejel/article/view/1927/1890.

[21] Sweller, John. "Cognitive Load During Problem Solving: Effects on Learning." Cognitive Load During Problem Solving: Effects on Learning - ScienceDirect, 2 Dec. 1998, https://doi.org/10.1016/0364-0213(88)90023-7.

8. Appendix

8.1 Google Form:

Grade? (because its summer please put the grade you are going into) *

○ 6
○ 7
○ 8
○ 9
○ 10
○ 11
○ 12
○ College
○ Graduated
○ Other: _____

What is your unweighted GPA? *

Your answer

What is your weighted GPA? *

Your answer

How much of your GPA is dependent on your environment? *

	0 1 2 3 4 5 6 7 8 9 10	
Not depe ndent	○ ○ ○ ○ ○ ○ ○ ○ ○ ○ ○	Completely dependent (teachers/classes/grading system/etc.)

What is your general opinion about school? (Excluding the social-interaction portions of school such as hanging out with friends or participating in clubs) *

	0 1 2 3 4 5 6 7 8 9 10	
Hate it	○ ○ ○ ○ ○ ○ ○ ○ ○ ○ ○	Love it

Part 2

How many hours per day do you spend on homework? (round to the nearest hour) *

Your answer

How important are your grades to you? *

	0 1 2 3 4 5 6 7 8 9 10	
Not important	○ ○ ○ ○ ○ ○ ○ ○ ○ ○ ○	Very important

They are that important because... *

☐ They're important for my future
☐ My parents expect good grades
☐ I like having good grades
☐ My friends have good grades
☐ Other: _____

Back   Next   Clear form

Never submit passwords through Google Forms.

This content is neither created nor endorsed by Google. Report Abuse - Terms of Service - Privacy Policy

Google Forms

Part 3

How often do you google answers for classwork or homework? (Be honest!) *

	0	1	2	3	4	5	6	7	8	9	10	
Never	○	○	○	○	○	○	○	○	○	○	○	Always

Please explain your previous score *

Your answer

How often do you ask your friends for answers to classwork or homework? (Be honest!) *

	0	1	2	3	4	5	6	7	8	9	10	
Never	○	○	○	○	○	○	○	○	○	○	○	Always

Please explain your previous score *

Your answer

How often do you ask friends for hints of what kinds/types of questions will be on a test or quiz? (questions about test format such as multiple choice or short answer doesn't count) *

	0	1	2	3	4	5	6	7	8	9	10	
Never	○	○	○	○	○	○	○	○	○	○	○	Always

Please explain your previous score *

Your answer

How often do you ask friends for hints of what kinds/types of questions will be on a test or quiz? (questions about test format such as multiple choice or short answer doesn't count) *

	0	1	2	3	4	5	6	7	8	9	10	
Never	○	○	○	○	○	○	○	○	○	○	○	Always

Please explain your previous score *

Your answer

How often do you cheat on tests? (Be honest!) *

	0	1	2	3	4	5	6	7	8	9	10	
Never	○	○	○	○	○	○	○	○	○	○	○	Always

Please explain your previous score *

Your answer

Back   Next   Clear form

Never submit passwords through Google Forms.

This content is neither created nor endorsed by Google. Report Abuse - Terms of Service - Privacy Policy

Google Forms

And so the path diverges...

Please pick 1 or 2 *

○ 1

○ 2

Math

Please open this link
click here!

Pretend you're in class. What is your first reaction to receiving what was attached *
in the link as part of your mandatory homework on top of a busy day's worth of
homework and classwork?

	0	1	2	3	4	5	6	7	8	9	10	
Not excited	○	○	○	○	○	○	○	○	○	○	○	Very excited

Please explain your previous answer *

Your answer

Knowing that the answers to the worksheet can be found online and that there *
are no consequences to searching them up, what would be your reaction?

○ Search up the answers

○ Will not search up the answers

Do you think searching or not searching up the answers will have a drastic impact *
on your grade in the class?

○ Yes

○ No

Please explain your previous answer *

Your answer

Back   Next   Clear form

Bio

Please open this link
click here!

Pretend you're in class. What is your first reaction to receiving what was attached *
in the link as part of your mandatory homework on top of a busy day's worth of
homework and classwork?

	0	1	2	3	4	5	6	7	8	9	10	
Not Excited	○	○	○	○	○	○	○	○	○	○	○	Very Excited

Please explain your previous answer *

Your answer

Knowing that the answers to the worksheet can be found online and that there *
are no consequences to searching them up, what would be your reaction?

○ Search up the answers

○ Will not search up the answers

Do you think searching or not searching up the answers will have a drastic impact *
on your grade in the class?

○ Yes

○ No

Please explain your previous answer *

Your answer

Back   Next   Clear form

Never submit passwords through Google Forms

Busy Work

What are your opinions on the overall workload of honors or AP classes? *

○ Too little

○ Just right

○ Too much

Please elaborate on your previous response *

Your answer

Do you often find that much of the work you do is "busy" work that doesn't provide any value to your understanding of the subject? *

○ Yes

○ No

How often do you have to do "busy work"? (Past class experiences also count) *

	0	1	2	3	4	5	6	7	8	9	10	
Never	○	○	○	○	○	○	○	○	○	○	○	Always

When faced with busy work, how likely is it for you to search up the answers? *

	0	1	2	3	4	5	6	7	8	9	10	
Never	○	○	○	○	○	○	○	○	○	○	○	100% will search it up

Do you think that some homework or review is useful to gain understanding of a subject? *

○ Yes

○ No

Back   Submit   Clear form

8.2 Math & Bio Worksheets:

AP Calculus BC Review

1 Open Response Questions

These are the types of questions that should be more similar to the MCQs on the AP Exam. However, since this is meant to review all past concepts from the year, I thought that it would work better if I left them as open-response questions. Also, use a calculator if the numbers seem messy, otherwise do not use one. I hope this helps you all in your preparation!

1. Determine
$$\int \left(\frac{\cos t}{\sqrt{1-\sin^2 t}}\mathbf{i} - \sec t \tan t \mathbf{j} + \frac{\ln t}{t}\mathbf{k}\right)dt.$$

2. Evaluate $\lim_{h\to 0}\frac{\ln(6+h)-1}{h}$.

3. Find the area bounded by the polar curve $r = 2\cos 2\theta$ and $r = 1$ (inside the rose curve but outside the circle).

4. The sum
$$\sum_{n=0}^{\infty}\frac{x^{2n}}{n!}$$
is the power series representation of which function?

5. Find $\frac{dy}{dx}$ given that $y = \ln(e^x + \cos x)$.

6. Find $f'(x)$ given that $f(x) = \frac{6^x \cdot \ln x}{x^2 + 2x + 1}$.

7. Find the volume of the solid generated by revolving the area bounded by $f(x) = -x^2 + 2x - 1$ and the x-axis around $y = 2$.

8. The expression
$$\int_0^4 \sqrt{1 + \sec^2 x}\,dx$$
calculates the arc-length on the interval $x \in [0,4]$ of which function?

9. Determine the particular solution to the differential equation $\frac{dy}{dx} = yx$ through the point $(1,2)$.

10. A particle's position is defined by $\vec{r} = \arcsin(2^t)\mathbf{i} + \frac{1}{1+t^2}\mathbf{j}$. What is the magnitude of the acceleration vector at $t = 3$?

11. The area of a circle increases at a rate of 2 units² per second. Determine the rate of change of the radius when $r = 3$.

12. Evaluate
$$\int_0^{\pi} \sec x\,dx.$$

13. Evaluate $\lim_{x\to 0}\frac{\sin(4x)\sin(3x)}{x\sin(5x)}$.

14. Find the slope of the line tangent to the parametrically-defined curve $x(t) = t^2\sin t$ and $y(t) = \ln(t^2 + \sin t)$ at $t = 3$.

15. The function $f(x) = x^3 + 4x^2 + 2x - 4$ is concave up on which of the following intervals?

16. Evaluate
$$\int_0^{\pi} x\arctan(x^2)dx.$$

17. Determine the length of the curve defined by the curve $\vec{r} = (\pi\sin(4t), \pi\cos(4t))$ on $t \in [0,\pi]$.

18. Evaluate $f'(x)$ given that $f(x) = \sec^{-1}(\cos(x))$.

19. Evaluate the error bound resulting from approximating $f(x) = e^x$ on $|x| \le 1$ using a third degree Maclaurin Series.

20. Determine the slope of the line tangent to $r = 2\sin 2\theta$ at $\theta = \frac{\pi}{3}$.

21. Given that f and g are inverse functions, and that $g(3) = 1$ and that $g'(3) = -2$, determine $f'(1)$.

22. Evaluate $\lim_{x\to\infty}\frac{6^x\cos x + \sin x}{5^x}$.

23. Evaluate
$$\int_0^{\pi} x^3\sin x\,dx.$$

24. The cost to produce strawberries can be written as a function in terms of the number of buckets of strawberries produced, times 100 minus the square of the number of buckets of strawberries. Determine the amount of buckets of strawberries the company should produce to minimize the cost of the strawberries, given that they can produce no more than 10000 buckets of strawberries.

25. Find the area that lies inside of both the rose curve and the circle, with equations $r = 3\sin 4\theta$ and $r = 2$.

26. with initial position $(3,0)$ has velocity defined as $\vec{V} = (t, t^2)$. Determine the magnitude of the particle's displacement after $t = 3$ seconds.

27. The rate of change of a penguin population is given as $\frac{dP}{dt} = .00001P(1000 - P)$. What is the population of the penguins when the rate of change of their population is the greatest?

28. Estimate $y(.2)$ given that $\frac{dy}{dx} = x - y$ and that $y(0) = 2$.

29. Determine the radius of convergence of the power series
$$\sum_{n=0}^{\infty}\frac{x^{n+1}n!}{e^n(2n)!}$$

30. A runner's velocity is defined as $\vec{V} = \cos t\sin t\mathbf{i} + \cos t e^{\sin t}\mathbf{j}$. The runner starts at position $(0,2)$. Determine the position of the runner at $t = 4$ (a). Then, determine the acceleration vector of the runner at $t = 10$ (b). Finally, determine the magnitude of the velocity vector at time $t = 7$, and explain the physical significance of this value (c).

31. Evaluate $\lim_{x\to 0}\frac{\sqrt{x+4}-1-\frac{x}{4}}{x^2}$.

32. A 10 m ladder is leaning against a wall and sliding towards the floor. The top of the ladder is sliding down the wall at a rate of 8 m/sec. How fast is the base of the ladder sliding away from the wall when the base of the ladder is 8 m from the wall?

Page 2

33. Determine the average value of the function $f(x) = \sin(x)$ on the interval $x \in [0, \frac{3\pi}{4}]$.

34. Find $f''(x)$ given that $f(x) = \tan(x^2)$.

35. Determine the total distance travelled on $t \in [0, 3]$ by the particle defined parametrically by $x(t) = t^2$ and $y(t) = e^{-t}$.

36. Make a conclusion on the convergence or divergence of
$$\sum_{n=1}^{\infty} \frac{2^n n!(-1)^n}{(2n+1)!}$$

37. Determine the volume of the solid formed by isosceles triangle cross sections perpendicular to the x-axis, of the region bounded by $f(x) = e^x$ and $f(x) = x^2$ in the first quadrant.

38. Find $\frac{dy}{dx}$ given the relation $x^2 \sin y + y^2 \sin x = 1$.

2 Free Response Questions

1. 2012 AP Calculus BC FRQ 1: Calculator Active

t (minutes)	0	4	9	15	20
$W(t)$ (degrees Fahrenheit)	55.0	57.1	61.8	67.9	71.0

1. The temperature of water in a tub at time t is modeled by a strictly increasing, twice-differentiable function W, where $W(t)$ is measured in degrees Fahrenheit and t is measured in minutes. At time $t = 0$, the temperature of the water is 55°F. The water is heated for 30 minutes, beginning at time $t = 0$. Values of $W(t)$ at selected times t for the first 20 minutes are given in the table above.

   (a) Use the data in the table to estimate $W'(12)$. Show the computations that lead to your answer. Using correct units, interpret the meaning of your answer in the context of this problem.

   (b) Use the data in the table to evaluate $\int_0^{20} W'(t)\, dt$. Using correct units, interpret the meaning of $\int_0^{20} W'(t)\, dt$ in the context of this problem.

   (c) For $0 \le t \le 20$, the average temperature of the water in the tub is $\frac{1}{20}\int_0^{20} W(t)\, dt$. Use a left Riemann sum with the four subintervals indicated by the data in the table to approximate $\frac{1}{20}\int_0^{20} W(t)\, dt$. Does this approximation overestimate or underestimate the average temperature of the water over these 20 minutes? Explain your reasoning.

   (d) For $20 \le t \le 25$, the function W that models the water temperature has first derivative given by $W'(t) = 0.4\sqrt{t}\cos(0.06t)$. Based on the model, what is the temperature of the water at time $t = 25$?

2. 2019 AP Calculus BC FRQ 2: Calculator Active

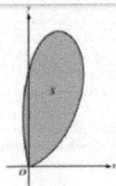

2. Let S be the region bounded by the graph of the polar curve $r(\theta) = 3\sqrt{\theta}\sin(\theta^2)$ for $0 \le \theta \le \sqrt{\pi}$, as shown in the figure above.

   (a) Find the area of S.

   (b) What is the average distance from the origin to a point on the polar curve $r(\theta) = 3\sqrt{\theta}\sin(\theta^2)$ for $0 \le \theta \le \sqrt{\pi}$?

   (c) There is a line through the origin with positive slope m that divides the region S into two regions with equal areas. Write, but do not solve, an equation involving one or more integrals whose solution gives the value of m.

   (d) For $k > 0$, let $A(k)$ be the area of the portion of region S that is also inside the circle $r = k\cos\theta$. Find $\lim_{k\to\infty} A(k)$.

3. 2017 AP Calculus BC FRQ 4: No Calculators

4. At time $t = 0$, a boiled potato is taken from a pot on a stove and left to cool in a kitchen. The internal temperature of the potato is 91 degrees Celsius (°C) at time $t = 0$, and the internal temperature of the potato is greater than 27°C for all times $t > 0$. The internal temperature of the potato at time t minutes can be modeled by the function H that satisfies the differential equation $\frac{dH}{dt} = -\frac{1}{4}(H - 27)$, where $H(t)$ is measured in degrees Celsius and $H(0) = 91$.

   (a) Write an equation for the line tangent to the graph of H at $t = 0$. Use this equation to approximate the internal temperature of the potato at time $t = 3$.

   (b) Use $\frac{d^2H}{dt^2}$ to determine whether your answer in part (a) is an underestimate or an overestimate of the internal temperature of the potato at time $t = 3$.

   (c) For $t < 10$, an alternate model for the internal temperature of the potato at time t minutes is the function G that satisfies the differential equation $\frac{dG}{dt} = -(G - 27)^{2/3}$, where $G(t)$ is measured in degrees Celsius and $G(0) = 91$. Find an expression for $G(t)$. Based on this model, what is the internal temperature of the potato at time $t = 3$?

4. 2021 AP Calculus BC FRQ 6: No Calculators

6. The function g has derivatives of all orders for all real numbers. The Maclaurin series for g is given by
$$g(x) = \sum_{n=0}^{\infty} \frac{(-1)^n x^n}{2e^n + 3}$$ on its interval of convergence.

   (a) State the conditions necessary to use the integral test to determine convergence of the series $\sum_{n=0}^{\infty} \frac{1}{e^n}$. Use the integral test to show that $\sum_{n=0}^{\infty} \frac{1}{e^n}$ converges.

   (b) Use the limit comparison test with the series $\sum_{n=0}^{\infty} \frac{1}{e^n}$ to show that the series $g(1) = \sum_{n=0}^{\infty} \frac{(-1)^n}{2e^n + 3}$ converges absolutely.

   (c) Determine the radius of convergence of the Maclaurin series for g.

   (d) The first two terms of the series $g(1) = \sum_{n=0}^{\infty} \frac{(-1)^n}{2e^n + 3}$ are used to approximate $g(1)$. Use the alternating series error bound to determine an upper bound on the error of the approximation.

5. 2016 AP Calculus BC FRQ 5: No Calculators

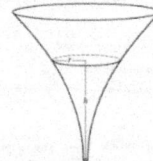

5. The inside of a funnel of height 10 inches has circular cross sections, as shown in the figure above. At height h, the radius of the funnel is given by $r = \frac{1}{20}(3 + h^2)$, where $0 \le h \le 10$. The units of r and h are inches.

   (a) Find the average value of the radius of the funnel.

   (b) Find the volume of the funnel.

   (c) The funnel contains liquid that is draining from the bottom. At the instant when the height of the liquid is $h = 3$ inches, the radius of the surface of the liquid is decreasing at a rate of $\frac{1}{5}$ inch per second. At this instant, what is the rate of change of the height of the liquid with respect to time?

Gene Expression—Translation

How do cells synthesize polypeptides and convert them to functional proteins?

Why?

The message in your DNA of who you are and how your body works is carried out by cells through gene expression. In most cases this means synthesizing a specific protein to do a specific job. First, mRNA is transcribed from the DNA code. Then, the mRNA sequence is translated into a polypeptide sequence.

Model 1 – Codons

mRNA nucleotides   Amino acids

Second Base

First Base	U	C	A	G	Third Base
U	UUU Phe UUC Phe UUA Leu UUG Leu	UCU Ser UCC Ser UCA Ser UCG Ser	UAU Tyr UAC Tyr UAA stop UAG stop	UGU Cys UGC Cys UGA stop UGG Trp	U C A G
C	CUU Leu CUC Leu CUA Leu CUG Leu	CCU Pro CCC Pro CCA Pro CCG Pro	CAU His CAC His CAA Gln CAG Gln	CGU Arg CGC Arg CGA Arg CGG Arg	U C A G
A	AUU Ile AUC Ile AUA Ile AUG Met (start)	ACU Thr ACC Thr ACA Thr ACG Thr	AAU Asn AAC Asn AAA Lys AAG Lys	AGU Ser AGC Ser AGA Arg AGG Arg	U C A G
G	GUU Val GUC Val GUA Val GUG Val	GCU Ala GCC Ala GCA Ala GCG Ala	GAU Asp GAC Asp GAA Glu GAG Glu	GGU Gly GGC Gly GGA Gly GGG Gly	U C A G

1. Model 1 defines the code scientists have discovered that relates the nucleotide sequence of mRNA to the amino acid sequence of polypeptides.

   a. What do the letters U, C, A, and G in Model 1 represent?

   b. What do the abbreviations such as Phe, Ile, Ala, and Gly in Model 1 represent?

   c. The language of mRNA is often described as a "triplet code." Explain the significance of this reference.

2. If an mRNA molecule had 300 nucleotides in the coding region of the strand, how many amino acids would be in the polypeptide that was synthesized? Show mathematical work to support your answer.

3. Consider the information in Model 1.

   a. How many different **codons** (triplets) code for the amino acid Proline (Pro)?

   b. Compare all of the codons for Proline. What are the similarities and differences?

   c. Considering that mistakes can occur during transcription and DNA replication, what advantage is there for an organism to have multiple mRNA sequences code for the same amino acid?

4. Using the mRNA codon chart in Model 1, complete the following:

   DNA →   TAC   CTT   CGG   ATG   GTC   ACT

   mRNA →

   polypeptide sequence →

5. According to the table in Model 1, what amino acid is at the beginning of every polypeptide?

6. The codons shown in Model 1 are used in all species on Earth with very little variation. What might scientists conclude from this?

Model 2 – Translation

Initiation   Elongation

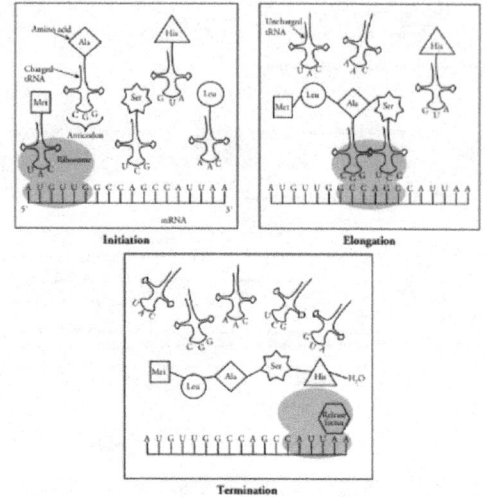

Termination

7. Refer to Model 2.

   a. What are the three stages of translation?

   b. Define each of the terms used in your answer to part a as they are used in everyday language.

8. According to Model 2, when the mRNA leaves the nucleus, to which cellular organelle does it attach?

9. The mRNA attaches to the organelle at the sequence AUG. What is the significance of this sequence of nucleotides?

10. Describe the movement of the ribosome as translation occurs.

Read This!

The ribosome is a large complex of ribosomal RNA (rRNA) and proteins. It consists of two subunits. The smaller subunit binds to the mRNA strand and the larger subunit holds the tRNA molecules in place while the covalent peptide bond is formed between the amino acids. Several ribosomes can attach to an mRNA molecule simultaneously. This allows for many polypeptide chains to be synthesized at once.

11. The tRNA molecules in a cell are short sequences of nucleotides (about 80 bases) that contain an **anticodon** and carry a specific amino acid.

   a. Find the tRNA in Model 2 that is carrying the Histidine (His). What sequence of nucleotides makes the anticodon on this tRNA molecule?

   b. What codon on mRNA would match this anticodon?

   c. Verify that the codon you wrote in part b codes to Histidine by looking at the table in Model 1.

   d. What anticodon would be found on a tRNA molecule carrying Glycine (Gly)? (Note: There are several correct answers here.)

12. The "t" in tRNA is short for transfer. In a complete sentence, explain why this molecule is called transfer RNA.

13. During elongation, how many tRNA molecules are held in the ribosome at the same time?

14. What will happen to the unattached tRNA once it has delivered its amino acid?

15. Describe two things that occur during termination as illustrated in Model 2.

16. Explain how the term "translation" applies to the synthesis of proteins from DNA instructions.

(STOP)

Gene Expression—Translation   5

Extension Questions

17. The codons of mRNA are a set of three nucleotides with four possible bases in combination.
    a. Show mathematically that there are 64 permutations possible when three bases are used.

    b. Show mathematically that two bases as a codon would not be sufficient to code for all 20 known amino acids.

18. A silent mutation is one that does not affect protein structure. Write a code for an original DNA strand containing at least 12 bases, and then mutate the original DNA so that the final protein is unaffected.

19. In prokaryotic cells, translation begins before transcription is finished. Give two reasons why this would not be possible in eukaryotic cells.

Gene Expression—Transcription

How is mRNA synthesized and what message does it carry?

Why?

DNA is often referred to as a genetic blueprint. In the same way that blueprints contain the instructions for construction of a building, the DNA found inside the nuclei of cells contains the instructions for assembling a living organism. The DNA blueprint carries its instructions in the form of genes. In most cases the genes direct the production of a polypeptide, from which other more complex proteins, such as enzymes or hormones, may be constructed. These polypeptides and other molecules run the organism's metabolism and, in multicellular organisms, dictate what each cell's job is. So, what is the language of these instructions and how are they read and decoded by the cellular organelles? This activity will focus on the decoding of genes in eukaryotes.

Model 1 – Transcription

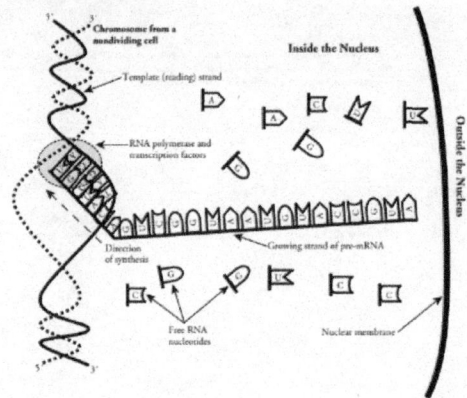

Gene Expression—Transcription   1

1. Consider the eukaryotic cell in Model 1.
   a. Where in the cell is the DNA found?

   b. Where in the cell does transcription take place?

2. Refer to Model 1.
   a. What polymer is synthesized during transcription?

   b. What monomers are used to construct this polymer and where are they found?

3. According to Model 1, what enzyme is required for transcription? (*Hint:* Think about how enzymes are named. What ending is used for enzyme names?)

4. Refer to Model 1.
   a. What is the base-pair rule for a DNA strand matching an RNA strand?

   b. Compare this base-pair rule with that of two DNA strands.

5. Which strand of the DNA contains the "blueprint" for the pre-mRNA?

6. Consider Model 1.
   a. In which direction is the DNA molecule read?

   b. The DNA strand and pre-mRNA strand are anti-parallel. With this in mind label the 3' and 5' ends of the pre-mRNA strand in Model 1.

   c. In which direction is the pre-mRNA molecule constructed?

7. Before printing presses were available, books had to be transcribed in order to share the information in them. Consider the definition of transcription and explain why the process in Model 1 is described using that word.

Read This!

In eukaryotes the enzyme **RNA polymerase** joins with several **transcription factor** proteins at the promoter, which is a special sequence of base pairs on the DNA template strand that signals the beginning of a gene. The transcription factor proteins, along with the RNA polymerase, is called the **transcription initiation complex**. This moves along the DNA template strand at about 40 base pairs per second producing pre-mRNA. When the RNA polymerase reaches the **terminator** sequence of base pairs on the DNA template strand, it completes the production of pre-mRNA and releases it into the nucleoplasm.

8. What parts make up the transcription initiation complex?

9. Where on the DNA strand does the transcription initiation complex form?

10. Nearly all cells in an organism contain identical DNA, and each DNA strand may contain hundreds or thousands of individual genes. Is it likely that a cell would transcribe all the genes within its nucleus simultaneously? Justify your answer using complete sentences.

11. Considering the many types of cells in a multicellular organism, and their different functions, is it likely that all cells transcribe all their genes at some point in their lifetime? Justify your answer using complete sentences.

Gene Expression—Transcription 3

Model 2 – mRNA Processing

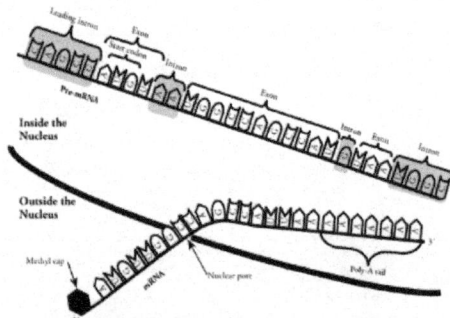

12. Compare the pre-mRNA to the mRNA leaving the nucleus in Model 1.

   a. What has been removed from the pre-mRNA to make it into mRNA?

   b. What has been added to the mRNA that was not present in the pre-mRNA, and where on the mRNA strand are the additional items located?

13. Identify the structure through which the mRNA leaves the nucleus.

14. The nucleotides on the mRNA will be "read" in the next step to producing a polypeptide. What sequence of bases indicates the starting point for the polypeptide "blueprint"?

15. The "m" in mRNA is short for "messenger." Why is this molecule called messenger RNA?

4

POGIL™ Activities for AP* Biology

Read This!

Introns are sections of pre-mRNA that are noncoding. That is, they don't provide useful information for the production of the polypeptide being synthesized. There is evidence that suggests these introns allow certain sections of DNA to code for different polypeptides when different sections are removed. The removal of specific sections is triggered by a signal response in the cell. The portions of the pre-mRNA that remain are called **exons**. The methyl cap (sometimes called the GTP cap or 5′ cap) helps the mRNA molecule move through the nuclear pore and attach to a ribosome, its final destination. mRNA is a short-lived molecule. Once in the cytoplasm the mRNA will be subject to **exonucleases** that immediately start removing individual nucleotides from the 3′ end of a nucleic acid. The individual mRNA nucleotides will then be free to be used again during the process of transcription.

16. The human genome contains about 25,000 genes and yet produces about 100,000 different polypeptides. Propose an explanation of how this is possible.

17. Using the information in the *Read This!* box, develop a hypothesis to explain the advantage of the poly-A tail added to the 3′ end of the mRNA.

18. Different mRNA molecules can have poly-A tails of different lengths. Considering the purpose of adding the poly-A tail (from the previous question), why are some tails longer than others? Justify your answer using complete sentences.

19. Summarize the steps of transcription.

Gene Expression—Transcription 5

Extension Questions

20. What type of biological molecule is an exonuclease?

21. Free nucleotides must be available in a cell's nucleus to produce mRNA strands. Where do these free nucleotides come from?

22. Even though bacterial cells do not contain a nucleus, transcription occurs in a similar way to eukaryotic cells. How might biologists use transcription mechanisms to support the theory of evolution?

6

POGIL™ Activities for AP* Biology

Franklin Education Foundation
Journal of Quantitative and Qualitative Research

From Food Waste to Food Guard: Creating a Novel Chitosan Bioplastic with Nanoparticle
Coating and Its Unique Effect on Water Resistance and Food Preservation
Henry Yao

From Food Waste To Food Guard: Creating A Novel Chitosan Bioplastic With Nanoparticle Coating And Its Unique Effect On Water Resistance And Food Preservation

Henry Yao

Abstract

Plastics, despite their benefits in transforming our lives in multiple aspects, have caused serious environmental and aquatic pollution. The objective of this project is to create low-cost and sustainable chitosan bioplastic, design a novel approach to solve the water permeability challenge, and evaluate its effectiveness as an environmental-friendly bio-alternative to conventional petroleum-based plastics. Due to the unique antimicrobial property of chitosan, this project is also designed to explore the application of chitosan film in antimicrobial and antifungal effectiveness. Prior works have explored chitosan as a biofilm alternative, however, few have developed a full study on a nanoparticle-coated chitosan biofilm and testing its effectiveness in mechanical properties, biodegradability, and water resistance. This project has successfully developed chitosan-based bioplastic composite and identified SiO_2 nanoparticle coating to resolve the water permeability challenge facing most bioplastic films. Both chitosan films and nanoparticle-coated chitosan films have demonstrated significant biodegradability advantages in hydrolysis and home compost compared to commercially available polyethylene resin films and PLA corn films. After biodegradation, both biofilms have shown no phytotoxicity, and instead, enhanced plant growth. In addition, chitosan films have shown unique antimicrobial effect in prolonging shelf-life of perishable foods. As a thin film and composite that is low cost, biodegradable, and antimicrobial, the chitosan bioplastic film developed from this project has its unique and superior advantages as the next-gen bioplastic alternative that can be used for food wraps, grocery bags, food package and storage, and other containers. In addition, solving the water resistance challenge through nanoparticle coating has the potential of broadening the commercial application of chitosan bioplastic, and can be applied to other bioplastic films to change biofilm usage from single-use to multiple-use, generating further economic benefits. Therefore, chitosan bioplastic films with nanoparticle coating created from this project have proven to be a unique and highly viable bioplastic option for food packaging and preservation industry and beyond.

Keywords: chitosan, biodegradability, water resistance, nanoparticle coating, antimicrobial

Franklin Education Foundation

Journal of Quantitative and Qualitative Research

From Food Waste to Food Guard: Creating a Novel Chitosan Bioplastic with Nanoparticle
Coating and Its Unique Effect on Water Resistance and Food Preservation

Henry Yao

1. Introduction

The proliferation of plastic usage in packaging, storage, retailing, to product design and engineering has generated serious environmental problems due to its nature of non-renewable, non-biodegradable, and release of toxic dioxins, phthalates, vinyl chloride, and lead into the environment [1]. If current production and waste management trends continue, twelve billion tons of plastic waste will end in landfills or natural environment by 2050 [2].

Extensive research has been conducted to search for a suitable biopolymer material to substitute for chemically manufactured plastics. The most widely utilized synthetic biopolymer is polylactic acid filament (PLA), mostly sourced from renewable resources and biowaste with recycling capability [3]. However, PLA has significant challenges in its high temperature stability and slow degradation rate [4]. Further research was conducted on cellulose, the most abundant source of biopolymer, as another common option for bioplastics [5][6]. However, the hydrophilic nature and semi-crystalline structure of cellulose make their bioproducts more susceptible to moisture and temperature differences [6]. Bioplastics based on these biopolymers are less applicable in packaging and transportation, an industry heavily dominated by petroleum-based plastic wraps.

Chitin, derived from exoskeletons of crustaceans, is the second most abundant biopolymer. Chitin is commonly considered and isolated as food waste in food processing. The large amount of chitin-rich byproduct is discarded and creates contamination problems if not properly treated or utilized [7]. Chitosan processes D-glucosamine and N-acetyl glucosamine, with a large number of hydroxyl and amino groups in its structure [7]. Cross-linking chitosan with other biopolymers such as starch provides significant structural benefits to the brittle rigidity structure of chitosan, caused by the rigid D-glucosamine [8]. Chitosan's proven antimicrobial and antifungal effects make chitosan-based biofilms uniquely applicable in food packaging and transportation. As verified by studies by Holley et al. (2000), and Fernandez-Saiz et al. (2009), the protonated fraction of chitosan that is released upon contact with liquids in antimicrobial testing acts as a bio-killing agent, protonating nitrenium groups of chitosan which interacts with negatively charged membranes of bacteria, effectively causing membrane rupture and cytoplasm overflow [9][10]. Previous studies have been conducted to incorporate and test chitosan in other biofilm products. Additional studies in 2000, 2008, and 2020 analyzed chitosan's antimicrobial and antifungal capabilities, but never worked towards applying other polymers and coatings to improve quality [9][11][12]. A study conducted in 2019 worked to incorporate chitosan into a modified tapioca flour bioplastic, analyzing its effects on tensile strength and biodegradability [13]. Through these studies, issues were observed with the water permeability properties of chitosan incorporated films, which resulted in further research on NP coatings for improved water resistance. In November 2020, a study was conducted to observe the effects of an added silver hydrophobic NP coating, and test the coated biofilm on antimicrobial activity and mechanical activity [14]. However, a full study on a developed chitosan-NP coated biofilm, incorporating a wide range of tests on mechanical properties, biodegradability, and water resistance, has yet to be completed, leaving room for significant improvement.

The objective of this project is to create chitosan-based bioplastic film and test its efficacy as an environmental-friendly bio-alternative to conventional petroleum-based plastics. Due to the unique antimicrobial property of chitosan, this project is also designed to explore the application of chitosan film in antimicrobial and antifungal effectiveness. In addition, this project takes a novel approach in resolving the water permeability challenge of chitosan bioplastic though nanoparticle coating, which can be applied to other bioplastic products.

1.1 QUESTIONS

Can chitosan be used as base material to create bioplastic?

How to solve the water permeability challenge of chitosan and most bioplastics?

How does chitosan bioplastic compare to conventional plastics?

What is the unique application of chitosan bioplastic in food preservation?

2. Methods

This project is designed into four parts. Part 1 focuses on synthesis of chitosan bioplastic films. Part 2 employs nanoparticle coating to improve water resistance of the chitosan films. Part 3 tests tensile strength, biodegradability, and water permeability of the chitosan films created. Part 4 explores antimicrobial application of the chitosan films.

2.1 Synthesis of Chitosan Bioplastic Films

Chitosan powder was combined with acetic acid, glycerin, water, and starch to form chitosan bioplastic films. Material

Franklin Education Foundation

Journal of Quantitative and Qualitative Research

From Food Waste to Food Guard: Creating a Novel Chitosan Bioplastic with Nanoparticle
Coating and Its Unique Effect on Water Resistance and Food Preservation

Henry Yao

concentration levels were tested for best durability and malleability. A final concentration of 14g chitosan, 14g starch, 190 mL water, 10mL glycerin, and 10ml acetic acid was selected as the most viable option. Chitosan was mixed with starch powder at 65-75°C for 20 minutes, combined with glycerin as plasticizer to enhance thermal stability and improve malleability and firmness. Acetic acid was added as a catalyst in breaking down branching of amylopectin, facilitating hydrogen-bonding with glycerin and decreasing brittleness. All films were cooled at room temperature of 25°C for even crystallization.

2.2 Synthesis of Nanoparticle-Coated Chitosan Bioplastic Films

99.5% surface modified SiO_2 (10-20 nm) nanoparticles were mixed with acetone, 99% isopropyl alcohol, and sodium lauryl sulfate at 1500 RPM for 30 minutes in 25°C environment. 20%, 30%, and 40% of SiO_2 nanoparticles were tested for optimal suspension quality. A final 0.01 grams of SiO_2 was selected for optimal quality. Acetone (40 mL) was added for phase transfer of modified SiO_2 nanoparticles into non-aqueous isopropyl alcohol (100 mL), dissolving free silica nanoparticles and removing the layer of linear-chained polystyrene. This was then followed with sodium lauryl sulfate, with final testing showing an optimal amount of 0.04g. Dried chitosan composites were subsequently immersed perpendicularly in the dispersion for 30 seconds, allowing sufficient time for complete wetting of the substrate. Water contact angle tests were conducted on dried nanoparticle-coated films to measure hydrophobicity of coated films vs non-coated films.

2.3 Testing Chitosan Bioplastic Film Efficacy

Chitosan (CH) bioplastic films and nanoparticle (NP) coated CH film created from the project were tested on tensile strength, biodegradability in water and soil, degradability rate through mass loss test, water permeability and humidity test; compared with polyethylene resin bag as the control group and PLA corn film as a commercially available option of biofilms.

Tensile Strength Test
To measure the physical properties, tensile strength testing was conducted on 5 x 2.5 cm strips of each bioplastic film, compared with polyethylene films and PLA corn films.

Water and Soil Degradability Examined by SEM Analysis
Hydrolysis testing was conducted to observe effects of liquids on composite structure. Four films (CH films and

NP-coated CH films created from this project, polyethylene resin films and PLA corn films purchased from commercial marketplace) were immersed in beakers filled with DI water, with temperatures held constant by a heated water bath at 40°C for five days.

Home composting was used to observe soil degradability of the four films. Each film was cut into 5 x 2 cm strip, placed between acrylic sheets, and planted into the soil of each home composting bin.

Scanning Electron Microscope (SEM) analysis examined the effect of hydrolysis and soil composting on the surface structure of exposed and non-exposed composites.

Mass Loss Testing
Mass loss testing measured the rate of degradation in home composting bins, with 10 grams of each type of four films buried in 150 grams of potting soil. Mass loss was measured every three days for a duration of four weeks, adjusted for soil loss in the plastic film bin.

Phytotoxicity Testing
Phytotoxicity testing assessed phytotoxicity of the biofilms by measuring plant growth in the biodegraded soils. Five mung bean seeds and five red bean seeds were planted in each of the four compost bins after biodegradation tests. Each bean growth was measured every week for four weeks to assess plant growth and phytotoxicity of the biodegraded films in the compost bins.

Water Permeability and Humidity Testing
To analyze films' retention capability of liquids, water permeability and humidity tests were conducted under controlled environments for periods of up to six hours. Small beakers of water were placed upside-down in a closed environment with corresponding film composites tightly covering the opening. Humidity meters were placed into the closed environment and observed over a period of six hours at multiple intervals.

2.4 Antimicrobial Testing of Chitosan Films
Highly perishable fruits such as strawberries and raspberries were selected to test food preservation capability of chitosan bioplastic film vs polyethylene resin film, PLA corn film, and self-developed starch composite. Each fruit was placed in four separate containers, with each container covered tightly with the respective film. Observation of freshness was recorded and photographed every day over a duration of ten days. Pictures from the tests were taken as part of data collection, in addition to the daily log of changes in color, decay, mold, and juice leakage, etc. Due to

Franklin Education Foundation

From Food Waste to Food Guard: Creating a Novel Chitosan Bioplastic with Nanoparticle
Coating and Its Unique Effect on Water Resistance and Food Preservation

Journal of Quantitative and Qualitative Research

Henry Yao

the subjective nature of the experiment, tests were conducted in excess, with multiple types of fruits, to ensure accuracy of results.

3. Results and Discussion

3.1 Synthesis of Chitosan Bioplastic Films

A ratio of 12% chitosan, 80% water, 4% glycerin, and 4% acetic acid was determined through multiple testing, producing a thin and flexible sheet of translucent light yellow film composite. Tests were conducted to analyze the properties against competitive thin films in the market: polyethylene resin films, and PLA corn films as commercially available biofilm.

3.2 Nanoparticle Coating of Chitosan Biofilm Indicated Successful Improvement in Hydrophobicity

To counteract the low water resistance capability of chitosan, silicon dioxide (SiO_2) nanoparticle coating was added to boost chitosan's water resistance. Water contact angles of the coated films were measured at 107 to 115 degrees after coating, compared to 46 - 60 degrees water contact angle of uncoated films. This indicated the water resistance level of the uncoated film changed from hydrophilic (< 90 degrees) to hydrophobic (>90 degrees) with nanoparticle coating.

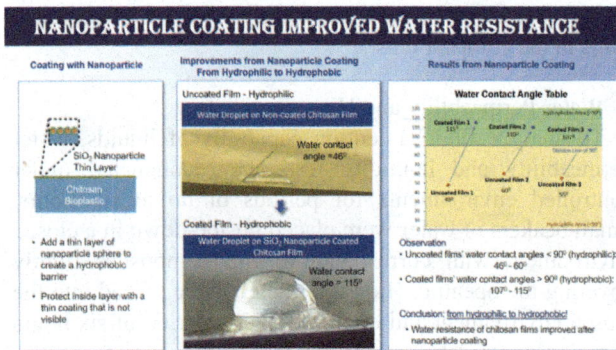

Figure 1: Water Contact Angles

3.3 Chitosan Biofilm and NP-Coated Chitosan Biofilm Demonstrated Significant Advantages in Biodegradability While Preserving Sufficient Tensile Strength

3.3.1 Tensile Strength Testing Demonstrated the Effectiveness of Chitosan-Starch composite

To boost the physical properties (flexural strength and malleability) of the developed chitosan films, multiple ratios

of starch were added for testing. On average, 50/50 ratios demonstrated the best quality and strength, and were subsequently used in tests against other competitive thin films. Physical stress tests of the films under a force sensor indicated that chitosan film and NP-coated chitosan film, created from this project, doubled the tensile strength of PLA corn film, as indicated in figure 2.

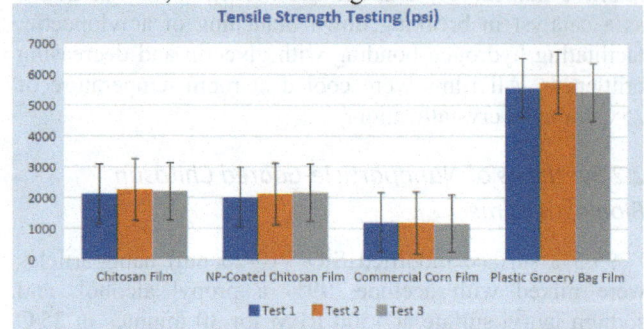

Figure 2: Tensile Stress Testing Result

3.3.2 NP-Coated Chitosan Biofilms and Chitosan Biofilms Showed Significantly Faster Soil and Water Degradability

Following one week of 40°C hydrolysis controlled in a water bath environment and two weeks of home composting environment, scanning electron micrographs (SEM) were taken at 1000x to examine structural changes of the composites.

In soil degradation, both CH film and NP-coated CH films have shown visible pores and filamentous microbe growths, while PLA corn film showed no visible signs of degradation and commercial polyethylene film indicated slight surface ruptures. Similar structural pores and breakage were visible for chitosan and NP-coated chitosan films from hydrolysis, in contrast to lack of visible degradation for PLA corn films and polyethylene films.

Franklin Education Foundation
Journal of Quantitative and Qualitative Research

From Food Waste to Food Guard: Creating a Novel Chitosan Bioplastic with Nanoparticle
Coating and Its Unique Effect on Water Resistance and Food Preservation

Henry Yao

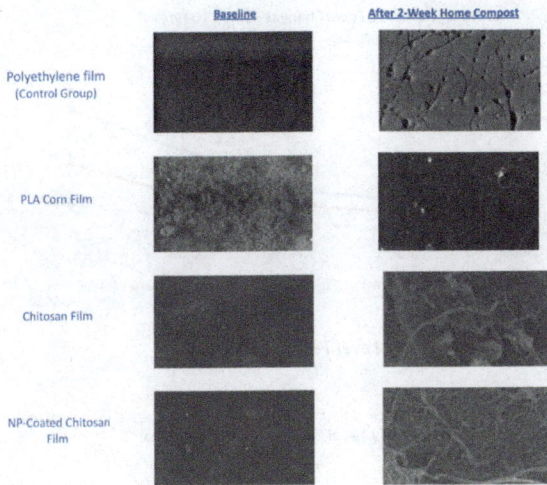

Figure 3: SEM Analysis Images of Soil Degradation

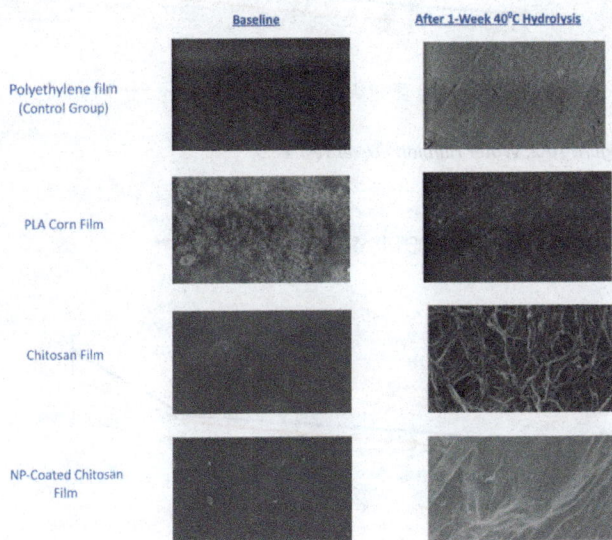

Figure 4: SEM Analysis Images of Hydrolysis

3.3.3 Mass Loss Testing Indicated Faster Degradation of Chitosan Biofilms and NP-Coated Chitosan Biofilms Compared with Polyethylene Films and PLA Corn Films

Mass loss test was conducted to compare the rate of degradation of these biofilms vs polyethylene film and PLA corn film over a period of four weeks. On day 27, chitosan biofilm mass loss was measured at 89-91% and NP-coated chitosan biofilm at 69-73%, as compared to PLA corn film's mass loss at 37-43%.

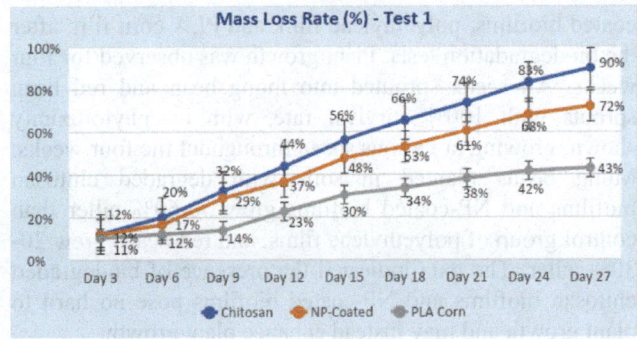

Figure 5: Mass Loss Rate – Test 1 (adjusted for soil mass loss)

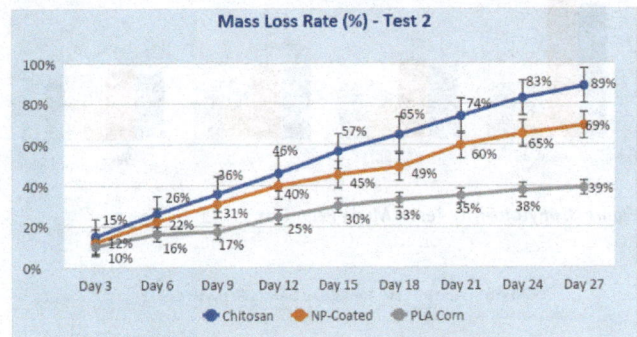

Figure 6: Mass Loss Rate – Test 2 (adjusted for soil mass loss)

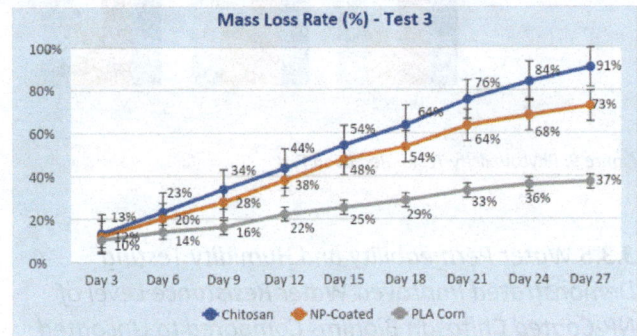

Figure 7: Mass Loss Rate – Test 3 (adjusted for soil mass loss)

3.3.4 Chitosan Biofilms and NP-Coated Chitosan Biofilms Posed No Harm to Plant Growth through Phytotoxicity Testing

Degradation of chemicals can often times release toxic by-products which can cause harm to crop growth in the field. To assess environmental impact from biodegradation of chitosan biofilms and NP=coated films, phytotoxicity testing was conducted. Five mung bean seeds and five red bean seeds were planted in each of the four compost bins containing soils with biodegraded chitosan biofilms, NP-

Franklin Education Foundation

Journal of Quantitative and Qualitative Research

From Food Waste to Food Guard: Creating a Novel Chitosan Bioplastic with Nanoparticle
Coating and Its Unique Effect on Water Resistance and Food Preservation

Henry Yao

coated biofilms, polyethylene film, and PLA corn film after the biodegradation tests. Plant growth was observed for four weeks. All seeds sprouted into mung bean and red bean sprouts with 100% survival rate, with no phytotoxicity shown, growing at various speed throughout the four weeks. Mung beans planted in soils with degraded chitosan biofilms and NP-coated biofilms grew 50-60% taller than control group of polyethylene films, and red beans grew 20-30% taller. The data indicated the presence of biodegraded chitosan biofilms and NP-coated biofilms pose no hard to plant growth and may instead enhance plant growth.

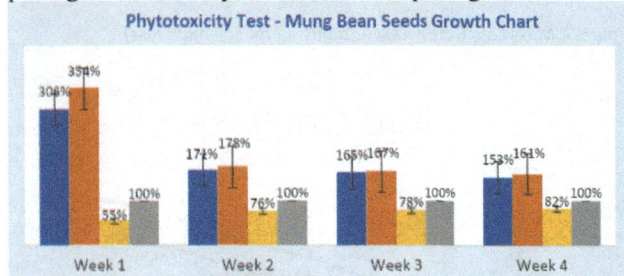

Figure 8: Phytotoxicity Test – Mung Bean Test

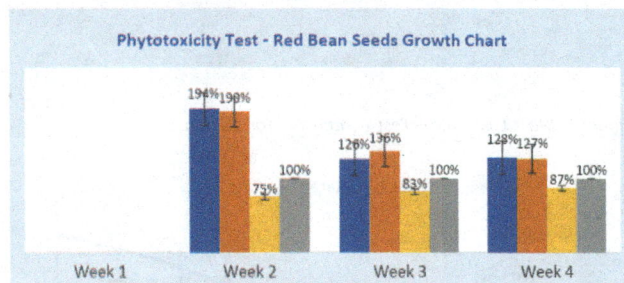

Figure 9: Phytotoxicity Test – Red Bean Test

3.3.5 Water Permeability and Humidity Testing Demonstrated Improved Water Resistance Level of NP-Coated Chitosan Biofilms Compared to Uncoated Chitosan Biofilms and PLA Corn Films

Water permeability and humidity testing observed humidity level increase and film breakage with water exposure over a six-hour period. NP-coated films showed 31-35 degrees increase over 6 hours, compared to 46-54 degrees increase for non-coated films. Neither of the coated or non-coated chitosan films broke in the six-hour testing period. As a comparison, the PLA corn film broke within 15 minutes of testing, with humidity level rising to 64-82 degrees. Polyethylene film performed the strongest water resistance, with less than 20 degrees humidity increase over the six-hour testing period.

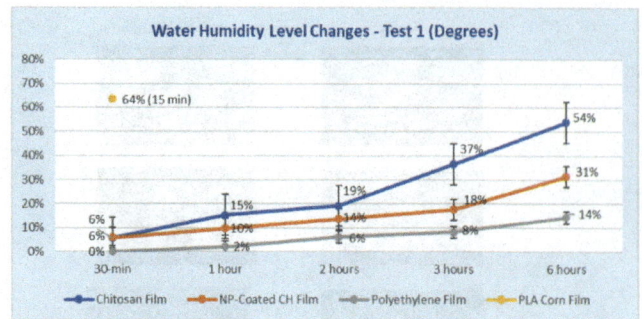

Figure 10-1: Water Humidity Level Test 1

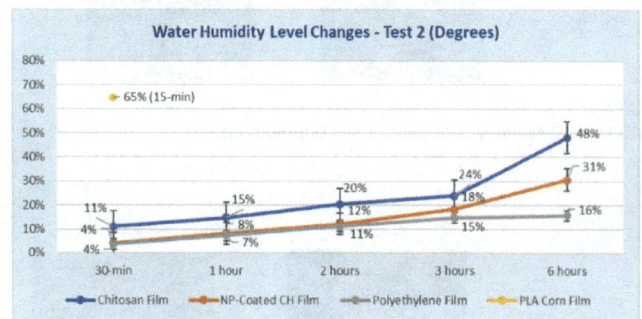

Figure 10-2: Water Humidity Level Test 2

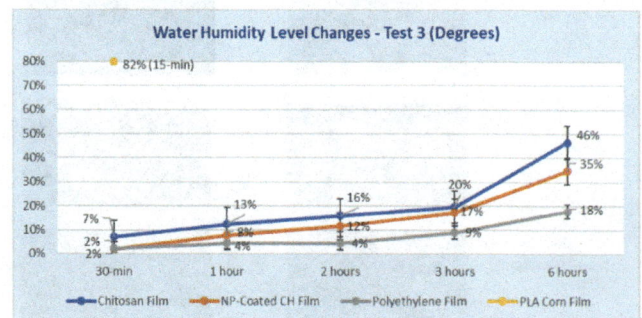

Figure 10-3: Water Humidity Level Test 3

3.4 Antimicrobial Testing of Chitosan Biofilms

Chitosan's antimicrobial and antifungal properties are mainly attributed to its bio-killing agent, which breaks open the cell wall of bacterium. Tests were conducted to observe the unique effect of chitosan films in preserving shelf-life of perishable foods.

In fruit preservation test 1 and 2 using strawberries, the strawberry covered by plastic film and commercial corn film broke out with white and black mold dots on day 2. The strawberry covered by starch film broke out with black

Franklin Education Foundation

Journal of Quantitative and Qualitative Research

From Food Waste to Food Guard: Creating a Novel Chitosan Bioplastic with Nanoparticle
Coating and Its Unique Effect on Water Resistance and Food Preservation

Henry Yao

mold on day 3. The strawberry covered by chitosan film kept its freshness until day 10 when one white mold dot emerged. In raspberry preservation test, except for the chitosan-covered raspberry, mold dots emerged on all other raspberries covered by starch film, commercial corn film, or plastic film on day 3. On day 8, white mold dot emerged on the raspberry covered with chitosan film.

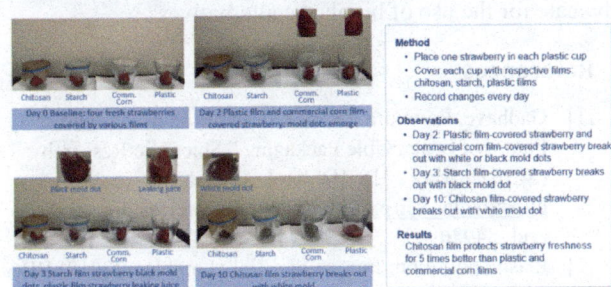

Figure 11: Strawberry Preservation Test

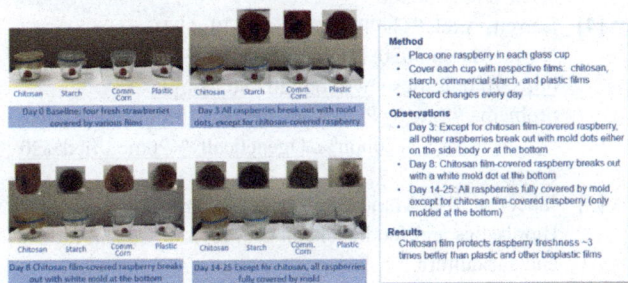

Figure 12: Raspberry Preservation Test

4. Discussion

The objective of this project was to create chitosan-based bioplastic films, in the expectation to replace conventional petroleum-based plastics, and to reduce white pollution. This project also attempted to identify a novel approach to resolve the water resistance challenge of bioplastics using nanoparticle coating and conducts multiple tests to validate the effectiveness of chitosan biofilms and nanoparticle-coated biofilms in terms of tensile strength, biodegradability, and water resistance level. In addition, this project also explored the application of chitosan bioplastic in preserving food for longer shelf-life due to its unique antimicrobial property.

Through multiple iterations, chitosan and starch were used as the base materials with addition of glycerin, acetic

acid, and water to produce a thin biofilm composite with translucent light-yellow color.

In search of improving water permeability of chitosan films, applying silicon dioxide (SiO_2) nanoparticle coatings to the chitosan films have shown to be very effective in increasing water resistance of chitosan films. Water contact angles rose from 46-60 degrees as in uncoated films to up to 115 degrees in coated films. This indicated the water resistance level of the uncoated film changed from hydrophilic (< 90 degrees) to hydrophobic (>90 degrees) with nanoparticle coating. The improvement in water resistance level was further validated by water permeability and humidity tests. NP-coated films showed slower humidity level increase, with 31-35 degrees increase over six hours, compared to 46-54 degrees increase for non-coated films, indicating a 33-43% improvement in water resistance. This can be taken as a potential approach to increase hydrophobicity of other bioplastic products.

Stress tests have suggested that chitosan biofilms and nanoparticle (NP) coated biofilms can sustain tensile strength better than commercially available PLA corn films with doubling psi measurement.

Water and soil degradation tests have demonstrated a significantly faster degradation rate of chitosan biofilms and NP-coated biofilms compared to PLA corn films and polyethylene films. After one week of water degradation in 40°C water bath environment and two weeks of soil degradation in home composting environment, scanning Electron Microscope (SEM) analyses have shown visible structural pores and filamentous microbe growths in NP-coated and uncoated chitosan biofilms. Meanwhile, PLA corn film and polyethylene films under the same testing environments have shown very little to no signs of degradation. Multiple mass loss tests over four weeks have validated the biodegradability advantages of the chitosan biofilms: chitosan biofilms degrade at almost double the rate of PLA corn films, and NP-coated biofilms degrade at 60-80% faster than PLA corn films. In addition, phytotoxicity testing have indicated the chitosan and NP-coated biofilms cause no environmental harms to plants, and instead, might enhance plant growth.

With the discovery of chitosan's unique antimicrobial property during project research, repeated tests with perishable fruits have revealed the uniqueness of the chitosan bioplastic film in prolonging perishable foods' shelf-life by up to 5 times compared with polyethylene film. The antimicrobial effect of chitosan can generate additional

Franklin Education Foundation

Journal of Quantitative and Qualitative Research

From Food Waste to Food Guard: Creating a Novel Chitosan Bioplastic with Nanoparticle
Coating and Its Unique Effect on Water Resistance and Food Preservation

Henry Yao

economic values in commercial application, such as in food packaging and transportation.

Due to constraints of lab equipment, dip coating technique was used in a home-designed Langmuir-Blodgett trough. In an established lab facility, spin coating techniques can be applied to create a uniform layer of coating for potentially better and consistent results. Although physical stress tests indicated that chitosan films and NP-coated chitosan films doubled the tensile strength of PLA corn films, they still lag the tensile strength of the grocery shopping bags made from polyethylene films. Future research may expand to include further polymer blending options to improve tensile strength of chitosan biofilms.

5. Conclusion

This project successfully developed a novel chitosan-based bioplastic composite and identified SiO_2 nanoparticle coating to chitosan bioplastic film to resolve the water permeability challenge facing most bioplastic films. Both chitosan films and nanoparticle-coated chitosan films have demonstrated significant biodegradability advantages in hydrolysis and home compost compared to polyethylene resin film and PLA corn film as a viable bio-alternative to conventional plastic films. In addition, chitosan films have shown unique antimicrobial effects in prolonging shelf-life of perishable foods.

As a thin film and composite that is low cost, biodegradable, and antimicrobial, chitosan bioplastic has its unique and superior advantages as the next-gen bioplastic alternative that can be used for food wraps, grocery bags, food package and storage, and other containers. In addition, solving the water resistance challenge through nanoparticle coatings has the potential of broadening the commercial application of chitosan bioplastic, and can be applied to other bioplastic films to change biofilm usage from single-use to multiple-use, generating further economic benefits. Therefore, chitosan bioplastic film with nanoparticle coating created from this project has proven to be a unique and highly viable bioplastic option for food packaging and preservation industry and beyond.

6. Acknowledgment

I want to thank Creek Connection Actions Group (www.cleanacreek.org) for the collective community efforts to clean our environment and for persistently calling for community awareness for environmental protection. These events have sparked my interests in exploring bioplastic alternatives to conventional plastics. This project has firmed up my belief that we can make an impact in saving our environment.

I want to thank my science teacher Mr. Leung for his support of this research project. I also want to thank my parents for their unconditional support of my idea to pursue this project, letting me exploit home kitchen and garage for my experimentation, and showcasing the bioplastic films created from this project to their friends and co-workers to advocate for the use of bioplastic alternatives.

7. References

[1] Gadhave, Ravindra. "Starch-Based Bioplastics: The Future of Sustainable Packaging." Scientific Research (SCIRP). May 2018. [Online]. Available: https://www.scirp.org/journal/paperinformation.aspx?paperid=84926

[2] Plastic pollution: Images of a global problem (2018) BBC 25. [Online]. Available: https://www.bbc.com/news/science-environment-44215882

[3] Science Direct. [Online] Available: https://www.sciencedirect.com/topics/materials-science/polylactide

[4] Barrett, Axel. "The Problems with PLA" Bioplastics News. March 2020. [Online]. Available: https://bioplasticsnews.com/2020/03/14/pla-problems/#:~:text=PLA%20releases%20fewer%20GHGs%20from,%2C%20non%2Dgenetically%20modified%20crops.

[5] Jabeen Nafisa, Majid Ishrat, Nayik Ahmad Gulzar. (2015) Bioplastics and food packaging: A review. Cogent food and agriculture.

[6] Marichelvam, M.K. "Corn and Rice Starch-Based Bioplastics as Alternative Packaging Materials." MDPI. April 2019. [Online]. Available: https://www.mdpi.com/2079-6439/7/4/32/htm

[7] Iber, Benedict. "A Review of Various Sources of Chitin and Chitosan in Nature." Engormix. January 2022. [Online]. Available: https://en.engormix.com/feed-machinery/articles/review-various-sources-chitin-t48446.htm

[8] [8] Jiminez-Gomez, Carmen. "Chitosan: A Natural Biopolymer with a Wide and Varied Range of Applications." NCBI. September 2020. [Online]. Available: https://www.ncbi.nlm.nih.gov/pmc/articles/PMC7504732/

[9] Holley, Richard. "Inhibition of surface spoilage bacteria in processed meats by application of antimicrobial films prepared with chitosan." Academia. July 2000. [Online]. Available: https://www.academia.edu/42084885/Inhibition_of_surface_spoilage_bacteria_in_processed_meats_by_application

Franklin Education Foundation

Journal of Quantitative and Qualitative Research

From Food Waste to Food Guard: Creating a Novel Chitosan Bioplastic with Nanoparticle
Coating and Its Unique Effect on Water Resistance and Food Preservation

Henry Yao

of_antimicrobial_films_prepared_with_chitosan_a_b_a_a
_c?auto=citations&from=cover_page

[10] Fernandez-Saiz. "Optimization of the biocide properties
of chitosan for its application in the design of active films
of interest in the food area." ScienceDirect. May 2009.
[Online]. Available:
https://www.sciencedirect.com/science/article/abs/pii/S02
68005X0800132X

[11] [11] Raafat Dina, Sahl Hans-Georg. (2008, December 8)
Chitosan and its antimicrobial potential – a critical
literature survey. Society for Applied Microbiology and
Blackwell Publishing Ltd.

[12] Hüsnügül, Atay. "Antibacterial Activity of Chitosan-
Based Systems." NCBI. May 2020. [Online]. Available:
https://www.ncbi.nlm.nih.gov/pmc/articles/PMC7114974/
#:~:text=Chitosan%20is%20a%20natural%20antimicrobi
al,wall%20of%20filamentous%20fungus%2C%20R.

[13] Susilawati, Susilawati. "Characterization of Bioplastic
Packaging from Tapioca Flour Modified with the
Addition of Chitosan and Fish Bone Gelatin." 2019.
[Online]. Available:
https://bibliotekanauki.pl/articles/1065256

[14] Cao, Wenling. "Preparation and characterization of
catechol-grafted chitosan/gelatin/modified chitosan-AgNP
blend films." Science Direct. November 2020. [Online].
Available:
https://www.sciencedirect.com/science/article/abs/pii/S01
44861720308171

[15] Oever Martien, Molenveld Karin, Zee Maarten, Bos
Harriette. (2017, April 15) Bio-based and biodegradable
plastics – Facts and Figures. Wageningen Food &
Biobased Research.

[16] [16] "7+ Revealing Plastic Waste Statistics" Recycle
Coach. September 2021. [Online]. Available:
https://recyclecoach.com/resources/7-revealing-plastic-
waste-statistics-2021/

[17] Asma Qdemat, Emmanuel Kentzinger, Johan Buitenhuis,
Ulrich R¨ucker, Marina Ganeva and Thomas Bruckel.
(2020) Self assembled monolayer of silica nanoparticles
with improved order by drop casting.

[18] Cao, Muhan. "Dispersing hydrophilic nanoparticles in
nonaqueous solvents with superior long term stability."
Royal Society of Chemistry. May 2017. [Online].
Available:
https://pubs.rsc.org/en/content/articlehtml/2017/ra/c7ra03
472e

[19] Seven charts that explain the plastic pollution problem.
(2017) BBC 10. Retrieved October 10th, 2018 from
https://www.bbc.com/news/science-environment-
42264788

[20] Nina Tsydenova, Pawan Patil. (2021, November 9) 6
Reasons to Blame Plastic Pollution for Climate Change.
World Bank Blogs.

Gender, Fashion, Income, and Brand Image

Zexi Sun

1. Introduction

The popular quote "image is everything" has been said by numerous individuals, including Japanese writer Haruki Murakami and American tennis legendary champion Andre Agassi (Tignor, 2015). In the field of business, this idea can be exemplified by the brands of products or companies, as certain brands tend to conjure up particular images in many people's minds. For example, some brands tend to be associated with luxury items or extravagant lifestyles, while other brands are typically associated with cheaper products, practical items, healthy lifestyles, or environmental-friendly images.

As a marketing strategy, branding can be very effective. A number of factors can influence the success of a brand, such as the messages from advertisements and even its name (Rooney, 1995). The brand can help a company find its identity, create unique images, become more memorable in consumers' minds, differentiate its products from those of competitors, convey its aspirations, and establish its values for customers (Tarver, 2022). Thus, it is very important for an institution to build and maintain its brand.

The concept of brand equity further illustrates the importance of branding (Keller, 2003). Two products can be made from the same materials, but if you change the brand name, the price can be different, and even the perception of the products can be different. For instance, to some American and Asian young women, owning certain brands of luxury handbags is considered as a status signal and an identity symbol (Grotts & Johnson, 2013). As another example, one study (Robinson, Borzekowski, Matheson, & Kraemer, 2007) presented two bags of practically-identical french fries to children. When the children believed that one bag of fries was from McDonald's, most of them rated fries from that bag as better tasting, even though the two bags essentially had the same fries (Robinson et al., 2007).

Other researchers (Lee, Frederick, & Ariely, 2006) presented beer with a bit of added vinegar to college students at the Massachusetts Institute of Technology (MIT). Those who were told that the beer was "MIT brew" liked its taste, but those who were told that the beer was mixed with vinegar disliked its taste (Lee et al., 2006). These examples illustrate that how people evaluate products can be related to how they perceive brands. Given the importance of branding, the current study examines the brand images of five companies that sell clothes and/or shoes: Adidas, Louis Vuitton, Nike, Off-White, and Stussy.

2. Method

The survey method was used for the current study. First, to collect background information, the questionnaire asked about participants' age (free response), gender (i.e., Male, Female, or Other), cultural/ethnic background (i.e., Asian, Asian American, Black/African American, Latino/Latina, Native American, White/Caucasian or European American, and Other), and family income status (i.e., Lower Income, Middle Income, Upper-Middle Income, Upper Income, or Other). For gender, cultural/ethnic background, and family income status, the "Other:" category allowed participants to type-in free responses.

Second, to measure people's behavior and interests, the questionnaire asked three open-ended questions: "What is/are your favorite extracurricular activity/activities?", "What do you plan to do for your future career?", and "When shopping for clothes, what are the characteristics of clothing that are important to you?". Also, participants were asked how often they shopped for or bought (online and in-person) clothes (i.e., once per month or less, about 2-3 times per month, about 4-5 times per month, about 6-7 times per month, or more than 7 times per month) as well as how much they were generally into fashion from a scale of 0 (not at all) to 10 (very much).

Then, to assess participants' images and perceptions of five particular brands (Nike, Adidas, Louis Vuitton, Stussy, and Off-White), the questionnaire showed four pictures to the participants (Pictures A, B, C, and D).

Picture A

Picture B

Picture C

Picture D

For Picture A, the question was: "the clothes are most likely from which brand?". For Picture B, the question was: "the shoes are most likely from which brand?". For Picture C, the question was: "the suit is most likely from which brand?". For Picture D, the question was: "the clothes are most likely from which brand?". For each picture, participants were asked to indicate one answer from five possible choices of brands: Nike, Adidas, Louis Vuitton, Stussy, or Off-White.

Next, participants were asked to rate how much they liked each of the five brands (Adidas, Nike, Louis Vuitton, Stussy, and Off-White) in scales from 0 (not at all) to 10 (very much). Finally, participants were asked to pick their favorite brand and least-favorite brand (from the aforementioned five brands) as well as write one or two thing(s) on what they liked the most about their favorite brand and what they disliked the most about their least-favorite brand.

Forty-two participants completed the online questionnaire. Their ages ranged from 14 to 18, and the age frequency distribution was roughly normal (mean = 16.12, median = 16, and mode = 16). About 37% of them were males, about 61% of them were females, and one participant was gender-fluid. All of them were Asians or Asian-Americans, while one of them was part Asian and part White/European. In terms of family income status, 27.5% of them were in the middle-income group, 60% of them were in the upper-middle-income group, and 12.5% of them were in the upper-income group. None of them were in the lower-income group.

3. Results

Figure 1 shows how often the participants shopped for clothes. Most of the students from middle-income families bought/shopped for clothes approximately once per month or less than once per month. Students from upper-middle-income families were more likely to buy or shop for clothes about two-to-three times per month. Students from upper-income families bought or shopped with the highest frequency, and some of them even bought/shopped for clothes more than seven times per month. Generally, the higher the income group, the higher the shopping frequency.

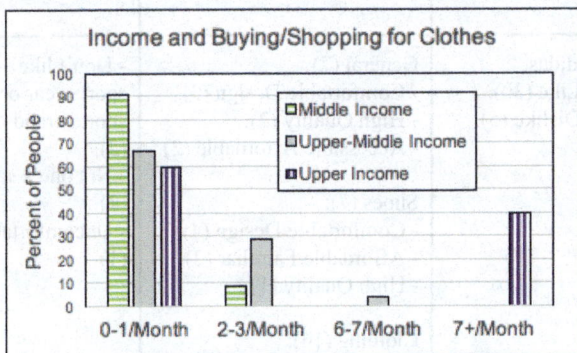

Figure 1: Income Groups and the Frequency of Buying/Shopping for Clothes.

Figure 2 shows the level of interest in fashion for males and females. Females (mean = 5.80, SD = 2.81) were likely to be slightly more interested in fashion than males (mean = 4.33, SD = 3.15) were, and this difference was approaching statistical significance , $t(38) = 1.53$, $p = 0.06$.

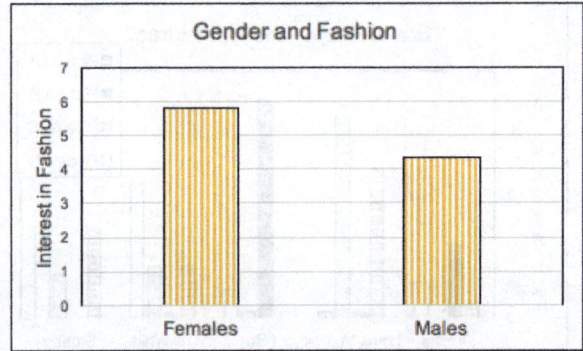

Figure 2: The Levels of Interest in Fashion for Males and Females.

Figure 3 shows the level of interest in fashion for the three income groups: middle-income, upper-middle-income, and upper-income families. There was no significant difference in interest between upper-middle and upper-income families. However, students from upper-income families were likely to be more interested in fashion than students from middle-income families, $t(14) = 1.89$, $p < 0.05$, and those upper-middle-income families were also likely to be more interested in fashion than those from middle-income families, $t(33) = 2.04$, $p < 0.05$.

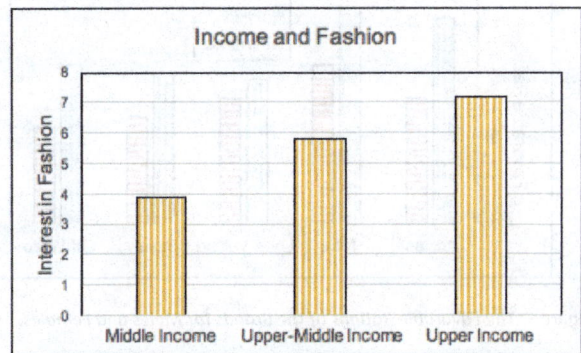

Figure 3: The Levels of Interest in Fashion for Middle-Income, Upper-Middle-Income, and Upper-Income Families.

Figure 4 shows participants' responses for each of the pictures (A, B, C, and D). Picture A was thought to be from Louis Vuitton (48.8%) by almost half of the participants, though some of them thought that it was from Stussy (29.3%) or Off-White (17.1%). Picture B was overwhelmingly thought to be from Nike (70.7%) by the majority of the participants, followed by Adidas (24.4%) responses. Picture C was thought to be from Louis Vuitton (65.9%) by most of the participants, followed by responses of Off-White (17.1%) or Stussy (14.6%). Picture D was mostly thought to be from Off-White (43.9%) and Stussy (31.7%).

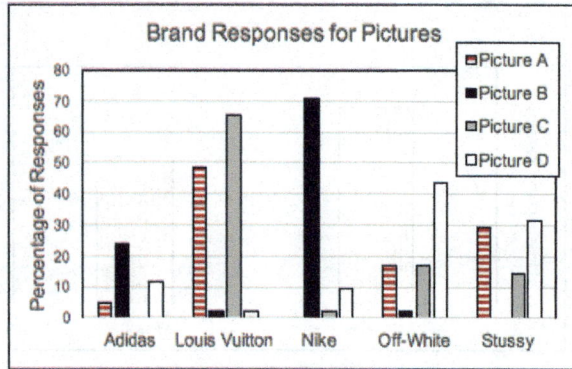

Figure 4: The Participants' Responses for Each of the Pictures (A, B, C, and D).

Figure 5 shows the participants' favorable ratings for each of the five brands (Adidas, Nike, Louis Vuitton, Stussy, and Off-White). Overall, the males (mean = 6.15, SD = 2.07) generally gave higher ratings than the females (mean = 4.30, SD = 1.42) did, t(38) = 3.34, p < 0.01, and this difference was especially pronounced for Adidas.

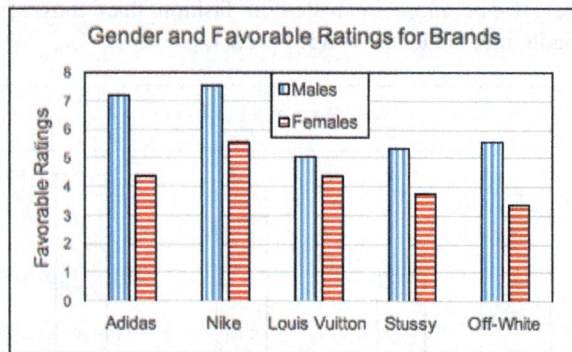

Figure 5: The Favorable Ratings of the Brands for Males and Females.

Figure 6 shows the participants' favorable ratings of the five brands for the three family-income groups (middle, upper-middle, and upper). There were no overall differences in ratings among the three family-income groups, F(2, 37) = 0.19, p = 0.83. However, those from the upper-income group gave higher ratings for Nike and Louis Vuitton; they also gave lower ratings for Stussy and Off-White.

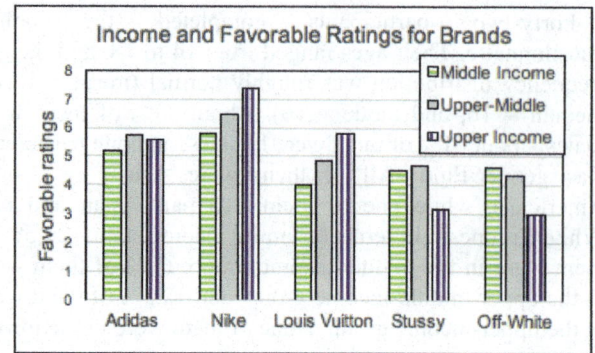

Figure 6: The Favorable Ratings of the Brands for Middle, Upper-Middle, and Upper Income Groups.

In terms of the qualitative thematic analyses, the participants were asked to pick their favorite brand and least-favorite brand as well as write one or two thing(s) on what they liked the most about their favorite brand and what they disliked the most about their least-favorite brand. Table 1 summarizes the qualitative results. The number of comments are included in the parentheses.

Brand	Favorite: Like (Comments)	Least-Favorite: Dislike (Comments)
Adidas - Like (30). - Dislike (5).	General (7): - Comfortable/Design (3). - High Quality (2). - Accessible/Affordable (2). Shoes (7): - Comfortable/Design (4). - Affordable/Familiar (2). - High Quality (1). Clothing (16): - Comfortable (3) / Design (7). - Flexible (2) / Affordable (2). - Good Quality (2).	- Don't like sportswear or sports brands (2). - Not one's style (2). - Uncomfortable (1).

Brand	Liked	Disliked
Louis Vuitton - Like (8). - Dislike (24).	General (2): - High-Quality (2). Design (6): - Stylish/Fancy (2); Cool (1). - Legitimate/Standard (2). - Simplistic but Elegant (1).	- Expensive (10). - Not into luxury brands (4); Doesn't fit one's style (3); Looks bad (2). - Uncomfortable (1); Not for daily wear (1). - Use to emit lots of greenhouse gasses (1); The logo/pattern is put everywhere (1). - N/A (1).
Nike - Like (26). - Dislike (5).	General (8): - Comfortable/Familiar/Design (4). - Good Quality (2). - Affordable (2). Shoes (12): - Comfortable (3); Design/Style (3). - High Quality (4). - Good for Exercise/Movement (2). Clothing (6): - Comfortable / Design (3). - Flexible (2). - Good for exercise (1).	- Don't like sportswear or sports brands (3). - Not one's style (1). - Quality of clothing is not good (1).
Off-White - Like (10). - Dislike (11)	Design (9): - Unique/Stylistic (2); Clean (2). - Aesthetic/Beautiful/Simple (3). - T-Shirts/General (2). Sounds Coolest (1).	- Never heard of it (2); Don't know much about it (2). - Not one's style (3). - Peculiar (1); Tacky (1); Basic (1); Showy (1).
Stussy - Like (12). - Dislike (21).	General (4): - Beautiful/Cool (3); Fitting (1). Style (2): - Graphic (1); Street (1). Clothes (6): - Comfort (2); Warm (1); Affordable (1); Stain-Resistant (1); Quality (1).	- Never heard of it (5); Don't know much about it (5). - Not one's style (6). - Lack Creativity/Variety (2); Basic (1); Punk/Street Style (1); Ugly (1).
Other Comments	None/Unsure or N/A (5). Don't Know Stussy or Off-White (1).	- Don't know or Unsure (3). - Don't have a least-favorite one (3). - N/A (2).

Table 1: Summary of What the Participants Liked about Their Favorite Brand and What They Disliked about Their Least-Favorite Brand.

4. Discussion

The current project has found a number of significant and meaningful results. Generally, people from higher income groups tended to shop more and be more interested in fashion (Also, females tended to be more into fashion than males). Furthermore, based on the data from participants answering questions about the pictures, it was possible to get a sense of their brand image. In particular, Louis Vuitton appeared to be associated with a luxury lifestyle. Both Nike and Adidas appeared to be associated with athletic/sports lifestyles, although Nike seemed to be more associated with basketball and basketball shoes. This finding is consistent with some popular opinions (Stuart, 2020; Rookie Road, n.d.), and it is also consistent with the current projects' qualitative findings; there were more Nike comments about shoes than Adidas comments about shoes. As for Stussy and Off-White, the patterns of responses were similar between these two brands, suggesting that people had somewhat similar brand images for Off-White and Stussy.

Generally, the males liked these five brands (Adidas, Nike, Louis Vuitton, Stussy, and Off-White) more than the females did, especially for Adidas. Also, participants from higher income groups tended to give higher ratings for Nike and Louis Vuitton as well as give lower ratings for Stussy and Off-White. Why were Adidas, Nike, and Louis Vuitton well-liked? Perhaps the qualitative results provide possible explanations. For people who liked these brands, it appeared that products from the brands of Nike, Adidas, and Louis Vuitton were perceived to be famous, fashionable, and high-quality (Nike and Adidas products were also perceived to be comfortable to wear). Why were Stussy and Off-White less likely to be favored? Maybe the participants did not know much about them. About 28 percent of the comments (i.e., 15 comments) regarding Stussy and Off-White indicated that the participant either had never heard of or did not know much about Stuffy and/or Off-White.

5. Conclusion

Every study has its own limitations, and the current study is no exception. In terms of methodology, the current project's survey is not an experiment, so causal inferences cannot be made. In terms of sampling, the current sample mostly consisted of Asian and Asian-American teenagers, so the results may not be generalized to people from other ethnic, cultural, or age groups.

Nevertheless, the current project's findings have practical implications for businesses. In particular, companies can use the findings to improve their brand images. For example, while Adidas and Nike generally garnered positive comments suggesting good brand images (especially from males), participants who disliked Louis Vuitton gave negative comments about the brand's association with overly-lavish extravagance. Furthermore, the current results found that Adidas was especially more popular among males than among females and that Adidas was more liked for its clothing, while Nike was more liked for its shoes (at least for Asian-American teenagers). Therefore, Adidas can improve by exerting more of its marketing efforts to focus on females and/or to promote its shoes. As for Off-White and Stussy, the patterns of responses were similar for these two brands, so perhaps more can be done to make their brand images unique and differentiate their brand images from each other. In addition, although people who favored Off-White and Stussy liked their specific styles or designs, many comments suggested that a lot of the participants did not know much about these two brands. Therefore, these companies can expand beyond niche marketing to increase their overall popularity and improve their general brand images.

Finally, for possible future directions, further research studies can examine the perception of brand images from other companies/products as well as test participants from other age, ethnic, cultural, and/or income groups.

6. References

[1] Grotts, A. S., & Johnson, T. W. (2013). Millennial consumers' status consumption of handbags. *Journal of Fashion Marketing and Management, 17*(3), 280-293.

[2] Keller, K. L. (2003). Understanding brands, branding and brand equity. *Interactive Marketing, 5,* 7-20.

[3] Lee, L., Frederick, S., & Ariely, D. (2006). Try it, you'll like it: The influence of expectation, consumption, and revelation on preferences for beer. *Psychological Science, 17*(12), 1054-1058.

[4] Robinson, T. N., Borzekowski, D. L. G., Matheson, D. M., & Kraemer, H. C. (2007). Effects of fast food branding on young children's taste preferences. *Archives of Pediatric and Adolescent Medicine, 161*(8), 792-797.

[5] Rookie Road (n.d.). Top 10 Basketball Brands. *Rookieroad.com.* https://www.rookieroad.com/basketball/top-10-brands/

[6] Rooney, J. A. (1995). Branding: A trend for today and tomorrow. *Journal of Product & Brand Management, 4*(4), 48-55.

[7] Stuart (2020, October 19). These 10 companies are the NBA's biggest sponsors and advertisers. *Interbasket.* https://www.interbasket.net/news/the-nbas-biggest-sponsors-and-advertisers/31519/

[8] Tarver, E. (2022, April 11). Brand identity: What it is and how to build one. *Investopedia.* https://www.investopedia.com/terms/b/brand-identity.asp

[9] Tignor, S. (2015, August 30). 1989: Image is everything – Andre Agassi's infamous ad. *Tennis.* https://www.tennis.com/news/articles/1989-image-is-everything-andre-agassi-s-infamous-ad

Franklin Education Foundation
Journal of Quantitative and Qualitative Research

Hidden Connections: The Factors That Are Associated With Public Familiarity and Opinions of Emerging, Prominent Medical Technologies

Anna Chen

Franklin Education Foundation

Journal of Quantitative and Qualitative Research

Hidden Connections: The Factors That Are Associated With Public
Familiarity and Opinions of Emerging, Prominent Medical Technologies

Anna Chen

1. Introduction

The world is in the middle of what scientists and leaders are calling a "technological revolution" (Wilkinson, 2022). The past few centuries have given rise to countless innovations across multiple fields, spanning from agriculture to architecture and everything in between. The medical sector especially has seen the development of several technological advancements that have pushed science forward to improve the quality of medicine and treatment. Innovations such as vaccines, anesthesia, antibiotics, and most recently, medical artificial intelligence, have revolutionized healthcare and greatly expanded our knowledge and practice of medicine (Hogg, 2021). While these developments undoubtedly benefit our society, the extent to which they can better our lives is greatly influenced by how accepting our communities are of their creation and effects.

For example, vaccines have played a significant role in eradicating certain diseases, reducing the mortality rates of preventable illnesses, and extending life expectancy (Rodrigues & Plotkin, 2020; Rughinis et al., 2022). However, they have simultaneously faced widespread skepticism and controversy ever since they were introduced into society (North, 2022). Debates about their effectiveness, utilization, and overall nature continue to stain the scientific community's efforts to inoculate full populations of people. This divide over the use of vaccinations was especially prevalent during the COVID-19 pandemic, where "successful campaigns to combat the COVID-19 pandemic depend[ed], in part, on people's willingness to be vaccinated" (Seddig et al., 2022).

The importance of public opinion in influencing a technology's effectiveness in society is exemplified not only by vaccines but also by many more recent medical procedures and innovations. Specifically, organ donation, genetic editing, and regenerative medicine are all showing promising potential to be essential parts of healthcare, but ongoing controversies surrounding each topic indicate that public opinion about them will play an integral part in how likely (or not) they are to be accepted into our society as they become more and more integrated into it. Knowing the general perceptions the public holds about these technologies and the factors that are related to certain perceptions can provide information that can help scientists and researchers predict their contributions to society and optimize their use in healthcare.

Therefore, this paper intends to investigate the factors that contribute to the formation of public familiarity and opinion regarding prominent, emerging medical technologies. Specifically, the topics of organ donation, genetic editing, and regenerative medicine will be focused on. Special attention will be paid to finding correlations between the extent of familiarity of one technology when compared to another, and the opinion of one technology when compared to another. Correspondingly, the main goals of this project are the following:

1) Analyze the factors that contribute to public knowledge and opinion on organ donation, genetic editing, and regenerative medicine
2) Find correlations between familiarity and opinion levels of each technology in comparison to one other

2. Literature Review

The process of this study was helped by several previous works by scholars that examine topics of related nature. In the following sections, existing studies focused on assessing public attitudes regarding organ donation, genetic editing, and regenerative medicine will be discussed.

2.1 Organ Donation

For organ donation, a study titled "Why are we Poor Organ Donors: A Survey Focusing on Attitudes of the Lay Public From Northern India" was examined (Panwar et al., 2016). This study was conducted to assess the reasons for poor organ-donation rates in India. The researchers used a 30-item questionnaire to assess participants' knowledge, views, and attitudes regarding organ donation and brain death. The survey garnered 352 responses, and, analyzing the data, the researchers concluded that lack of awareness was the biggest contributor to low donation rates, followed by religious beliefs/superstitions and lack of faith in the healthcare system (Panwar et al., 2016). The researchers noted that knowledge of the topic and willingness to donate was significantly associated with education level (ibid).

Another study titled "In their own words: the reasons why people will (not) sign an organ donor card" by Susan E. Morgan et al. revealed that the most common reasons in support of organ donation were religion and a desire to help those in need (Morgan et al., 2008).

2.2 Genetic Editing

In regards to genetic editing, a Pew Research Center survey conducted by Cary Funk et al., titled, "U.S. public opinion on the future use of gene editing" was examined (Funk et al., 2016). The survey assessed public opinion about the potential of gene editing in improving health and found that those who were familiar with the idea were much

Franklin Education Foundation

Journal of Quantitative and Qualitative Research

Hidden Connections: The Factors That Are Associated With Public
Familiarity and Opinions of Emerging, Prominent Medical Technologies

Anna Chen

more likely to want it for their baby when compared to those who were not familiar (ibid). Additionally, they found that the percentage of those who would want or support gene editing went down as the level of religious commitment went up (ibid).

2.3 Regenerative Medicine

For regenerative medicine, a study titled, "A comparative analysis of attitudes toward stem cell research and regenerative medicine between six countries," by Ryuma Shineha et al. was examined. This study assessed the differences in the public attitudes and interests of people regarding regenerative medicine across 6 countries by distributing an online questionnaire and collecting responses from 100 citizens per country (Shineha et al., 2022). The researchers discovered that the differences in interests toward regenerative medicine varied across countries and are influenced by political, social, and cultural contexts (ibid).

2.4 Gap

While previous research has been conducted on the factors that contribute to public familiarity and opinion on these three technologies, all of the studies have analyzed each topic separately, either assessing attitudes about organ donation, genetic editing, *or* regenerative medicine. This study combines all three subjects in order to find possible correlations between the familiarity and opinions of one medical technology and those of another. This way, the particular gap in research pertaining to the relationship between how well someone knows about and how well someone feels about one medical development and how well they know and feel about another can be filled, all while developing on the work of previous studies by analyzing the factors that may relate to those connections.

Additionally, this study examines possible factors of association that were not included in many previous studies. For example, not many previous works look closely at the age of the participants, and none have examined their favorite subject in relation to their familiarity and opinion about these medical technologies. This project addresses those aspects to find further factors that are associated with certain familiarity levels or opinions.

3. Method

This study aims to find correlations between familiarity levels and public opinion of certain technologies while examining the factors that contribute to those variables. Therefore, a mixed qualitative and quantitative correlational study was conducted. This allowed for a numerical comparison between specific factors and respective familiarity/opinion levels (quantitative), an analysis of the correlations between familiarity and opinion of all three technologies (quantitative), and a visualization of the resulting distributions of familiarity and opinion for all three technologies through graphical representations and analysis (qualitative).

3.1 Data Collection

For the method of data collection, an online survey was created due to a multitude of reasons: 1) many previous works (refer to Literature Review) used surveys/questionnaires to collect data, 2) a survey was the most effective way to gather a large number of responses about public perception due to its ability to efficiently collect and compile data about how much people know/how people feel about certain topics as well as its user-friendliness, 3) the survey was anonymous, which ensured that respondents would feel comfortable answering truthfully and can be straightforward with their responses, and 4) an experiment was not feasible to conduct for this study because the explanatory variables (which would include background information such as age, gender, favorite subject, etc.) cannot be manipulated.

3.2 Content of Survey

The survey was split into 4 different parts/pages.

The first page consisted of a list of questions on background information, the specifics of which were influenced by previous works (refer to Literature Review) as well as including several new factors that weren't asked about previously to contribute to existing scholarship on the subject. The following list displays the information about each individual that was obtained from the first part of the survey (see Appendix A for the full list of questions):

- Gender
- Age
- Favorite Subject
- Religious Status
- Education Level
- Whether the individual went to a public or private high school
- Whether the individual went to a religious or nonreligious high school
- The highest degree earned by either parent

The second, third, and fourth pages all followed the same format, the only difference being the topic each one focused on (the second page focused on organ donation, the third focused on genetic editing, and the fourth focused on

Franklin Education Foundation
Journal of Quantitative and Qualitative Research

Hidden Connections: The Factors That Are Associated With Public
Familiarity and Opinions of Emerging, Prominent Medical Technologies
Anna Chen

regenerative medicine). First, a short description of the topic was provided (see Appendix A for the descriptions). Then, respondents were asked to rate their familiarity with the topic on a scale of 0 to 10, with 0 being the lowest rating and 10 being the highest (see Appendix A for the descriptions used to describe the rating levels). Next, respondents were asked to rate their opinion on the topic on a scale of 0 to 10, with 0 being the lowest rating and 10 being the highest (note: the specific definition for "opinion" used in the survey was the level of support the individual felt about the topic, so the phrases "opinion ratings" and "support levels" will be used interchangeably throughout this paper; see Appendix A for the descriptions used to describe the rating levels).

3.3 Distribution

The online survey was distributed to participants via a link that was sent directly to the participant's preferred way of contact. Each survey was automatically saved upon submission and the data was collected and organized through Google Forms, which was also the platform used to create and distribute the survey.

3.4 Analysis

The data were later compiled into a spreadsheet for visualization and analysis. This was done by linking Google Forms to Google Sheets. Quantitative and qualitative analyses (including graphic representations, correlations, and statistics) were all calculated using these two platforms. Specifically, correlational research and causal-comparative research were used to analyze the variables and factors within this study.

4. Results

A total of 83 responses were obtained from the survey. The following information breaks down the demographics of the resulting sample: 54.2% of respondents were female, while 45.8% were male; 78.3% of respondents were under 25 years old, 8.4% were between 25 and 50 years old, and 13.2% were over 50 years old; 27.7% of respondents marked "science" as their favorite subject, 19.3% marked "math," 16.9% marked "art/music," 12% marked "English," 12% marked "social studies," and 12% marked "other" (responses in this category included computers/technology, foreign languages, law, forensics, and religion/philosophy); 54.2% of responses indicated that they did not follow a religion, while 45.8% indicated that they did; 77.1% of respondents were either currently attending or had completed high school as their highest education level, 7.2% had attained a Bachelor's degree, 13.3% had attained a Master's degree, and 2.4% had attained a Doctoral degree;

54.2% of respondents are attending/attended a private high school, while 45.8% are attending/attended a public high school; 55.4% of respondents are attending/attended a nonreligious high school, while 44.6% are attending/attended a public high school; 18.1% of respondents indicated that the highest degree of education earned by either of their parents was a high school diploma or lower, 6% indicated that the highest degree earned was an Associate degree, 30.1% marked a Bachelor's degree, 28.9% marked a Master's degree, and 16.9% marked a Doctoral degree.

An analysis of the distribution of the familiarity and support ratings for each of the three technologies was then performed. Figures 1 and 2 display the distributions of each sample of familiarity ratings and opinion ratings, respectively:

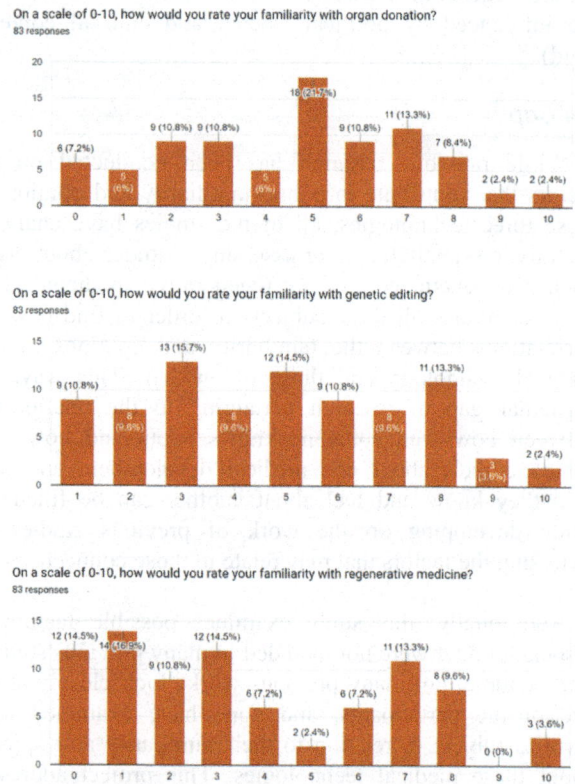

Figure 1: Distributions of Familiarity Ratings Across All Three Technologies

Hidden Connections: The Factors That Are Associated With Public
Familiarity and Opinions of Emerging, Prominent Medical Technologies

Anna Chen

Franklin Education Foundation

Journal of Quantitative and Qualitative Research

On a scale of 0-10, how would you rate your opinion on organ donation?
83 responses

On a scale of 0-10, how would you rate your opinion on genetic editing?
83 responses

On a scale of 0-10, how would you rate your opinion on regenerative medicine?
83 responses

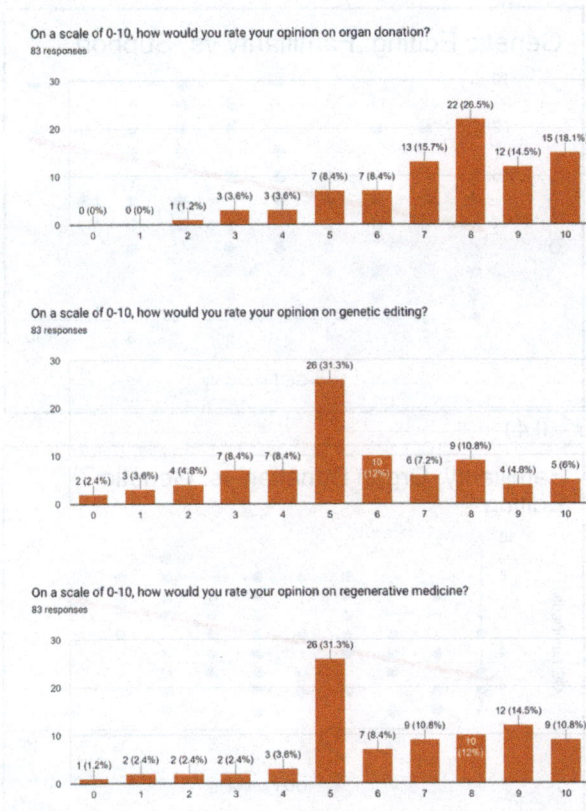

Figure 2: Distributions of Opinion Ratings Across All Three Technologies

Table 1 displays the shape, center (mean), and spread (standard deviation) of each sample:

		Shape of Distribution	Center (Mean Rating)	Spread (Standard Deviation)
Organ Donation	**Familiarity**	roughly symmetric	4.6	2.6
	Opinion	left-skewed	7.5	2.0
Genetic Editing	**Familiarity**	roughly symmetri	4.8	2.5
		c		
	Opinion	roughly symmetric	5.4	2.4
Regenerative Medicine	**Familiarity**	right-skewed	3.7	3.0
	Opinion	left-skewed	6.5	2.4

Table 1: Qualitative/Quantitative Analysis of the Samples of Familiarity and Opinion Ratings For All Three Technologies

4.1 Correlations Between Familiarity and Support

Next, the relationships between the familiarity and opinion ratings across all three technologies were graphed (there was a total of 9 combinations/graphs) and their respective correlation coefficients were calculated. Figure 3 displays the scatterplots of each relationship and their correlations:

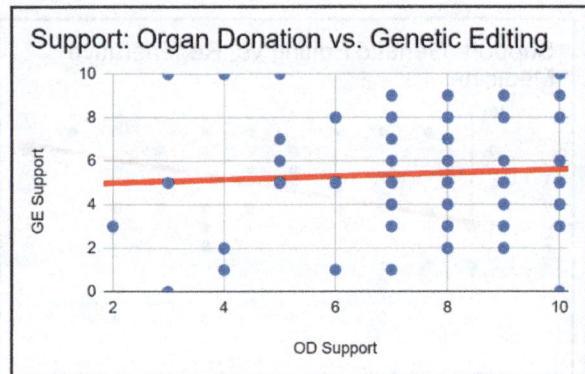

Support: Organ Donation vs. Genetic Editing

r = 0.06

Franklin Education Foundation
Journal of Quantitative and Qualitative Research

Hidden Connections: The Factors That Are Associated With Public
Familiarity and Opinions of Emerging, Prominent Medical Technologies

Anna Chen

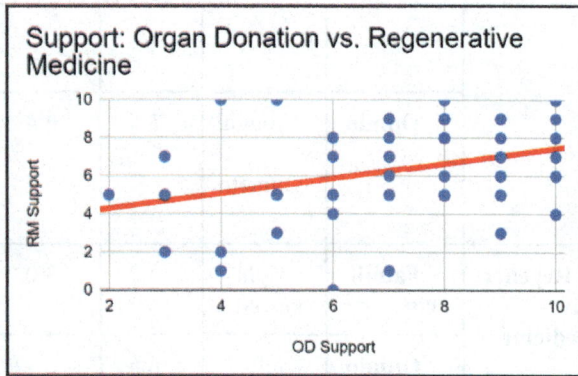

Support: Organ Donation vs. Regenerative Medicine

r = 0.33

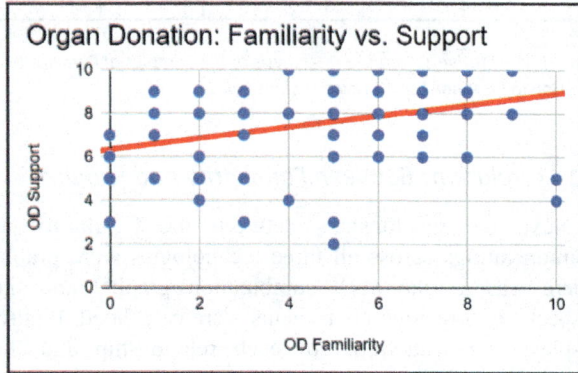

Organ Donation: Familiarity vs. Support

r = 0.34

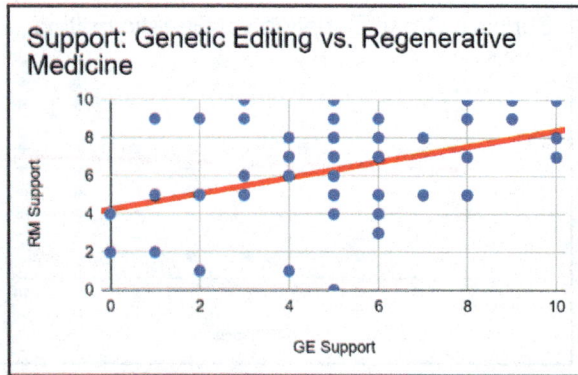

Support: Genetic Editing vs. Regenerative Medicine

r = 0.42

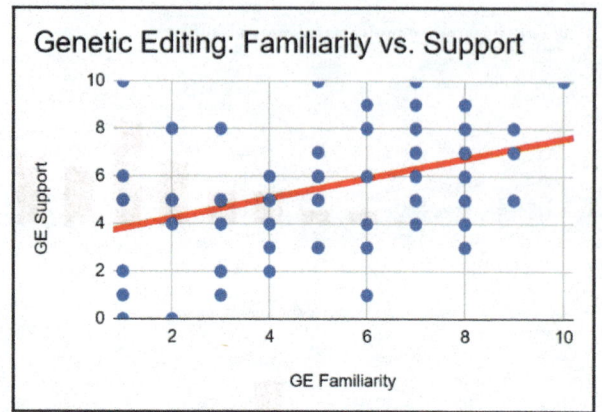

Genetic Editing: Familiarity vs. Support

r = 0.44

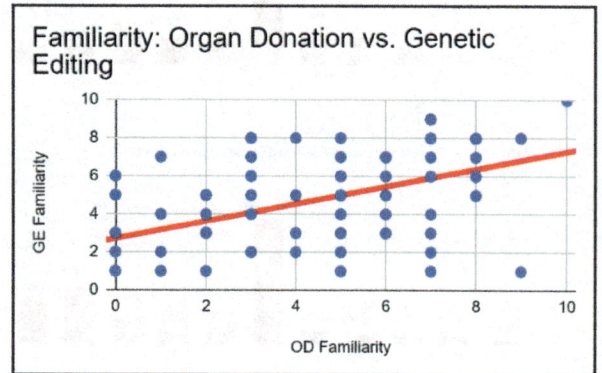

Familiarity: Organ Donation vs. Genetic Editing

r = 0.49

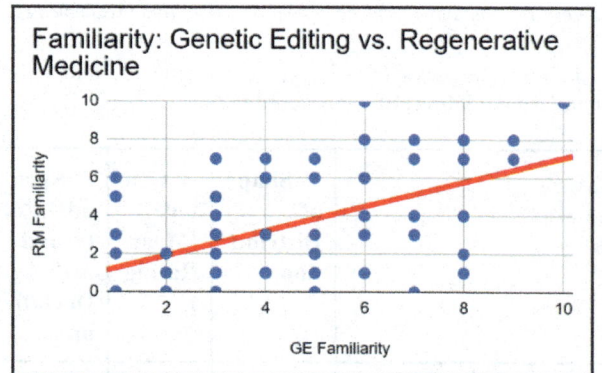

Familiarity: Genetic Editing vs. Regenerative Medicine

r = 0.54

Franklin Education Foundation

Journal of Quantitative and Qualitative Research

Hidden Connections: The Factors That Are Associated With Public
Familiarity and Opinions of Emerging, Prominent Medical Technologies

Anna Chen

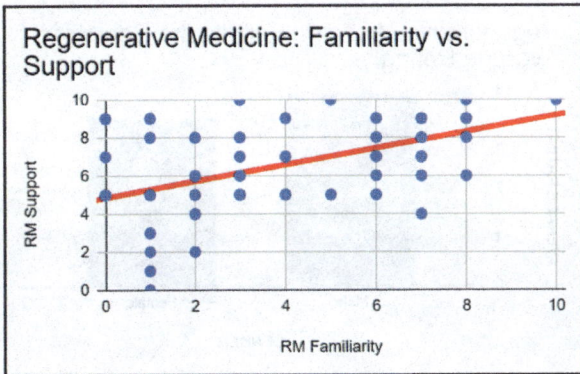

Regenerative Medicine: Familiarity vs. Support

r = 0.55

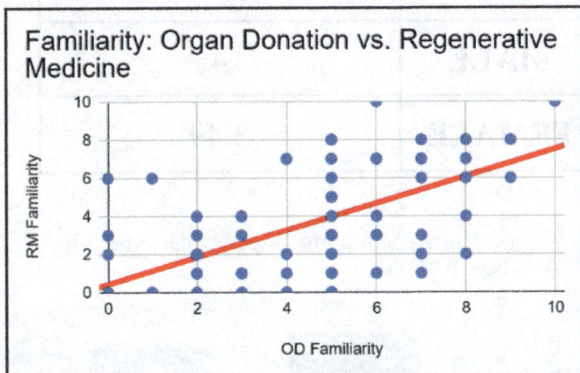

Familiarity: Organ Donation vs. Regenerative Medicine

r = 0.61

Figure 3: Scatterplots and Correlation Coefficients of Familiarity and Opinion Ratings Across All Three Technologies (in order from lowest to highest correlation)

4.2 Factors of Association

Next, each individual factor (the items asked for on the first page of the survey) and its relationship with the familiarity and opinion ratings for the three technologies was graphed and analyzed.

Figure 4 displays the relationships between gender and average familiarity/support ratings for each of the three technologies.

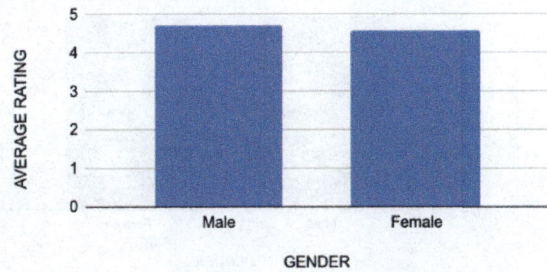

Organ Donation Familiarity: Gender vs. Average Rating

	AVERAGE RATING
MALE	4.71
FEMALE	4.58

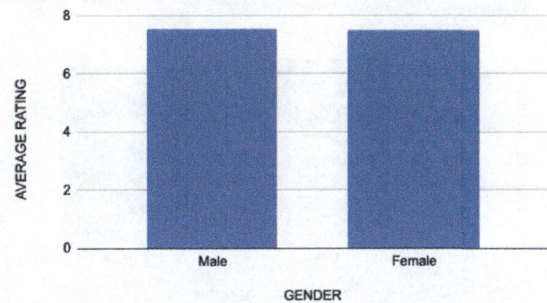

Organ Donation Support: Gender vs. Average Rating

	AVERAGE RATING
MALE	7.55
FEMALE	7.51

Franklin Education Foundation

Hidden Connections: The Factors That Are Associated With Public
Familiarity and Opinions of Emerging, Prominent Medical Technologies

Journal of Quantitative and Qualitative Research

Anna Chen

Genetic Editing Familiarity: Gender vs. Average Rating

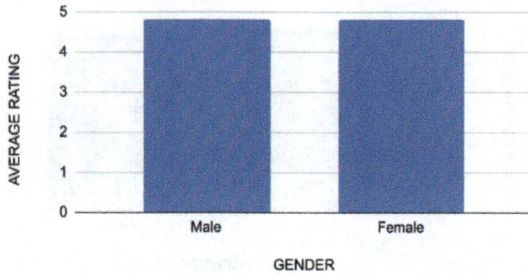

	AVERAGE RATING
MALE	4.84
FEMALE	4.82

Regenerative Medicine Familiarity: Gender vs. Average Rating

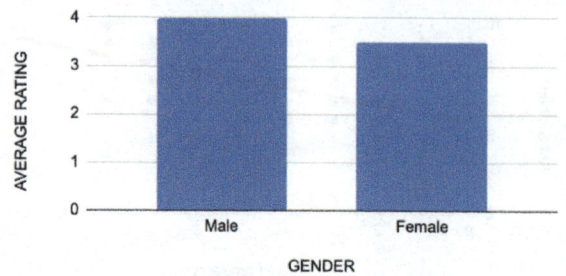

	AVERAGE RATING
MALE	4
FEMALE	3.49

Genetic Editing Support: Gender vs. Average Rating

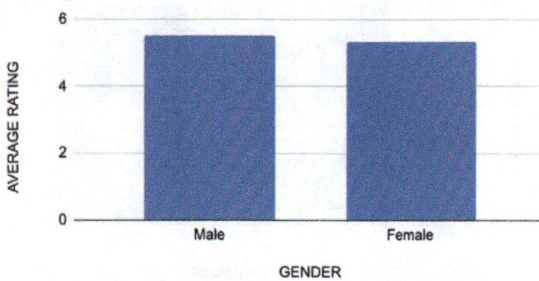

	AVERAGE RATING
MALE	5.52
FEMALE	5.33

Regenerative Medicine Support: Gender vs. Average Rating

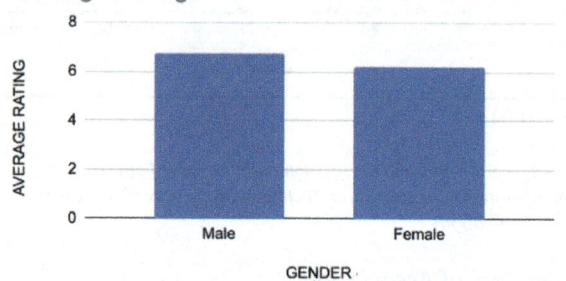

	AVERAGE RATING
MALE	6.74
FEMALE	6.24

Figure 4: Bar Graphs + Tables: Gender vs. Average Ratings

Figure 5 displays the relationships between age and average familiarity/support ratings for the three technologies.

Franklin Education Foundation
Journal of Quantitative and Qualitative Research

Hidden Connections: The Factors That Are Associated With Public
Familiarity and Opinions of Emerging, Prominent Medical Technologies
Anna Chen

Organ Donation Familiarity: Age vs. Average Rating

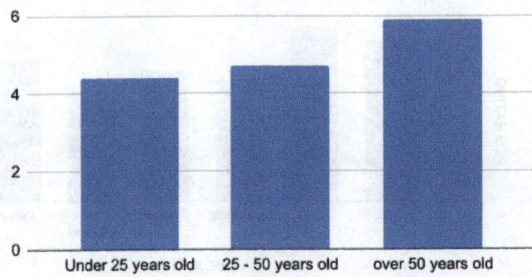

	AVERAGE RATING
<25	4.42
25 - 50	4.71
>50	5.91

Genetic Editing Familiarity: Age vs. Average Rating

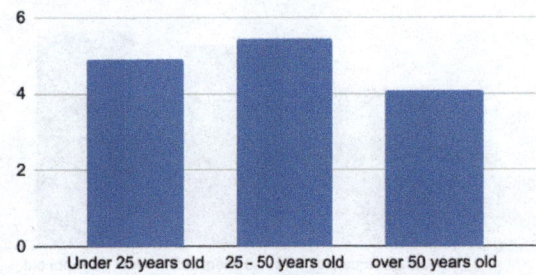

	AVERAGE RATING
<25	4.89
25 - 50	5.43
>50	4.09

Organ Donation Support: Age vs. Average Rating

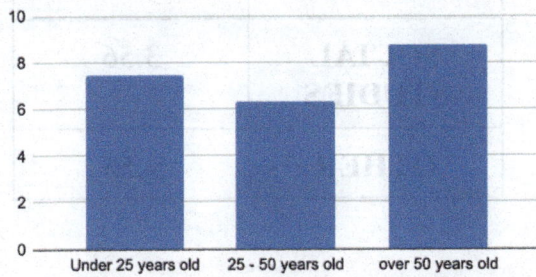

	AVERAGE RATING
<25	7.46
25 - 50	6.29
>50	8.73

Genetic Editing Support: Age vs. Average Rating

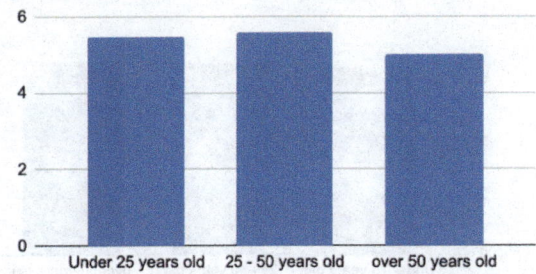

	AVERAGE RATING
<25	5.48
25 - 50	5.57
>50	5.00

Franklin Education Foundation
Journal of Quantitative and Qualitative Research

Hidden Connections: The Factors That Are Associated With Public
Familiarity and Opinions of Emerging, Prominent Medical Technologies
Anna Chen

Regenerative Medicine Familiarity: Age vs.
Average Rating

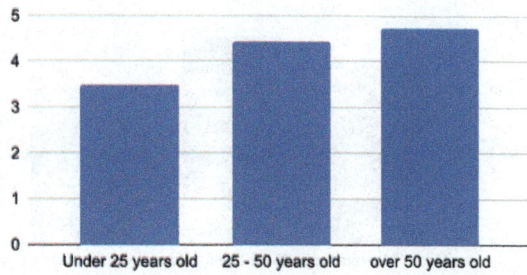

	AVERAGE RATING
<25	3.48
25 - 50	4.43
>50	4.73

Regenerative Medicine Support: Age vs.
Average Rating

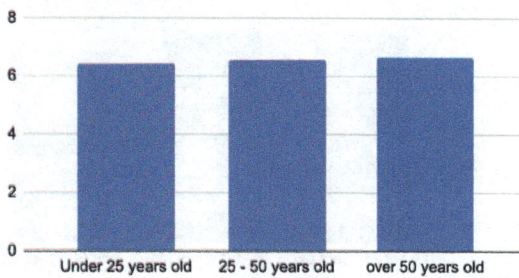

	AVERAGE RATING
<25	6.43
25 - 50	6.57
>50	6.64

Organ Donation Familiarity: Favorite Subject vs.
Average Rating

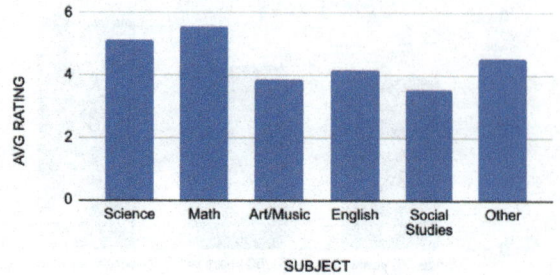

	AVERAGE RATING
SCIENCE	5.13
MATH	5.56
ART/MUSIC	3.86
ENGLISH	4.2
SOCIAL STUDIES	3.56
OTHER	4.55

Figure 5: Bar Graphs + Tables: Age vs. Average Ratings

Figure 6 displays the relationships between the respondents' favorite subject and the average familiarity/support ratings.

Franklin Education Foundation
Journal of Quantitative and Qualitative Research

Hidden Connections: The Factors That Are Associated With Public
Familiarity and Opinions of Emerging, Prominent Medical Technologies

Anna Chen

Organ Donation Support: Favorite Subject vs. Average Rating

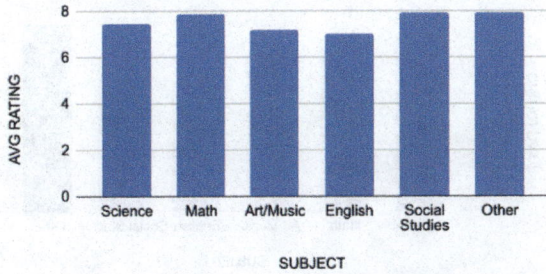

	AVERAGE RATING
SCIENCE	7.43
MATH	7.88
ART/MUSIC	7.14
ENGLISH	7.00
SOCIAL STUDIES	7.89
OTHER	7.90

Genetic Editing Familiarity: Favorite Subject vs. Average Rating

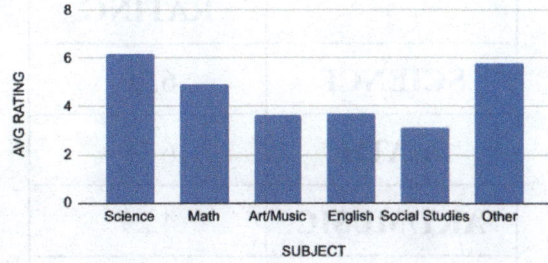

	AVERAGE RATING
SCIENCE	6.17
MATH	4.94
ART/MUSIC	3.64
ENGLISH	3.70
SOCIAL STUDIES	3.11
OTHER	5.82

Genetic Editing Support: Favorite Subject vs. Average Rating

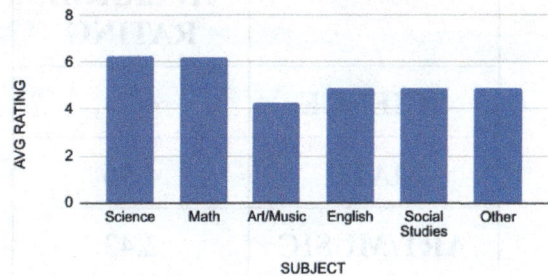

Franklin Education Foundation

Journal of Quantitative and Qualitative Research

Hidden Connections: The Factors That Are Associated With Public
Familiarity and Opinions of Emerging, Prominent Medical Technologies

Anna Chen

	AVERAGE RATING
SCIENCE	6.26
MATH	6.19
ART/MUSIC	4.29
ENGLISH	4.90
SOCIAL STUDIES	4.89
OTHER	4.90

Regenerative Medicine Familiarity: Favorite Subject vs. Average Rating

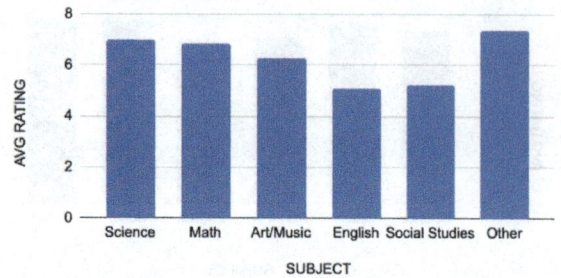

	AVERAGE RATING
SCIENCE	4.74
MATH	4.56
ART/MUSIC	2.43
ENGLISH	2.80
SOCIAL STUDIES	1.78
OTHER	4.46

Regenerative Medicine Support: Favorite Subject vs. Average Rating

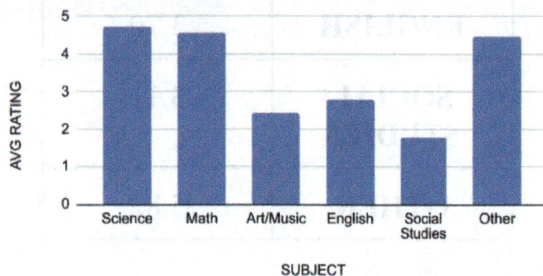

	AVERAGE RATING
SCIENCE	6.96
MATH	6.81
ART/MUSIC	6.29
ENGLISH	5.10
SOCIAL STUDIES	5.22
OTHER	7.36

Figure 6: Bar Graphs + Tables: Favorite Subject vs. Average Ratings

Figure 7 displays the relationships between whether the respondent was religious or not and the average familiarity/support ratings.

Franklin Education Foundation

Journal of Quantitative and Qualitative Research

Hidden Connections: The Factors That Are Associated With Public
Familiarity and Opinions of Emerging, Prominent Medical Technologies

Anna Chen

Organ Donation Familiarity: Religious Status vs. Average Rating

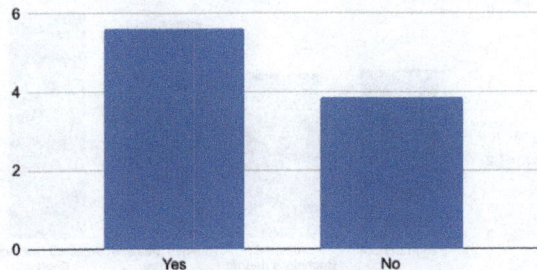

	AVERAGE RATING
RELIGIOUS	5.59
NOT RELIGIOUS	3.84

Genetic Editing Familiarity: Religious Status vs. Average Rating

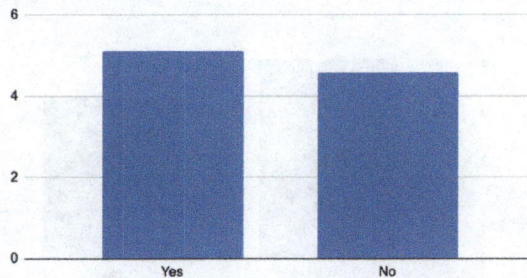

	AVERAGE RATING
RELIGIOUS	5.11
NOT RELIGIOUS	4.58

Organ Donation Support: Religious Status vs. Average Rating

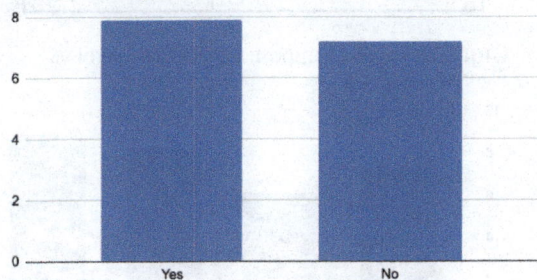

	AVERAGE RATING
RELIGIOUS	7.89
NOT RELIGIOUS	7.18

Genetic Editing Support: Religious Status vs. Average Rating

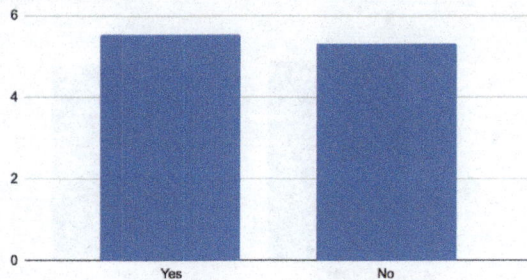

	AVERAGE RATING
RELIGIOUS	5.54
NOT RELIGIOUS	5.31

Franklin Education Foundation
Journal of Quantitative and Qualitative Research

Hidden Connections: The Factors That Are Associated With Public
Familiarity and Opinions of Emerging, Prominent Medical Technologies
Anna Chen

Regenerative Medicine Familiarity: Religious Status
vs. Average Rating

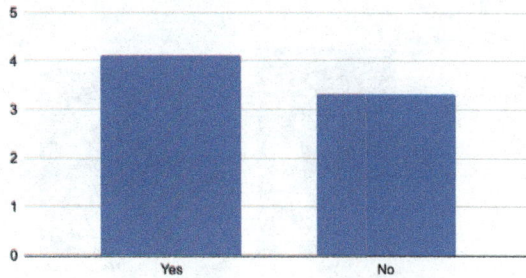

	AVERAGE RATING
RELIGIOUS	4.11
NOT RELIGIOUS	3.31

Regenerative Medicine Support: Religious Status vs.
Average Rating

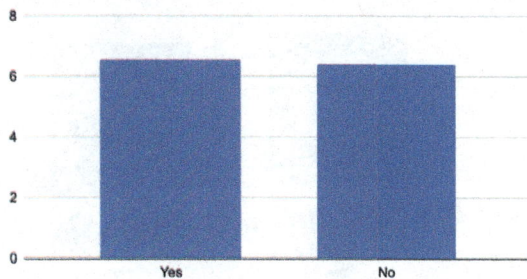

	AVERAGE RATING
RELIGIOUS	6.54
NOT RELIGIOUS	6.38

Figure 7: Bar Graphs + Tables: Religious Status vs. Average Ratings

Organ Donation Familiarity: Education Level vs.
Average Rating

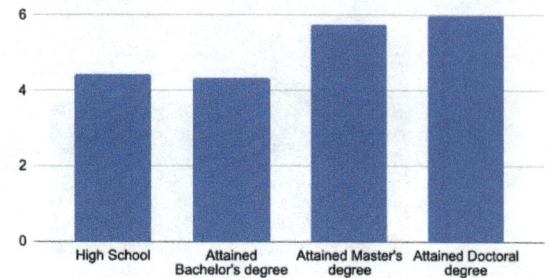

	AVERAGE RATING
HIGH SCHOOL	4.44
BACHELOR'S	4.33
MASTER'S	5.73
DOCTORAL	6.00

Organ Donation Support: Education Level vs.
Average Rating

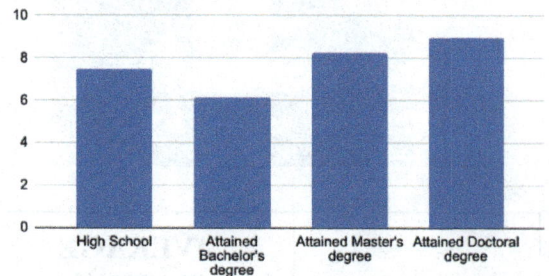

	AVERAGE RATING
HIGH SCHOOL	7.48
BACHELOR'S	6.17
MASTER'S	8.27
DOCTORAL	9.00

Figure 8 displays the relationships between the education level (of the respondents) and the average familiarity/support ratings.

Franklin Education Foundation

Hidden Connections: The Factors That Are Associated With Public
Familiarity and Opinions of Emerging, Prominent Medical Technologies

Journal of Quantitative and Qualitative Research

Anna Chen

Genetic Editing Familiarity: Education Level vs. Average Rating

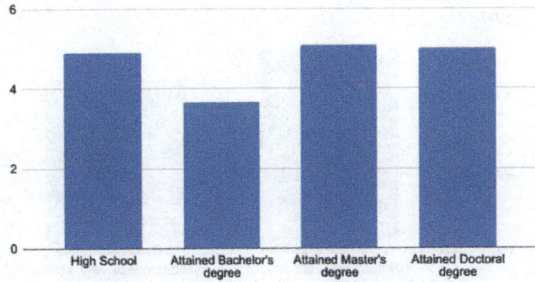

	AVERAGE RATING
HIGH SCHOOL	4.89
BACHELOR'S	3.67
MASTER'S	5.09
DOCTORAL	5.00

Regenerative Medicine Familiarity: Education Level vs. Average Rating

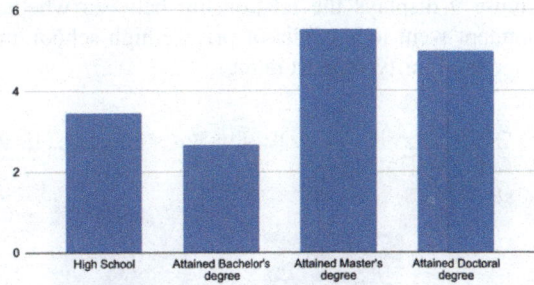

	AVERAGE RATING
HIGH SCHOOL	3.49
BACHELOR'S	2.67
MASTER'S	5.55
DOCTORAL	5.00

Genetic Editing Support: Education Level vs. Average Rating

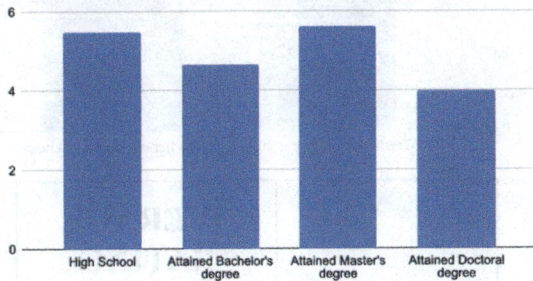

	AVERAGE RATING
HIGH SCHOOL	5.50
BACHELOR'S	4.67
MASTER'S	5.64
DOCTORAL	4.00

Regenerative Medicine Support: Education Level vs. Average Rating

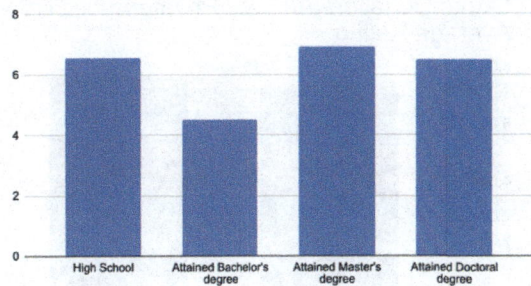

	AVERAGE RATING
HIGH SCHOOL	6.58
BACHELOR'S	4.50
MASTER'S	6.91
DOCTORAL	6.50

Franklin Education Foundation

Journal of Quantitative and Qualitative Research

Hidden Connections: The Factors That Are Associated With Public
Familiarity and Opinions of Emerging, Prominent Medical Technologies

Anna Chen

Figure 8: Bar Graphs + Tables: Education Level vs. Average Ratings

Figure 9 displays the relationship between whether the respondent went to a public or private high school and the average familiarity/support ratings.

Organ Donation Familiarity: Private/Public HS vs. Average Rating

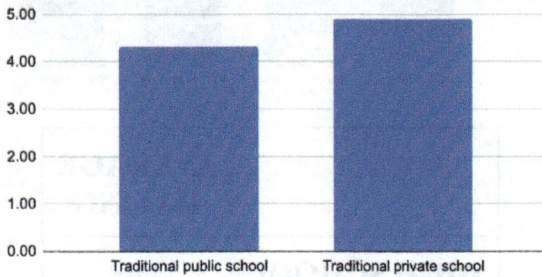

	AVERAGE RATING
PUBLIC	4.32
PRIVATE	4.91

Organ Donation Support: Private/Public HS vs. Average Rating

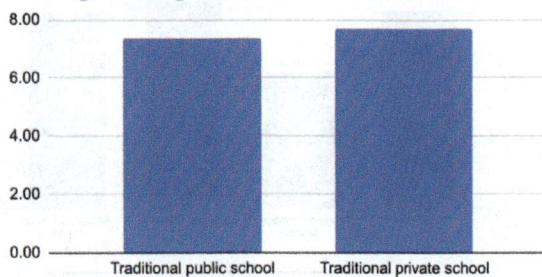

	AVERAGE RATING
PUBLIC	7.34
PRIVATE	7.69

Genetic Editing Familiarity: Private/Public HS vs. Average Rating

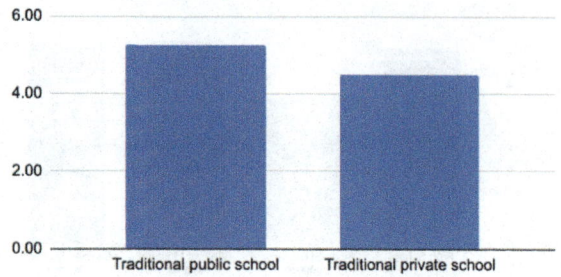

	AVERAGE RATING
PUBLIC	5.24
PRIVATE	4.49

Genetic Editing Support: Private/Public HS vs. Average Rating

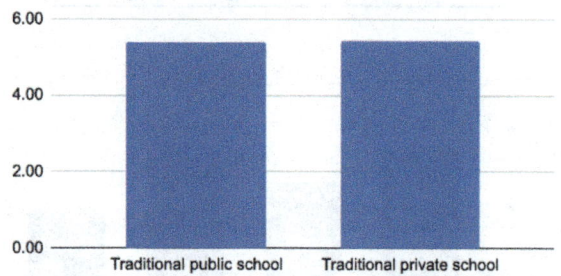

	AVERAGE RATING
PUBLIC	5.39
PRIVATE	5.44

Franklin Education Foundation
Journal of Quantitative and Qualitative Research

Hidden Connections: The Factors That Are Associated With Public
Familiarity and Opinions of Emerging, Prominent Medical Technologies
Anna Chen

Regenerative Medicine Familiarity: Private/Public HS vs. Average Rating

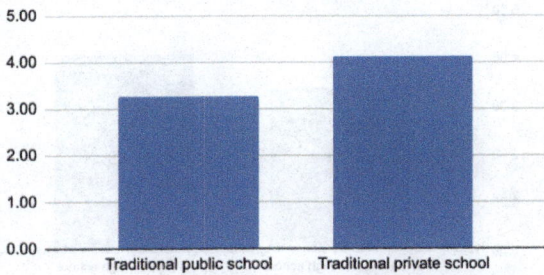

	AVERAGE RATING
PUBLIC	3.26
PRIVATE	4.11

Regenerative Medicine Support: Private/Public HS vs. Average Rating

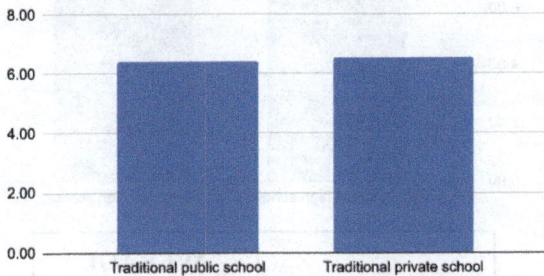

	AVERAGE RATING
PUBLIC	6.42
PRIVATE	6.51

Organ Donation Familiarity: Nonreligious/Religious HS vs. Average Rating

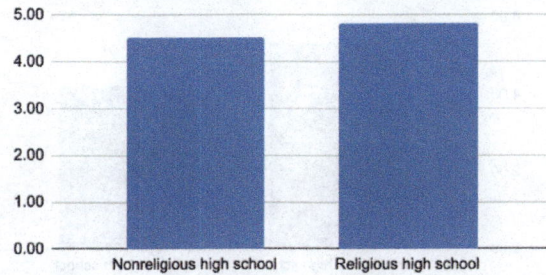

	AVERAGE RATING
NONRELIGIOUS	4.50
RELIGIOUS	4.81

Organ Donation Support: Nonreligious/Religious HS vs. Average Rating

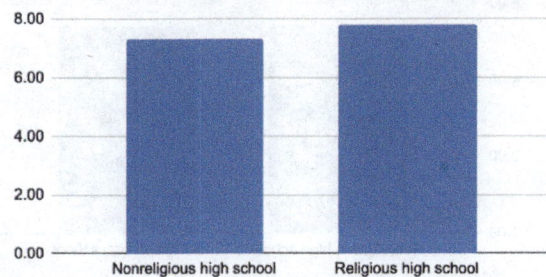

	AVERAGE RATING
NONRELIGIOUS	7.30
RELIGIOUS	7.81

Figure 9: Bar Graphs + Tables: Public or Private High School vs. Average Ratings

Figure 10 displays the relationships between whether the respondent went to a nonreligious or religious high school and the average familiarity/support ratings.

Franklin Education Foundation
Journal of Quantitative and Qualitative Research

Hidden Connections: The Factors That Are Associated With Public
Familiarity and Opinions of Emerging, Prominent Medical Technologies

Anna Chen

Genetic Editing Familiarity:
Nonreligious/Religious HS vs. Average Rating

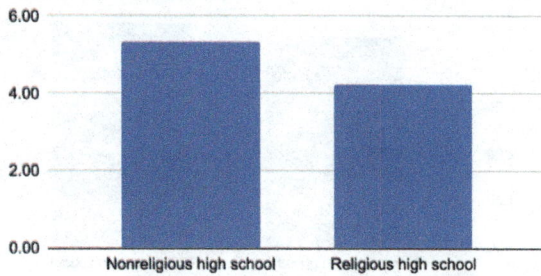

	AVERAGE RATING
NONRELIGIOUS	5.33
RELIGIOUS	4.22

Regenerative Medicine Familiarity:
Nonreligious/Religious HS vs. Average Rating

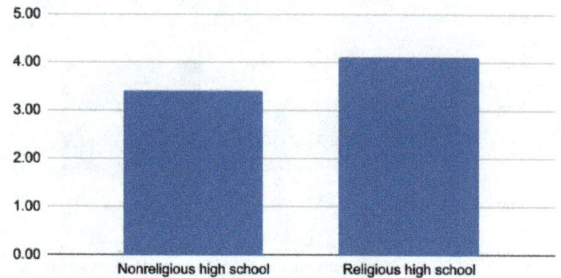

	AVERAGE RATING
NONRELIGIOUS	3.41
RELIGIOUS	4.11

Genetic Editing Support:
Nonreligious/Religious HS vs. Average Rating

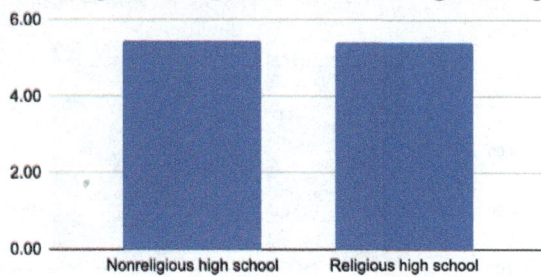

	AVERAGE RATING
NONRELIGIOUS	5.43
RELIGIOUS	5.41

Regenerative Medicine Support:
Nonreligious/Religious HS vs. Average Rating

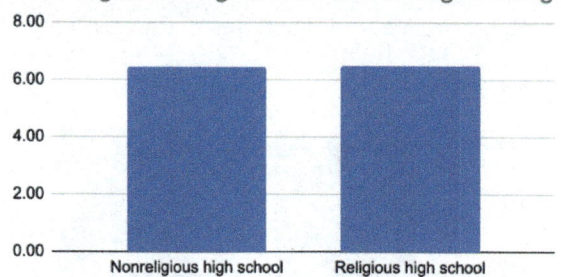

	AVERAGE RATING
NONRELIGIOUS	6.43
RELIGIOUS	6.51

Figure 10: Bar Graphs + Tables: Nonreligious or Religious High School vs. Average Ratings

Figure 11 displays the relationship between the highest degree of education earned by either of the respondents' parents and the average familiarity/support ratings.

Franklin Education Foundation
Journal of Quantitative and Qualitative Research

Hidden Connections: The Factors That Are Associated With Public
Familiarity and Opinions of Emerging, Prominent Medical Technologies
Anna Chen

Organ Donation Familiarity: Highest Parent Degree vs.
Average Rating

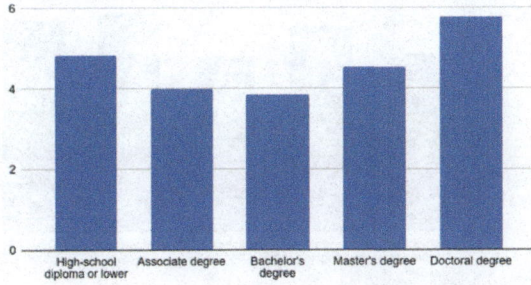

Organ Donation Support: Highest Parent Degree vs.
Average Rating

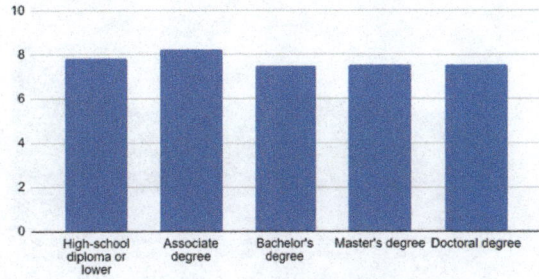

	AVERAGE RATING
HIGH SCHOOL OR LOWER	4.82
ASSOCIATE'S	4.00
BACHELOR'S	3.84
MASTER'S	4.54
DOCTORAL	5.79

	AVERAGE RATING
HIGH SCHOOL OR LOWER	7.82
ASSOCIATE'S	8.20
BACHELOR'S	7.48
MASTER'S	7.50
DOCTORAL	7.50

Franklin Education Foundation
Journal of Quantitative and Qualitative Research

Hidden Connections: The Factors That Are Associated With Public
Familiarity and Opinions of Emerging, Prominent Medical Technologies

Anna Chen

Genetic Editing Familiarity: Highest Parent Degree vs.
Average Rating

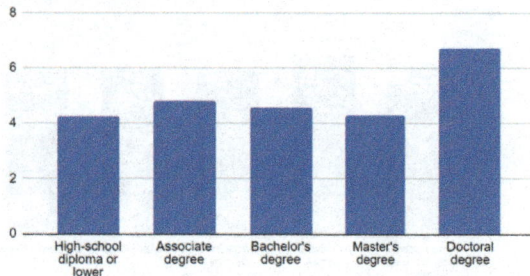

	AVERAGE RATING
HIGH SCHOOL OR LOWER	4.27
ASSOCIATE'S	4.80
BACHELOR'S	4.56
MASTER'S	4.29
DOCTORAL	6.71

Genetic Editing Support: Highest Parent Degree vs.
Average Rating

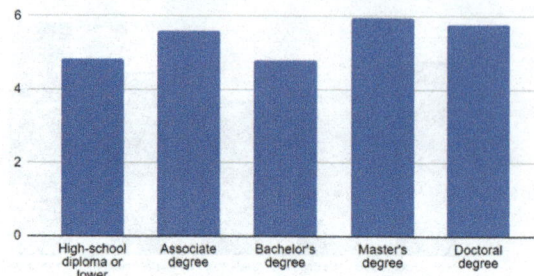

	AVERAGE RATING
HIGH SCHOOL OR LOWER	4.82
ASSOCIATE'S	5.60
BACHELOR'S	4.80
MASTER'S	5.96
DOCTORAL	5.79

Franklin Education Foundation
Journal of Quantitative and Qualitative Research

Hidden Connections: The Factors That Are Associated With Public
Familiarity and Opinions of Emerging, Prominent Medical Technologies
Anna Chen

Regenerative Medicine Familiarity: Highest Parent Degree
vs. Average Rating

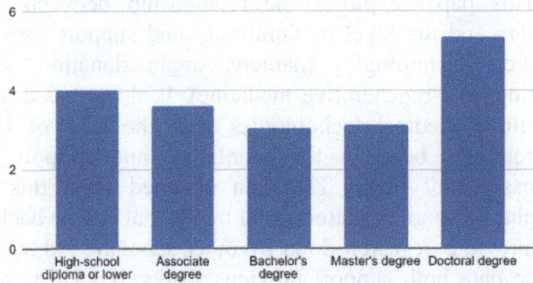

	AVERAGE RATING
HIGH SCHOOL OR LOWER	4.00
ASSOCIATE'S	3.60
BACHELOR'S	3.04
MASTER'S	3.13
DOCTORAL	5.36

Regenerative Medicine Support: Highest Parent Degree vs.
Average Rating

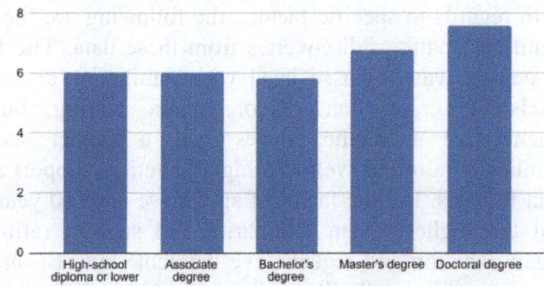

	AVERAGE RATING
HIGH SCHOOL OR LOWER	6.00
ASSOCIATE'S	6.00
BACHELOR'S	5.80
MASTER'S	6.75
DOCTORAL	7.57

*Figure 11: Bar Graphs + Tables: Highest Degree of Education Earned By
Either Parent vs. Average Ratings*

4.3 Summary

The correlation coefficients for all of the relationships
between familiarity and opinion ratings across the three
technologies were positive, which can lead us to the
following conclusions: 1) more familiarity of one
technology is associated with more familiarity of another
technology, 2) more support for/a more positive opinion on
one technology is associated with more support for/a more
positive opinion on another technology, and 3) more
familiarity of one technology is associated with more
support for/a more positive opinion on that technology. All
of the correlation values were significant except for one
(which belongs to the relationship between support for
organ donation and support for genetic editing, in which
case the r value is only 0.06). The relationship with the
highest correlation was between the familiarity with organ
donation and the familiarity with regenerative medicine, in
which case the r value was 0.61. The technology that had
the strongest correlation between familiarity levels and

Franklin Education Foundation

Journal of Quantitative and Qualitative Research

Hidden Connections: The Factors That Are Associated With Public Familiarity and Opinions of Emerging, Prominent Medical Technologies

Anna Chen

support levels was regenerative medicine, in which case the r value was 0.55.

In regards to specific factors, the following are the most significant patterns/discoveries from these data. The factor of gender was not associated with familiarity or support levels for organ donation or genetic editing, but for regenerative medicine, males had a higher average familiarity rating as well as a higher average support rating than females. For the factor of age, those over 50 years old had the highest mean familiarity and support rating for organ donation and regenerative medicine but also had the lowest mean familiarity and support rating for genetic editing. Respondents who indicated their favorite subject was STEM-based (such as science or math) almost always had a higher average familiarity and support rating for all three technologies than respondents who indicated their favorite subject fell under liberal arts (such as art/music, English, or social studies). Religious respondents had a higher average rating for familiarity and opinion for all three technologies than nonreligious respondents. Those with either a Master's or a Doctoral degree generally had higher average familiarity and opinion ratings for all three technologies than those with a high school education or a Bachelor's degree (with one exception being the support levels for genetic editing). Whether or not someone attended a private or public school did not seem to make a significant difference in support levels for any of the technologies, though those who attended/are currently attending a private high school had a higher average familiarity rating for organ donation and regenerative medicine while those who attended/are currently attending a public high school had a higher average familiarity rating for genetic editing. Additionally, attending a religious high school was associated with higher familiarity ratings for organ donation and regenerative medicine, as well as a higher support rating for organ donation. On the other hand, attending a nonreligious high school was associated with a higher familiarity rating for genetic editing, while the support ratings for genetic editing as well as regenerative medicine remained roughly even no matter the type of high school. Lastly, respondents who had at least one parent whose highest degree is a Doctoral degree tended to have higher familiarity ratings for organ donation, genetic editing, and regenerative medicine, but the support levels remained roughly even no matter the highest degree earned by either parent of the respondent.

It is important to note that the general trend found within these data is that factors such as these tended to be associated more with certain familiarity ratings than opinion/support ratings.

5. Discussion

This paper explores the relationship between certain factors and the level of familiarity and support for certain medical technologies (namely, organ donation, genetic editing, and regenerative medicine). It also cross-examines all three medical technologies with the goal of finding correlations between the familiarity and support levels across all of them. The data obtained from this study displays important patterns and trends that can be backed up by previous research done by other scholars. Additionally, these data both support previous works as well as present new findings that broaden the scope of the research done on public attitudes about organ donation, genetic editing, and regenerative medicine.

5.1 Familiarity and Opinion

The results (as shown above in Results) indicate that familiarity and opinion levels across all three technologies are positively associated with each other, meaning that if an individual is more familiar with a certain technology, they will not only have a higher chance of being more supportive of the advancement, but they also increase their chances of becoming more familiar with or supportive of another technology. The conclusion that familiarity is associated with support is backed up by Cary Funk, Brian Kennedy, and Elizabeth Sciupac's 2016 study on public opinion regarding genetic editing (refer to Literature review), where they indicated that the more someone was familiar with the idea, the more likely they were to use it themselves. The results of this paper add on to that conclusion by showing how familiarity and support levels of one technology can contribute to familiarity and support levels of other technologies (Funk et al., 2016).

With this in mind, the following sections discuss the significance of this study's findings as they relate to organ donation, genetic editing, and regenerative medicine.

5.2 Organ Donation

Based on having the highest mean rating (7.5), the public seems to be much more supportive of organ donation than both genetic editing (5.4) and regenerative medicine (6.5), indicating that more education on the benefits of the latter two is needed in order for society to become more receptive of them (as it was concluded in the previous section that familiarity, which can be achieved through more education about these topics, is positively associated with support levels). Additionally, it was discovered that respondents who indicated they followed a religion tended to have higher familiarity and opinion ratings for all three

Hidden Connections: The Factors That Are Associated With Public
Familiarity and Opinions of Emerging, Prominent Medical Technologies

Anna Chen

Franklin Education Foundation

Journal of Quantitative and Qualitative Research

technologies than those who indicated otherwise, including for organ donation. This was a surprising finding, considering previous research such as Rajesh Panwar et al.'s 2016 study on the reasons behind poor organ donation rates in India (refer to Literature Review) specifically cited religious beliefs as one of the main causes for unwillingness to support organ donation (in the form of donating their own organs) (Panwar et al., 2016). However, previous works, such as Susan Morgan et al.'s 2008 study on why people won't sign organ donor cards (refer to Literature Review) mention religion as a reason "for wanting to help sick people," more often than as a reason to not support organ donation, indicating that society may still be able to move towards a path where these technologies are seen as a way to exemplify the values that many religions see as vital parts of their practice and lifestyles (Morgan et al., 2008). This finding is particularly significant in building a much-needed bridge between religion and science.

5.3 Genetic Editing

Genetic editing scored the lowest mean opinion rating (5.4), which can point to a need for scientists to address the factors that may be contributing to this in order to make the topic more approachable and acceptable to the public. The presence of stigma or controversies surrounding genetic editing (such as disparities in access or ethical considerations), as mentioned by organizations such as the National Humane Genome Research Institute, suggests that the scientific community must work to absolve social issues and skepticism about this technology if they wish to increase levels of support for it (NHGRI).

5.4 Regenerative Medicine

Regarding regenerative medicine, this technology scored the lowest mean familiarity rating (3.7), but this study's results also indicated that age was a factor that contributed to this variable. Because the average familiarity rating for regenerative medicine increased with each age category (refer to Results), this suggests that introducing the technology to younger audiences may be beneficial to increase awareness about the topic.

5.5 Correlations Between the Technologies

An analysis of the differences between the familiarity and opinion ratings for each medical technology revealed that there was a much stronger correlation between familiarity levels across the three technologies than between support levels. In other words, how much someone supported a specific topic was less likely to be related to how much they supported another while how much they were familiar with a topic seemed to be able to indicate,

generally, how familiar they were with another. The connection between familiarity levels shows that education on scientific technologies as a whole is related to one another, and in order to publicize these medical innovations, it's important to spread knowledge about them together in order to increase the chances of understanding as a whole. For example, the strongest correlation in the data was between the familiarity with organ donation and the familiarity with regenerative medicine (0.61), which could mean that the two topics come off as closely related to the public. The combination of working with or teaching both subjects in settings such as business or education can facilitate greater understanding and support for both topics.

6. Conclusion

6.1 Implications

The findings of this study have multiple implications in the real world. First, from a public health perspective, understanding the different factors that are associated with knowledge and opinion about organ donation, genetic editing, and regenerative medicine can give an idea about the groups of people that will be more likely to know about and accept certain medical technologies as well as those who will not. Public health officials can use this information to, for instance, aid in figuring out which populations to target for educational campaigns about new innovations. That way, they can formulate expectations about the distribution of acceptance of new medical technologies in order to cater their promotional or educational materials to certain populations. For example, the results of this study highlight regenerative medicine as a technology in need of more recognition (due to having the lowest average familiarity rating amongst all three topics). The findings of this study can also be used to find certain topics with a correlation to regenerative medicine that can be used to facilitate education on the topic. For instance, it was found that the highest correlation from all the combinations of data was between familiarity with regenerative medicine and familiarity with organ donation, so the scientific community can use education about organ donation to promote knowledge about regenerative medicine in order to boost the overall popularity of the subject.

The results of this study also have applications within the political and business fields. Medical companies can use this information to target specific audiences or improve their products to make them more appealing to certain populations, and politicians can use these data to preview their constituents' thoughts about controversial, scientific advancements.

Franklin Education Foundation
Journal of Quantitative and Qualitative Research

Hidden Connections: The Factors That Are Associated With Public
Familiarity and Opinions of Emerging, Prominent Medical Technologies

Anna Chen

In an educational setting, the findings of this study can be applied to classrooms in order to boost overall awareness of these technologies within certain populations. Because it was discovered that respondents whose favorite subjects were liberal arts-focused tended to have lower familiarity and support ratings for each technology, teachers and educators can use this information as an opportunity to create lessons that integrate these technologies into the regular coursework for these specific classes. In this way, students who may not necessarily be as interested in these medical technologies can become further exposed to them in an environment that they enjoy and are comfortable with.

6.2 Limitations

It is important to note that this project has its limitations. 75% of the survey respondents were Asian, and about the same percentage were under 25 years old, so the sample does not capture the diversity of our population. The sample was also not a Simple Random Sample, meaning the findings cannot be generalized to a greater population. Voluntary response bias may have swayed survey responses because participants were given a choice of whether or not to participate. The data was also obtained from a convenience sample, or the sample that was the most accessible to survey. Lastly, possible wording bias may have been introduced with the descriptions that were used for the subtopics during the survey, but careful work was done to minimize this by using credible sources and descriptions that didn't show visible signs of bias.

6.3 Areas of Future Research

To expand on the depth of this study, many aspects of this paper can be further explored through various areas of future research.

An interesting sequel to this study would be figuring out the types of educational programs that could be implemented in order to introduce more types of medical technologies to the public. How we educate our communities about controversial but important advancements is extremely crucial to how well they end up understanding and accepting them when they themselves are being affected. Additionally, because it was concluded that familiarity was associated with support, finding effective educational programs to teach the public about medical advancements will not only raise awareness for these technologies but also promote acceptance of them throughout our communities.

Another expansion of this study would be to apply it to different parts of the world in order to diversify the resulting sample and increase the chances of finding stronger evidence of correlations or new factors of association that may affect variables. This will allow us to highlight the differences and similarities within the factors that are associated with familiarity and support for different populations/parts of the world so that the scientists/researchers of each region can understand how to cater best to their respective communities.

This study can also be easily applied to other advancements, and it can be expanded to include those outside of the medical sector. Finding new factors that are connected to knowledge level and opinions about any topic will help our society effectively improve on its efforts to spread knowledge and awareness about important subjects and advancements to the people who will be affected by them most.

7. References

[1] Funk, C., Kennedy, B., & Sciupac, E. P. (2020, August 20). *2. U.S. public opinion on the future use of gene editing*. Pew Research Center Science & Society. Retrieved April 2023, from https://www.pewresearch.org/science/2016/07/26/u-s-public-opinion-on-the-future-use-of-gene-editing/

[2] Hogg, P. (2021, June 21). *The top 10 medical advances in history*. Proclinical.com. Retrieved from https://www.proclinical.com/blogs/2021-6/the-top-10-medical-advances-in-history

[3] Morgan, S. E., Harrison, T. R., Afifi, W. A., Long, S. D., & Stephenson, M. T. (2008). In their own words: The reasons why people will (not) sign an organ donor card. *Health Communication, 23*(1), 23–33. https://doi.org/10.1080/10410230701805158

[4] National Institute of Health. (2017, August 3). *What are the ethical concerns of genome editing?* National Human Genome Research Institute. Retrieved from https://www.genome.gov/about-genomics/policy-issues/Genome-Editing/ethical-concerns

[5] North, A. (2022, March 4). *The long, strange history of anti-vaccination movements*. Vox.

[6] Retrieved from https://www.vox.com/the-goods/22958419/covid-vaccine-mandate-pandemic-history

[7] Panwar, R., Pal, S., Dash, N. R., Sahni, P., Vij, A., & Misra, M. C. (2016). Why are we poor organ donors: A survey focusing on attitudes of the lay public from Northern India. *Journal of Clinical and Experimental Hepatology, 6*(2), 81–86. https://doi.org/10.1016/j.jceh.2016.04.001

[8] Rodrigues, C. M., & Plotkin, S. A. (2020). Impact of vaccines; Health, economic and Social

114

Franklin Education Foundation

Journal of Quantitative and Qualitative Research

Hidden Connections: The Factors That Are Associated With Public
Familiarity and Opinions of Emerging, Prominent Medical Technologies

Anna Chen

Perspectives. *Frontiers in Microbiology, 11.*
https://doi.org/10.3389/fmicb.2020.01526

[9]   Rughiniș, C., Vulpe, S.-N., Flaherty, M. G., & Vasile, S. (2022). Vaccination, life expectancy,
and trust: Patterns of COVID-19 and measles vaccination rates around the world. *Public Health, 210*, 114–122.
https://doi.org/10.1016/j.puhe.2022.06.027

[10] Seddig, D., Maskileyson, D., Davidov, E., Ajzen, I., & Schmidt, P. (2022). Correlates of
covid-19 vaccination intentions: Attitudes, Institutional Trust, fear, conspiracy beliefs, and vaccine skepticism. *Social Science & Medicine, 302*, 114981.
https://doi.org/10.1016/j.socscimed.2022.114981

[11] Shineha, R., Inoue, Y., & Yashiro, Y. (2022). A comparative analysis of attitudes toward stem
cell research and regenerative medicine between six countries – a pilot study. *Regenerative Therapy, 20*, 187–193. https://doi.org/10.1016/j.reth.2022.04.007

[12] Wilkinson, F. (2022, June 2). *Industrial Revolution and Technology.* National Geographic.
Retrieved from
https://education.nationalgeographic.org/resource/industrial-revolution-and-technology/

APPENDICES

Appendix A: *The Survey Content: Questions, Descriptions, and Parameters*

Part I: Background Information

1)   What is your gender?
   a.   Male
   b.   Female
   c.   Nonbinary
   d.   Prefer not to say
2)   What is your age?
   a.   Under 25 years old
   b.   25 - 50 years old
   c.   Over 50 years old
3)   What is your favorite subject?
   a.   Science
   b.   English
   c.   Math
   d.   Social Studies
   e.   Art/Music
   f.   Other
4)   Do you follow a religion?
   a.   Yes
   b.   No
5)   What is your education level?
   a.   Currently attending/completed high school
   b.   Attained Bachelor's degree
   c.   Attained Master's degree
   d.   Attained Doctoral degree

6)   Are you attending/did you attend a public or private high school?
   a.   Traditional public school
   b.   Traditional private school
7)   Are you attending/did you attend a religious or nonreligious high school?
   a.   Religious high school
   b.   Nonreligious high school
8)   What is the highest degree of education earned by either of your parents?
   a.   High school diploma or lower
   b.   Associate degree
   c.   Bachelor's degree
   d.   Master's degree
   e.   Doctoral degree

Part II: Organ Donation

Description: "Organ donation is the process of surgically removing an organ or tissue from one person (the organ donor) and placing it into another person (the recipient). Transplantation is necessary because the recipient's organ has failed or has been damaged by disease or injury." - Cleveland Clinic

1)   On a scale of 0-10, how would you rate your familiarity with organ donation? *[Note: Participants were provided with a scale that included all the numbers between 0 and 10, inclusive.]*
   a.   0 = "Before this question, I knew next to nothing about organ donation."
   b.   10 = "I could teach a whole class about this."
2)   On a scale of 0-10, how would you rate your opinion on organ donation?*[Note: Participants were provided with a scale that included all the numbers between 0 and 10, inclusive.]*
   a.   0 = "I am completely disgusted by this topic and refuse to believe humans could ever participate in such an act."
   b.   10 = "I trust and support the potential of organ donation to revolutionize the world with my life and soul."

Part III: Genetic Editing

Description: "Genome editing is a method for making specific changes to the DNA of a cell or organism. It can be used to add, remove or alter DNA in the genome." - World Health Organization

1)   On a scale of 0-10, how would you rate your familiarity with genetic editing? *[Note: Participants were provided with a scale that included all the numbers between 0 and 10, inclusive.]*
   a.   0 = "Before this question, I knew next to nothing about genetic editing."
   b.   10 = "I could teach a whole class about this."
2)   On a scale of 0-10, how would you rate your opinion on genetic editing?*[Note: Participants were provided with a scale that included all the numbers between 0 and 10, inclusive.]*

Franklin Education Foundation

Journal of Quantitative and Qualitative Research

Hidden Connections: The Factors That Are Associated With Public
Familiarity and Opinions of Emerging, Prominent Medical Technologies

Anna Chen

a. 0 = "I am completely disgusted by this topic and refuse to
    believe humans could ever participate in such an act."
b. 10 = "I trust and support the potential of genetic editing to
    revolutionize the world with my life and soul."

Part IV: Regenerative Medicine

*Description: "Regenerative medicine may be defined as the
process of replacing or 'regenerating' human cells, tissues or
organs to restore or establish normal function." - Association for
the Advancement of Blood & Biotherapies*

*"Stem cell therapy, also known as regenerative medicine,
promotes the repair response of diseased, dysfunctional or injured
tissue using stem cells or their derivatives. It is the next chapter in
organ transplantation and uses cells instead of donor organs,
which are limited in supply." - Mayo Clinic*

1) On a scale of 0-10, how would you rate your familiarity with
    regenerative medicine? *[Note: Participants were provided
    with a scale that included all the numbers between 0 and 10,
    inclusive.]*
a. 0 = "Before this question, I knew next to nothing about
    regenerative medicine."
b. 10 = "I could teach a whole class about this."
2) On a scale of 0-10, how would you rate your opinion on
    regenerative medicine? *[Note: Participants were provided
    with a scale that included all the numbers between 0 and 10,
    inclusive.]*
a. 0 = "I am completely disgusted by this topic and refuse to
    believe humans could ever participate in its study."
b. 10 = "I trust and support the potential of regenerative
    medicine to revolutionize the world with my life and soul."

Franklin Education Foundation
Journal of Quantitative and Qualitative Research

Know Keto or No Keto? A Meta-Analysis of the Ketogenic Diet
Lucia Liu

Know Keto or No Keto? A Meta-Analysis of the Ketogenic Diet

Lucia M. Liu

Abstract

The current study conducted a meta-analysis on the advantages and the disadvantages of the Ketogenic (Keto) Diet. First, the Introduction section discusses and compares a number of dietary methods, including the Paleo Diet, intermittent fasting, the Atkins Diet, and the Keto Diet. Next, the Method section explains the processes of the meta-analysis, such as collecting, reviewing, summarizing, and analyzing articles before compiling the advantages and the disadvantages. Then, the Results section presents the findings to provide a more comprehensive understanding. Furthermore, the Discussion section examines the results regarding various aspects of the Keto Diet, especially its weight-loss mechanisms, possible side effects, and long-term effectiveness as well as its likely effects on epilepsy, neurodegenerative diseases, LDL cholesterol, and type II diabetes. Finally, the Conclusion section evaluates the findings, addresses potential implications, suggests dietary recommendations, and indicates future research directions for the fields of nutrition and food science.

Franklin Education Foundation
Journal of Quantitative and Qualitative Research

Know Keto or No Keto? A Meta-Analysis of the Ketogenic Diet
Lucia Liu

1. Introduction

A famous phrase states that "you are what you eat," so it may be hard for some people to digest the paradox claiming that a high-fat diet may actually help individuals lose weight. Such is the belief that some scholars have regarding the Ketogenic (or Keto) Diet, which typically contains more fats than proteins and carbohydrates. When the levels of carbohydrates (and proteins) are low (e.g., during fasting), the liver (specifically, through the actions of its hepatocytes) converts some fats to ketones, and the human body supposedly burns fat by using more ketones for energy (Sumithran & Proietto, 2008). However, although a Ketogenic Diet may possibly be effective for losing weight, it is hard to conduct rigorous studies to test this diet, so further research is needed to understand more about its effects (Drabińska, Wiczkowski, & Piskuła, 2021).

Of course, Keto was not the first dietary method to attract the attention of researchers. Indeed, the fields of nutrition and food science have always been concerned with the topic of how food consumption is related to health. The links between specific food and certain health conditions have been observed or hypothesized (and even tested) in a number of ancient medical systems, including those of Egyptian, Greek, Indian, Chinese, and Native-American origins. As an example, ginger (*Zingiber officinale*) has been used in Chinese food and in traditional Chinese medicine for at least hundreds of years. Specifically, it was used to help treat or manage arthritis, rheumatism, and general muscular aches. Moreover, modern research has confirmed its nutritional and medicinal benefits: several compounds in ginger (such as gingerol and shogaol) have been identified to be antioxidants as well as have anti-inflammatory or anti-tumor properties (Shahrajabian, Sun, & Cheng, 2019). Other examples include the link between oranges (specifically vitamin C) and the treatment of scurvy (Dresen, Lee, Hill, Notz, Patel, & Stoppe, 2023) as well as the link between iodine and goitre/goiter (Zimmermann, 2008).

In the modern era, a number of dietary methods have been popularized for health reasons. Famous starting in the middle of the 1900s, the Paleolithic (or Paleo, or Stone-Age) Diet is a dietary method containing food items that supposedly mimic the food consumed by humans in the Paleolithic era. The exact items of food differ among the followers of this diet, but they typically include "natural" food (such as vegetables, fruits, eggs, and meat) and exclude processed food, dairy products, grains, added sugar, salt, and alcohol (Johnson, 2015). The Paleo Diet's advantages and disadvantages are somewhat controversial. For example, although some scholars believe that this diet may be beneficial for weight loss and general metabolism, it may increase the risk of calcium deficiency or even osteoporosis (Pitt, 2016).

Another famous dietary method is intermittent fasting, which can possibly change people's metabolic processes and lifestyle patterns. Popular starting in the 1960s, intermittent fasting is based more on the timing of food consumption and less on the specific food items. Typically, the length of restriction from eating is about 16 to 18 hours of fasting (or more) per day, and it may cause the body to use more ketones for energy (de Cabo & Mattson, 2019). Although the exact length or the timing of fasting may be controversial, some versions of intermittent fasting may help lower blood pressure, decrease weight, manage diabetes for some patients, reduce inflammation, increase resistance to stress, and promote other health benefits in the long run (Patterson & Sears, 2017; de Cabo & Mattson, 2019; Malinowski, Zalewska, Węsierska, Sokołowska, Socha, Liczner, Pawlak-Osińska, & Wiciński, 2019).

Then came the trend of eating low-carbohydrate diets. Developed in the 1960s and gained popularity starting in the 1970s, the Atkins Diet (or the Atkins Nutritional Approach) was originally created by cardiologist Robert Atkins (Mayo Clinic, 2022). Typically, this dietary method limits the consumption of carbohydrates (especially food items that have white sugar, white flour, and other refined carbohydrates) while encouraging the consumption of more fats and proteins. Even though versions or phases of this diet change overtime, it aims to control "net carb," which is the total amount of carbohydrates minus the amount of fiber (though the phases of some versions allow a gradual increase in carbohydrate consumption). However, although it may help some people lose weight (Miller, Bertino, Reed, Burrington, Davidson, Green, Gartung, & Nafziger, 2003), reduce seizures (Kossoff & Dorward, 2008), or even reduce epileptic medications (Kossoff, Krauss, McGrogan, & Freeman, 2003), it may lead to complications (Chen, Smith, Rosenstock, & Lessnau, 2006), and its benefits may be no better than other types of weight-loss diets (Mayo Clinic, 2022). In terms of its disadvantages, besides the possible side effects of mental fatigue or dizziness, the Atkins Diet allows the consumption of large amounts of fats and proteins from animal sources; some scholars believe that this eating habit may increase one's risk of getting heart disease or cancer. Moreover, it has been recommended that people with severe kidney disease and women who are pregnant or breastfeeding should not follow the Atkins Diet (Mayo Clinic, 2022).

The Ketogenic Diet is also a low-carbohydrate and high-fat dietary method. Keto is somewhat similar to the Atkins Diet in the sense that both can induce ketosis, promoting the

Franklin Education Foundation

Journal of Quantitative and Qualitative Research

Know Keto or No Keto? A Meta-Analysis of the Ketogenic Diet

Lucia Liu

human body to use more ketones for energy instead of glucose (Kossoff, Krauss, McGrogan, & Freeman, 2003); this process can influence the inhibitory and the excitatory neurotransmitter systems in the brain, possibly changing the processes of energy metabolism (Hartman, Gasior, Vining, & Rogawski, 2007; Swink, Vining, & Freeman, 1997). However, the Keto Diet typically allows less carbohydrate intake and less protein intake than the Atkins Diet, possibly causing the body to stay in ketosis for longer periods of time. Also, Keto tends to be more restrictive, allowing less food variety as well as less fruits and vegetables to be consumed (Shoemaker, 2023). In addition, although some modified versions of the Atkins Diet are similar to the Keto Diet, Keto can allow even more fat consumption; up to 90% calorie intake can come from fats (Kossoff & Dorward, 2008; Kossoff, Cervenka, Henry, Haney, & Turner, 2013). The current study focuses on the Ketogenic Diet. It was first created by physicians in the 1920s to help treat epilepsy, and it appeared to improve patients' seizure conditions before the development of anticonvulsant medications decreased its popularity (Wheless, 2008). However, starting in the 1990s and in the 2000s, its popularity surged again. As the prevalence of obesity increased, more people became interested in Keto as a possible way to lose weight (Swink, Vining, & Freeman, 1997; Wheless, 2008). The current study evaluates its possible benefits and drawbacks.

2. Methods

Given the degrees of controversy surrounding the Ketogenic Diet, there is a need to understand the findings of researchers from various sides. The current study applies meta-analysis to assess the viewpoints of the scientific community. In order to get a broader picture of researchers' assessments of the Ketogenic Diet, the current meta-analysis reviews and summarizes articles regarding this dietary method, compiling its advantages and its disadvantages. By treating each article as a data point or articles as data points, this endeavor provides a more complete picture of how the Keto is perceived by researchers in the scholarly literature.

First, a wide variety of articles regarding the Ketogenic Diet were collected from various sources. Search engines were used, especially Google Scholar, and efforts were taken to make sure that all sides were represented. Second, all of the articles were summarized and analyzed. Third, the findings from each of the articles were extracted and listed in a table. To show the results of the meta-analysis, a table presents the sources, the advantages, and the disadvantages regarding the Ketogenic Diet. The advantages and the disadvantages are based on the perspective of health; typically, advantages improve the functioning of any part of

the human body, while disadvantages disrupt the normal functioning of any part of the human body.

After the presentation of the results, the Discussion section evaluates the significance of the findings and makes suggestions or recommendations accordingly. Finally, the Conclusion section addresses the current study's practical limitations, potential implications, and possible future directions.

3. Results

The following table presents the results of the meta-analysis. Ketogenic Diet is abbreviated as KD.

Sources	Advantages	Disadvantages
Harvard Health Publishing (2022)	- It reduces children's seizures. - It can lead to faster weight loss - It can improve blood-sugar levels in diabetic patients (at least for the short term).	- It can be hard to follow. - It can include fatty, salty, and unhealthy food. - Patients with kidney disease need to be cautious because this diet could worsen their condition. Additionally, some patients may feel a little tired in the beginning, while some may have bad breath, nausea, vomiting, constipation, and sleep problems. - Weight loss disappears over time.
Harvard Health Publishing (2020)	- It reduces children's epileptic seizures. - Produces short-term weight loss results (mixed results for long-term)	- It can be high in saturated fat. - It is associated with an increase in LDL cholesterol levels, which is linked to heart disease. - Possible nutrient deficiency (from not eating a wide variety of vegetables and fruits). - It may have too much fat for the liver to

Franklin Education Foundation
Journal of Quantitative and Qualitative Research

Know Keto or No Keto? A Meta-Analysis of the Ketogenic Diet
Lucia Liu

		metabolize (bad for existing liver conditions). - It may have too much protein for the kidneys to metabolize, causing kidney problems. - It can be low in fiber (from grains and legumes), which helps prevent constipation. - Low-carb diets can lead to confusion/irritability (sugar from healthy carbohydrates helps the brain function).	decrease in seizures. - More effective than epileptic drugs (children failed at least 2 epileptic drugs before trying the ketogenic diet).		
Hartman, Gasior, Vining, and Rogawski (2007)	- It can be an important therapeutic approach for epilepsy, especially in children. - It may have neuroprotective properties.		Cervenka, Henry, Felton, Patton, and Kossoff (2016)	- Not only effective in reducing epilepsy in children, but in adults. - Effective short-term: After 3 months, 36% of patients had a 50% seizure reduction, and 16% were seizure-free. - Effective long-term: after 4 years, 21% of patients had a 50% seizure reduction, and 7% were seizure-free. - 19% of patients had weight loss.	- 39% of patients suffered hyperlipidemia (high levels of lipids in the bloodstream).
Swink, Vining, and Freeman (1997)	- It successfully controls a wide range of seizure types. - It can be better than some medications (with higher success rate, lower price, and fewer side effects).		Gardner, Landry, Perelman, Petlura, Durand, Aronica, Crimarco, Cunanan, Chang, Dant, Robinson, and Kim (2022)	- Both the KD and Mediterranean diets were successful in lowering blood-sugar levels in patients w/ Type II Diabetes. - Compared to the Mediterranean diet, the KD resulted in a greater decrease in triglycerides. - Greater weight loss in the KD (8% decrease).	- Compared to the Mediterranean diet, the KD had lower nutrient intake (provided less fiber, thiamin, phosphorus, vitamins B6, C, D, and E) - The KD had lower rates of adherence than the Mediterranean diet. - Levels of LDL cholesterol increased after being on the KD.
Vining, Freeman, Ballaban-Gil, Camfield, Holmes, Shinnar, Shuman, Trevathan, and Wheless (1998)	- Extremely effective in decreasing epilepsy in children. - Observed that 40% of children (suffering >10 seizures a week) who were on the KD had >50%		Harvard T. H.	- Increased satiety	- Most KDs allow foods

Franklin Education Foundation

Journal of Quantitative and Qualitative Research

Know Keto or No Keto? A Meta-Analysis of the Ketogenic Diet

Lucia Liu

Source	Column 1	Column 2
Chan School of Public Health (2023)	due to the higher fat content. - Decreased level of appetite-stimulating hormones (ex. Insulin, ghrelin). - Reduced insulin resistance, high blood pressure, cholesterol, triglyceride levels.	high in saturated fat. - Possible side effects include: hunger, fatigue, low mood, irritability, constipation, headaches, and brain fog. - Increased risk of kidney stones, osteoporosis (decreased bone density), gout.
Bueno, de Melo, de Oliveira, and Ataide (2013)	- Compared to the low-fat diet, the KD had a greater weight loss and greater decrease in triglycerides and blood sugar.	- After one year, the KD had a greater increase in HDL and LDL cholesterol. - Compliance with the KD decreased after 2 years.
Yancy, Jr., Foy, Chalecki, Vernon, and Westman (2005)	- Improved glycemic control in patients w/ Type II Diabetes. - Out of 21 participants, diabetes medications were: Discontinued in 7 participants Reduced in 10 participants Unchanged in 4 participants - Weight loss, decrease in waist circumference and body fat percentage.	- Increased serum LDL and HDL cholesterol.
Kinzig, Honors, and Hargrave (2010)	- Insulin resistance of the KD was reversed upon cessation of the diet.	- Mice on the KD experienced insulin resistance and impaired glucose tolerance (can lead to Type II diabetes).
Al-Reshed, Sindhu, Madhoun,		- Low-carb diets (<45% of total energy) are associated with
Bahman, AlSaeed, Akhter, Malik, Alzaid, Al-Mulla, and Ahmad (2023)		increases in insulin resistance - Consumption of 45-65% carbohydrates are necessary to maintain normal glucose homeostasis
Phillips, Murtagh, Gilbertson, Asztely, and Lynch (2018)	- Parkinson's Disease patients experienced improvements in motor and nonmotor skills in both the low-fat and ketogenic diets. - Patients on KD had greater improvements in non-motor skills (i.e. depression, urinary problems, pain, fatigue) than the low-fat diet group.	- Patients on KD experienced increases in HDL and LDL cholesterol. - Most common symptoms of the KD group were tremors and rigidity.
Krikorian, Shidler, Dangelo, Couch, Benoit, and Clegg (2010)	- 23 participants with Alzheimer's disease symptoms (such as memory loss) - Improved verbal memory performance for the participants who followed the low-carbohydrate diet. - Decrease in weight, waist circumference, glucose, and insulin. - Several patients noted having "more mental energy and feeling more clear-headed."	- Patients reported that maintaining KD was difficult.
Paoli, Bianco,	- Long-term (12	

Franklin Education Foundation
Journal of Quantitative and Qualitative Research

Know Keto or No Keto? A Meta-Analysis of the Ketogenic Diet
Lucia Liu

Grimaldi, Lodi, and Bosco (2013)	months) weight loss success (>10% decrease) when combining the KD with the Mediterranean diet - Stable decrease in total cholesterol, LDL cholesterol, triglycerides and glucose levels - Compliance with the diet was high throughout the 12 months.	
Tabaie, Reddy, and Brahmbhatt (2022)	- Improved cognitive abilities and quality of life of patients with mild to severe Alzheimer's disease. - Improved several types of memory once ketosis was reached.	- High amounts of medium-chain triglycerides in the KD might cause gastrointestinal issues.
Bostock, Kirkby, Taylor, and Hawrelak (2020)	- Effective in treating epilepsy in children and adults.	- 7 most common symptoms of "keto flu" include: Flu Headache Fatigue Nausea Dizziness Brain Fog Gastrointestinal discomfort - Median range of "Keto flu" is 9.5 days, with some extreme cases lasting a whole month.
Schmidt, Harmon, Kludtke, Mickow, Simha, and Kopecky (2023)	- Effective tool for rapid weight-loss.	- Tested patients w/ a genetic predisposition to cholesterol metabolism dysregulation. - After being on the KD for 12.3 months, patients had an average increase of 245% in LDL

		cholesterol. - When patients stopped following the KD, their LDL cholesterol decreased by 220%.
Wibisono, Rowe, Erin Beavis, Kepreotes, Mackie, Lawson, and Cardamone (2015)	After being on the KD for 2 years: - 3 (6%) patients became seizure free - 35 patients (73%) had a <50%-90% in seizures - 10 (21%) had a 0%-50% decrease in seizures	- 65% of participants suffered from constipation - Kidney stones were present in 1 patient prior to administering potassium citrate - 2 patients who didn't take the potassium citrate supplements developed hypercalciuria (excess calcium in urine → can lead to kidney stones)
Schmidt, Pfetzer, Schwab, Strauss, and Kämmerer (2011)	- LDL and HDL cholesterol levels decreased significantly after 6 weeks of the KD. - All patients, except one, demonstrated decreased blood glucose levels. - Improved "emotional functioning." - Less insomnia.	- Temporary constipation and fatigue. - Out of the 16 participants, 4 stated that the feasibility of the diet was poor to moderate. - No significant impact on tumors of cancer patients.

4. Discussion

4.1 Weight Loss:

Numerous studies have shown that the Ketogenic Diet (KD) is effective for rapid weight loss (Cervenka, Henry, Felton, Patton, & Kossoff, 2016; Bueno, de Melo, de Oliveira, & Ataide, 2013; Yancy, Jr., Foy, Chalecki, Vernon, & Westman, 2005). There are several ways that the body does this:

1. Initial water loss - Each gram of glycogen (stored form of glucose) is stored with three grams of water. Thus, as the body burns through its remaining consumed carbohydrates

Franklin Education Foundation
Journal of Quantitative and Qualitative Research

Know Keto or No Keto? A Meta-Analysis of the Ketogenic Diet
Lucia Liu

and into its glycogen stores, the water attached to each glycogen molecule is also being released (Elía, Ortega, Nelson, & Mora-Rodriguez, 2015). As a result, many users will often experience higher levels of thirst and urination while on the KD (Song, Zechner, Hernandez, Cánovas, Xie, Sondhi, Wagner, Stadlbauer, Horvath, Leber, Hu, Moe, Mangelsdorf, & Kliewer, 2019).

2. Fat loss - Since carbohydrates are the easiest to break down out of the three macronutrients, the body burns carbohydrates for energy first. However, because the KD is a low-carb diet, carbohydrates in the body are not being replenished. Thus, the body must rely on the best alternative energy source: fat stores (proteins are the last resort since they take the longest to break down). Stored fat is broken down into ketones, which the body can then use for energy (Christiansen-Bullers, 2023).

3. Suppresses appetite - Studies have shown that the KD suppresses hunger through the appetite-stimulating hormones: ghrelin and leptin (Amicis, Leone, Lessa, Foppiani, Ravella, Ravasenghi, Trentani, Ferraris, Veggiotti, Giorgis, Tagliabue, Battezzati, & Bertoli, 2019). However, whether the KD is effective long-term is not as clear. Because of the restrictive nature of the diet, many participants in studies reported the diet to be difficult to follow (Harvard Health Publishing, 2022; Gardner, Landry, Perelman, Petlura, Durand, Aronica, Crimarco, Cunanan, Chang, Dant, Robinson, & Kim, 2022; Bueno, de Melo, de Oliveira, & Ataide, 2013; Krikorian, Shidler, Dangelo, Couch, Benoit, & Clegg, 2010). There have been several studies where the KD was combined with the Mediterranean diet to provide sustainable long-term weight loss. In one study, participants switched between the two diets for one year and showed high success rates for weight loss (>10%) and compliance (Paoli, Bianco, Grimaldi, Lodi, & Bosco, 2013).

4.2 Epilepsy

Originally, the KD was developed as a method to treat children with epilepsy. The ketones produced during ketosis were observed to have an anti-seizure effect (Meira, Romão, do Prado, Krüger, Pires, & da Conceição, 2019). In one study, results showed a 50% decrease in seizure occurrences in 40% of the original patients (69% of patients still remained on the diet) after six months (Vining, Freeman, Ballaban-Gil, Camfield, Holmes, Shinnar, Shuman, Trevathan, & Wheless, 1998). Not only is the KD effective for children, it has also shown to be effective in reducing seizures long-term for adults (Cervenka, Henry, Felton, Patton, & Kossoff, 2016).

4.3 Neurodegenerative Diseases

Following the successful results on epilepsy, the KD has been tested on patients with neurodegenerative diseases, such as Alzheimer's Disease and Parkinson's Disease. One common characteristic among neurodegenerative diseases is glucose hypometabolism, in which the brain is not consuming enough glucose. As such, by providing an alternative source of energy for the brain in the form of ketone bodies, this may slow disease progression or even prevent the disease (Jensen, Wodschow, Nilsson, & Rungby, 2020). While there have not been many large-scale studies conducted, the few studies conducted thus far have shown promising results. As a result of the KD, patients experienced improvements in nonmotor skills, such as memory, urination, fatigue, etc. (Phillips, Murtagh, Gilbertson, Asztely, & Lynch, 2018).

4.4 Type II Diabetes

Due to the low-carbohydrate characteristic of the KD, many doctors recommend the KD for patients suffering from type II diabetes. In type II diabetes, body cells develop a resistance towards insulin, the hormone used to let glucose into cells. As a result of insulin not regulating glucose properly, blood sugar levels rise (Centers for Disease Control and Prevention, 2023).

Since the KD is a low-carb diet, this helps to regulate blood sugar levels as well as promote weight loss (Gardner, Landry, Perelman, Petlura, Durand, Aronica, Crimarco, Cunanan, Chang, Dant, Robinson, & Kim, 2022; Yancy, Jr., Foy, Chalecki, Vernon, & Westman, 2005). However, some studies conducted on mice have suggested the contrary (Kinzig, Honors, & Hargrave, 2010): Low-carb diets, such as the KD, increased insulin resistance because the diet did not allow the body to properly use insulin. However, whether these results hold the same for humans are still unclear.

4.5 Increase in LDL Cholesterol

One risk of the KD associated with some studies is an increase in LDL cholesterol. Unlike HDL ("good") cholesterol that is metabolized in the liver, LDL ("bad") cholesterol is taken directly to the arteries, where plaque can build up. As a result, high levels of LDL cholesterol are associated with greater risk for cardiovascular diseases (Gidding & Allen, 2019). Although the majority of studies showed an increase in LDL cholesterol (Harvard Health Publishing, 2020; Gardner, Landry, Perelman, Petlura, Durand, Aronica, Crimarco, Cunanan, Chang, Dant, Robinson, & Kim, 2022; Bueno, de Melo, de Oliveira, & Ataide, 2013; Phillips, Murtagh, Gilbertson, Asztely, &

Franklin Education Foundation
Journal of Quantitative and Qualitative Research

Know Keto or No Keto? A Meta-Analysis of the Ketogenic Diet
Lucia Liu

Lynch, 2018; Schmidt, Harmon, Kludtke, Mickow, Simha, & Kopecky, 2023), several studies actually showed a decrease in LDL cholesterol (Paoli, Bianco, Grimaldi, Lodi, & Bosco, 2013; Schmidt, Pfetzer, Schwab, Strauss, & Kämmerer, 2011). This difference in results could be due to the type of fat consumed in the diet, as saturated fats tend to lead to increases in LDL cholesterol, while unsaturated fats lead to increases in HDL cholesterol (Siri-Tarino, Sun, Hu, & Krauss, 2010).

4.6 Other Side Effects

One of the primary concerns of the KD is nutrient deficiency. Because the level of carbohydrates is so low, the diet cuts out many fresh fruits and vegetables that have carbohydrates. In doing so, many nutrients such as vitamins, minerals, and fiber are lacking. Specifically, the lack of fiber may lead to constipation among practitioners, since fiber helps to soften and increase the size of stool (Ho, Tan, Daud, & Seow-Choen, 2012). Plus, because the diet relies heavily on high-protein animal products such as eggs, meat, and cheese, this makes the urine more acidic, which can cause kidney stones. This can typically be resolved through taking potassium citrate supplements (Wibisono, Rowe, Beavis, Kepreotes, Mackie, Lawson, & Cardamone, 2015).

The so-called "keto flu" is also a common symptom during the first few days of the diet. As the body transitions from using carbohydrates to ketones as its primary energy source, the body may experience flu-like symptoms. Possible symptoms can include: flu, headache, fatigue, nausea, dizziness, brain fog, and gastrointestinal discomfort. The majority of symptoms typically appeared on days 3-4 upon starting the diet, with most going away after nine days. However, there were rare cases in which symptoms lasted for up to a month (Bostock, Kirkby, Taylor, & Hawrelak, 2020).

5. Conclusion

The results of the meta-analysis lead to several general conclusions. First, the Ketogenic Diet can be beneficial for people who already have certain underlying conditions (e.g., epilepsy, diabetes, Alzheimer's disease, Parkinson's disease, etc.), but it may not be very beneficial for the "average" person, unless he or she wants to drastically lose weight. Second, before an individual adopts the Ketogenic Diet, he or she may want to take into account any genetic predispositions (if possible) and check the functions of his or her kidney.

Third, perhaps the distinction between "healthy fats" and "unhealthy fats" can help explain some of the discrepancies in research regarding the Ketogenic Diet. Given that Keto

allowed a large percentage of calorie intake to come from fats, perhaps more consumption of "healthy fats" might have resulted in some of its benefits, while more consumption of "unhealthy fat" might have resulted in some of its disadvantages. Fourth, in terms of possible recommendations, to offset possible nutrient deficiency and encourage long-term weight loss, Keto may be combined with another diet such as the Mediterranean Diet (plus supplements of vitamins, fiber, calcium, etc.), creating a combination diet that can be adjusted in timing, length, and nutritional variety.

Finally, promising future research can examine the Ketogenic Diet by varying the different ratios of fats, carbohydrates, and proteins for the purpose of making this dietary method more standardized. Other research can compare different dietary methods regarding how effective they are for weight loss and/or in terms of their retention rates (in the short run or in the long run). Also, the length of time can be examined as a factor for evaluating dietary methods. Another possibility is to assess the advantages and the disadvantages of diets that are combined with each other in various proportions. After all, the more researchers know about the Ketogenic Diet, the more likely it can be optimized, eventually offering food-for-thought that fuels the science of nutrition as much as providing healthy benefits that can be safely absorbed.

6. References

[1] Al-Reshed, F., Sindhu, S., Madhoun, A. A., Bahman, F., AlSaeed, H., Akhter, N., Malik, M. Z., Alzaid, F., Al-Mulla, F., & Ahmad, R. (2023). Low carbohydrate intake correlates with trends of insulin resistance and metabolic acidosis in healthy lean individuals. *Frontiers in Public Health, 11.* https://doi.org/10.3389/fpubh.2023.1115333

[2] Bostock, E. C. S., Kirkby, K. C., Taylor, B., & Hawrelak, J. (2020). Consumer reports of "Keto flu" associated with the ketogenic diet. *Frontiers in Nutrition, 7.* https://doi.org/10.3389/fnut.2020.00020

[3] Bueno, N. B., De Melo, I. S. V., De Oliveira, S. L., & Da Rocha Ataíde, T. (2013). Very-low-carbohydrate ketogenic diet v. low-fat diet for long-term weight loss: a meta-analysis of randomised controlled trials. *British Journal of Nutrition, 110*(7), 1178–1187. https://doi.org/10.1017/s0007114513000548

[4] Cervenka, M. C., Henry, B., Felton, E. A., Patton, K., & Kossoff, E. H. (2016). Establishing an Adult Epilepsy Diet Center: Experience, efficacy and challenges. *Epilepsy & Behavior, 58,* 61-68. https://doi.org/10.1016/j.yebeh.2016.02.038

[5] Chen, T.-Y., Smith, W., Rosenstock, J. L., & Lessnau, K.-D. (2006). A life-threatening complication of Atkins diet. *Lancet, 367,* 958.

Franklin Education Foundation

Journal of Quantitative and Qualitative Research

Know Keto or No Keto? A Meta-Analysis of the Ketogenic Diet

Lucia Liu

[6] Christiansen-Bullers, A. (2023, January 24). What to know about the keto diet from experts at KU Medical Center who study it. *KU Medical Center.* https://www.kumc.edu/about/news/news-archive/keto-diet-research.html#:~:text=In%20keto%20diets%2C%20where%20carbs,of%20carbs%20%E2%80%94has%20been%20achieved.

[7] De Amicis, R., Leone, A., Lessa, C., Foppiani, A., Ravella, S., Ravasenghi, S., Trentani, C., Ferraris, C., Veggiotti, P., De Giorgis, V., Tagliabue, A., Battezzati, A., & Bertoli, S. (2019). Long-term effects of a classic Ketogenic Diet on ghrelin and leptin concentration: A 12-month prospective study in a cohort of Italian children and adults with GLUT1-deficiency syndrome and drug resistant epilepsy. *Nutrients, 11*(8). doi: 10.3390/nu11081716.

[8] de Cabo, R., & Mattson, M. P. (2019). Effects of intermittent fasting on health, aging, and disease. *The New England Journal of Medicine, 381,* 2541-2551.

[9] Diet Review: Ketogenic diet for weight loss. (2019, May 22). *The Nutrition Source.* https://www.hsph.harvard.edu/nutritionsource/healthy-weight/diet-reviews/ketogenic-diet/#:~:text=A%20study%20of%2089%20obese,weight%20regain%20at%20one%20year

[10] Drabińska, N., Wiczkowski, W., & Piskuła, M. K. (2021). Recent advances in the application of a ketogenic diet for obesity management. *Trends in Food Science & Technology, 110,* 28-38.

[11] Dresen, E., Lee, Z.-Y., Hill, A., Notz, Q., Patel, J. J., & Stoppe, C. (2023). History of scurvy and use of vitamin C in critical illness: A narrative review. *Nutrition in Clinical Practice, 38*(1), 46-54.

[12] Fernández-Elías, V. E., Ortega, J. F., Nelson, R. K., & Mora-Rodriguez, R. (2015). Relationship between muscle water and glycogen recovery after prolonged exercise in the heat in humans. *European Journal of Applied Physiology, 115*(9), 1919–1926. https://doi.org/10.1007/s00421-015-3175-z

[13] Gardner, C. D., Landry, M. J., Perelman, D., Petlura, C., Durand, L. R., Aronica, L., Crimarco, A., Cunanan, K., Chang, A. C. Y., Dant, C., Robinson, J. L., & Kim, S. H. (2022). Effect of a ketogenic diet versus Mediterranean diet on glycated hemoglobin in individuals with prediabetes and type 2 diabetes mellitus: The interventional Keto-Med randomized crossover trial. *The American Journal of Clinical Nutrition, 116*(3), 640–652. https://doi.org/10.1093/ajcn/nqac154

[14] Gidding, S. S., & Allen, N. B. (2019). Cholesterol and atherosclerotic cardiovascular disease: a lifelong problem. *Journal of the American Heart Association, 8*(11). https://doi.org/10.1161/jaha.119.012924

[15] Hartman, A. L., Gasior, M., Vining, E. P. G., & Rogawski, M. A. (2007). The neuropharmacology of the ketogenic diet. *Pediatric Neurology, 36*(5), 281-292.

[16] Harvard Health Publishing (2022, August 9). Ketogenic diet: Is the ultimate low-carb diet good for you? *Harvard Medical School.* https://www.health.harvard.edu/blog/ketogenic-diet-is-the-ultimate-low-carb-diet-good-for-you-2017072712089

[17] Harvard Health Publishing (2020, August 31). Should you try the keto diet? *Harvard Medical School.* https://www.health.harvard.edu/staying-healthy/should-you-try-the-keto-diet

[18] Ho, K.-S., Tan, C. Y. M., Daud, M. A. M., & Seow-Choen, F. (2012). Stopping or reducing dietary fiber intake reduces constipation and its associated symptoms. *World Journal of Gastroenterology, 18*(33), 4593. https://doi.org/10.3748/wjg.v18.i33.4593

[19] Jensen, N. J., Wodschow, H. Z., Nilsson, M., & Rungby, J. (2020). Effects of ketone bodies on brain metabolism and function in neurodegenerative diseases. *International Journal of Molecular Sciences, 21,* 8767. doi: 10.3390/ijms21228767.

[20] Johnson, A. R. (2015). The paleo diet and the American weight loss utopia, 1975-2014. *Utopian Studies, 26*(1), 101-124.

[21] Kinzig, K. P., Honors, M. A., & Hargrave, S. L. (2010). Insulin sensitivity and glucose tolerance are altered by maintenance on a ketogenic diet. *Endocrinology, 151*(7), 3105–3114. https://doi.org/10.1210/en.2010-0175

[22] Kossoff, E. H., Cervenka, M. C., Henry, B. J., Haney, C. A., & Turner, Z. (2013). A decade of the modified Atkins diet (2003–2013): Results, insights, and future directions. *Epilepsy & Behavior, 29*(3), 437-442.

[23] Kossoff, E. H., & Dorward, J. L. (2008). The modified Atkins Diet. *Special Issue: Ketogenic Diet and Related Dietary Treatments, 49*(8), 37-41.

[24] Kossoff, E. H., Krauss, G. L., McGrogan, J. R., & Freeman, J. M. (2003). Efficacy of the Atkins diet as therapy for intractable epilepsy. *Neurology, 61*(12), 1789-1791.

[25] Krikorian, R., Shidler, M. D., Dangelo, K., Couch, S. C., Benoit, S. C., & Clegg, D. J. (2012). Dietary ketosis enhances memory in mild cognitive impairment. *Neurobiology of Aging, 33*(2), 425.e19-425.e27. https://doi.org/10.1016/j.neurobiolaging.2010.10.006

[26] Malinowski, B., Zalewska, K., Węsierska, A., Sokołowska, M. M., Socha, M., Liczner, G., Pawlak-Osińska, K., & Wiciński, M. (2019). Intermittent fasting in cardiovascular disorders – An overview. *Nutrients, 11*(3). https://doi.org/10.3390/nu11030673

[27] Mayo Clinic (2022). Atkins Diet: What's behind the claims? https://www.mayoclinic.org/healthy-lifestyle/weight-loss/in-depth/atkins-diet/art-20048485

Franklin Education Foundation
Journal of Quantitative and Qualitative Research

Know Keto or No Keto? A Meta-Analysis of the Ketogenic Diet
Lucia Liu

[28] Meira, I. D., Romão, T. T., do Prado, H. J. P., Krüger, L. T., Pires M. E. P., & da Conceição, P. O. (2019). Ketogenic Diet and epilepsy: What we know so far. *Frontiers in Neuroscience, 13*(5). doi: 10.3389/fnins.2019.00005. eCollection 2019.

[29] Miller, B. V., Bertino, J. S., Reed, R. G., Burrington, C. M., Davidson, L. K., Green, A., Gartung, A. M., & Nafziger, A. N. (2003). An evaluation of the Atkins' Diet. *Metabolic Syndrome and Related Disorders, 1*(4), 299-309.

[30] Paoli, A., Bianco, A., Grimaldi, K., Lodi, A., & Bosco, G. (2013). Long term successful weight loss with a combination biphasic Ketogenic Mediterranean Diet and Mediterranean Diet maintenance protocol. *Nutrients, 5*(12), 5205–5217. https://doi.org/10.3390/nu5125205

[31] Patterson, R. E., & Sears, D. D. (2017). Metabolic effects of intermittent fasting. *Annual Review of Nutrition, 37*, 371-393.

[32] Phillips, M., Murtagh, D. K. J., Gilbertson, L., Asztely, F., & Lynch, C. D. (2018). Low-fat versus ketogenic diet in Parkinson's disease: A pilot randomized controlled trial. *Movement Disorders, 33*(8), 1306–1314. https://doi.org/10.1002/mds.27390

[33] Pitt, C. E. (2016). Cutting through the Paleo hype: The evidence for the Palaeolithic diet. *Australian Family Physician, 45*, 35-38.

[34] Schmidt, T., Harmon, D., Kludtke, E., Mickow, A., Simha, V., & Kopecky, S. L. (2023). Dramatic elevation of LDL cholesterol from ketogenic-dieting: A case series. *American Journal of Preventive Cardiology, 14*, 100495. https://doi.org/10.1016/j.ajpc.2023.100495

[35] Schmidt, M., Pfetzer, N., Schwab, M., Strauss, I., & Kämmerer, U. (2011). Effects of a ketogenic diet on the quality of life in 16 patients with advanced cancer: A pilot trial. *Nutrition & Metabolism, 8*(1). https://doi.org/10.1186/1743-7075-8-54

[36] Shahrajabian, M. H., Sun, W., & Cheng, Q. (2019). Clinical aspects and health benefits of ginger (Zingiber officinale) in both traditional Chinese medicine and modern industry. *Acta Agriculturae Scandinavica, Section B - Soil & Plant Science, 69*(6), 546-556.

[37] Shoemaker, S. (2023, June 23). What's the difference between Keto and Atkins? *Healthline.* https://www.healthline.com/nutrition/atkins-vs-keto#bottom-line

[38] Siri-Tarino, P. W., Sun, Q., Hu, F. B., & Krauss, R. M. (2010). Saturated fatty acids and risk of coronary heart disease: modulation by replacement nutrients. *Current Atherosclerosis Reports, 12*(6), 384–390. https://doi.org/10.1007/s11883-010-0131-6

[39] Song, P., Zechner, C., Hernandez, G., Canovas, J. M., Xie, Y., Sondhi, V., Wagner, M., Stadlbauer, V., Horvath, A., Leber, B., Hu, M., Moe, O. W., Mangelsdorf, D. J., & Kliewer, S. A. (2018). The hormone FGF21 stimulates water drinking in response to ketogenic diet and alcohol. *Cell Metabolism, 27*(6), 1338-1347.e4. https://doi.org/10.1016/j.cmet.2018.04.001

[40] Sumithran, P., & Proietto, J. (2008). Ketogenic diets for weight loss: A review of their principles, safety and efficacy. *Obesity Research & Clinical Practice, 2*(1), 1-13.

[41] Swink, T. D., Vining, E. P., & Freeman, J. M. (1997). The ketogenic diet: 1997. *Advances in Pediatrics, 44*, 297-329.

[42] Tabaie, E. A., Reddy, A. J., & Brahmbhatt, H. (2021). A narrative review on the effects of a ketogenic diet on patients with Alzheimer's disease. *AIMS Public Health, 9*(1), 185–193. https://doi.org/10.3934/publichealth.2022014

[43] Type 2 diabetes. (2023, April 18). *Centers for Disease Control and Prevention.* https://www.cdc.gov/diabetes/basics/type2.html

[44] Vining, E. P. (1998). A multicenter study of the efficacy of the ketogenic diet. *Archives of Neurology, 55*(11), 1433. https://doi.org/10.1001/archneur.55.11.1433

[45] Wheless, J. W. (2008). History of the ketogenic diet. *Epilepsia, 49*(Suppl. 8), 3-5.

[46] Wibisono, C., Rowe, N., Beavis, E., Kepreotes, H., Mackie, F., Lawson, J. A., & Cardamone, M. (2015). Ten-year single-center experience of the Ketogenic Diet: factors influencing efficacy, tolerability, and compliance. *The Journal of Pediatrics, 166*(4), 1030-1036.e1. https://doi.org/10.1016/j.jpeds.2014.12.018

[47] Yancy, W. S., Foy, M. E., Chalecki, A. M., Vernon, M. C., & Westman, E. (2005). A low-carbohydrate, ketogenic diet to treat type 2 diabetes. *Nutrition & Metabolism, 2*(1). https://doi.org/10.1186/1743-7075-2-34

[48] Zimmermann, M. B. (2008). Iodine requirements and the risks and benefits of correcting iodine deficiency in populations. *Journal of Trace Elements in Medicine and Biology, 22*(2), 81-92.

Library Liability: Analyses on Age, Gender, Book Content, and Opinions of Censorship

Lindsey Jiang

Abstract

This study addresses the gap in the field of educational research regarding public responses to school library censorship. Its findings surround the overarching question: "How are age, gender, book content, and frequency of reading related to one's opinion on which type of book content should be censored in elementary, middle, and high school libraries?" The survey focused on two main book topics: LGBTQ+ themes or protagonists and content with drugs, profanity, or offensive language. A survey was implemented; participants were asked to rate their agreement with the censorship of these topics in elementary, middle, and high schools on a scale of 1 to 10. Additional questions collected data regarding participant backgrounds and supplemental information to identify potential correlations with censorship opinion. Overall, the study reported significant correlations between levels of censorship agreement with both age and gender. Age had a significant positive correlation with censorship agreement for LGBTQ+ content across elementary, middle, and high schools. Age had a significant positive correlation only for middle and high schools for drug, profanity, or offensive language content. Males generally reported higher levels of agreement for censorship of both topics than females. Other findings suggested that factors such as book content encountered may also correlate with general opinion of censorship. The results of this study may guide administrations, educators, and librarians to form more holistic policies when making censorship decisions.

Keywords: book censorship, library, elementary school, middle school, high school

1. Introduction

There has long existed a correlation between reading and higher academic performance. Reading has always been of fundamental importance in the United States education system, and it may have a more significant impact on a child's performance in school than their financial background (Pearson, 2015).

Providing access to literary materials and information which may supplement student learning, school libraries play a critical role in the educational development of students. With the vast range of these materials available for student consumption, American schools must choose which literary works to keep. When administrators face this act of conscious selection, patterns emerge among the books that are commonly thrown out (Oltmann, 2016).

Despite the relaxation of social mores in the 20th and 21st centuries, book challenges remain more prevalent than ever. Under the First Amendment, government censorship of books, magazines, and newspapers is forbidden for all U.S. residents, with students having the same rights, regardless of the school library setting. However, the Supreme Court has ruled that community standards may be considered when evaluating the obscenity of materials. Thus, the unclear circumstances in which book censorship should occur creates conflict between those against book banning and those who believe it is essential.

Researchers Friedman and Johnson report that, during the 2021–22 academic year, minor book challenges confined within schools developed into a "full-fledged social and political movement" powered on a national scale. The majority of the targeted books contain content relating to race and racism, LGBTQ+ identities, or sex education (Friedman & Johnson, 2022). Political pressures in relatively conservative U.S. states—Texas, South Carolina, Wisconsin, Georgia—have been tied to the most significant figures in book bans across the country. One major factor in the unprecedented scope of censorship is the proliferation of organized efforts, such as the organization Moms for Liberty, which boasts over 200 chapters nationwide. Since their formation, organized groups pushing for book bans have played a role in over 50 percent of book bans within the U.S. during the 2021-2022 school year (Friedman & Johnson, 2022). Attempted bans of books, even in schools today, tend to have devastating effects on librarians, especially those who do not want to be involved with controversial material (Blakemore, 2022).

In 2021, the American Library Association (ALA) reported 729 censorship attempts toward library resources. The Over 1,500 books were targeted—the greatest number of attempted book bans in more than twenty years (ALA, 2022). However, in 2022, from January to the end of August, the ALA recorded 681 attempts trying to ban or restrict library resources, and 1,651 unique book titles were targeted. Additionally, more than 70 percent of 600-plus efforts to hinder access to resources in libraries were directed at multiple books. These figures highlight a shift from past censorship, where the majority of challenges only sought to restrict single books (ALA, 2022). Deborah Caldwell-Stone, director of the American Library Association's Office of Intellectual Freedom, described the movements to ban books as campaigns motivated by political agendas to restrict educational access and marginalize certain groups (Hellerstein, 2022).

As the societal roles of the younger generation become increasingly prevalent, the effect censorship may have on students with direct access to school libraries is crucial to analyze. As one article mentions, "It is imperative that students have access to texts depicting all types of ideas and people—including ones like themselves and ones unlike themselves" (Carlson, 2018). Especially in rural areas where students do not have access to reliable internet and digital resources (Mardis, 2016), restricting certain books may severely limit one's developing understanding of the world around them.

Still, in many cases, schools attempt to minimize controversy and potential lawsuits by conceding to general community consensus (Dawkins, 2018). With the study aiming to determine the influences behind censorship, a clearer path to analyzing and combatting its potential adverse effects must be observed.

2. Literature Review

2.1 Search Strategies

Studies were located via the database Google Scholar, with the requirement of peer-reviewed studies to ensure credibility. Public news articles were reviewed thoroughly to gain insight into social and political climates.

Keywords used while researching were: school library, book censorship, and public opinion.

2.2 Types of Media in School Libraries

Many school libraries have undergone significant alterations with the rise of ebooks and digital technologies in the twenty-first century. The increasing dominance of technology in literature—observed through eBooks, Kindles, and a multitude of internet library archives—makes the effects of digital reading in diminishing the roles of libraries critical to the discussion of censorship regarding these institutions. Still, studies have found that despite the presence of digital devices, core instructional practices have remained largely unchanged, and the school library systems will accordingly continue their distribution of physical reading materials (Collins & Halverson, 2010).

Beyond that, a study that examined reading under time pressure found that using hard-copy resources was more efficient (Ackerman & Lauterman, 2012). The results reinforce the inferiority of digital learning and the sustained role of school libraries in supporting education. Therefore, librarians' role in censoring hard-copy books will likely remain significant despite the increased technology in schools. A plethora of research exists documenting the developments of school libraries and their materials across the U.S. (e.g., Hopkins & McAfee, 2000; Johnson, 2018), but few make the connection to potential digital and physical censorship by these educational institutions.

2.3 Sociological Perspective on Library Use

Many studies found that people tend to read less and have more negative attitudes toward reading as they progress from childhood to their teenage years (Clark, 2019; Wilkinson et al., 2020). Existing bodies of evidence support the notion that being able to access book-oriented environments is linked to children developing academic skills for education and occupation. Data from 31 societies that participated in the Programme for the International Assessment of Adult Competencies (PIAAC) between 2011 and 2015 show that training related to books that encourage the development of reading skills helps young people acquire knowledge that they will use throughout their lives (Sikora et al., 2018).

However, these positive trends do not correlate with an increase in teenage library use; in fact, less than 20 percent of American teenagers indicated that they read regularly for pleasure, while over 80 percent of them indicated that they access social media daily. Digital media use has recently experienced substantial increases. Among twelfth-graders, the use of the Internet in their free time increased 100 percent (from one to two hours per day) during the span of 2006-2016. Internet usage also went up for tenth and eighth graders, by 75 and 68 percent respectively (Twenge et al., 2018). With the prompt shift away from traditional library uses, the efforts made to sustain libraries as attractive places of learning for teenagers must be thoroughly reconsidered.

2.4 Controversial Book Topics

Of the existing research regarding censorship in American school libraries, frequently censored controversial themes are recurring topics. Pre-existing research suggests that books with LGBTQ+ themes or protagonists, racial slurs, drug use, and violence are censored most frequently in school libraries (Rosearynandira & Asmiyanto, 2020). Out of these topics, quantitative data from over one hundred American public school libraries revealed that libraries in schools generally tended to have significantly fewer books with LGBTQ+ themes compared to other controversial works (Garry, 2015). Researcher Dawkins noted that when North Carolina school librarians were asked to predict the discomfort of principals on a scale of 1 to 7 to controversial materials, violence (4.94), LGBTQ content (4.83), and offensive language (4.78) were ranked first, second, and third, respectively.

2.5 Views of Influential Parties on Library Censorship

As schools play a critical role in developing students' minds, libraries may have the responsibility to help students choose books that are appropriate for them.

For research connecting censorship to the critical function of libraries, self-censorship on behalf of librarians is widely recognized. A librarian's fear of backlash distinguishes self-censorship from actual censorship. Second-guessing motivates covert acts, such as "removing or misplacing a book" or "restricting its access." This form of censorship is harder to quantify, as no "challenge" exists and thus cannot undergo the standard review process in which other parties are involved (Dawkins, 2018).

However, while a plethora of studies document librarian experiences and identify the books being challenged, there remains a lack of research regarding individual factors such as race, gender, and age in these evaluations. To add, despite established educational criteria for libraries and value judgments by librarians, school administrations and community consensus were more relevant in removing materials in multiple analyses of school library collections (Rickman, 2010).

Administrators can use their authority to discriminate intentionally and unintentionally in discretion. As of February 2022, 42 American states have attempted to prevent the teaching of critical race theory or disallow teachers from discussing sexism and racism in school (Shearer, 2022). Representative Matt Krause of Texas even made a list of more than 800 books; he thought that those books could cause students to feel guilty or uncomfortable because of their gender or background. Shearer notes that 97 out of the first 100 books were authored by females, members of racial minorities, or LGBTQ+ individuals, and argues that the removal of race-related materials is against the First Amendment because the voices of minorities have the right to be heard (Shearer, 2022). Perceived public opinion influences administrative decisions during the book selection process (Dawkins, 2018), making it likely that states with rampant book bans may be prone to increased censorship.

Despite this concession, existing research largely neglects the factor of public opinion while considering censorship. This observed correlation of community dissent with censorship decisions of librarians and administrations makes it essential to examine further different factors that may impact public opinion on these widely-contested topics. However, these studies were either isolated to elementary or high schools or mentioned the American school system in general without analyzing the progression of opinion from elementary to middle to high school. Additionally, few studies included the students' point of view regarding censorship, and when adolescents were involved, it was limited to the topic of reading in general. These gaps in the existing base of research regarding library censorship allowed for the development of the research question:

"How are age, gender, book content, and frequency of reading related to one's opinion on which type of book content should be censored in elementary, middle, and high school libraries?"

The project aims to develop a comprehensive understanding of the multiple perspectives on the issue of censorship. The results of this inquiry may provide schools with a more transparent framework regarding censorship limitations in their libraries. Defining the factors behind public opinion will open up further discussion of book bans across the U.S.

3. Methodology

This study explores the connection between the factors of age and gender to beliefs regarding censorship and the school library system.

The survey was conducted through Google Forms. The survey method was optimal for investigating the correlation of age with opinions on censorship of varying topics, enabling the respondents' opinions to be studied thoroughly and efficiently due to its simplicity and ability to collect data from a larger sample size. It also allowed for participants to submit their results anonymously. If an observational study or an in-person interview had been conducted, the lack of anonymity may have decreased the

accuracy of the results. Questions were a mix of multiple choice, select all that apply, and short-answer responses. Also, experiments are not feasible for this project because it is impossible or impractical to manipulate and control factors such as age, gender, the frequency of reading, and the school libraries for students.

The first three questions collected participant data regarding age, gender, and ethnicity. Responses were anonymous, but this information was collected to observe if these factors may have caused discrepancies in the results.

Participants were then asked to rate their reading frequency on a scale of 1-10, with 1 being never and 10 being every day. The range of choices eliminated inconsistencies in interpreting the question by clarifying the timeframes at the highest and lowest points and allowed the range in reading frequency among the respondents to be more accurately pinpointed.

Participants were asked to respond to a long-answer response question with three ways school libraries could be improved to assess general opinion on libraries. The restriction of school libraries was placed to make the results concurrent with censorship occurring at elementary, middle, and high schools across the U.S.

Opinions regarding specific topics were then discerned, with the first three statements surrounding the topic of whether books with LGBTQ+ themes or protagonists should be censored. Respondents inputted their answers on a scale of 1 to 10, with 1 representing strong disagreement with the statement and 10 representing strong agreement. The first topic, LGBTQ+ materials, was split into three statements: one being that they should be censored in elementary schools, one addressing middle schools, and one being high schools. The next topic, which included profanity, offensive language, and mentions of drug use, was also split into three questions, each addressing the different levels of education (Figure 1). Participants were once again asked to rank their agreement on a scale of one to ten, this time regarding profanity, offensive language, or mentions of drug use.

Figure 1. Survey Questions.

The survey then asked respondents to rank their agreement with the statement, "School libraries should restrict students from accessing certain books upon receiving complaints from parents." The survey asked participants to explain their response in a short-answer question to assess differences in opinion which may have ultimately determined the differences in answers to previous scale questions. An example of the long-answer question format is shown in Figure 2.

Figure 2. Long Answer Response.

Finally, to assess whether the types of materials participants read impacted their opinions of what topics should be censored, participants were asked to select all the book topics they encountered while reading. Some of the options correlated to the topics which had been previously mentioned in the quantitative questions, with other sensitive topics included as well to make the question more general. The options included: graphic depictions of violence, racial or derogatory slurs, LGBTQ+ themes or characters, drug use or abuse, sexual assault, and profanity (Figure 3).

Figure 3. Final Question (select all that apply).

In total, survey participants answered three short-answer response questions, nine quantitative questions, and two questions in long-answer response form. The survey was not split into sections, as the questions represented a natural documentation of opinions regarding a variety of topics. All questions were required to ensure the equal valuation of each response among each question.

After 61 participants were surveyed, survey data were transferred to a spreadsheet in Microsoft Excel, where statistical analyses were performed.

4. Results

4.1 Age and Views Regarding Books with LGBTQ+ Content in School Libraries

The following figures show the relationships between the participants' ages and their levels of agreement regarding the censorship of books with LGBTQ+ themes or protagonists in school libraries. Figure 4 shows this relationship for LGBTQ+ books in elementary school libraries (r = 0.539), Figure 5 shows this relationship for middle school libraries (r = 0.628), and Figure 6 shows this relationship for high school libraries (r = 0.575). In all of these three analyses, there was a moderate positive correlation between age and the level of agreement in censorship.

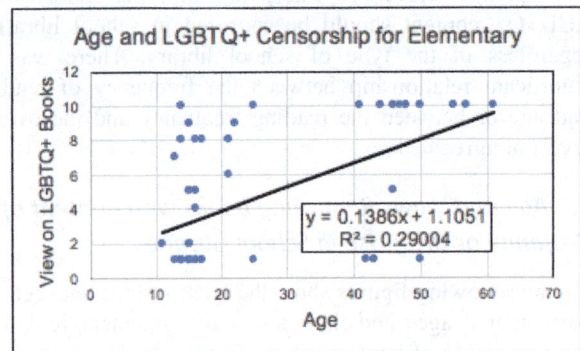

Figure 4: Age and the Level of Agreement on Censoring Books with LGBTQ+ Content in Elementary School Libraries.

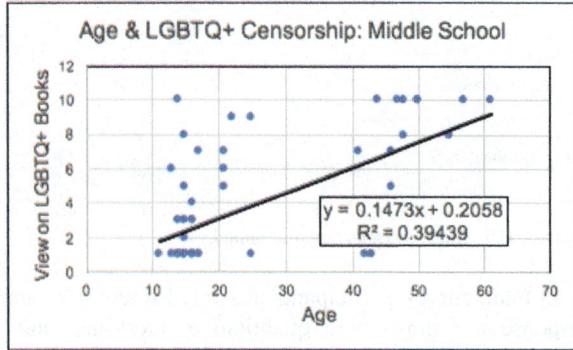

Figure 5: Age and the Level of Agreement on Censoring Books with LGBTQ+ Content in Middle School Libraries.

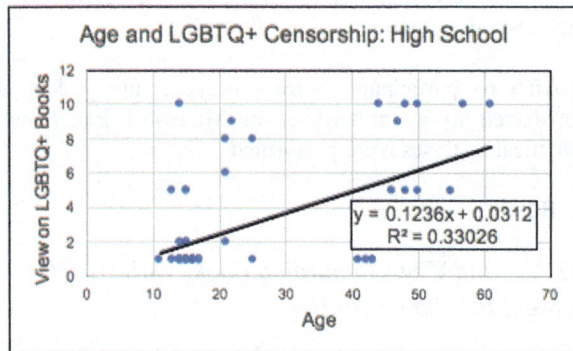

Figure 6: Age and the Level of Agreement on Censoring Books with LGBTQ+ Content in High School Libraries.

The slope of the regression line was significant for elementary school [t(60) = 4.91, p < 0.01], middle school [t(60) = 6.20, p < 0.01], and high school [t(60) = 5.39, p < 0.01] libraries. In addition, an analysis of variance (ANOVA) found no significant differences among the average levels of agreement across the three types of school libraries. Taken together, these results suggested that older participants were more likely to think that books with LGBTQ+ content should be censored in school libraries, regardless of the type of school library. There was no significant relationship between the frequency of reading and age or between the reading frequency and the overall levels of agreement.

4.2 Age and Views Regarding Books with Content of Profanity or Drug Use in School Libraries

The following figures show the relationships between the participants' ages and their levels of agreement regarding the censorship of books with profanity, offensive language, or mentions of drug use in school libraries. Figure 7 shows this relationship for elementary school libraries, Figure 8 shows this for middle school libraries, and Figure 9 shows this relationship for high school libraries. There were positive correlations between age and the level of agreement in censoring books with profanity/drug content for middle school libraries (r = 0.332) and for high school libraries (r = 0.449).

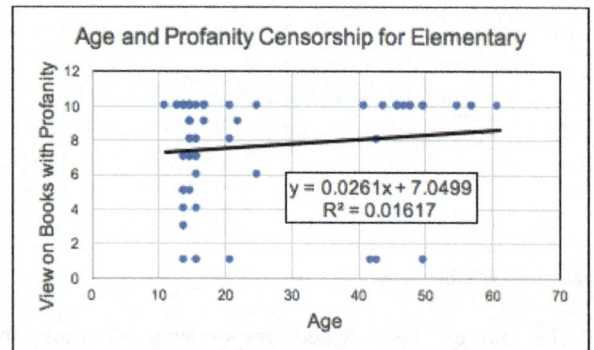

Figure 7: Age and the Level of Agreement on Censoring Books with Profanity/Drug-Use Content in Elementary School Libraries.

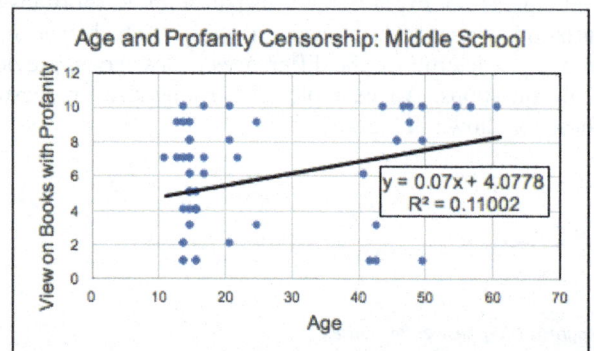

Figure 8: Age and the Level of Agreement on Censoring Books with Profanity/Drug-Use Content in Middle School Libraries.

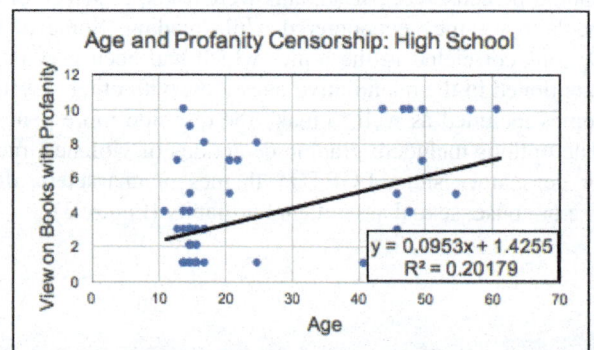

Figure 9: Age and the Level of Agreement on Censoring Books with Profanity/Drug-Use Content in High School Libraries.

However, there was no such significant correlation for elementary school libraries (r = 0.127); as can be seen in the corresponding figure, the agreement levels were generally high in this condition, regardless of age. The slope of the regression line was significant only for middle school [t(60) = 2.70, p < 0.01] and high school [t(60) = 3.86, p < 0.01] libraries. Interestingly, ANOVA showed an overall significant difference among the average levels of agreement across the three types of school libraries, F(2, 180) = 24.6, p < 0.01. Figure 10 shows these differences.

Specifically, the overall agreement level on censoring books with profanity/drug content for elementary school libraries was significantly higher than the agreement level for middle school libraries, t(60) = 8.32, p < 0.01, and the agreement on censoring such books for middle school libraries was significantly higher than that of high school libraries, t(60) = 8.26, p < 0.01. Taken together, these results suggested that participants generally thought that books with profanity/drug content should be censored in elementary school libraries (regardless of age), but older participants were more likely to think that such books should be censored in middle school and high school libraries. There was no significant relationship between reading frequency and the level of agreement on book censorship in any of these conditions.

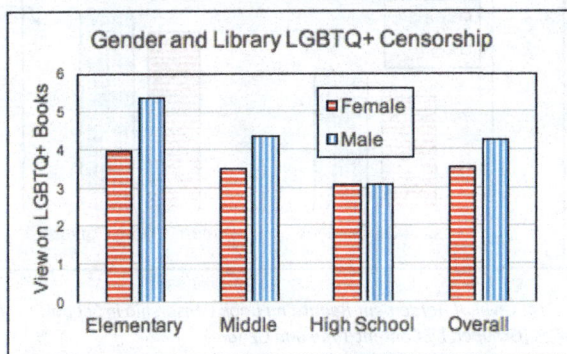

Figure 10: Levels of Agreement on Censoring Books with Profanity/Drug-Use Content in School Libraries.

4.3 Age and General Views Regarding the Restriction of Certain Books in School Libraries

When asked how strongly they believed that school libraries should restrict students from accessing certain books upon receiving complaints from parents (in a general sense), participants' responses to this question were related to their ages. There was a positive correlation (r = 0.450) between age and the level of agreement; the slope of the

regression line was significantly greater than zero, t(60) = 3.87, p < 0.01 (Figure 11).

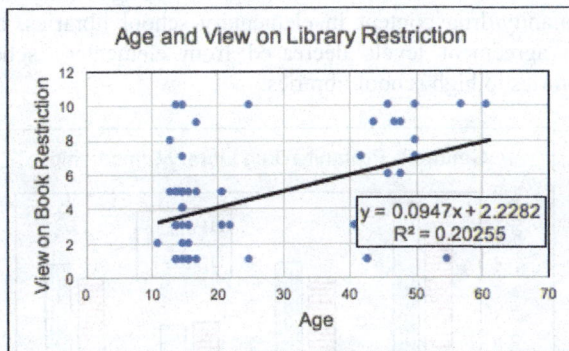

Figure 11: Age and the Level of Agreement on Restricting Certain Books in School Libraries Upon Receiving Complaints from Parents.

4.4 Gender and Views on Censoring Books in School Libraries

Figure 12 shows the participants' gender and their levels of agreement regarding the view on whether books with LGBTQ+ themes or protagonists should be censored in school libraries. Overall, there was no significant difference between females (mean = 3.52, SD = 3.31) and males (mean = 4.25, SD = 3.33) in the agreement levels. However, males generally had higher levels of agreement, particularly regarding censoring LGBTQ+ books in elementary school libraries, and the agreement levels decreased from elementary school libraries to high school libraries.

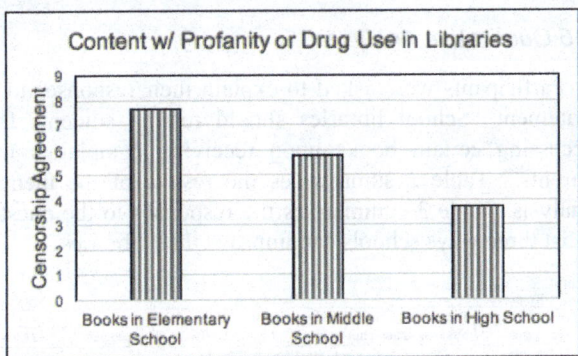

Figure 12: Gender and the Level of Agreement Regarding LGBTQ+ Book Censorship in School Libraries (Grouped by the Type of School Library).

Figure 13 shows the participants' gender and their agreement levels regarding the view on whether books with profanity/drug content should be censored in school libraries. A similar pattern emerged. Again, there was no significant difference between females (mean = 5.57, SD =

2.87) and males (mean = 6.17, SD = 2.56) in the levels of agreement. However, males generally had higher levels of agreement, particularly regarding censoring books with profanity/drug content in elementary school libraries, and the agreement levels decreased from elementary school libraries to high school libraries.

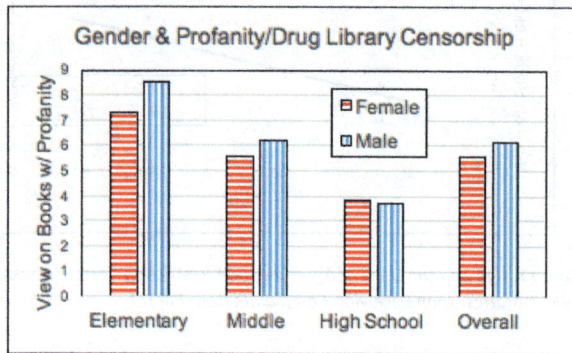

Figure 13: Gender and the Level of Agreement Regarding Censorship of Books With Profanity/Drug Content in School Libraries (Grouped by the Type of School Library).

Figure 14 shows the levels of censorship agreement grouped by book content and gender. The agreement levels on book censorship of profanity/drug content (mean = 5.82, SD = 2.74) were significantly higher than the agreement levels on censorship of LGBTQ+ content (mean = 3.83, SD = 3.31), t(59) = 6.29, p < 0.01, for both females and males.

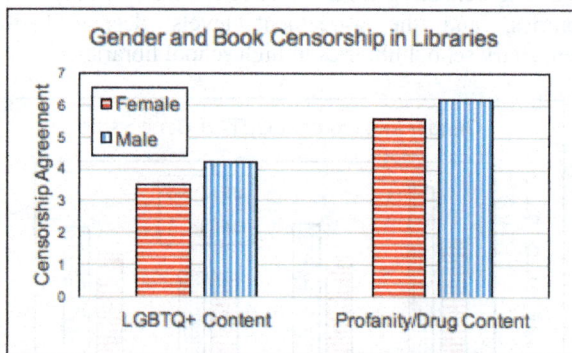

Figure 14: Level of Agreement Regarding Book Censorship in School Libraries (Grouped by Content Type and Gender).

4.5 Age and Book Contents Encountered While Reading

Figure 15 and Table 1 summarize the results in terms of the percentage of people who have encountered various book contents while reading. For all of the specific types of book content (violence, LGBTQ+, slurs, drug use/abuse,

profanity, and sexual assault), a significantly higher percentage of the youths (ages 11-17) encountered them more than the adults (ages 21-61) did, and the differences were greatest for contents related to profanity, drug use/abuse, and LGBTQ+ themes/characters.

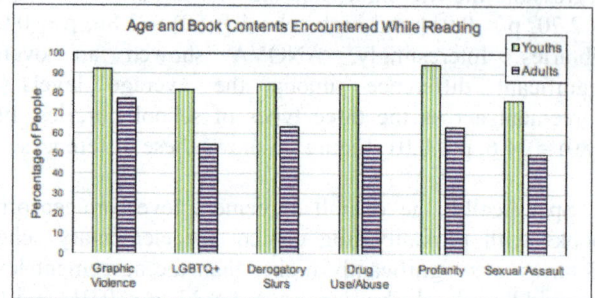

Figure 15: Age and Book Contents.

	Youths	Adults	Difference	two-proportion z-test
Graphic Violence	92.3%	77.3%	15.0%	z = 1.67, p < 0.05 *
LGBTQ+ Themes/Characters	82.0%	54.5%	27.5%	z = 2.30, p < 0.05 *
Racial/Derogatory Slurs	84.6%	63.6%	21.0%	z = 1.87, p < 0.05 *
Drug Use/Abuse	84.6%	54.5%	30.1%	z = 2.30, p < 0.05 *
Profanity	94.8%	63.6%	31.2%	z = 3.16, p < 0.01 **
Sexual Assault	76.9%	50.0%	26.9%	z = 2.15, p < 0.05 *

Table 1: Percentages of Book Contents Encountered by Respondents.

4.6 Qualitative Analyses

Participants were asked to explain their responses to the statement "School libraries should restrict students from accessing certain books upon receiving complaints from parents." Table 2 summarizes the results of the thematic analysis. Table 3 summarizes the responses to the question "List three ways schools can improve their libraries."

Response	Examples	Number
Agree	Parents should decide, judge, or be involved in education	14 (17%)
Agree	Subjects "should not be taught"; Criticize offensive/drug content	4 (4.9%)
Agree	Children/students need "good/positive" books	3 (3.7%)
In Middle	Consider student intention; Schools/teachers/librarians should decide	11 (13.5%)
In Middle	Depends on content: censor profanity/drug content, but not LGBTQ+	7 (8.5%)
In Middle	Depends on the school levels, the student ages, or the specific schools	6 (7.3%)
Disagree	Some parents are not the best judges; They might be "bigoted, over-protective, religious, politically-motivated, paranoid, or overly-strict"	12 (14.6%)
Disagree	The right or freedom for students to learn or discover things	7 (8.5%)
Disagree	Be open-minded; Understand what people may face in the world	7 (8.5%)
Disagree	Others: Banning is ineffective; No need to be afraid of the info., etc.	6 (7.3%)
Nonsense	"Nothing" or "lol."	5 (6.1%)

Table 2: Responses to the statement "School libraries should restrict students from accessing certain books upon receiving complaints from parents."

Response	Examples	Number
General	Better environment (12) or furniture/seating (4); More funding/resources (4); More study rooms/area (2); Snack machines/stores (1); Printers (1)	24 (13.6%)
Books	More or newer (quality/relevant) books/updates (37)	37 (21.0%)
Book Content	Wider range/selection of authors, books, or genres (17); More cultural diversity or general diversity (9)	26 (14.8%)
Book Content	For other languages or ages (6); Other formats: audiobooks, braille books, media (4); For English learners (3)	14 (8.0%)
Book Content	Censor sexual content/orientation (2) or drug use (1); Note biases of authors/books/contexts (2); Eliminate religious/political censorship (1)	6 (3.4%)
Services: Access	Easier book access / more intuitive check-in/out system / digitize processes (11); Better borrowing/quota system (5); More book collection/donation (2); Recommendation system (2)	20 (11.4%)
Services: Events	More reading/community groups/events/activities (6); More social area/interactions (1); Accepting student book suggestions (7)	14 (8.0%)
Services: People	More volunteers (3); Hire more librarians or paying librarians more (2); Get more support/donations (2); Friendlier staff (1)	8 (4.5%)
Services: Others	Advertisement about services (3); Teach research or have more lectures (2); Free news subscription (1); Incentive to use non-book related services (1); Homework center (1); Get rid of worn books (1)	9 (5.1%)
Time or Schedule	Have longer operating hours (9); Always be open (1); Be open during the summer break (1)	11 (6.2%)
N/A	Nothing / Don't know (4); Libraries are not needed (2); Non-sense (1)	7 (4.0%)

Table 3: Suggested Ways That Schools Can Improve Their Libraries.

5. Discussion

Overall, the current findings successfully address the research questions regarding the factors that are related to opinions on the issue of censoring books in school libraries, and they met the project goal of understanding people's views on this issue. In this sense, many of the results from the current project have practical significance. For example, it was found that older participants had more traditional views, but regardless of age or gender, most participants generally wanted to censor books with profanity/drug content more than they wanted to censor books with LGBTQ+ content. These results suggest a cultural shift in views, especially for younger participants regarding LGBTQ+ content. The younger generation was more influenced by this shift in views, and teenagers are becoming more accepting of LGBTQ+ people. Indeed, this shift coincides with a number of recent high-profile LGBTQ+ events in mainstream media. For example, LGBTQ+ content is being added to children's books (Zeng, 2021), Sesame Street created a married gay couple in 2021 (Kochi, 2021), and even one of Disney's animated movies ("Strange World") featured an LGBTQ protagonist in 2022 (Zee, 2022).

As for the general issue of whether libraries should restrict students from accessing certain books, older participants were more likely to agree with parental complaints, while younger students were more likely to emphasize the freedom of choice. Also, what might have influenced the participants' views was less likely to be how much they read but more likely to be the types of content that they read, as the younger participants were more likely to have encountered book content related to LGBTQ+, drugs, and profanity. These findings are important for educational leaders and school managers, who should take

them into consideration when making decisions regarding libraries in schools.

Next, regardless of gender, for books with both LGBTQ+ content and profanity/drug content, the level of censorship agreement tended to decrease from elementary school libraries to middle school libraries, then to high school libraries. However, males were more likely to have higher levels of censorship agreement than females. These findings are consistent with previous research showing that young females were more likely to identify themselves as liberal compared to young males (De Vise, 2022).

The qualitative analyses were consistent with the quantitative findings. Most of the adults believed that parents could decide what books should be restricted in libraries or taught in schools, while most of the students believed that students' ideas or feedback should be taken into account.

Moreover, the word-based qualitative findings added depth. Given that few previous studies have addressed this issue from the perspectives of teenagers, Table 1 adds to the discussion of this topic, especially regarding the views of high school students. Table 2 is also important because it presents people's ideas on how to actually improve libraries, and some of them were ideas that many others might have yet to consider. Examples included adding braille content, recommendation systems, streamlined processes, non-book services, etc. At a time when more and more libraries are struggling to survive (Morel, 2021), the current study's findings offer possible ways to help traditional libraries to reinvent themselves.

6. Results

The current research process generated new understandings by showing how factors such as age, gender, the type of reading content, and the type of school libraries are related to people's views on book censorship. However, no study is perfect, and there are limitations. First, correlation does not imply causation. Given that it is not possible/feasible to experimentally manipulate the aforementioned factors and control for all potentially confounding variables, one cannot conclude that these factors caused differences in participants' views. For example, differences between younger and older people could have been due to cohort effects, and differences between genders could have been due to sociocultural factors. As for the factor of book content, it could be that being exposed to certain contents caused people to feel a specific way, or it could be that feeling a specific way led to seeking-out certain books, or it could be that another factor (e.g. environmental exposure to profanity) caused people to both feel a specific way and seek-out certain books.

Furthermore, there are limitations regarding sampling. The data were collected through convenient sampling, and most of the responses came from Asian-American or Asian participants. The results' generalizability may be restricted, so comparing the findings with data from other ethnic groups may represent a greater scope of demographics in U.S. schools. In addition, another limitation is the survey's somewhat unclear wording, which might have led to various interpretations. Specifically, the questions about books with profanity, offensive content, and drug use as one topic might have decreased the reliability of participant feedback, as respondents may have had conflicting opinions regarding each one. Greater accuracy could be ensured by addressing each of the topics in isolation.

Nevertheless, despite the limitations, this study poses significant implications for educators, as its results may guide them toward creating a tangible framework to decide which pieces of literature should or should not be allowed in the classroom. Implementing this type of framework into school districts is highly encouraged in order to establish consistency and accountability in the different sides involved in this debate. Also, by understanding the conflicting viewpoints surrounding book censorship, teachers must evaluate how to effectively control this situation. As the views between younger and older demographics on the involvement of parents in the book selection process largely conflict, a moderate method to regulate student reading, such as the requirement of parent signatures for books containing offensive content, may discourage parent protests while eliminating both teacher-parent conflict and parent-child conflict. General suggestions regarding the improvement of libraries may also be taken into consideration by librarians in order to increase the accessibility of school libraries, and in turn, encourage student use.

There are also implications for politicians. Information regarding the factors of age and gender may help politicians make informed decisions about their constituents. With conservative states such as Florida recently introducing book bans, taking into account the additional perspective of how the students view potential reforms may help politicians develop a holistic view of the nuanced debate of censorship. Political influence on the passing of laws makes it critical for politicians to understand which point of view corresponds with the group they are trying to cater towards.

Finally, with guiding data from research, future studies could include extra factors to narrow down explanations for certain viewpoints. For example, sexuality could be an important factor to research, as one of the topics dealt with LGBTQ+ themes and protagonists. In addition, future research could ensure greater diversity of respondents, in order to gather enough data to include more people from different ethnicities, cultures, and socioeconomic backgrounds. Moreover, future directions can examine people's viewpoints regarding books with certain types of sensitive topics, such as sexual content and graphic violence. After all, author Sarah Maas once wrote that "libraries were full of ideas – perhaps the most dangerous and powerful of all weapons" (Maas, 2012, p. 51). It would be wise to understand how to harness their powers and use these intellectual weapons responsibly.

7. Bibliography

[1] Ackerman, R., & Lauterman, T. (2012). *Taking reading comprehension exams on screen or on paper? A metacognitive analysis of learning texts under time pressure.* American Psychological Association. Retrieved April 29, 2023, from https://psycnet.apa.org/record/2012-14696-001

[2] Blakemore, E. (2022*). The history of book bans-and their changing targets-in the U.S. Culture.* Retrieved February 7, 2023, from https://www.nationalgeographic.com/culture/article/history-of-book-bans-in-the-united-states

[3] Carlson, C. (2018). *Jazz, Drama, and a Librarian: Advocating Against Book Censorship in Public Schools.* View of jazz, drama, and a librarian: Advocating against book censorship in public schools. Retrieved February 7, 2023, from https://journals.wichita.edu/index.php/ke/article/view/198/203

[4] Clark, C. (2018). *Children and Young People's Reading in 2017/18: Findings from our annual literacy survey. National Literacy Trust Research Report.* National Literacy Trust. Retrieved December 12, 2023, from https://eric.ed.gov/?id=ED598400

[5] Collins, A., & Halverson, R. (2010). *The Second Educational Revolution: Rethinking Education in the Age of Technology.* Journal of Computer Assisted Learning. Retrieved April 30, 2023, from https://onlinelibrary.wiley.com/doi/abs/10.1111/j.1365-2729.2009.00339.x

[6] Dawkins, A.M. (2018). The decision by school librarians to self-censor: The impact of perceived administrative discomfort. Teacher Librarian, 45(3),8-12.

[7] De Vise, D. (2022). Young women are trending liberal. Young men are not. *The Hill.* https://thehill.com/homenews/campaign/3675477-young-women-are-trending-liberal-young-men-are-not/

[8] Friedman, J., & Johnson, N. F. (2023). *Banned in the USA: The Growing Movement to Ban Books*. PEN America. Retrieved February 7, 2023, from https://pen.org/report/banned-usa-growing-movement-to-censor-books-in-schools/

[9] Garry, C. (2015). *Selection or censorship? school librarians and LGBTQ resources*. School Libraries Worldwide. Retrieved December 29, 2022, from https://journals.library.ualberta.ca/slw/index.php/slw/article/view/6884

[10] Hellerstein, E. (2022). *America's culture warriors are going after librarians*. Coda Story. Retrieved February 7, 2023, from https://www.codastory.com/rewriting-history/war-on-librarians-united-states/

[11] Kochi, S. (2021). Love is love: Sesame Street features first married same-sex couple to have recurring spots on show. *USA Today*. https://www.usatoday.com/story/entertainment/tv/2021/06/22/sesame-street-recurring-same-sex-couple-make-history/5303670001/

[12] Maas, S. J. (2012). *Throne of Glass*. United States: Bloomsbury Publishing.

[13] Mardis, M. (2016). *Beyond the glow: Children's broadband access, digital learning ...* Journal of Educational Multimedia and Hypermedia. Retrieved April 29, 2023, from https://mardis.cci.fsu.edu/01.RefereedJournalArticles/1.12mardis.pdf

[14] Morel, K. (2021). 'It's sad to see.' School libraries are increasingly eliminated. *New Jersey Herald*. https://www.njherald.com/story/news/2021/08/11/school-libraries-transition-media-centers-but-they-endangered/5504506001/

[15] Oltmann, S. (2016) Public Librarians' Views on Collection Development and Censorship, Collection Management, 41:1, 23-44, DOI: 10.1080/01462679.2015.1117998

[16] Pearson UK. (2015). Why is reading so important? Retrieved December 29, 2022, from http://uk.pearson.com/enjoyreading/why-is-reading-so-important.html

[17] Rickman, W. (2010). *A Study of Self-Censorship by School Librarians*. Research Journal of the American Association of School Libraries. Retrieved April 30, 2023, from https://www.ala.org/aasl/sites/ala.org.aasl/files/content/aaslpubsandjournals/slr/vol13/SLR_StudyofSelf-Censorship_V13.pdf

[18] Rosearynandira, A., & Asmiyanto, T. (2020). *Librarian's dualist attitude on censorship practices in primary and ...* PalArch's Journal of Archeology of Egypt. Retrieved March 12, 2023, from https://www.researchgate.net/publication/347879087_LibrarianS_Dualist_Attitude_On_Censorship_Practices_In_Primary_And_Secondary_Education--Palarch's

[19] Shearer, M. (2022). *Banning books or banning BIPOC?* SSRN. Retrieved January 7, 2023, from https://papers.ssrn.com/sol3/papers.cfm?abstract_id=4188196

[20] Sikora, J., Evans, M. D. R., & Kelley, J. (2018). *Scholarly culture: How books in adolescence enhance adult literacy ...* Social Science Research. Retrieved April 29, 2023, from https://www.researchgate.net/publication/328034646_Scholarly_culture_How_books_in_adolescence_enhance_adult_literacy_numeracy_and_technology_skills_in_31_societies

[21] Twenge, J. M., Martin, G. N., & Spitzberg, B. H. (2018). *Trends in U.S. adolescents' media use, 1976–2016*. American Psychological Association. Retrieved February 25, 2023, from https://www.apa.org/pubs/journals/releases/ppm-ppm0000203.pdf

[22] Wilkinson, K., Andries, V., Howarth, D., Bonsall, J., Sabeti, S., & McGeown, S. (2020). *Reading During Adolescence: Why Adolescents Choose (or Do Not Choose) Books*. Journal of Adolescent & Adult Literacy. Retrieved January 16, 2023, from https://ila.onlinelibrary.wiley.com/doi/10.1002/jaal.1065

[23] Zee, M. (2022). 'Strange World' cast and creators on the Disney film's biracial, LGBTQ character: 'You don't have to normalize normal. It just is.' *Variety*. https://variety.com/2022/film/news/strange-world-gay-biracial-character-jaboukie-young-white-1235432785/

[24] Zeng, C. (2021). Children's and YA LGBTQ books: Spring 2021. *Publishers Weekly*. https://www.publishersweekly.com/pw/by-topic/childrens/childrens-book-news/article/86191-children-s-and-ya-lgbtq-books-spring-2021.html

On Wind Energy Circuits: Performance Comparison and Enhancement

Jingwen Zheng

Abstract

Nowadays, wind power - as one of the renewable energies - is being promoted widely across the world. Still, how to achieve a higher efficiency in wind power generation is one of the hot topics experts are still exploring. Among which, circuit design is a key issue in the generation of wind power, and different circuits may achieve various generation performance. This paper first reviews a circuit design that contains a bridge rectifier and a boost converter regarding its efficiency. As the circuit fails to boost the output voltage, we improve the circuit to overcome the shortage of the original circuit. The improved circuit, however, still cannot make the output voltage stable over time. Hence we devise a circuit with a simpler design. By simulation, we find that the output voltage of the new circuit will reach a constant value quickly and can boost the voltage to the desired value. We use the Multisim software to simulate the circuits and explain their operation ideas.

1. Introduction

In the recent decade, there has been a rapid growth of wind power generation in many countries all over the world, such as China, Germany, India, etc., and it has accounted for a large proportion of the overall power generation. For example, its proportion exceeded 9.0% of total power generation in the United State in 2021[1]. To further promote its applications, it is meaningful to explore efficient methods of wind power generation, and one of the fundamental issues is the circuit design.

We introduce the main components of a wind power generation circuit and their roles for the power generation in the following. Fig. 1 gives an illustration of a common wind power generation circuit.

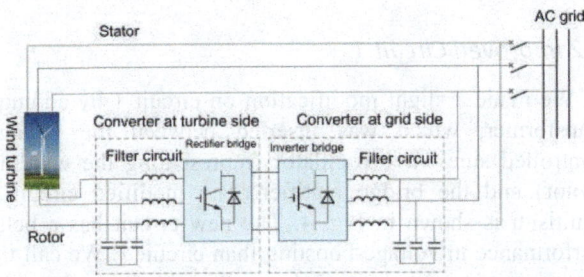

Fig. 1 Illustration of a wind power generation circuit

First, wind turbines generate energy from the wind. A wind turbine consists of three parts: the rotor, nacelle, and the tower. The rotor is made of three blades and a hub. The hub is the central part that connects the blades. As the wind rotates the rotor, the rotor spins a generator connected to it through a shaft, which then generates electricity by converting the kinetic energy into electrical energy. In the nacelle, which is the component container behind the rotor, multiple components work together to harvest energy. A typical nacelle consists of a generator, gearbox or direct drive system, yaw drive and yaw motor, pitch system, control and monitoring systems, transformer, cooling system, anemometer and wind vane, and lightning protection, each of which has a role in producing power and maximizing produced power. The tower is the structure that supports the nacelle and raises it high from the ground. However, the electricity harvested from the wind turbine cannot be directly used, because it does not have a constant voltage level. Its value varies with the speed of the wind. Therefore, a circuit that can stabilize the voltage is necessary. In this paper, we will specifically review the circuit that contains a bridge rectifier that converts AC to DC, and a boost converter that stabilizes and boosts the voltage.

Secondly, a diode is a semiconductor device that can control the direction of a current. In a conventional diode, the current would only be able to flow one way, and flowing in the other way damages the diode. However, in a Zener diode, conventional current is able to flow in one direction freely, and the reverse current is also possible under special conditions, usually when the reverse voltage reaches a certain value. In this paper, we will mostly be using Zener Diodes. Diodes, including Zener diodes, are constructed in a clever way. They're constructed by joining two types of silicon, P-Type, and N-Type. P-Type is made by adding aluminum, which decreases the number of electrons. N-Type is made by adding N-type material such as phosphorus, increasing the number of electrons. The two materials join to form a P-N junction. At this junction, some of the excess electrons of the N-type side will move to the P-type side which lacks electrons. This migration will create an electric field and prevents more electrons from moving across. Therefore, a typical diode has a 0.7 Volts barrier, under which the electrons can't make the jump to the other side.

Thirdly, a capacitor is a device that can store electrical energy. Fourthly, a transistor is similar to a diode, it is also a semiconductor device with PNP or NPN construction, and it acts like a switch. Finally, we are using 555 Timer IC as the integrated circuit in this work.

2. Method and Models

We used the Multisim software to build our circuits. All the components were also provided by Multisim. In the rest of this section, we present three circuit designs, called circuit 1, improved circuit 1, and circuit 2, respectively.

2.1 Circuit 1

The first circuit, which is called circuit 1, is a bridge rectifier and boost converter circuit, and Fig. 2 shows its picture[4].

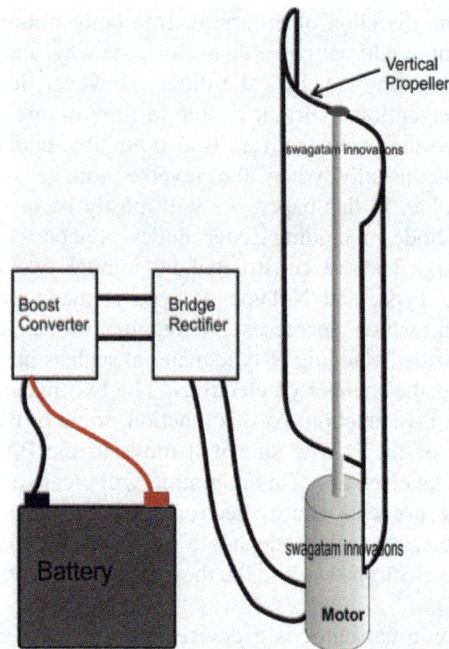

(a) circuit diagram

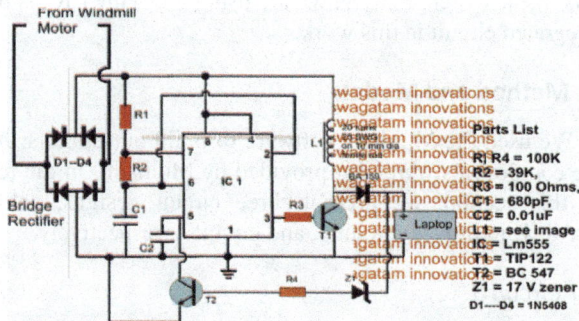

(b) the detailed physical circuit

Fig. 2 Circuit 1 of wind power generation

In this circuit, the group of 4 diodes is known as a diode bridge, which is a bridge rectifier circuit. As previously stated, this bridge rectifier takes AC as input and outputs DC.

We construct the above circuit in the Multisim software, shown below in Fig. 3. On the upper left corner of Fig. 3, the output of the windmill motor is represented by a voltage-controlled sine wave oscillator. Its output voltage varies between 0V and 12V. The Zener diode connecting to the oscillator controls the direction of a current and the voltage. The Zener diode together with the rest components

on the left side of the battery works to output a stable and boosted voltage. To test the simulation result, we use two multimeters on the rightmost of the figure to measure the magnitude of current and voltage, respectively.

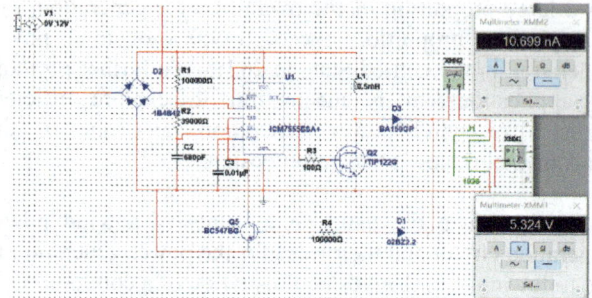

Fig. 3 Circuit 1 in Multisim

2.2 Improved Circuit 1

We made a slight modification on circuit 1 by adding a transformer, which was inserted between the voltage-controlled sine wave oscillator (representing the windmill motor) and the bridge rectifier. The modified circuit in Multisim is shown in Fig. 4. The new circuit has a better performance in voltage-boosting than circuit 1. We call this new circuit improved circuit 1. For the added transformer in improved circuit 1, the ratio of the number of turns between the primary coil and the secondary coil is set to 1:10. Later on we will make a sensitivity analysis on the output voltage in terms of the ratio.

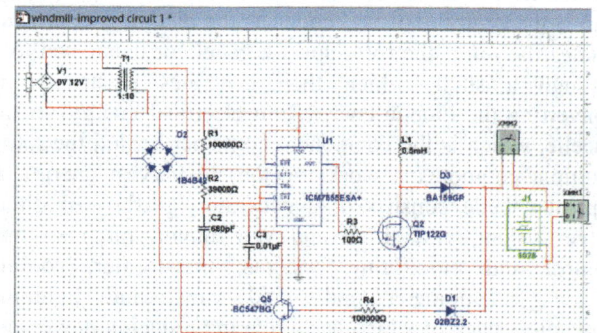

Fig. 4 Improved Circuit 1 in Multisim

2.3 Circuit 2

Now we construct another circuit with a different idea, and called it circuit 2, which is illustrated in Fig. 5. The circuit seems much simpler than improved circuit 1. It consists of only five components, i.e., a voltage-controlled sine wave oscillator that denotes the windmill motor, a transformer, a Zener diode, a resistor, and a battery. Similar to the improved circuit 1, the minimum and maximum output voltages of the oscillator were set to 0V and 12V, respectively. The ratio of the number of turns between the primary coil and the secondary coil of the double coil inductor is also set to 1 to 10. The resistor has a resistance of 100Ω.

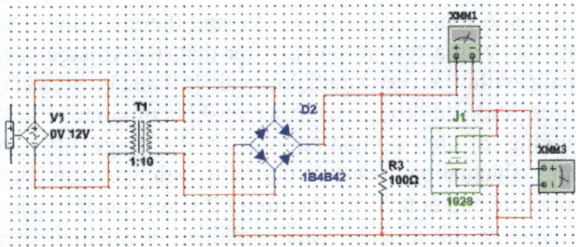

Fig. 5 Circuit 2 in Multisim

For the above circuits, circuit 1 and improved circuit 1 are similar in design, while circuit 2 is different from those designs and also simpler. In the next section we will test their performance in Multisim and make a comparative analysis.

3. Simulation and Discussion

In this section we conduct simulations via Multisim for the three established circuits, and observe their performance in voltage boosting and voltage-stabilizing.

We started the simulation by testing circuit 1, and unfortunately found that circuit 1 did not work as intended. Here are the following two negative observations for this circuit.

First, the voltage outputs of circuit 1 were not boosted and also unstable. Given the input voltage by the windmill motor fluctuating between 0V and 12V, the output voltage of the circuit also varied in the same interval. Moreover, the fluctuation was also large. Hence, this circuit did not satisfy the expected target.

Secondly, in several runs of simulation, a simulation error always occurs and terminates the simulation abnormally when the voltage rose from 5.000V to around 9.000V in less than 10 seconds. Note that the current varies between 10.000nA and 20.000nA during the simulation. The error could not be resolved by running the convergence assistant, which is the software's built-in detection and repair function.

Next we redid the simulation for the improved circuit 1. We found that the simulation error which appeared in circuit

1 did not occur within the 150-seconds simulation. We obtained the following observations during the simulation.

First, in improved circuit 1, its output voltages fluctuated mostly between 550.00mV and 102.50V. More precisely, the output voltages fell into two disjoint intervals: 0.550V to 5.5V and 65V to 102.5V during the simulation. Fig. 6(a) and 6(b) give two screenshots with two different voltages (720.07mV and 102.02V) at the beginning of improved circuit 1's simulation. However, the latter interval narrowed down to 65V to 75V after a few loops of voltage fluctuation. Hence, we can conclude that there were significant jumps in voltage changes, and the voltage fluctuations were limited to two disjoint intervals. We believe that the phenomenon of voltage jumps should be caused by the self-inductance of the double coil inductor in the circuit. Unfortunately, we did not find out the reason for the large jump.

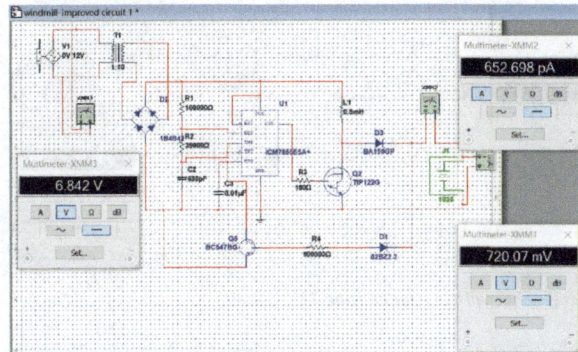

(a) screenshot with output voltage 720.07mV

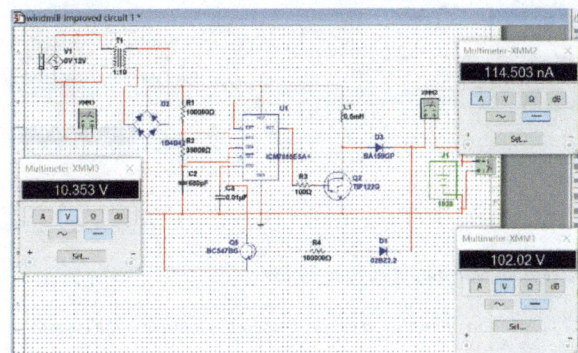

(b) screenshot with output voltage 102.02V

Fig. 6 Illustration of improved circuit 1 at the beginning

Secondly, the maximum input voltage of the double coil inductor is set to 12V, and the number of turns in the secondary coil is 10 times of that of the primary coil, which means that the output voltage should be boosted 10 times.

141

Therefore, its output voltage is theoretically up to 120V(=12×10). In the simulation, however, the observed maximum instant voltage is always less than 102V, giving a nearly 15% gap between the experimental maximum voltage and the theoretical maximum voltage. A reasonable explanation for the gap is energy loss through wires and components.

Thirdly, the input voltage of the inductor converges to 5.999V in several simulations, as shown in the multimeter readings on the left side of Fig. 7(a) and 7(b). The multimeter readings on the right side of the figures indicate that the output voltage keeps on varying in the intervals (0.550V, 5.5V) and (65V, 75V).

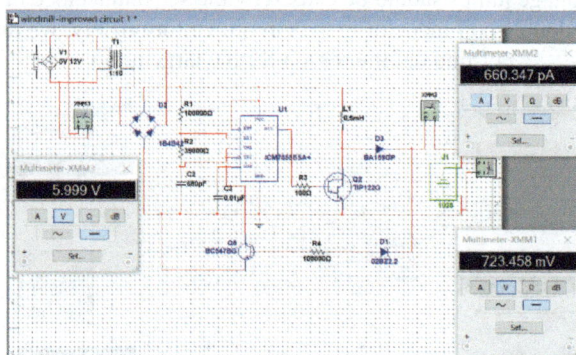

(a) screenshot with output voltage 723.458mV

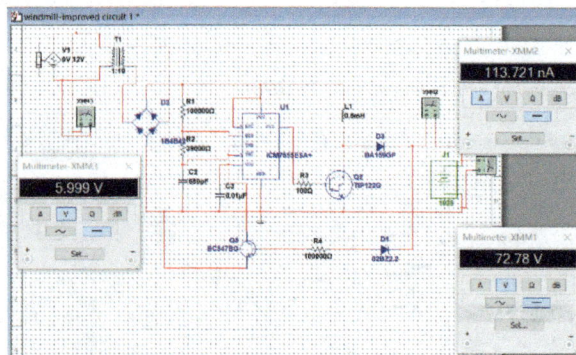

(b) screenshot with output voltage 72.78V

Fig. 7 Illustration of improved circuit 1 when the input voltage is stable

According to the above observations, we can conclude that improved circuit 1 cannot stabilize voltage. Notice that in improved circuit 1, the current changed along with the voltage and varied within (500pA, 120nA) during the simulation.

Now we perform the simulation again on circuit 2 in Multisim, and we obtain the following two observations.

First, the input voltage on the left side of the double coil inductor is initially about 7.4V, then it quickly approaches 6V while accompanied by slight oscillations, and then remains unchanged at 5.999V. Similarly, the output voltage starts at a value between 60V and 80V, then quickly decreases to some value below 35V and then rebounds back to over 59V in a few seconds. After that, the voltage keeps varying within a very small interval: [59.832V, 59.834V]. Figures. 8(a) and 8(b) give the screenshots of circuit 2 at the beginning of the simulation and at the stage of stable voltage fluctuation, respectively. Through the simulation, we observe and conclude that circuit 2 takes much less time to converge to a stable and smaller fluctuation range compared to improved circuit 1.

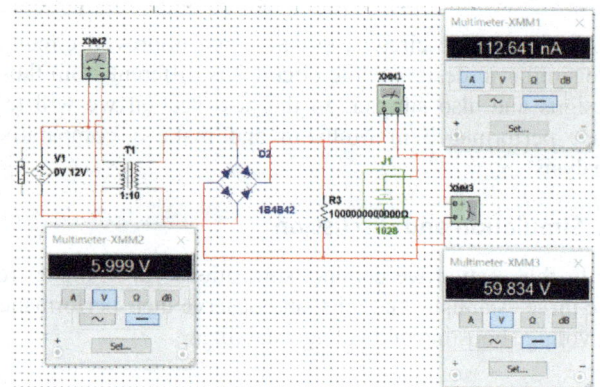

(a) screenshot at the beginning

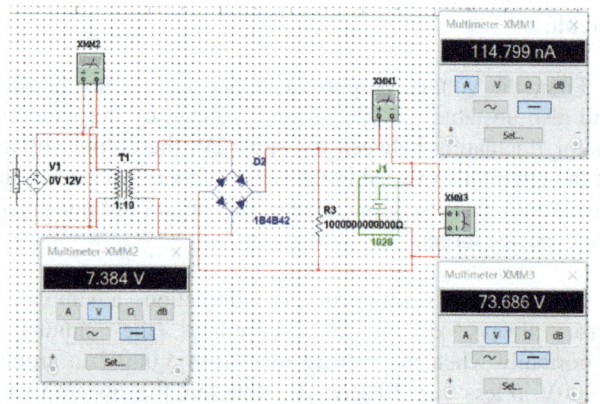

(b) screenshot with stable output voltage

Fig. 8 Screenshots of circuit 2 in Multisim

Secondly, the stable fluctuation range [59.832V, 59.834V] in circuit 2 has smaller lower and upper bounds than the second variation interval of the improved circuit 1 i.e., (65V, 75V), and the range was much narrower. It implied that the former has a slightly weaker voltage boost intensity. However, circuit 2 converged to a single and narrow fluctuation range, while the improved circuit 1 had two broader variation ranges, i.e., (550.00mV, 5.5V) and (65V, 75V). Therefore, we can conclude that circuit 2 outperforms improved circuit 1 in voltage-boosting and voltage stability.

However, in terms of current in the stable stage, circuit 2 had a larger current fluctuation range than improved circuit 1, varying within (5.0pA, 186.0nA). A possible explanation is there were fewer resistors and other components used for current buffering and splitting in circuit 2.

4. Sensitivity Analysis

In the previous simulations, it is shown that both improved circuit 1 and circuit 2 can boost voltage and converge to relatively small fluctuation ranges, outperforming circuit 1. In this section we further conduct sensitivity analysis on the ratio of the number of turns between the primary coil and the secondary coil of the double coil inductor for the two circuits.

We first consider the improved circuit 1, and change the above ratio from 1:2 to 1:18, as shown in Table 1. Recall that for this circuit, there are two voltage fluctuation ranges. In the table, L1 and U1 represent the lower and upper bound of the first fluctuation range, and L2 and U2 are those for the second fluctuation range. We observe that in the second column of the table, the input voltage stabilizes to 5.999V, which is exactly the output voltage of the windmill motor. We use line charts to depict the fluctuation trend of the output voltages in the stable stage, as given in Fig. 9. In the figure, we can intuitively see that when the ratio changed from 1:2 to 1:18, the first fluctuation range (L1, U1) remains almost unchanged. For the second fluctuation range (L2, U2), however, both the values of L2 and U2 increased with the ratio, and the fluctuation range, i.e., U2-L2, also increased overall. Therefore, we can conclude that the voltage-stability of improved circuit 1 decreases in general as the ratio increases.

Ratio	Input Voltage	L1	U1	L2	U2
1:18	5.999	0.64	5.3	76	117
1:16	5.999	0.63	5.3	75	112.5
1:14	5.999	0.63	5.3	73	106
1:12	5.999	0.62	5.4	68	80
1:10	5.999	0.65	5.5	65	75
1:08	5.999	0.59	5.5	57	64
1:06	5.999	0.57	5.5	43	49
1:04	5.999	0.53	5.52	16	34
1:02	5.999	0.5	5.6	10	16.5

Table 1 Voltage fluctuation range in stable stage for improved circuit 1

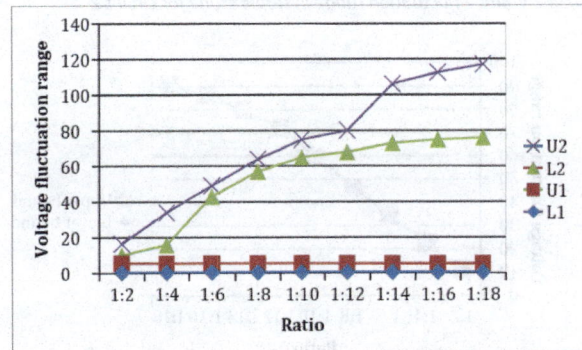

Fig. 9 Trend of voltage fluctuation range for improved circuit 1

Now we conduct the same experiment for circuit 2. The experimental results are given in Table 2. As shown in the second column of the table, the input voltage of circuit 2 converges to 5.999V in the stable stage. Circuit 2 has a single voltage fluctuation range that is nearly negligible, especially for the last cases with ratios 1:8, 1:6, 1:4, and 1:2, where the lower bound matched the upper bound. Fig. 10 shows the line charts of the variation trend of the output voltages in the stable stage. We have the following observations.

First, when the ratio changed from 1:2 to 1:18, the upper and lower bounds of the voltage fluctuation range are almost the same. It implies that the output voltages were quite stable with negligible fluctuations, and thus circuit 2 performs very well in output voltage stabilization.

Secondly, the output voltage in the stable stage increases nearly linearly with the ratio. It indicates that the expected output voltage can be estimated with the ratio of the number of turns between the primary coil and the secondary coil of the double coil inductor. This observation is helpful for the decision-maker to design the double coil inductor according to the required output voltage in practice.

Ratio	Input Voltage	Lower bound	Upper bound
1:18	5.999	90.479	90.481
1:16	5.999	85.891	85.892
1:14	5.999	79.783	79.784
1:12	5.999	71.83	71.831
1:10	5.999	59.832	59.834
1:08	5.999	46.14	46.14
1:06	5.999	34.226	34.226

1:04	5.999	22.343	22.343
1:02	5.999	10.541	10.541

Table 2 Voltage fluctuation range in stable stage for circuit 2

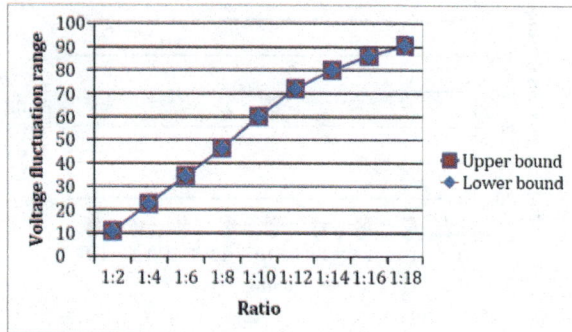

Fig. 10 Trend of voltage fluctuation range for circuit 2

5. Conclusion

In a world where global warming, deforestation, pollution, etc. are real and emergent problems, clean energy is especially important. Wind power generation is one of the most important clean energy supplies. Therefore, it is useful to study the way a wind energy circuit works and dive deeper into it. In this paper we reviewed one of the possible circuit designs. To achieve the objectives of stable and boosted output voltages, we presented an improved circuit based on the previous one, and then proposed circuit 2 with new design ideas. Simulation results showed that circuit 2 can successfully output the expected stable and boosted voltages. Sensitivity analysis further supported the above conclusion, and gave some valuable practical references for the decision-maker.

6. References

[1] Department of Energy, DOE finds record production and job growth in U.S. wind power sector[EB/OL]. Energy.Gov, 08-16-2022, https://www.energy.gov/articles/doe-finds-record-production-and-job-growth-us-wind-power-sector.

[2] [2] CWC20 NAU technical design report[R]. https://www.energy.gov/sites/prod/files/2020/10/f80/nau-technicaldesignreport.pdf.

[3] [3] L Zhao, Y Yang, Toward small-scale wind energy harvesting: design, enhancement, performance comparison, and applicability[J]. Shock and Vibration, 2017: 3585972, https://www.hindawi.com/journals/sv/2017/3585972/#conclusions.

[4] [4] Homemade Circuit Projects, Simplest windmill generator[EB/OL]. https://www.homemade-circuits.com/simplest-windmill-generator-circuit/.

Possible Solutions to Homelessness for Californians with Mental Health Issues

Zhaosen Qu

Abstract

This study provides an overview of problems facing the homeless population in California, primarily drug addiction and mental illness, and investigates potential solutions to the homeless crisis. By examining and evaluating past reports and articles, this study provides a general background on the causes of mental issues among the homeless. Relevant literature consists of previous studies as well as reports from government agencies and nonprofit organizations. This study uses demographic statistics to introduce the issues of the California homeless. Next, this study analyzes possible causes and the correlation between mental illness and homelessness. Finally, this study explores potential solutions such as housing assistance and community funded mental health services.

Keywords: mental illness, shelters, rental assistance, homelessness, supportive housing

1. Introduction

Homelessness has grown in the United States for many years without substantial efforts to find effective solutions. The magnitude of the issue is often underestimated, particularly when regarding the relationship between mental illness and homelessness. According to the Orange County Homeless Management Information System, more than 12,000 people in Orange County do not have proper housing, including 5,313 in Central Orange County, 4,964 in North Orange County, and 1,953 in South Orange County (HMIS Information, 2021). The growth of homelessness is magnified in California's metropolitan areas of Los Angeles and San Francisco.

Although many research papers examine homelessness, few have specifically studied the impact of mental illness on homeless population growth. Without sufficient research on the causes of homelessness, it is difficult to take specific actions. This study is intended to provide a pathway to possible solutions.

According to the National Alliance on Mental Illness, 20.5% of homeless individuals in the United States are affected by mental illness (HUD 2019 Continuum of Care Homeless Assistance Programs Homeless Populations and Subpopulations, 2019). The HMIS data for Orange County reveals that over 200 veterans require housing expense assistance and 69 need emergency shelter (HMIS Information, 2021). The prevalence of mental illness among veterans and homeless individuals contributes to the yearly increases of the homeless population in Orange County.

Government agencies are a primary source of research as well as aid for the homeless. A total of 19 federal member agencies are involved in the United States Interagency Council on Homelessness including the Department of Agriculture for food stamps, the Department of Commerce for census and business, the Department of Education for free and reduced meals, the Veterans Administration to provide healthcare and psychiatric services for veterans, and Housing and Urban Development. With the efforts of USICH, 82 communities and three states have ended veteran homelessness, and four communities have ended chronic and veteran homelessness (Communities That Have Ended Homelessness, 2021). USICH is not the only organization that plays a role in the effort to help the homeless; nonprofits and other organizations such as the National Alliance to End Homelessness, the Coalition for the Homelessness, and even private landlords deliver aid where possible.

To identify solutions through studies, reports, and journals from various sources, it is imperative to address the following questions:

1) Why is mental illness so prevalent in the California homeless population?

2) Is there a strong correlation between mental illness and poverty?

3) What current solutions are reporting the best results?

For clarification, the term 'veteran homelessness' means persons who have served in the armed forces who are homeless or living without access to secure and appropriate accommodation (Department of Veterans Affairs 2013). The term 'chronic homelessness' refers to people who have experienced homelessness for at least a year — or repeatedly — while struggling with a disabling condition such as a serious mental illness, substance use disorder, or physical disability" (Chronically Homeless, National Alliance to End Homelessness, 2021).

2. Methodology

This study is a meta-analysis of current research on homelessness, particularly among those with mental health issues, and homeless intervention programs. Current research on the homelessness crisis facing California is cited to investigate the efficacy of possible solutions. A variety of sources are collected including information from nonprofit organizations, government agencies, academics, and others.

The three questions outlined in the introduction are the framework which potential solutions are evaluated through. This study acknowledges that there is no single solution for homelessness and approaches must vary per homeless individual.

3. Results

3.1 Causes of Mental Illness-Related Homelessness

In regards to this study's first question, an in-depth analysis points to a variety of reasons why mental illness leads to homelessness. According to a report by the city of Santa Ana, "some [people] have lost their homes due to the loss of a job or loved one, while others are fleeing domestic violence. Other contributing factors may include the lack of affordable housing, low wages, substance abuse or mental health issues... a 2017 study... [found that]... securing or retaining jobs with sustainable wages and finding or retaining affordable housing... [were] the number one and two most identified reasons for homelessness… These two circumstances alone account for 76 percent of the basis for homelessness." (Why Are People Homeless, 2018)

John Begin, the Homelessness Initiative Director for Trellis, a Costa Mesa faith-based consortium, explains that "there's no one reason for homelessness and there's no one solution." Begin explains that many other factors contribute to living on the street, ranging from a job loss or a rent increase to drug addiction (Money, L., Pinho, F. E., Davis, H. E., & Vega, P. E, 2019). Loss of a job and sudden rent increases are financial factors that, in combination with drug addiction, lead to mental health issues and ultimately homelessness.

Ultimately, many factors contribute to mental illness-related homelessness: high cost of living in California, lack of access to healthcare, substance abuse, unemployment, and housing supply shortages. Without proper assistance, people with mental illnesses are likely to lose their housing and struggle to break the cycle of homelessness.

3.2 Correlation Between Mental Illness, Poverty, and Homelessness

There is also a strong connection between mental health and homelessness. Increased use of alcohol or drugs in addition to violent behavior often results in mental illness and homelessness (Tarr, P. 2018). According to a report by SAMHSA, 18.4% of adults with mental illness also experience "substance use disorder" (Substance Abuse and Mental Health Services Administration, 2020).

The requirements of sustaining adequate housing, specifically earning a stable income and carrying out daily and routine activities, are difficult for individuals suffering from mental illnesses. An inability to function in the workplace and earn an affordable living for themselves leads to poverty and ultimately homelessness (Housing and Shelter, 2020). According to the United Nations, adequate housing must have the following characteristics: "adequate privacy, adequate space, adequate security, adequate lighting and ventilation, adequate basic infrastructure, and adequate location with regard to work and basic facilities— all at a reasonable cost" (Leckie, 1992). Stable income is best defined as income that is paid in a set or fixed amount from the same source on a regular basis(Creek, C., 2021). The American Psychiatric Association, in defining mental illness as "health conditions involving changes in emotion, thinking, or behavior (or a combination of these)," concurs that mental illnesses associated with distress or problems of functioning in society do play a significant role in homelessness (Parekh, R. 2018, August).

As people afflicted with mental health issues are demonstrably incapable of carrying out daily tasks on their own, they must rely on help from family or friends. Those with no visible support systems are left with few alternatives other than to seek food and shelter on their own and potentially live on the California streets. Thus, there is a strong connection between the mental health issues that make ordinary employment impossible and homelessness.

3.3 Current Solutions and Successes

Several initiatives found some success in preventing individuals from becoming homeless. Although it does not specifically target the mentally ill, California's eviction moratorium extension is helping some from becoming homeless. This was enacted recently due to the COVID-19 pandemic, whereby Governor Gavin Newsom signed an order shielding all renters who were unable to pay rent from eviction. This order continues through September 30, 2021, and rental assistance extends to March 2022 for tenants earning less than 80% of the area median income (Tobias, M. M. 2021). This means that there will be fewer people, some with mental health issues, who become homeless due to an inability to pay rent.

Another possible solution is community-based mental health services, which play an important role in reducing homelessness. Overall, mental health services decrease the severity of mental illness in overall populations. Some services can specifically increase access to supportive housing as well as provide other basic necessities. People with mental health issues encounter more barriers, such as employment, and tend to be in poorer health compared to the overall homeless. Housing outreach is a service that provides a safe place to live and is a vital component of stabilizing mental illness and helping individuals on their journey to recovery (Mental Health, 2021). Jamboree Housing Corporation also made an effort to reduce homelessness, stating that "permanent supportive housing results in better outcomes and is more cost-effective than supporting homeless people on the streets. Why? Simply put, permanent supportive housing is permanent. It gives men, women, children, and families experiencing homelessness a place to call home permanently…not temporarily or transitionally" (Permanent Supportive Housing Statistics, Benefits, Studies, and Evidence, 2021). According to a report by the USICH, "there is a growing body of evidence that people experiencing homelessness can achieve stability in permanent housing when they are provided the appropriate level of tailored services and support. These approaches are both cost effective and create stronger outcomes" (Culhane, D., and Byrne, T., 2010).

Questions	Why is mental illness so prevalent in the California homeless population?	Is there a strong correlation between mental illness and poverty?	What current solutions are reporting the best results?
Results	A variety of factors contribute to mental illness-related homelessness such as job loss, unaffordable housing, low wages, and substance abuse.	Many activities that facilitate adequate housing, such as earning a stable income, can be difficult for individuals with mental illnesses.	California's eviction moratorium extension under the impact of COVID-19, long-term housing support for long-term effects, funded health programs.

Simple summary table of the results section

4. Discussion

This study sought to find the causes of homelessness among those with mental illness, the correlation between mental illness and homelessness, and current solutions that are reporting the best results. As summarized above, the findings shown in this paper agree with previous research, that homelessness is a direct result of poverty which can be caused by mental illness. This provides a general cause and possible solutions to mentally ill homelessness.

In researching homelessness, scope is limited because all information is based on a literature review of various reports from government agencies and other organizations. It is important to note that this study did not conduct in-person surveys of homeless communities and relies on reported information.

While it appears that the studied initiatives are working effectively, the overall homelessness crisis continues to grow. These initiatives must continue to grow and the situation continuously evaluated. More detailed research that builds on these conclusions with increasing specificity, such as a focus on homeless veterans with mental illnesses, will provide a better framework to evaluate solutions.

This research provides an overall background on homelessness in California, its connection to mental illness, and possible solutions. Future research could benefit from personal observations, interviews, and surveys.

5. Conclusion

Homelessness is not only a growing crisis in California, but also the entire world. Studying mental illness and applying that information to homelessness is a good start. An improvement in government funding, research, and overall concern is a necessity to create a lasting impact on homelessness. This information can be used as a foundation for future research on homelessness. The three questions of this study are focused on the cause of homelessness, the link between homelessness and mental illness, and the solutions to homelessness. This framework is necessary to evaluate the hopefully increasing efforts to reduce homelessness.

6. References

[1] Chronically Homeless - National Alliance to End Homelessness. (2021, March 6). National Alliance to End Homelessness. endhomelessness.org/homelessness-in-america/who-experiences-homelessness/chronically-homeless/

[2] United States Interagency Council on Homelessness (USICH). (2021). Communities That Have Ended Homelessness. usich.gov/communities-that-have-ended-homelessness

[3] Creek, C. (2021). What is A Stable Income & How Does It Affect Your Mortgage? https://www.cherrycreekmortgage.com/blog/article/getting-a-mortgage-what-is-income-stability

[4] Culhane, D. and Byrne, T. (2010). Ending Chronic Homelessness: Cost-Effective Opportunities for Interagency Collaboration. University of Pennsylvania ScholarlyCommons.

[5] Department of Veterans Affairs. (2013, October 22). Homeless Veterans. https://www.benefits.va.gov/persona/veteran-homeless.asp

[6] Housing and Shelter. (2020, April 15). samhsa.gov/homelessness-programs-resources/hpr-resources/housing-shelter

[7] HUD 2019 Continuum of Care Homeless Assistance Programs Homeless Populations and Subpopulations. U.S. Department of Housing and Urban Development. (2019, September 20). https://files.hudexchange.info/reports/published/CoC_PopSub_NatlTerrDC_2019.pdf.

[8] Leckie, S. (1992). From Housing Needs to Housing Rights: An analysis of the right to adequate housing under international human rights law. International Institute for Environment and Development, London, United Kingdom.

[9] Money, L., Pinho, F. E., Davis, H. E., & Vega, P. E. (2019, December 30). Unsheltered, Part 1: Why does Orange County have a homeless problem and how can it be solved? Daily Pilot.

latimes.com/socal/daily-pilot/news/story/2019-12-30/part-1-why-does-orange-county-have-a-homeless-problem-and-how-can-it-be-solved

[10] Parekh, R. (2018, August). What Is Mental Illness? psychiatry.org/patients-families/what-is-mental-illness

[11] Permanent Supportive Housing Statistics, Benefits, Studies & Evidence. (2021). Jamboree Housing Corporation. jamboreehousing.com/pages/what-we-do-resident-services-permanent-supportive-housing-stats-and-studies

[12] Substance Abuse and Mental Health Services Administration (SAMSA). (2020). Key substance use and mental health indicators in the United States: Results from the 2019 National Survey on Drug Use and Health (HHS Publication No. PEP20-07-01-001,

[13] NSDUH Series H-55). Rockville, MD: Center for Behavioral Health Statistics and Quality, Substance Abuse and Mental Health Services Administration. https://store.samhsa.gov/sites/default/files/SAMHSA_Digital_Download/PEP20-07-01-001-PDF.pdf

[14] Tarr, P. (2018, November 19). Homelessness and Mental Illness: A Challenge to Our Society. Brain & Behavior Research Foundation. https://bbrfoundation.org/blog/homelessness-and-mental-illness-challenge-our-society

[15] The Homeless Hub. (2021). Mental Health. homelesshub.ca/about-homelessness/topics/mental-health

[16] Tobias, M. M. (2021, June 25). California's eviction moratorium extension: What's in it for tenants and landlords? CalMatters. https://calmatters.org/housing/2021/06/california-eviction-moratorium-deal/

[17] 211 OC. (2021, March 31). HMIS information. https://www.211oc.org/coc/hmis-information.html.

[18] Why are people homeless? The City of Santa Ana. (2018, April 12). https://www.santa-ana.org/homelessness/why-are-people-homeless.

Recommendation Algorithms: Process of Implementation and Accuracy

Ethan Chen

Abstract

Ever since e-commerce business became more and more popular in modern world society, companies such as Netflix, YouTube, and Amazon grew, began to implement customer specific, or what is known as the recommendation engine, to calibrate to their customers' preferences and tastes. These recommendation engines revolve around comparing and contrasting user's old viewing histories on items or videos and based on that information, providing suggestions or similar recommendations to the users. However, with more and more recommendation algorithms emerging in the past few years, the need to determine the best fit algorithms with the highest accuracy in predicting customer preferences became a crucial element. By having an accurate prediction algorithm, customers would be able to discover more items or products that they would enjoy, and thus creating more incentive for them to stay and continue using products from the companies. By simulating the process using a set of data that would be able to represent the customer population, testing out the accuracy of each individual algorithm, and comparing the accuracy between all tested algorithms, the paper exemplifies how companies determine the best-fit algorithms to implement into their recommender system.

Keywords: Recommendation Engine, Collaborative Filtering, Algorithms, RMSE, MAE.

1. Introduction

When the internet was introduced, the drastic increase in online information and product choices made it difficult for users and consumers to decide and purchase their ideal products. This problem further rose as a serious issue as websites like Tao Bao and Amazon were introduced, further introducing thousands and thousands of choices ranging from cosmetics to everyday essentials. Even streaming services like Netflix and Disney Plus have diverse movie choices, making it difficult for users to find and select their perfect movies, leading to the importance of having reliable recommendation systems calibrated for each user.

In this paper, a dataset from MovieLens would be evaluated by several different algorithms such as Singular Value Decomposition (SVD), SlopeOne, and K-Nearest Neighbors Basic (KKNBasic), serving as a sample of how the recommendation engine from famous sites like Netflix and Amazon determines the best selection algorithm to be used in their recommendation engine. 11 algorithms in total are classified into four different categories: Basic Algorithms, KNN-Inspired Algorithms, Matrix Factorization Algorithms, and Miscellaneous Algorithms. They are then applied to the dataset and based on their RMSE and MAE, we will evaluate each algorithm's accuracy and conclude on which algorithm is the best selection algorithm. This paper will go into detail about the background of the recommendation engines, introduce the dataset (and the cleaning process), implement each algorithm and find their respective RMSE and MAE, then conclude based on our findings.

2. Background

2.1 Recommendation Engines

In the past few years, demands for accurate recommendation engines and algorithms have increased greatly due to the circumstances of websites and apps needing them to filter out options and choices. Websites like Netflix, Amazon, and Spotify all use complicated recommendation engine systems to ensure their users will be able to discover products and items that they would enjoy.

For reference, a recommendation engine is a type of filtering tool that can filter out options and recommend the user with the most relevant items from their preference. With the implementation of recommendation engines, users would be able to find and discover preferred products faster and easier, allowing less time to be spent scrolling through products one after another, and more ideal products to be found and purchased, generating more revenue and income for the companies.

2.2 Types of Recommendation Engine

There are two main types of recommendation engines: collaborative filtering, and content filtering, both of which filter out the best recommendations and send them to the users, through different methods and comparisons. A collaborative filtering recommendation engine collects data from other users that share similarities with the original user, and uses the data comparison to filter out options that would be most relevant to the user. On the other hand, a content-based filtering recommendation engine collects data from the items that the user had recently purchased or viewed, and uses the data to recommend the user with the most suitable item. While the two engines use significantly different methods, they are both efficient in being able to find similar recommendations for the user.

Aside from the two usual types of recommendation engines, there is also a third type: the hybrid model recommendation engine. This type of recommendation engine is a hybrid of both collaborative filtering and content filtering and also looks at both implicit and explicit data. Because of these qualities, the hybrid model outperformed both collaborative and content-based filtering recommendation engines.

2.3 Algorithms Classification

In this paper, the type of recommendation engine I worked with was the collaborative filtering recommendation engine, which includes a lot of various algorithms that can effectively filter out and recommend the best options for the user. Common algorithms for collaborative filtering include the Nearest Neighbors Algorithm, also known as the KNN-Inspired Algorithms, the Matrix Factorization Algorithms, and the Optimization Algorithms. Each of the 11 algorithms used in my code are classified into their respective classes, as shown below in figure 1.

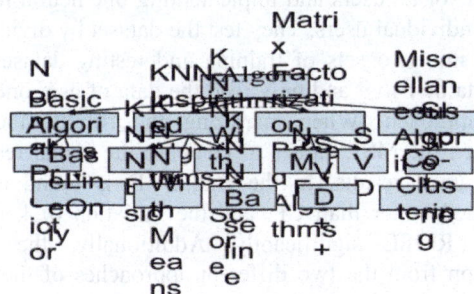

Figure 1: Different classes and types of Algorithms evaluated

The basic algorithms represent the algorithms that predict a random rating based on the distribution of the training set, which is assumed to be normal. While they aren't efficient and don't do much, they are used in the coding for comparing accuracies with the other classes. The KNN, or the K-nearest neighbors algorithms, predict the correct recommendation from the test data by calculating the distance between the test data and all the training points, select the K number of points, then calculate the probability of test data falling into the items of each K and returns the one with the highest probability. Matrix Factorization, on the other hand, determines the association between users and movie matrices to find similarity and make a prediction based on both item and user entities. It considers both similarities and associations between items and users in order to predict accurate recommendations. Lastly, the Miscellaneous Algorithms, consisting of SlopeOne, which creates a linear relation between item preferences, and Co-Clustering, which group matrices into rows and columns that exhibit similar traits to each other. Since the two algorithms use different methods than that of KNN and matrix Factorization, I chose to group the two under the miscellaneous category. I will be going into more detail of how each algorithms perform in *section 4.3: Algorithms*

3. Related Works

My paper had been largely inspired by Mojdeh Saadati and his team's research. In their paper, *Movie Recommender Systems: Implementation and Performance Evaluation*, the team performed a similar experiment on a larger dataset which consists of 1,000,209 rows from the Movielens website. By using RMSE, the team evaluated the performance of the 1 million-plus dataset and compared them to a particular userID-3. The second method they did was to implement the SVD algorithm using python language to find the root mean square error based on different values of k in which k is the number of features. The last method was to use a neural network to predict the movie ratings. The team used two approaches, one neural network for all users and implementing one neural network for all individual users. They test the dataset by dividing the dataset into two sets of training and testing datasets with user data of 1 to 9 and only feed the data of user one in the other approach. When analyzing the results, the team examined the MSE values to compare the actual results to the obtained results. In the end, SVD is found to have performed better than CF, and the variation of k did not change RMSE significantly. Additionally, the "tanh" activation from the two different approaches of the neural network is found to be better than the others. Just like their work, my experiment would evaluate the performance of

different methods, consisting of 11 algorithms, and examine which algorithms would have the highest accuracy and best result.

4. Process and Methods

4.1 Dataset

The dataset that I've chosen to download and us to evaluate the algorithms was from Kaggle. This dataset consists of all the movies and the ratings that were used in the famous Netflix prize competition in 2009, which was held back in 2006 for 4 the following years. The original dataset includes a total of 17,337,458 rows, and a total of 3 columns labeling under user id, movie id, and rating. The dataset was large enough to represent the population of Netflix users and their ratings.

4.2 Cleaning

Since my dataset consists of over 17 million data, which would have easily crashed my entire system if I just ran the code using my original dataset, I had to clean out and shrink my dataset so my program would not crash when I compile the coding. Since there aren't any rows and data that are wrong or displaced, I chose to clean out my dataset by randomly selecting 26,000 rows from my huge dataset using the pandas sample function, organizing them into one smaller dataset, and removing the rest from the dataset. By using random selection, I was able to secure a dataset that wasn't biased and big enough to ensure normality, I was left with a much smaller dataset which would allow my code to run smoothly without crashing my whole program.

4.3 Algorithms

As mentioned before, the different algorithms that I applied to this dataset were the various algorithms from the scikit-surprise prediction algorithm package: the basic algorithms, the KNN-inspired Algorithms, the Matrix Factorization Algorithms, and other Miscellaneous Algorithms.

4.3.1 Basic Algorithms

From the scikit surprise prediction algorithm packages, the first section, the basic algorithms, includes two prediction algorithms: Normal Predictor, and BaselineOnly. The Normal Predictor predicts a random rating from the dataset while assuming the dataset is normal. This algorithm uses the maximum likelihood estimation to estimate a user's preference and recommends items based on the results. On the other hand, the BaselineOnly model predicts the baseline estimate for the given user and the item.

4.3.2 KNN-Inspired Algorithms

The KNN-inspired algorithms predict the results by finding the similarity between the new data and the available data in the dataset and predict based on the previous information. The KNN algorithms I used include the KNNBasic Algorithm, KNNWithMeans Algorithm, KNNWithZScore Algorithm, and KNNBaseline Algorithm.

The KNNBasic algorithm is the most basic collaborative filtering algorithm in the KNN category, and KNNBaseline, while similar to KNNBasic, takes into account a baseline rating, just like the BaselineOnly algorithm. On the other hand, KNNWithMeans Algorithm and KNNWithZScore algorithm both are basic collaborative filtering algorithms that take into account the mean ratings of each user and the z-score normalization of each user.

4.3.3 Matrix Factorization-Based Algorithms

Matrix Factorization Algorithms generate latent features when multiplying two different kinds of entities. The three algorithms that were evaluated include the SVD algorithm, the SVD++ Algorithm, and the NMF algorithm. The SVD algorithm is known for being used by Simon Funk during the Netflix Prize, which is the same dataset that I'll be using. The SVD++ Algorithm is a more extended version of SVD that takes into not only explicit ratings but also implicit ratings. The last algorithm, NMF, is a collaborative filtering algorithm based on Non-negative Matrix Factorization, which is very similar to the SVD algorithm.

4.3.4 Miscellaneous Algorithms

This category includes two algorithms: SlopeOne and Co-Clustering. SlopeOne on surprise is a straightforward algorithm that is just the implementation of the SlopeOne algorithm, while Co-clustering is a collaborative filtering algorithm based on co-clustering

5. Experiment Results

In this experiment, RMSE, or the root mean square error, and MAE, or the mean absolute error, are the two types of errors that were measured in this experiment. To find out the most accurate algorithm to test on the dataset, the RMSE and MAE values that the algorithm has must be the smallest out of all of the tested algorithms. In Figure 2, the algorithms are listed below with their respective RMSE values and MAE values. For all algorithms, their RMSE values range from 1.06 to 1.444, with the normal predictor having the highest RMSE and KNNWithZScore and KNNWithMeans having the lowest. On the other hand, the algorithm's MAE values range from 0.828 to 1.158, with

the normal predictor also having the highest MAE value and KNNBaseLine and BaseLineOnly having the lowest MAE value. The figure shows that the BaselineOnly and KNNBaseline are the most accurate two algorithms to use on this dataset, since they have the lowest MAE values as well as low RMSE values, where MAE is more important in this scenario because it is an unbiased error estimator. The two algorithms are almost as accurate as each other because they both take into account the baseline rating.

Algorithm	Rmse	Mae
NormalPredictor	1.444	1.158
SVD	1.022	0.838
SVDpp	1.023	0.84
BaselineOnly	1.016	0.828
SlopeOne	1.117	0.912
CoClustering	1.101	0.908
NMF	1.109	0.918
KNNBasic	1.062	0.891
KNNWithZScore	1.06	0.883
KNNWithMeans	1.06	0.885
KNNBaseline	1.016	0.828

Figure 2: RMSE and MAE results of each algorithms

In Figure 3, while considering the NormalPredictor algorithm as an outlier, the graph shows the difference between each algorithm. Similarly, KNNBase and BaseLineOnly exhibit the lowest data point out of the 11 algorithms, which means that they are the most accurate prediction algorithms out of the 11 algorithms.

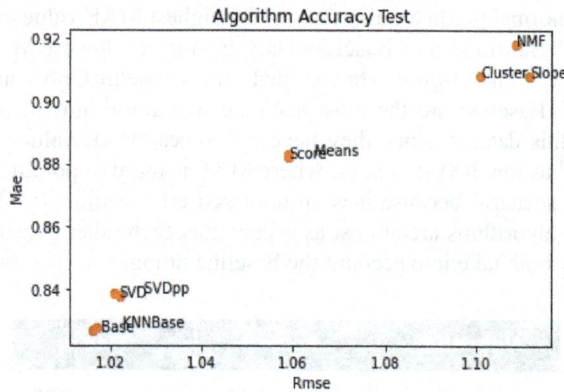

Figure 3 Algorithm Accuracy Test Graph

6. Discussion

From this experiment, I learned many useful python coding skills that would be very useful in future projects and experiments, especially the kinds that are related to engineering and computer science. I also gained knowledge on different topics such as machine learning and data analysis, which I used to help improve my paper quality and result evaluation. From the trials that were conducted above, the best way to analyze the dataset I got from Kaggle is by using the BaselineOnly algorithm and the KNNBaseline algorithm. These two algorithms have the lowest possible RMSE and MAE, meaning that they will have the lowest errors in predicting suitable recommendations for consumers, making them the most accurate algorithms out of the 11 I tested. If I had more time in this experiment, the things that I would want to accomplish are to be able to analyze my dataset in more than one way as well as perform more trials in order to generate more accurate results and eliminate any possibilities that the results could be affected by other factors. I also want to implement and test more diverse algorithms since I did not have enough time to find and utilize other different algorithms.

7. Completion

Recommendation Engines are used more and more in the present day, and many more various algorithms are created to be used in those engines. However, the important part remains that people should be using the most accurate algorithms in their recommendation engines to ensure the best and most relevant results can always be recommended to its users. This is especially important for the websites and companies that focus on selling and advertising their products online because it is in their best interests to keep their users satisfied with the best items/choices possible. In the experiment, the most accurate algorithms are both the KNNBaseline and BaselineOnly algorithms, having the

lowest errors out of the 11 that I tested. However, since I've only performed a few trials, the test results may not be the most accurate. Furthermore, different companies that promote different products or items would also have different choices and needs for different algorithms, so while KNNBaseline and BaselineOnly could've been the most accurate algorithms for this scenario, it may not be as accurate if implemented by other companies such as Amazon or Target.

8. Reference

[1]   Christopher, A. (2021, February 3). *K-Nearest Neighbor*. Medium. Retrieved May 7, 2023, from https://medium.com/swlh/k-nearest-neighbor-ca2593d7a3c4

[2]   Chen, D. (2020, July 9). *Recommendation system-matrix factorization*. Medium. Retrieved May 7, 2023, from https://towardsdatascience.com/recommendation-system-matrix-factorization-d61978660b4b

[3]   Saadati, M. (2019, September 16). *Movie Recommender Systems: Implementation and Performance Evaluation*. ArXiv.Org. https://arxiv.org/abs/1909.12749

[4]   *Kaggle: Your Machine Learning and Data Science Community*. (n.d.). Kaggle. Retrieved October 3, 2021, from https://www.kaggle.com

[5]   *Netflix Prize: Home*. (2009). Netflix. https://www.netflixprize.com/

[6]   *prediction_algorithms package — Surprise 1 documentation*. (n.d.). Surprise. Retrieved October 2, 2021, from https://surprise.readthedocs.io/en/stable/prediction_algorithms_package.html#

[7]   *Basic algorithms — Surprise 1 documentation*. (n.d.). Surprise. Retrieved October 2, 2021, from https://surprise.readthedocs.io/en/stable/basic_algorithms.html

[8]   *k-NN inspired algorithms — Surprise 1 documentation*. (n.d.). Surprise. Retrieved October 2, 2021, from https://surprise.readthedocs.io/en/stable/knn_inspired.html

[9]   *Matrix Factorization-based algorithms — Surprise 1 documentation*. (n.d.). Surprise. Retrieved October 2, 2021, from https://surprise.readthedocs.io/en/stable/matrix_factorization.html

[10] *Slope One — Surprise 1 documentation*. (n.d.). Surprise. Retrieved October 2, 2021, from https://surprise.readthedocs.io/en/stable/slope_one.html

[11] *Co-clustering — Surprise 1 documentation*. (n.d.). Surprise. Retrieved October 2, 2021, from https://surprise.readthedocs.io/en/stable/co_clustering.html

The Effectiveness of Motorsports Advertisements on Current Adolescent Race Fans Compared to New Adolescent Fans

Chun Po Lee

Abstract

The study examines the effectiveness of Formula One (F1) marketing strategies that encourage adolescent race fans and non-race fans to watch F1 races. The research uses qualitative methods – interviews conducted with a sample size of 15 adolescents. These adolescents responded to open-ended questions to identify common patterns of where adolescents get exposure to F1 racing. The research also uses quantitative methods – surveys given to a sample size of 113 adolescents. These participants responded to a survey testing three forms of advertisement (Drive to Survive, Independently Produced Marketing videos, and F1-Produced Marketing videos). Ultimately, the findings showed that adolescents were more compelled to watch F1 races after watching dramatic and cliffhanger-type videos. Overall, increasing exposure to the sport through social media or fashion-brand collaborations will increase the likelihood for adolescents to start watching F1 races. Data collected from this research will be invaluable for the marketing teams of motor-series companies desiring to advertise to the adolescent demographic.

1. Introduction

Motorsport is a popular form of entertainment and a lucrative industry with a global audience attracting millions of fans. Motorsports have been an attractive platform for advertisers to promote various products, from automobile brands to fashion. In the 21st century, in order to expand viewership, advertisers at Formula One (F1) are moving in the direction of social media and have embraced digital marketing. However, the effectiveness of these advertisements on different demographics of the motorsports audience is not fully understood. Although long-time race fans are a critical audience for advertisers, new fans (particularly adolescents) represent an essential demographic for the growth and sustainability of the sport. However, these new fans have different expectations and preferences. They are more receptive to innovative and interactive advertising techniques that appeal to their digital-savvy and socially-conscious nature. Thus, this research paper investigates the effectiveness of F1 advertisements on adolescents and the likeness of watching an F1 race after exposure to F1 marketing or F1 content. It is important to provide advertisers with the most effective method to attract the younger generation to watch an F1 race.

2. Literary Review

Generally, the effectiveness of advertisements from major companies (Geico, McDonald, Chevrolet, NFL) is thoroughly researched, and promotional materials target the entire population for their revenue. However, analysis of motorsport advertisements and their effects on race fans and new fans is sparse, with current research focusing on older viewers. Just like any other sport, motorsports require persistent viewership in order to maintain sponsorships. If viewers drop, then motor racing is at risk of losing sponsors, and eventually the sport may not be able to sustain itself. The future of motorsports needs to attract the younger generation of viewers who have the potential to become lifelong fans, allowing motorsports to tap into a stream of revenue that is currently untouched. This requires more in-depth research evaluating how much advertisements continue to attract current fans and influence new fans to watch the sport to provide marketing teams with a precise analysis of their efficacy. With in-depth research on which forms of mediums can attract the most fans to watch actual races, motorsports advertisers can approach the targeted group of audiences most effectively; this can help them acquire a new stream of revenue while attracting a new demographic of young viewers that may potentially become lifelong fans.

F1 has become the fastest-growing motor racing series, with 1.9 million views on the season opener in Bahrain in 2020, a 39% increase compared to 2019. Compared to Nascar with a 6% increase and Indy Car with a 5% increase, F1 is taking the initiative to market to a wider and ever more diverse audience. F1 has concluded that when promoting its series, it is forced to "keep it real" with long-time race fans while making it intriguing for new fans. The fans look for inclusivity and interactions with the racing action. Prior to 2017, F1 undertook a strict limitation on its media presence, limiting broadcasting rights and exposure drivers could post on social media. Resulting in an all-time low of 350 million viewers (average per year, that year) from its height of 600 million in 2008, however, in January 2017 F1 changed its broadcast management. Liberty Media gained sole commercial rights to F1 from the Formula One Group and the change in management brought in a new era of racing with new media rights extended to more channels, and increased media exposure by the drivers. Subsequently, in September 2017, F1 held a global survey of 14,000 participants that identified themselves as F1 fans based on their interest levels in the sports.

Formula 1 is an incredibly rich sport, mixing many elements, including technology, human interest, heroism, and glamour into a really exciting package... This survey confirms to us that no two fans are the same. Everyone interacts with the sport in different ways and it's our job to deliver a sport that appeals to the particular interest of all of our fans.

This survey confirmed how F1 advertisements developed after Liberty Media's acquisition, by attracting new fans and old fans flirting with the idea of continuing to watch the series. After Liberty Media's takeover numbers confirmed by data from third-party sources like ESPN, show the season-starting Bahrain Grand Prix in 2021 had an average viewership of 1,357,737; making it the 15th most-watched all-time race. However, detailed research on what advertisement strategy was the most effective for the increase in viewership remains unmeasured. The data that do exist provide little insight into the effectiveness of advertisements due to their lack of specificity and general range of investigation. F1 and other motorsports series have recognized its rapid growth but lack real-world testing on the effectiveness of ad campaigns and their appeal to old and new race fans. Current studies lack variables determining how effective a motorsports advertisement is on an entirely new age range of viewers with no prior knowledge of motor racing.

Motorsports encompass a wide variety of racing series spanning the globe, from NASCAR and Indy Car in the US to F1 and Le-Mans in Europe. Other racing series look towards F1 for inspiration to expand their advertising campaigns. The most noticeable advertisement campaign that F1 and Liberty Media adopted is their partnership with Netflix. Production of the docuseries Drive to Survive (DTS) provided current fans with behind-the-scenes action at races and created a reality-type show to attract new fans. Netflix and F1 spokespersons both claim in interviews with motorsports blogs that DTS is a huge success with Netflix citing over 4 million viewers of the new docu-series. However, the number of viewers that watched the show does not reflect the numbers that would watch an actual F1 race. If F1 cannot determine the number of viewers that would watch an actual race after watching the show, then it cannot determine the effectiveness of the show. Other methods of advertising, like shorter Tik Tok edits, could prove to be more effective, but without comparative analysis, there lies a gap in research.

The success of marketing F1 with dramatic storylines, such as reality shows, has increased new viewers but has also led current race fans struggling to keep up. Current race fans have called Netflix's DTS series "overdramatized", claiming that the show creates rivalries that ruin the true sportsmanship between drivers and that Netflix has edited the footage with unnecessary plot points. Ultimately, this leads to the actual racing being distorted. According to fan forums that give first-hand accounts of the reaction of viewers,

The series got off to an electric start with a 90% rating on Rotten Tomatoes for season one, and it maintained a healthy rating in 2019 with 84%. ... Season four was much-anticipated, given the incredibly epic and dramatic title battle between seven-time world champion Lewis Hamilton and Max Verstappen in 2021, but the series' rating has plummeted. At the time of writing (March 22, 2022), its score sits at a paltry 14%.

DTS was an instant success in bringing in more viewers due to its novelty, as a first of its kind to document the inner workings of motorsports, but its downfall occurred drastically within four seasons. Guenther Steiner, team principal of the Haas F1 team, puts it best in Season 1, Episode 1 of DTS, "Why do you watch Formula 1? You want to see action. You want to see drama. You want to see the underdog making a good result." The drastic disconnect from reality has turned the exciting, hair-raising drama into far-fetched fantasies that belong in Hollywood films. While the target audience for Netflix is to attract new fans, the negative reviews and criticism have dissuaded new fans from watching the show and ultimately watching races. F1 needs to ensure that this trend does not continue as it strives

to preserve current race fans while taking an innovative approach for new fans.

Ultimately, there is an absence of research on maintaining high view counts that will entice new viewers while keeping current race fans happy. Considering that motorsports series attract sponsorships, which advertise their sports paying upwards of $35 million dollars, there is a need for motorsports series to test the effectiveness of their campaigns in reaching the younger generation of new fans and attempting to maintain veteran fans. As more racing series look to F1 for marketing techniques, there needs to be a battery of real-world surveys and questionnaires to determine the threshold of innovative advertisements that are effective compared to the over-dramatization of this high-stakes sport.

My paper had been largely inspired by Mojdeh Saadati and his team's research. In their paper, *Movie Recommender Systems: Implementation and Performance Evaluation*, the team performed a similar experiment on a larger dataset which consists of 1,000,209 rows from the Movielens website. By using RMSE, the team evaluated the performance of the 1 million-plus dataset and compared them to a particular userID-3. The second method they did was to implement the SVD algorithm using python language to find the root mean square error based on different values of k in which k is the number of features. The last method was to use a neural network to predict the movie ratings. The team used two approaches, one neural network for all users and implementing one neural network for all individual users. They test the dataset by dividing the dataset into two sets of training and testing datasets with user data of 1 to 9 and only feed the data of user one in the other approach. When analyzing the results, the team examined the MSE values to compare the actual results to the obtained results. In the end, SVD is found to have performed better than CF, and the variation of k did not change RMSE significantly. Additionally, the "tanh" activation from the two different approaches of the neural network is found to be better than the others. Just like their work, my experiment would evaluate the performance of different methods, consisting of 11 algorithms, and examine which algorithms would have the highest accuracy and best result.

4. Process and Methods

This research applies quantitative and qualitative methods through the use of surveys that are distributed among the students in high school. The study aims to provide real-world tests that directly evaluate the effectiveness of F1 marketing strategies on adolescents and is able to identify areas of improvement to increase the appeal of F1 racing to this demographic of young teens. Prior to starting the interview and survey, all respondents were given a consent form; it states that the responses (including their personal opinions and preferences on advertisements and F1 racing) are voluntary. All respondents who proceeded with this experiment agreed to the consent form (Appendix B).

Interviewees are selected through criterion sampling where passionate race fans, individuals already watching F1 races, were eliminated from the sample pool. Initially, 15 adolescents who are not F1 fans were chosen for the preliminary interview to identify where adolescents primarily get their information on F1 racing. The interview was conducted in person or via video call and lasted for 10-15 minutes, responding to five open-ended questions. The interview questions explored the participants' perceptions, attitudes, and interests in F1 racing based on the marketing and social media content they encountered before this interview. Questions included:

1) Have you encountered any advertisements about F1, heard about F1 on the radio, or seen ads posted in physical locations? If so, where?
2) Have you heard or seen anyone mention the name "Lewis Hamilton," "Sebastion Vettel," or "Charles Leclerc"? If so, where?
3) Take something you are interested in, a sport or a music concert. Where would you want to see advertisements for their games or shows? EG: Tik Tok ads, YouTube Ads...
4) What type of advertisements is most likely to attract your attention? Short and fast-paced? Long but descriptive? or "If it's in front of something I want to watch, please get it out of my face"?
5) When browsing Netflix or YouTube and you come across a new show or video related to motorsports or F1 racing, would you be interested in clicking it and giving it a quick look?

By using open-ended questions, participants can express and articulate opinions that may be extreme, unusual, or omitted from the data collection surveys. The responses from the interview lead to the initial hypothesis that "Teens are more compelled to watch an F1 race after watching dramatic and cliffhanger-type videos that generate interest and motive to continue watching races." The researcher will use quantitative and qualitative research methods to test the effectiveness of F1 marketing strategies on adolescents encouraging them to watch an F1 race. The study aims to provide a comprehensive understanding of the effectiveness of F1 marketing strategies on adolescents and to identify

areas for improvement to increase the appeal of F1 racing to this demographic of young teens.

There was a sample pool of 113 adolescents between the ages of 12 to 18. The survey assessed the participants' likeliness to watch an F1 race after being exposed to different forms of promotional material. The qualitative data were collected from the respondents through a self-administered survey of the advertisements consisting of Netflix Drive to Survive clips, independent marketing videos, and F1-produced marketing videos. According to the preliminary interview, these are the most common forms of advertisement and media in which F1 content is featured and the most probable way respondents have come in contact with F1 content. Researcher Marieke Danne from Malo University used a similar approach when she analyzed "How do fans perceive authenticity in the Netflix documentary series' Drive to Survive'?". She used detailed surveys to acquire data from respondents and used open-ended qualitative interview questions, which allowed her to determine patterns of similarity between two data sets with which she concluded the fan's perceptions of the advertisements based on her initial hypothesis. While my project presents similarities to Danne's research, the main difference is the age group of the sample set. Danne's research had a more mature group of respondents, whereas my research focused on adolescents which would allow this research to close the research gap with data on adolescent preferences when it comes to F1 racing. In addition, the research methods of this experiment differ from Danne's approach. In this experiment, the respondents' answer choice consists of multiple-choice responses on a scale of 1-10 (Appendix B). This divergence is based on an assessment conducted by the Journal of Management Information Systems, which concluded that multiple choice is the best method to collect quality data when a mass collection is needed. The videos consist of a balance of short and long advertisements to ensure engagement from the respondents. Using a mix of shorter clips (30-1:00) with upbeat music and slightly longer clips (1:30-2:30) that never exceed three minutes was found to be the best balance for engagement.

Furthermore, adopting the format of a short clip followed by the 1-10 scale of interest questions allows for pattern analysis when the researcher interprets the data. Building off Marieke Danne's research, the researcher collects a large sample size and compares it to the original hypothesis formulated from the controlled preliminary interviews. Using descriptive and inferential statistics such as logistic regression allowed the researcher to identify patterns and relationships between the different advertising styles and how likely a respondent was to watch an F1 race.

5. Limitation

The sample of adolescents was limited to a group from similar demographics with a high socioeconomic and education level; hence it lacks representation from an entire population of adolescents across the nation with various backgrounds, possibly creating biased results. In addition, the research did not include a control group because of limited resources and a sample population. As a result, the self-reported nature of the data would limit the study due to inherent bias either for or against watching F1. However, the skewed data were compensated for by the large sample size. Finally, the study was limited to a cross-sectional design, which did not allow the researcher to establish causality between the marketing strategies and the adolescents' interest in watching an F1 race over time because the survey was given at one point in a respondent's life. This means that their opinions may change over time, and longitudinal trends will not be depicted in the data set.

While it is feasible that there may be bias in the data, the collection of robust data due to the large group size minimizes the bias. In addition, all results are placed into a spreadsheet to eliminate outlier data, which can potentially skew the data. Ultimately, the findings of this study can inform the F1 organization and marketing professionals on how to target adolescents in order to increase the viewership of F1 races among this demographic.

6. Data Analysis

The preliminary interview was conducted with 15 respondents who stated they were non-race fans out of the total of 25 possible respondents. The questions consisted of five open-ended questions, and the following are direct quotes from the responses:

1) Have you encountered any advertisements about F1, heard about F1 on the radio, or seen ads posted in physical locations? If so, where?
   a) Respondent 1 stated, "I have seen F1 advertisements from youtube commercials and shopping at stores. Pacsuns were selling F1 branded clothing. I've also heard my dad who watches F1 religiously talk about it all the time"
   b) Respondent 2 stated, "Not really. I've heard other friends talk about it but I have never seen an ad about F1."
2) Have you heard or seen anyone mention the name "Lewis Hamilton," "Sebastian Vettel," or "Charles Leclerc"? If so, where?
   a) Respondent 5 stated, "I've heard these names somewhere before, either from a fashion brand or Tik Tok videos. I know the name Lewis Hamilton sounded familiar, I'm certain I saw it in a Tik Tok video once."
   b) Respondent 7 stated, "Yes, I've heard and seen Charles Leclerc too many times. I know Ferrari posts him on their social media on Instagram and Twitter."
3) Take something you are interested in, a sport or a music concert. Where would you want to see advertisements for their games or shows? EG: Tik Tok ads, YouTube Ads...
   a) Respondent 11 stated, "I'm into tennis so I hope to see shorter edits of matches or highlights on Tik Tok. Since I watch tennis matches already, I dont think a youtube ad will keep me away from continuing to watch. I just want to see highlights of good match points"
   b) Respondent 10 stated, "My friends talk about F1 a lot but I'm never that interested. Since I spend a lot of time on youtube, seeing ads that pop up there might be the most intuitive option for me"
4) What type of advertisements is most likely to attract your attention? Short and fast-paced? Long but descriptive? or "If it's in front of something I want to watch, please get it out of my face"?
   a) Respondent 6 stated, "All of the above I guess? I don't have a preference, but if the ad catches my eyes then I'd be more likely to not tune it out."
   b) Respondent 4 stated, "I like dramatic ads. Something that adds suspense like horror movie ads. Honestly anything that is different from all the happy bright ads I see all the time."
5) When browsing Netflix or YouTube and you come across a new show or video related to motorsports or F1 racing, would you be interested in clicking it and giving it a quick look?
   a) Respondent 15 stated, "I mean if I have time or I'm so bored. My parents talk about F1 so much, I might watch something so I have something to talk to them about."
   b) Respondent 13 stated, "Eh I don't know. My friends are into that stuff, and if an video has an interesting headline or the first few seconds can keep me from falling asleep I guess I would watch more."

The responses from the preliminary survey are categorized into groups through discourse analysis. This allows the researcher to examine how respondents reply based on different social contexts and different social backgrounds that surround individuals as a singular person. Thus, the researcher grouped them into unique groups that can be applied to the wider society. The 15 respondents are grouped into the following groups:

- **Group 1: High Exposure and Familiarity** - Respondents 1 and 5 makeup have been exposed to F1 prior to this experiment ranging from advertisements on YouTube, fashion brands, TikTok or word of mouth. Therefore, these respondents are more likely to have a higher interest in F1 races and become fans of the sport.

- **Group 2: Low Exposure, Familiar with Race Car Drivers Social Media** - Respondents 2 and 7 have heard of F1 racing through social media posts (Instagram and Twitter) from the Ferrari show and prompt drivers like Charles Leclerc. However, they have not encountered F1 advertisements on other media platforms and have very limited knowledge of F1 and its drivers. Hence these respondents who are only familiar with F1 drivers and have little to no interest in motorsports racing are less susceptible to watching an F1 race after viewing an F1 ad.

Franklin Education Foundation The Effectiveness of Motorsports Advertisements on Current Adolescent Race Fans Compared to New Adolescent Fans

Journal of Quantitative and Qualitative Research Chun Po Lee

- **Group 3: Moderate Exposure, Preference for TikTok and YouTube** - Respondents 10 and 11 express interest in viewing F1 advertisements on Tik Tok and YouTube. Suggesting these respondents have high exposure to F1 advertisements and are invested in the F1 content on these platforms, confirmed by their patterns of usage, making them more likely to watch an F1 race, after viewing the advertisement.

- **Group 4: Ad Preference for Attention-Grabbing Ads** - Respondents 4 and 6 express preferences for dramatic ads or ads that catch their attention. This suggests the respondents like the suspense and intrigue of racing and are likely to respond positively to the F1 advertisements, but will be flighty F1 fans.

- **Group 5: Moderate Interest, Limited Time Constraints** - Respondents 13 and 15 express moderate interest in F1 content but indicate they may only click on and engage with the content if they have time or if the content is interesting enough to keep their attention. Suggesting, these respondents will not actively seek out F1-related content but may engage with it out of convenience. Hence, these respondents are willing to race fans contingent on convenience.

Five of the respondents' statements were omitted in the final grouping. These respondents provided outlier answers that were strongly based on personal opinions against watching an F1 race completely. These outliers are beyond the measurable effectiveness of different F1 ads no matter the social situation and type of advertisement given. Discourse analysis allows for the open-ended questions to be applied to the understanding of preferences in the larger society of teens. Thus, it is conclusive that 26% of the teen population who are exposed to F1 racing and advertisements through social media will become racing fans. 13% of the teen population who are exposed to ads and social media demonstrate little interest in becoming an F1 fan. Finally, 26% of the teen population who are exposed to ads and social media will become fans based on specific preferences or conveniences.

The second part of the research was an advertisement survey consisting of 113 respondents. The respondents were separated into two groups. The first group consisted of current race fans with 55 respondents (48.7%) having prior motorsports or F1 knowledge. The second group consisted of non-race fans with 58 respondents (51.2%) who had no

prior exposure to F1 racing. There was equal representation for both measurable groups. Respondents were given a 1-10 response choice (1 least likely to watch and 10 most likely to watch) to the questions "How likely are you to watch an F1 race after looking at this advertisement?" and asked to choose how likely they are to watch a race based on the advertisement they just saw. The three forms of advertisements consisted of the Netflix-produced Drive to Survive (DTS), independently produced marketing from broadcasting groups like ESPN, Sports Star, SkyNews Sports, etc, and F1-produced marketing, consisting of promotional race films through social media. This gives a conclusive response to the overall research question "How effective are different types of advertisements on adolescent race fans compared to new fans." Since this is correlational research, the preliminary interview is done through qualitative analysis, and the second part of the advertisement survey is quantitative analysis.

The results from the survey are shown in the following pie charts.

Current race fans displayed the following data:

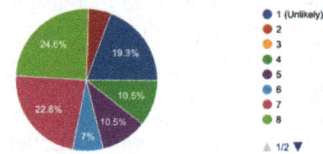

Figure 1.1

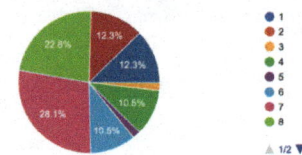

Figure 1.2

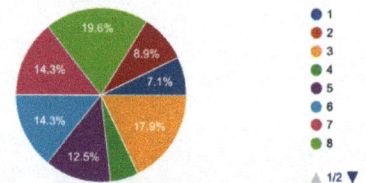

Figure 1.3

Figure 3.1

Figure 3.2

Figures 1.1, 1.2, and 1.3 show how likely a current race fan, with knowledge of racing, will watch an F1 race based on Drive to Survive (DTS) promotional materials. 3.1 is an image of the advertisement.

Figures 1.4, 1.5, and 1.6 show how likely a current race fan, with knowledge of racing, will watch an F1 race based on independent third-party (e.g. ESPN, Sports Star, SkyNews Sports) promotional materials. 3.2 is an image of the advertisement.

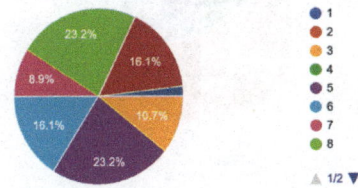

Figure 1.4

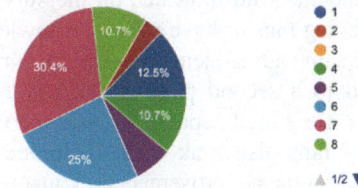

Figure 1.7

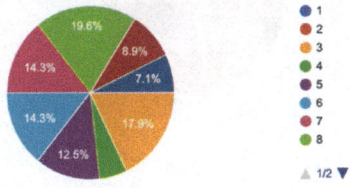

Figure 1.5

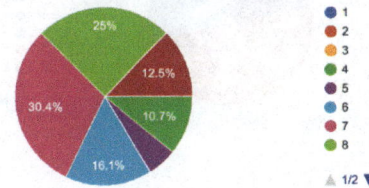

Figure 1.8

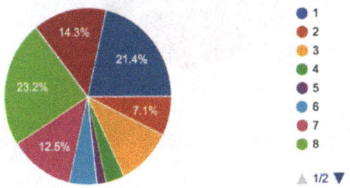

Figure 1.6

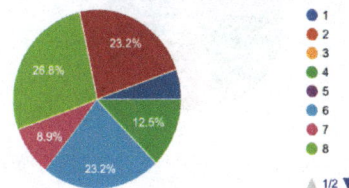

Figure 1.9

Figure 3.3

Figures 1.7, 1.8, and 1.9 show how likely a current race fan, with knowledge of racing, will watch an F1 race based on promotional material produced by Formula 1 itself. 3.3 is an image of the advertisement.

Respondents who indicated on the survey they were not current racing fans or have no prior knowledge of racing are given the same advertisement videos as current race fans but redirected to a second page of the survey so this group's responses are stored separately from the current race fans. Non-Race fans also rank their likelihood to watch an F1 race based on the advertisement they just watched on a scale of 1-10, 1 being unlikely and 10 being highly likely.

57 responses

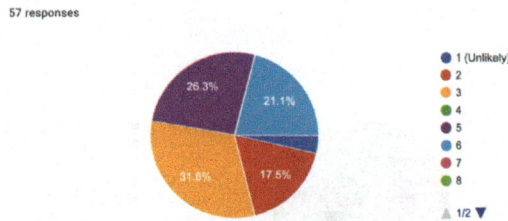

Figure 2.1

57 responses

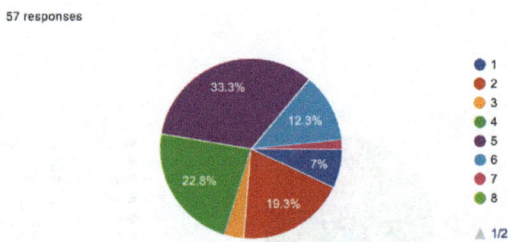

Figure 2.2

57 responses

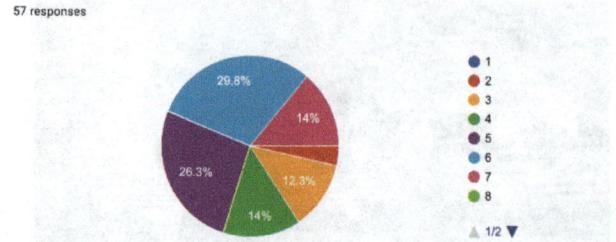

Figure 2.3

Figures 2.1, 2.2, and 2.3 show how likely a new race fan, with no knowledge of racing, will watch an F1 race based on Drive to Survive (DTS) promotional materials. Reference 3.1 for a screen capture of the advertisement

57 responses

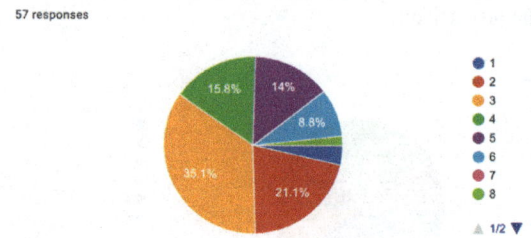

Figure 2.4

57 responses

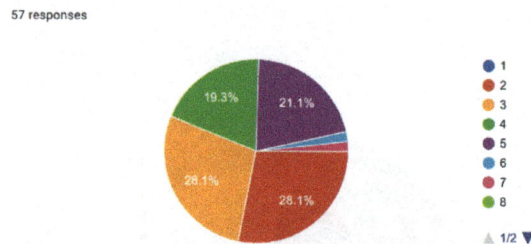

Figure 2.5

57 responses

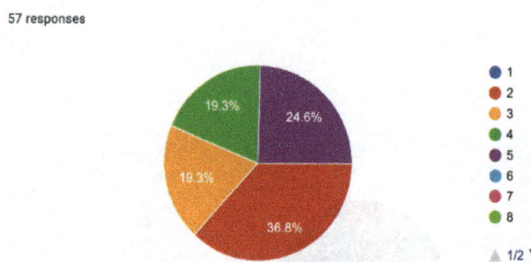

Figure 2.6

Figures 2.4, 2.5, and 2.6 show how likely a new fan, with no knowledge of racing, will watch an F1 race based on independent third-party (e.g. ESPN, Sports Star, SkyNews

Sports) promotional materials. Reference 3.2 for a screen capture of the advertisement.

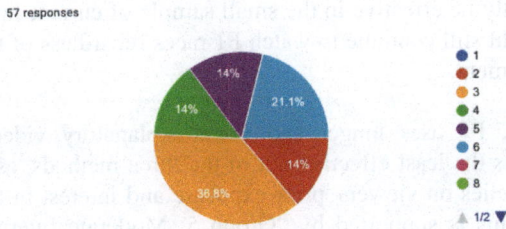

57 responses

Figure 2.7

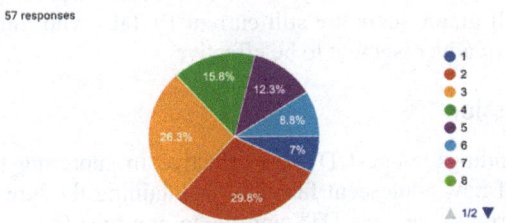

57 responses

Figure 2.8

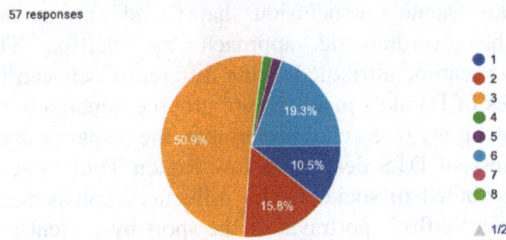

57 responses

Figure 2.9

Figures 2.7, 2.8, and 2.9 show how likely a current race fan, with no knowledge of racing, will watch an F1 race based on promotional material produced by Formula 1 itself. Reference 3.3 for a screen capture of the advertisement.

Cross-tabulation is effective in analyzing comparisons between current race fans and non-race fans and their preference for different marketing approaches. Respondents were given 3 videos from each category of advertisements, with 9 videos in total, and they were asked to select the likelihood to watch F1 races after viewing the video on a scale of 1-10. Next, a cross-tabulation comparison of the data was used to identify the preferences for the 9 videos between the race fan group and non-race fan group. Initially, a pie chart was created to identify the frequency of each number from 1-10 on the likelihood of watching F1 races.

Then, with this data, a T-chart was created to compare the frequency of each number based on the race fan group and non-race fan group. Ultimately, with the data from the T-chart, a bar graph was created to illustrate the likelihood of choosing each number between the two groups.

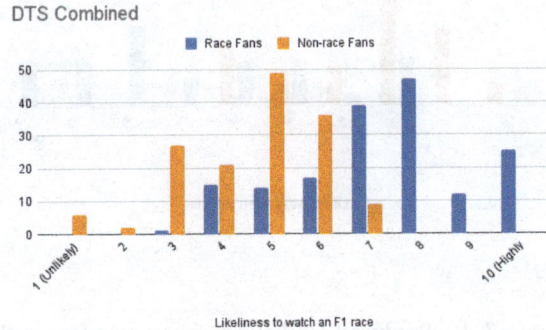

Figure 6.1

When examining the data presented in Figure 6.1, Netflix produced a DTS advertisement, which shows that race fans most frequently chose 8, with the majority of the responses distributed above 5. However, non-race fans chose 5 as their most frequent response with no respondents choosing above 7. A line of best fit, which connects the most frequent answer choice from both groups, shows that the majority of responses fall within a small range of 5 to 8 resulting in a positive skew and low standard deviation.

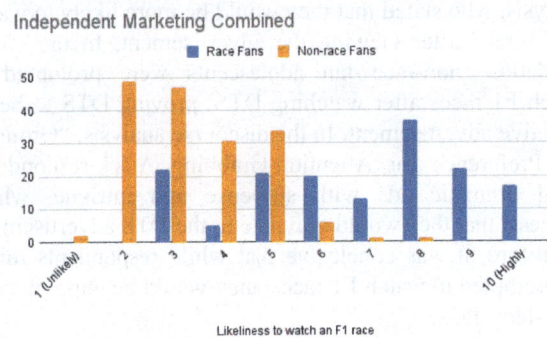

Figure 6.2

Moving on to Figure 6.2, Independent Marketing, race fans most frequently chose 8 but have a more distributed deviation of answers. Non-race fans responded similarly but most frequently chose 2 with a wide distribution all the way up to 8. All frequent points would range from 2 to 8, creating a high negative and high positive distribution at both ends of the graph. This pattern results in a high range and high standard deviation.

163

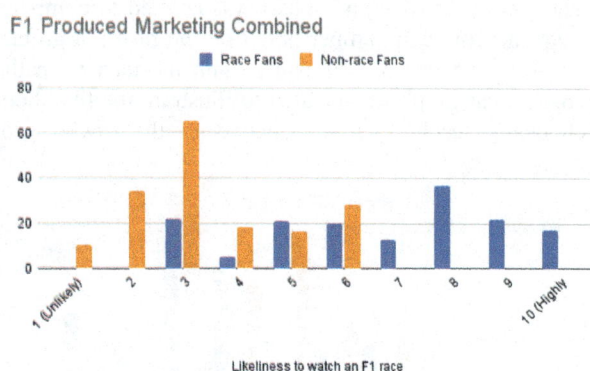

Figure 6.3

Figure 6.3, F1-Produced Marketing, shows race fans with a wide distribution of responses from 3 to 10 and most frequently choosing 8. Non-race fans most frequently chose 3 with no respondents choosing above 6. This creates a negative skew on the combined graph, resulting in a low standard deviation towards a negative skew and a high range.

The discourse analysis with the cross-tabulation rendered the cross-examining of the results. When it comes to current adolescent race fans, DTS is the most effective marketing approach, supported by "Group 3- Moderate Exposure, Preference for TikTok and YouTube" from the discourse analysis, who stated that they would be more likely to watch an F1 race after viewing the advertisement. In the cross-tabulation, non-race fan adolescents were prompted to watch F1 races after watching DTS, proving DTS to be an effective advertisement. In the discourse analysis, "Group 4: Ad Preference for Attention-Grabbing Ads" respondents liked dramatic ads with suspense and intrigue, which suggests that they would gravitate to the DTS advertisement. Therefore, it was conclusive that while respondents might be prompted to watch F1 races, they would be unpredictable long-term fans.

Independently produced marketing appears in shorter forms, making it more common on TikTok and YouTube ads like those mentioned in "Group 3: Moderate Exposure, Preference for TikTok and YouTube." These viewers are more likely to come across these ads while browsing social media, but there is a wide variety of effects as seen in the cross-tabulation analysis. Furthermore, independently produced marketing is also less effective than DTS. The cross-tabulation data suggest that independently produced advertisements are only effective for current race fans to be prompted to continue watching F1 races. Therefore, independently produced marketing heavily relies on

respondents' prior exposure to F1 content in order to capture their attention. Hence, independently produced marketing is less effective on the general adolescent population and would only be effective in the small sample of current fans, who might still continue to watch F1 races regardless of the advertisement.

Lastly, F1 uses longer and more explanatory videos, hence it is the least effective out of the three methods, as it heavily relies on viewers' prior exposure and interest in the sports. This is supported by "Group 5: Moderate Interest, Limited Time Constraints" in the discourse analysis, as respondents are willing to look at F1 ads if it does not take up too much time. However, F1-produced ads rely on previous exposure to build on the respondents' interests. While cross-tabulation analysis shows a negative skew for the overall graph, there are still current F1 fans who found this form of advertisement to be effective.

7. Discussion

The findings suggest DTS is effective in capturing the interest of new adolescent fans and maintaining the lure of F1 for current race fans. DTS appeals to non-race fans with its attention-grabbing elements and reality show-like production. DTS also appeals to current race fans, contrary to Marieke Danne's conclusion that found current fans dislike the overdramatic approach by Netflix. This discrepancy can be attributed to the difference between the preferences of Danne's more mature group compared to the adolescents in my research. Furthermore, the disparity in the effectiveness of DTS despite its low Rotten Tomato score can be attributed to social media influences and personal bias against Netflix's portrayal of the sport by current race fans, causing the show's low ratings. Overall, adolescent race fans and non-race fans agree that DTS is the most effective form of advertisement out of the three advertisements (DTS, independent marketing, and F1-produced promotional videos). The fact that adolescents found DTS to be compelling is a good sign for F1 and other motor racing series, suggesting that this niche sport is slowly gaining popularity. Ultimately, adolescents' preference for DTS as the primary advertisement motivating them to watch F1 is enlightening and contrary to known research, paving out a new direction that marketing teams need to explore to grab the attention of adolescents. The data collected will be invaluable for future marketing campaigns, not only for F1 but also for other motorsports like NASCAR, Indy Car, and Le-Mans, which are growing in size and popularity but lack data on how to capture the attention of the younger teen audience. Having the understanding of how to attract viewers from an early age will increase the likelihood that the racing series will gain

Franklin Education Foundation   The Effectiveness of Motorsports Advertisements on Current Adolescent Race Fans Compared to New Adolescent Fans

Journal of Quantitative and Qualitative Research   Chun Po Lee

lifelong fans, who can generate revenues for the series by watching races for much longer than a mature audience.

While the research closed the gap in the literature with new data on adolescents that were not present before and provided contrary results to other researchers' projects, there were some limitations to this research. First, the interview was limited to five questions with a small sample size; the results might not reflect the preferences of the overall adolescent population. Open-ended questions and disclosure analysis allow for a more comprehensive explanation of adolescent preferences for ads and where they might see them. Thus, more comprehensive research with a larger sample size of interview respondents could have yielded more specific and detailed groups through discourse analysis. Furthermore, digital media has a significant influence over adolescents but is not seen as an official form of "advertisement" for the F1 series, and it was therefore not measured in this study. Future research should address these limitations and explore the personal context influencing adolescents to watch F1 races.

Overall, the current study provides data and insights into the preferences of teenage audiences and measures the effectiveness of current motorsports' advertisements. The results close a gap in research on adolescent preferences for advertisements compared to the current data on the preferences of more mature race fans. It is time for motorsports to make their mark in history as a mainstream sport like football; taking the time and effort to research effective means of advertisements will be the first step towards this goal.

1. "Advertising: How It Influences Children and Teenagers," Raising Children Network, October 12, 2022, 1.

2. Paulsen, "Viewership on the Rise for NASCAR, IndyCar and F1," (Sports Media Watch, June 16, 2022), 2.

3. F1, "Formula 1 Reveals Details of Fan Segmentation Research," Formula 1 (Formula 1, July 3, 2018),1.

4. F1, "Formula 1 Reveals Details of Fan Segmentation Research," Formula 1 (Formula 1, July 3, 2018), 1.

5. Maury Brown, "ESPN Poised to Have the Highest U.S. Formula 1 Viewership, Ever," Forbes (Forbes Magazine, April 14, 2022), 1.

6. Bruce Schoenfeld, "'Drive to Survive' Made Americans Fall in Love with Formula 1," The New York Times (The New York Times, July 14, 2022), 1.

7. Andrew Gamble, "F1's Netflix Drive to Survive Ratings Plummet since 2019," Express.co.uk (Express.co.uk, March 31, 2022), 1.

8. Marieke Danne, "How Do Fans Perceive Authenticity in the Netflix Documentary Series 'Drive to Survive'?,"1.

9. Alain Pinsonneault and Kenneth L. Kraemer, "Survey Research Methodology in Management Information Systems: An Assessment," Journal of Management Information Systems 10, no. 2 (1993), 4.

10. Heather Wojton, Jonathan Snavely, and Justin Mary, "Introduction to Survey Design" (Institute for Defense Analyses, 2016), 6.

Appendix A

The information you will share with us if you participate in this study will be kept completely confidential to the full extent of the law. Participating in this study may not benefit you directly, but it will help us learn the effect of F1 advertisements.
- Yes, I consent
- No, I do not consent

Appendix B

After watching this short clip, on a scale of 1-10 how interested are you in F1? (DTS) *

○ 1 (Unlikely)
○ 2
○ 3
○ 4
○ 5
○ 6
○ 7
○ 8
○ 9
○ 10

8. Reference

[1] "Advertising: How It Influences Children and Teenagers." Raising Children Network, October 12, 2022. https://raisingchildren.net.au/toddlers/play-learning/screen-time-media/advertising-children.

[2] "TV Viewers of Formula One (F1) Worldwide 2021." Statista, March 14, 2022. https://www.statista.com/statistics/480129/cable-or-broadcast-tv-networks-formula-one-f1-racing-watched-within-the-last-12-months-usa/.

[3] Blake, Aaron. "Three Tiers of Sponsorship: Breaking down NASCAR's Sponsor Process." Front Office Sports, August 7, 2020. https://frontofficesports.com/three-tiers-of-sponsorship-breaking-down-nascars-sponsor-process/.

[4] Brown, Maury. "ESPN Poised to Have the Highest U.S. Formula 1 Viewership, Ever." Forbes. Forbes Magazine, April 14, 2022. https://www.forbes.com/sites/maurybrown/2022/04/01/espn-poised-to-have-the-highest-us-formula-1-viewership-ever/?sh=4766e03617a2.

[5] Danne, Marieke. "How Do Fans Perceive Authenticity in the Netflix Documentary Series 'Drive to Survive'?" Simple search, 2022. http://www.diva-portal.org/smash/search.jsf.

[6] Engle, Greg. "Most Recent Formula 1 Financials Seem to Show Motorsports Recovering Nicely." Forbes. Forbes Magazine, August 8, 2021. https://www.forbes.com/sites/gregengle/2021/08/08/most-recent-formula-1-financials-seem-to-show-motorsports-recovering-nicely/?sh=40182c4c265e.

[7] F1. "Formula 1 Reveals Details of Fan Segmentation Research." Formula 1. Formula 1, July 3, 2018. https://www.formula1.com/en/latest/article.formula-1-reveals-details-of-fan-segmentation-research.19u9fkhcB8cOocIwAacuow.html.

[8] Gamble, Andrew. "F1's Netflix Drive to Survive Ratings Plummet Since 2019." Express.co.uk. Express.co.uk, March 31, 2022. https://www.express.co.uk/sport/f1-autosport/1589182/F1-Netflix-Drive-to-Survive-ratings-plummet-2019-F1-news.

[9] Hallett, Lewis. "Motorsport Insights: How Effective Is F1 Sponsorship for a Brand?" National Motorsport Academy, November 12, 2021. https://motorsport.nda.ac.uk/news/the-power-of-sponsorship-in-f1/.

[10] Olmstead, Christopher. "NASCAR: Analyzing the Five Types of Fans in the Sport Today." FOX Sports. FOX Sports, March 4, 2020. https://www.foxsports.com/stories/nascar/nascar-analyzing-the-five-types-of-fans-in-the-sport-today.

[11] Paulsen. "Viewership on the Rise for NASCAR, IndyCar and F1." Sports Media Watch, June 16, 2022. https://www.sportsmediawatch.com/2022/06/nascar-ratings-fox-fs1-viewership-indycar-nbcsn-f1-espn-increase/.

[12] Pinsonneault, Alain, and Kenneth L. Kraemer. "Survey Research Methodology in Management Information Systems: An Assessment." *Journal of Management Information Systems* 10, no. 2 (1993): 75–105. http://www.jstor.org/stable/40398056.

[13] Schoenfeld, Bruce. "'Drive to Survive' Made Americans Fall in Love with Formula 1." The New York Times. The New York Times, July 14, 2022. https://www.nytimes.com/2022/07/14/magazine/formula-1-miami-drive-to-survive.html.

[14] Warner, Stanley L. "Randomized Response: A Survey Technique for Eliminating Evasive Answer Bias." *Journal of the American Statistical Association* 60, no. 309 (1965): 63–69. https://doi.org/10.2307/2283137.

[15] Wojton, Heather, Jonathan Snavely, and Justin Mary. "Introduction to Survey Design." Institute for Defense Analyses, 2016. http://www.jstor.org/stable/resrep22713.

[16] Wolkin, Joseph. "USA Network's New NASCAR Docuseries Aims to Compete with 'Drive to Survive'." Forbes. Forbes Magazine, September 2, 2022. https://www.forbes.com/sites/josephwolkin/2022/09/01/usa-networks-new-nascar-docuseries-aims-to-compete-with-drive-to-survive/?sh=83a488320acc.

Using SVM Analysis to Compare the Relative Importance of Unemployment on Technology Stocks and Retail Stocks

Using SVM Analysis to Compare the Relative Importance of Unemployment on Technology Stocks and Retail Stocks

Jiuxi Wang

Abstract

Unemployment is one of the most important macroeconomic indicators for performing stock price forecastings. Previous research found an inverse correlation between unemployment and the price of major stock indexes, but a research gap exists in comparing the impact of unemployment on the stock prices of various industries. This leads to the research question of this study: How does the impact of unemployment on the stock price of retail companies compare to its impact on the stock price of technology companies?

To examine the difference in unemployment's impact on the stock prices of technology companies and retail companies, a binary classification machine learning model using the SVM algorithm was created.

Out of the 8 features used in the study, unemployment was ranked at 6th for technology companies and 4th for retail companies. It was concluded that unemployment holds a more significant impact over the stock prices of retail companies than that of technology companies.

Keywords: Unemployment, Stock Prices, Technology Companies, Retail Companies, Feature Importance

Franklin Education Foundation   Using SVM Analysis to Compare the Relative Importance of Unemployment on Technology Stocks and Retail Stocks

Journal of Quantitative and Qualitative Research   Jiuxi Wang

1. Introduction

In the 21st century economy, stocks are closely tied to the welfare of the market and the wealth of consumers. According to the 2019 Survey of Consumer Finances, 53% of all American families hold possessions of publicly traded stocks in some form, a 21% increase from 1989 (Bhutta et.al 2020). It is therefore unsurprising that stock prices show a positive correlation with economic growth. In general, the performance of stocks are influenced by macroeconomic factors such as the federal interest rate, gross domestic product (GDP), Consumer Price Index (CPI), and inflation (e.g., Khan and Zaman 2012). One significant macroeconomic indicator in financial analysis is the unemployment rate, which measures the number of people in the workforce that are not employed and are actively looking for employment.

A high unemployment rate can negatively impact both company productivity and profits. When per-capita income drops, consumers typically spend less, ultimately weakening economic output. For open economies such as the United States, consumer spending comprised 67.9% of aggregate demand in quarter 4 of 2022 (FRED 2023). A decrease in consumption will result in a decrease in demand for consumer products. In addition, when unemployment rates are high, consumers invest less in stocks, and the decline in the demand for stocks further lowers stock prices. These considerations predict an inverse relationship between unemployment rate and stock prices, which indeed is confirmed by empirical studies that find a negative correlation (e.g., Esipov 2010).

From an investment perspective, unemployment data holds predictive power. In this age of data analysis, the Bureau of Labor Statistics publishes monthly unemployment data to all investors. By utilizing this short-term metric, investors can attempt to predict the trajectory of the economy in the near future. Unemployment's predictive power extends to the stock market as its effectiveness for predicting two kinds of return—aggregate and cross-sectional—last 36 months and 24 months, respectively (Khan and Zaman 2012). Thus, unemployment can be a significant factor in forecast modeling and in investors' decisions for purchasing or selling a stock.

2. Literary Review

As one of the main macroeconomic factors that influence the economy, unemployment impacts the stock market, and its effects have been examined by multiple studies. In a 2016 business research journal from the Clute Institute, Francisco Jareño and Loredana Negrut tested macroeconomic factors' correlation with the U.S. stock market. Jareño and Negrut used the Dow Jones Index, a portfolio that consists of one share of the 30 largest blue chip companies, to analyze the companies that held the most market power. Jareño and Negrut found an inverse relationship between unemployment and stock prices (Figure 1).

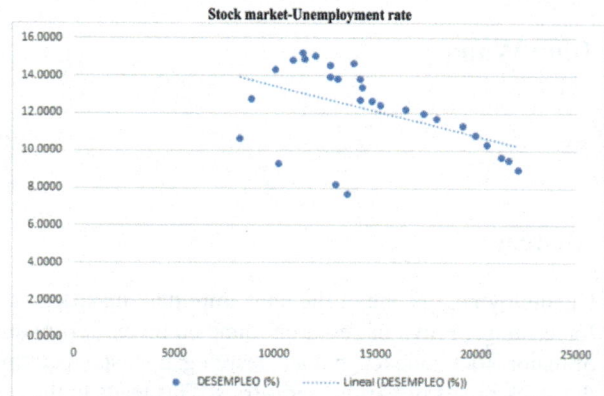

Figure 1: Graph of quarterly unemployment rate (Desempleo) in percentage against the price of the Dow Jones index (Jareño and Negrut 2016)

Negrut and Jareño measured the unemployment rate to have a "negative and statistically significant" (p-value 0.01) correlation with the price of the Dow Jones Index (Jareño and Negrut 2016). Thus, lower values of unemployment are associated with high prices of stock indexes. However, from an investor's perspective, this relationship is not bilateral. In a 2017 study, Pan performed a Granger causality test to examine the causal relationship between unemployment data and stock prices. A strong Granger causality is found from unemployment to stock prices as lagged values of unemployment are significant in predicting stock prices. This indicates that unemployment is helpful in predicting stock prices (Pan 2017). In comparison, the casual relationship from stock prices to unemployment is not significant. In a 2020 University of Calabria and Bonn University study, Algieri et al. confirmed that a Granger causality does not exist from stock prices to unemployment; the reverse causal relationship does exist from stock prices to unemployment, which is in agreement with the result of Pan's study (Algieri at el 2020). This one-way causal relationship from unemployment to stock prices means that investors should only use unemployment to predict stock prices and not vice versa.

Furthermore, studies conducted show how the expectedness of unemployment can change the outcome of a stock price forecast. In a 2005 finance journal from *The*

American Finance Association, Bernanke and Kuttner argue that unanticipated unemployment will negatively impact stock prices. As an increase in unemployment leads to a lower level of consumption, companies' balance sheets are negatively affected, resulting in a decrease in stock prices (Bernanke and Kuttner 2005). The negative consequences of unexpectedly high unemployment on stock prices are also supported by a 2021 University of California Berkeley study on unanticipated unemployment news' impact on the stock market. David Chi found that news about unanticipated unemployment led to fear among investors, which temporarily sent stock prices downward (Chi 2021). In contrast, anticipated unemployment can positively impact the stock market. The unemployment rate can be used to predict the interest rate, which can in turn be used for predicting stock prices. When the anticipated unemployment rate rises, the Federal Reserve lowers the interest rate. In a 2005 National Bureau of Economic Research study, Boyd et al found information about the interest rate to "dominate" the trend of the stock market (Boyd et al 2005). With lower interest rates, investors move money deposited in banks to buy stocks, resulting in an increase in stock prices. Anticipated unemployment will raise stock prices as it will lead to lower interest rates (Gonzalo and Taamouti 2017). Despite the difference caused by the unexpectedness of unemployment data, ultimately the general unemployment rate is more significant for financial analysis. By definition, the general unemployment rate is the combination of unanticipated and anticipated unemployment. Thus, the general unemployment rate's negative correlation with stock prices is more significant and can be utilized in predictions as it is reflective of the economic landscape.

Although a general conclusion can be made about the unemployment rate's inverse relationship with the price of major stock indexes, only a minimal number of studies have been conducted in examining the relationship between unemployment and the stock price of specific industries. One important result was obtained by John Osiemo, a graduate student at the University of Phoenix, who in 2016 examined the correlation between unemployment and the price of retail company stocks in Texas. Osiemo (2016) utilized the Pearson Correlation and factorial Analysis of Variance (ANOVA) to test the correlation, finding that unemployment is inversely related to the stock prices of retail companies in Texas (with a p-value of 0.01, sufficient to reject the null hypothesis of no relationship).

With recent advances in computing technology, financial studies increasingly incorporate support vector machine (SVM) analysis, which is a form of supervised machine learning. The objective of the support vector machine is to create a line or choice limit in n-dimensional space ("hyperplane") that can optimally separate labeled classes so that new data points can be allocated to the different classes with ease. The SVM picks the focuses and vectors that make the hyperplane, which are known as support vectors (Zoppis et al. 2019). In a 2007 California State University San Bernardino study, Shuo Han and Rung-Ching Chen tested the accuracy of using financial statements with support vector machine analysis when predicting the trend of stock prices. By inputting components of a financial statement such as Earnings Per Share (EPS), Book Value Per Share (BVPS), and Net Profit Growth Rate (NPGR) into their support vector machine analysis, Han and Chen achieved a higher accuracy in predicting the trend of stock prices than when they used raw support vector machine analysis to predict stock trends. Han and Chen conclude that the usage of financial indicators in performing support vector machine analysis will yield more accurate and promising stock price forecastings (Han and Chen 2007).

In a 2013 study, a marketing researcher at Sun Yat-sen University Zhen Hu et al used a support vector machine that incorporated the unemployment rate and other macroeconomic indicators to predict the trend of price change in stocks. The study utilized six macroeconomic factors in their support vector machine: consumer spending, consumer investment, unemployment rate, inflation rate, federal funds rate, and the price of the Dow Jones Index. 15 companies were randomly selected to create the samples for the study, with the focus on the time range from 1995 to 2002. In aggregate, this random selection created a total of 88 unique company-year observations. After creating the sample data, 10 stocks out of the data set were selected at random, with the remaining 78 company-year observations used as training data. Based on the macroeconomic indicators inputted, the support vector machine attempted to split the cluster of data into two sections: good investment and poor investment. A stock was classified as a good investment if its price rose over a given year while it was classified as a poor investment if its price did not rise over a given year. For the testing sample of 10 stocks, Hu at el's support vector machine demonstrated a classification accuracy of 70%, leading them to conclude that inputting macroeconomic factors such as unemployment into a support vector machine can yield satisfactory predictions when examining stock market trends (Zhu et al. 2013).

2.1 Research Gap and Hypothesis

While the aforementioned studies demonstrate a strong inverse relationship between unemployment and the stock prices of major stock indexes, and this negative correlation is also seen between unemployment and retail stocks in Texas, there is a research gap in comparing the impact of unemployment on the stock prices of various industries. More specifically, there appears to be no research that compares the impact of unemployment on the stock price of industry-leading retail companies and the stock price of industry-leading tech companies. In the previously mentioned studies, analysis was conducted on indexes without comparison between different industries. In my opinion, analysis on entire indexes cannot accurately reflect the correlation that unemployment has with the stock price of specific industries. For most of the studies mentioned above, the Standard and Poor's 500 and the Dow Jones Index are used for analysis. The S&P 500 is a stock market index that includes the 500 largest companies traded in the U.S stock market; the Dow Jones Index is a portfolio that contains the 30 largest blue chip companies that are traded in the New York Stock Exchange and Nasdaq. Due to how these indexes are formulated, analyzing them cannot present the correlation between unemployment and the stock price of specific industries as these indexes include stocks from multiple industries. When a significant change occurs in the unemployment rate, some stocks in the S&P 500 and Dow Jones Index could be more impacted than others, but this impact is not reflected, as the S&P 500 and Dow Jones Index are aggregate sums of these stocks.

In this experiment, I hypothesized that unemployment will have a greater impact on the stock price of retail companies than technology companies. This hypothesis leads to the guiding question of my research: How does the impact of unemployment on the stock price of retail companies compare to its impact on the stock price of technology companies? To answer my research question, I focused my study on unemployment's importance to price changes in stocks of four technology companies (Apple, Google, Microsoft, International Business Machines) and four retail companies (Walmart, Target, Kohl's Corporation, Amazon). Using Python programming language, I created a support vector machine algorithm that analyzes the feature importance of unemployment in determining the price change of the four retail company stocks and the four technology company stocks among a selected group of macroeconomic indicators (further explained in the Methodology section). By comparing the feature importance of unemployment in determining the price change of retail company stocks and technology company stocks, the difference between the relative importance of unemployment's impact on each industry's stock prices can be derived, thus providing a possible conclusion about which industry's stock prices unemployment has a greater impact on, and the degree of the difference in that impact.

3. Methodology

The technology sector and retail sector are suitable for this study due to their weight in the U.S economy. According to Yahoo Finance and Investopedia, the retail industry and technology industry are among the top 10 in terms of revenue, indicating that they are among the most significant industries for investors (Yahoo! Finance 2022). Employment in the technology sector and retail sector are vastly different. Under the International Standard Classification of Occupations (ISCO-08), retail workers are considered skill level 2, which requires a high school diploma or an associate degree. In comparison, technology workers are considered level 3, which requires a bachelor's degree and procedural knowledge in a specialized field. Thus, the comparison of unemployment's effects on the tech sector and its effects on the retail sector is reflective of unemployment's effects on high-skill industries versus low-skill industries. The companies selected are split into two groups: technology and retail. Stocks in the technology company section include Apple (AAPL), Google (GOOGL), The International Business Machines Corporation (IBM), and Microsoft (MSFT). All four stocks hold great market power as they are all among the top 30 largest U.S. tech companies in market cap (CompaniesMarketCap.com 2023). Stocks in the retail company section include Walmart (WMT), Target (TGT), Kohl's Corporation (KSS), and Amazon (AMZN). According to the Top 100 Retailers 2022 list created by the National Retail Federation, these four stocks also hold significant market power as they are ranked in the top 30 for revenue (NRF 2022). All the companies selected for the technology company section and the retail company section hold a significant share of market power, making fluctuations in their stock prices less likely to influence insignificant changes in unemployment levels. This concurs with Jareño and Negrut's criteria of analyzing companies with "more weight in the country" (Jareño and Negrut 2016).

3.1 Collecting Macroeconomic Indicators Data

The first step in building the model is gathering macroeconomic indicators data. To keep comparisons uniform, only data that starts between January of 1980 and November of 2022 is used for all macroeconomic indicators data.

3.1.1 Unemployment data

Seasonally adjusted monthly unemployment rate data is taken from the U.S. Bureau of Labor Statistics and uploaded into the model as a csv file (BLS 2023). The data is in the form of percentage and is rounded to the hundredth decimal

(Table 1).

	A	B
1	Date	Rate
2	1-Nov-22	3.70%
3	1-Oct-22	3.70%
4	1-Sep-22	3.50%
5	1-Aug-22	3.70%
6	1-Jul-22	3.50%
7	1-Jun-22	3.60%
8	1-May-22	3.60%
9	1-Apr-22	3.60%
10	1-Mar-22	3.60%
11	1-Feb-22	3.80%
12	1-Jan-22	4.00%

Table 1: Sample Data

This table shows a portion of the seasonally adjusted monthly unemployment rate

3.1.2 Federal Funds Rate

The non-seasonally adjusted monthly Federal Funds Effective Rate is imported from the Federal Reserve Bank of St. Louis' database and uploaded into the model as a csv file (FRED 2023). The data is the form of percentage and is rounded to the hundredth decimal (Table 2).

1980-01-01	13.82
1980-02-01	14.13
1980-03-01	17.19
1980-04-01	17.61
1980-05-01	10.98
1980-06-01	9.47
1980-07-01	9.03
1980-08-01	9.61
1980-09-01	10.87
1980-10-01	12.81
1980-11-01	15.85
1980-12-01	18.9

Table 2: Sample Data

This table shows a portion of the federal funds rate data

3.1.3 United States Monthly Coincident Economic Activity Index (USPHCI)

The seasonally adjusted monthly United States Coincident Economic Activity Index is imported from the Federal Reserve Bank of St. Louis' database and uploaded into the model as a csv file (FRED 2023). The data is in index form and is rounded to the hundredth decimal (Table 3).

1980-01-01	46.76
1980-02-01	46.86
1980-03-01	46.93
1980-04-01	46.84
1980-05-01	46.69
1980-06-01	46.61
1980-07-01	46.51
1980-08-01	46.59
1980-09-01	46.69
1980-10-01	46.81
1980-11-01	46.94
1980-12-01	47.13

Table 3: Sample Data

This table shows a portion of the federal funds rate data

3.1.4 Delinquency Rate on Consumer Loans, All Commercial Banks (DRCLACBS)

The seasonally adjusted quarterly delinquency rate on consumer loans is imported from the Federal Reserve Bank of St. Louis' database and uploaded into the model as a csv file (FRED 2023). For every monthly data point to have a delinquency rate value, the quarterly delinquency rate is used for all months of the quarter. The data is in the form of percentage and is rounded to the hundredth decimal (Table 4).

Franklin Education Foundation   Using SVM Analysis to Compare the Relative Importance of Unemployment on Technology Stocks and Retail Stocks

Journal of Quantitative and Qualitative Research   Jiuxi Wang

DATE	DRCLACBS
1987-01-01	3.35
1987-04-01	3.28
1987-07-01	3.29
1987-10-01	3.31

Table 4: Sample Data

This table shows a portion of the delinquency on consumer loans data

3.1.5 Chicago Board Options Exchange, CBOE Volatility Index: VIX (VIXCLS)

The non-seasonally adjusted daily Chicago Board Options Exchange Volatility Index is imported from the Federal Reserve Bank of St. Louis' database and uploaded into the model as a csv file (FRED 2023). For every monthly data point to have a VIXCLS value, the daily VIXCLS Index values are averaged over a monthly basis. This is attained by

Monthly VIXCLS value = sum of daily VIXCLS value over a certain month divided by number of days of that certain month.

The data is in index form and is rounded to the hundredth decimal (Table 5).

DATE	VIXCLS
1990-01-02	17.24
1990-01-03	18.19
1990-01-04	19.22
1990-01-05	20.11
1990-01-08	20.26
1990-01-09	22.2
1990-01-10	22.44
1990-01-11	20.05
1990-01-12	24.64
1990-01-15	26.34
1990-01-16	24.18
1990-01-17	24.16
1990-01-18	24.34
1990-01-19	22.5
1990-01-22	26.7
1990-01-23	24.72
1990-01-24	25.39
1990-01-25	25.63
1990-01-26	26.28
1990-01-29	26.44
1990-01-30	27.25
1990-01-31	25.36

Table 5: Sample Data

This table shows a portion of the daily CBOE Volatility Index

3.1.6 Market Yield on U.S. Treasury Securities at 10-Year Constant Maturity, Quoted on an Investment Basis (DGS10)

The daily non-seasonally adjusted market yield on U.S. Treasury Securities at 10-year constant maturity is imported from the Federal Reserve Bank of St. Louis' database and uploaded into the model as a csv file (FRED 2023). For every monthly data point to have a DGS10 value, the daily

DGS10 values are averaged over a monthly basis. This is attained by

Monthly DGS10 Value = sum of daily market yield percentage of a certain month divided by number of days of that certain month.

This data is in percentage form and is significant to the hundredth decimal (Table 6).

1980-01-02	10.5
1980-01-03	10.6
1980-01-04	10.66
1980-01-07	10.63
1980-01-08	10.57
1980-01-09	10.58
1980-01-10	10.51
1980-01-11	10.68
1980-01-14	10.7
1980-01-15	10.65
1980-01-16	10.65
1980-01-17	10.71
1980-01-18	10.82
1980-01-21	10.96
1980-01-22	10.85
1980-01-23	10.82
1980-01-24	11.01
1980-01-25	11.1
1980-01-28	11.15
1980-01-29	11.21
1980-01-30	11.16
1980-01-31	11.13

Table 6: Sample Data

This table shows a portion of the market yield on 10-year U.S. Treasury Bonds

3.1.7 Standard and Poor's 500 (S&P500)

The daily S&P 500 price is imported from Yahoo! Finance and uploaded into the model as a csv file (Yahoo! Finance 2023). For every monthly data point to have a S&P 500 value, the daily S&P 500 values are averaged over a monthly basis. This is attained by

Monthly S&P 500 price = sum of daily S&P 500 price over a certain month divided by number of days of that certain month.

The data is in index form and is rounded to the hundredth decimal (Table 7).

1/7/1980	106.8
1/4/1980	106.5
1/3/1980	105.2
1/2/1980	105.8
1/1/1980	107.9

Table 7: Sample Data

This table shows a portion of the S&P 500 Index

3.2 Additional Features

Aside from the seven macroeconomic indicators listed in the section above, two additional features are used during the process of evaluating feature importance. The first feature is the percentage change of a selected stock's price between the previous month and two months prior. This feature is measured in percentage and is attained by

Percent stock price change =

$$\frac{(previous\ monthly\ average\ stock\ price - monthly\ average\ stock\ price\ two\ months\ ago)}{previous\ monthly\ average\ stock\ price} \times 100$$

This feature is selected because, according to a study from the Jaypee Institute Of Information Technology, previous stock prices are efficient for predicting future prices (Vijh et al. 2020). The second feature added is the percentage change of S&P 500's price between the previous month and two months ago. This feature is measured in percentage and is attained through the equation

Percent S&P 500 price change =

$$\frac{(previous\ monthly\ average\ S\&P\ 500\ price - monthly\ average\ S\&P\ 500\ price\ two\ months\ ago)}{previous\ monthly\ average\ S\&P\ 500\ price} \times 100$$

This feature is selected due to the S&P 500's ability to reflect the trend of the economy.

3.3 Uploading Stock Price

The stock prices for all ten companies are downloaded from Yahoo! Finance. For companies whose stocks were publicly traded before 1980, the data is cut to fit the time range of January 1980 to November 2022. For companies whose stocks began to be publicly traded after 1980, the data ranges from their start date to November of 2022. All stock prices used are monthly opening prices and are downloaded from Yahoo! Finance. The use of opening price is justified by Vijh's study, as he concluded that opening prices hold predictive power in forecasting future stock prices (Vijh et al. 2020). All stock data exported are in the csv format. A sample of each company's stock prices is displayed below.

Date	Open
1997-06-01	0.075521
1997-07-01	0.077083
1997-08-01	0.117188
1997-09-01	0.117188
1997-10-01	0.221875
1997-11-01	0.260938
1997-12-01	0.211979

Table 8: Amazon Stock Price (AMZN)

Date	Open
1985-01-01	0.130022
1985-02-01	0.129464
1985-03-01	0.110491
1985-04-01	0.098772
1985-05-01	0.094866
1985-06-01	0.075893
1985-07-01	0.080915
1985-08-01	0.070871
1985-09-01	0.066964
1985-10-01	0.070313
1985-11-01	0.083147
1985-12-01	0.089844

Table 9: Apple Stock Price (AAPL)

Date	Open
2004-09-01	2.557912
2004-10-01	3.257789
2004-11-01	4.820681
2004-12-01	4.531764
2005-01-01	4.916571

Table 10: Google Stock Price (GOOGL)

174

Franklin Education Foundation   Using SVM Analysis to Compare the Relative Importance of Unemployment on Technology Stocks and Retail Stocks

Journal of Quantitative and Qualitative Research   Jiuxi Wang

1980-01-01	15.057361
1980-02-01	16.40177
1980-03-01	15.176864
1980-04-01	13.32457
1980-05-01	13.11544
1980-06-01	13.234943
1980-07-01	14.041587
1980-08-01	15.595124
1980-09-01	15.654876
1980-10-01	15.326243
1980-11-01	15.953633
1980-12-01	16.25239

Table 11: IBM Stock Price (IBM)

Date	Open
1986-04-01	0.095486
1986-05-01	0.111979
1986-06-01	0.121528
1986-07-01	0.106771
1986-08-01	0.098958
1986-09-01	0.098958
1986-10-01	0.09809
1986-11-01	0.135417
1986-12-01	0.172743

Table 12: Microsoft Stock Price (MSFT)

Date	Open
1985-01-01	1.1875
1985-02-01	1.421875
1985-03-01	1.429688
1985-04-01	1.398438
1985-05-01	1.46875
1985-06-01	1.671875
1985-07-01	1.742188
1985-08-01	1.5625
1985-09-01	1.613281
1985-10-01	1.492188
1985-11-01	1.648438
1985-12-01	1.84375

Table 13: Walmart Stock Price (WMT)

Date	Open
1985-01-01	2.645833
1985-02-01	3
1985-03-01	3.083333
1985-04-01	3.25
1985-05-01	3.135417
1985-06-01	3.666667
1985-07-01	3.520833
1985-08-01	3.270833
1985-09-01	3.291667
1985-10-01	3.166667
1985-11-01	3.260417
1985-12-01	3.75

Table 14: Target Stock Price (TGT)

Date	Open
1992-06-01	1.96875
1992-07-01	2.3125
1992-08-01	2.421875
1992-09-01	2.703125
1992-10-01	2.8125
1992-11-01	3.25
1992-12-01	3.734375

Table 15: Kohl's Corporation Stock Price (KSS)

3.4 Applying Support Vector Machine Analysis

To analyze unemployment's effects on each individual company, a binary classification machine learning model using the SVM algorithm was created. We explored three types of algorithms: Decision Tree classification, a Gaussian Naive Bayes classification, and an SVM classification; of these, the SVM algorithm provided the highest test accuracy and therefore was utilized to complete the study. Google Colab was used to build the machine learning model, as it is an open source application and can directly access the macroeconomic indicator csv data files stored in Google Drive. The SVM binary classification analysis conducted attempts to categorize all data points for a specific company into two classifications: stock prices that would grow by more than 1% in the next month, and those that would not. Then, the model calculated the rank of unemployment in the feature importance of the model for that company by using permutation-based importance. Permutation-based importance takes the values of a feature and shuffles them randomly to examine how much those shuffles degrade the model. If shuffling a feature degrades the model to a great extent, then that feature is significant to what the model examines. After unemployment's feature importance was established for every company, the rank of unemployment's feature importance out of the total 8 features in the model was averaged for the four technology companies and four retail companies. Lastly, the average ranks and the error on the average ranks for the two sectors were compared.

4. Results

First, I confirmed the anti-correlation between S&P 500 stock prices and unemployment by plotting their values as a function of time. When the unemployment rate rises, the price of the S&P 500 falls in accordance (Figure 2),

verifying the relationship found by Jareño and Negrut (2016).

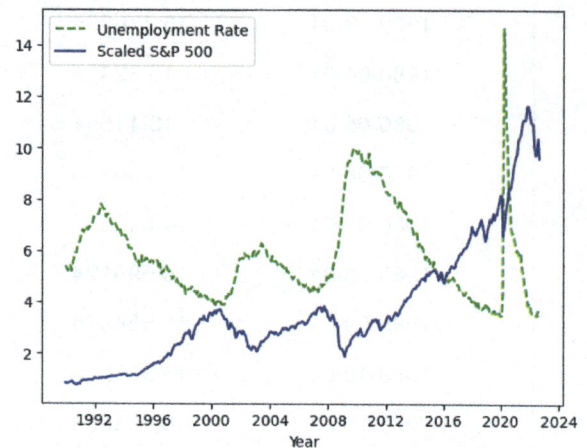

Figure 2: Unemployment and S&P 500 Anti-correlation Graph

Next, I investigated the relationship between stock prices and unemployment within the Tech and Retail sectors through constructing SVM models. A confusion matrix and feature importance plot was created for every individual stock (see example in Figure 3). After comparing the ranking of unemployment's feature importance in predicting the stock price of technology companies and retail companies, it was found that unemployment has a greater impact on the stock price of retail companies in comparison to technology companies. For each technology company, the relative importance of unemployment in predicting the stock price of the company was ranked at 7, 6, 6, 5 (Table 16). For each retail company, the relative importance of unemployment in predicting the stock price was ranked at 7, 2, 4, 3 (Table 16). The model's accuracy for each company and the average accuracy for each industry is shown in Table 15.

176

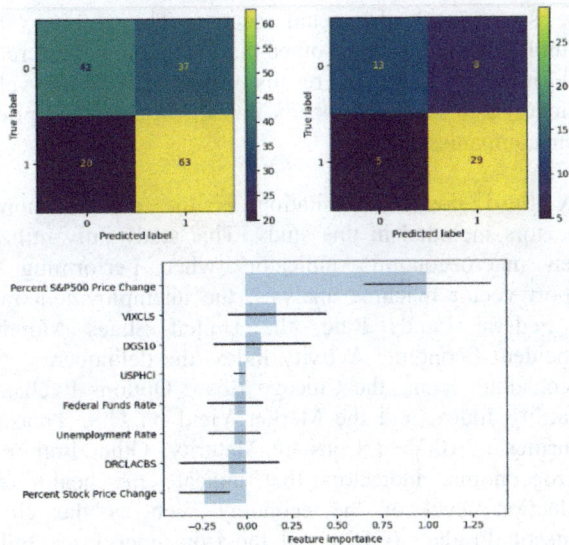

Figure 3: Train and Test Confusion Matrix and Feature Importance Plot (GOOGL)

All variables are defined in the methodology

Company:	Unemployment's Feature Importance Rank	Accuracy (Sgnificant to two places after the decimal)
AAPL	7	0.61
GOOGL	6	0.76
IBM	6	0.61
MSFT	5	0.65
WMT	7	0.52
TGT	2	0.58
KSS	4	0.52
AMZN	3	0.64
Average for Tech (AAPL, GOOGL, IBM, MSFT)	4.0 +/- 0.35	0.66
Average for Retail (WMT, TGT, KSS, AMZN)	6.0 +/- 0.94	0.57

Table 16: Unemployment Feature Importance Ranking and Accuracy Table

Table 16 demonstrates unemployment's feature importance for every company examined. The accuracy of the SVM model for each company is also provided

The average rank of unemployment's feature importance for retail companies is 4 and the average rank of unemployment's feature importance for technology companies is 6 (Figure 4).

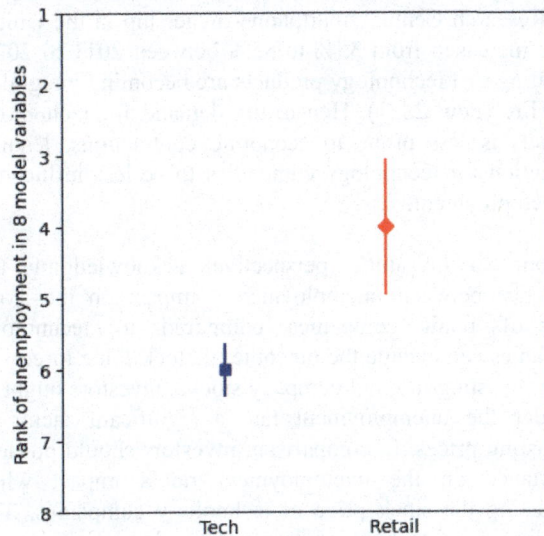

Figure 4: Average Unemployment Feature Importance Ranking

Figure 4 demonstrates the average ranking of unemployment's feature importance in predicting the stock prices of the companies in each of the three company sections

5. Discussion

The relative ranking of unemployment's feature importance in predicting future stock prices shows that unemployment has a greater impact on the stock prices of retail companies compared to technology companies. For technology companies, the unemployment rate ranks as the 6th most important out of eight indicators, indicating that the unemployment only holds a minimal impact over the stock price of technology companies. In comparison, the unemployment rate ranks as the 4th most important out of eight indicators for retail companies, indicating that unemployment has a moderate impact over the stock prices of retail companies. Ranking 6th and 4th indicate a significant difference, leading to the conclusion that the

177

Franklin Education Foundation   Using SVM Analysis to Compare the Relative Importance of Unemployment on Technology Stocks and Retail Stocks

Journal of Quantitative and Qualitative Research   Jiuxi Wang

unemployment rate holds more impact on the stock prices of retail companies than on technology companies.

One possible explanation is the difference in employment between the two industries; the technology industry employs less than one-fifth (18.6%) of the number of workers as the retail industry. Also, tech workers tend to possess a higher skill set. Hence, lower employment numbers and a higher employee skill level appear to insulate technology companies from the effects of unemployment in terms of output. Another possible explanation is the increasing demand for technology products. According to Pew Research Center, smartphone ownership in the United States increased from 35% to 85% between 2011 to 2021, indicating that technology products are becoming integral in daily life (Pew 2021). Hence, the demand for technology products is less prone to economic contractions, leading production for technology companies to be less influenced by unemployment.

From an investor's perspective, acknowledging the difference between unemployment's impact on the stock price of retail companies compared to technology companies can change the outcome of stock price forecasts. When investing in retail company stocks, investors ought to consider the unemployment rate a significant factor in forecasting prices. In comparison, investors should put less importance on the unemployment rate's impact when forecasting the stock price of technology companies. The accessibility of technology has resulted in an increase in retail purchasing online, leading technology companies' revenues may be less impacted by unemployment, meaning that investors can consider technology companies as a safer investment option during economic contractions.

6. Limitation

Although my hypothesis is affirmed by the results of my study, there are limitations worth acknowledging. Firstly, my support vector machine analysis is not as accurate as the one conducted in Zhu's study. In contrast, Zhu's analysis had an average accuracy of 70% (Zhu et. al 2013), while my support vector machine analysis had an average accuracy of around 60%. The lower accuracy of my analysis can potentially indicate that my results are not as significant as is stated in the discussion section. When I was conducting the support vector machine analysis, there were no forewarnings of my model's accuracy prior to obtaining my results.

Another potential limitation is the type of unemployment data used in the study. My unemployment dataset consisted of the entire U.S. economy instead of being specific to the

tech sector and the retail sector. This means that unemployment in sectors other than technology and retail could have influenced the results of this study to overvalue or undervalue unemployment's impact on the stock prices of the companies studied.

A third possible limitation is the macroeconomic indicators included in this study. This study only utilized seven macroeconomic indicators when performing its support vector machine analysis: the unemployment rate, the Federal Funds Rate, the United States Monthly Coincident Economic Activity Index, the delinquency rate on consumer loans, the Chicago Board Options Exchange Volatility Index, and the Market Yield on U.S. Treasury Securities at 10-Year Constant Maturity. Other important macroeconomic indicators that indicate the health and production level of the economy such as the Gross Domestic Product (GDP) and the Consumer Price Index (CPI) were not used in this study. Not all major macroeconomic indicators were utilized, potentially leading to skewed results.

Lastly, not all major companies in the retail and technology sector were examined. I selected companies based on my familiarity. The companies examined in this study varied widely within the top 30 in terms of market share for their respective industries. Future studies could incorporate more macroeconomic indicators, use sector-specific unemployment data if possible, and attempt to build a more accurate model.

7. Future Studies

More research should be conducted to address the potential flaws in this study. Future research could have a more comprehensive use of macroeconomic data when building their models to perform support vector machine analysis. In addition, future studies should examine a wider variety of companies in order to test the validity of the results derived in this study. Lastly, future studies should design their models to achieve a higher accuracy.

I plan to build on my research by addressing the limitations of my study. For future analysis, I will still focus on analyzing the stock price of specific companies, although I would select multiple other large firms in the technology and retail sector to test the validity of the results derived by my study. This would more accurately reflect the difference of unemployment's impact on the stock prices of technology and retail company stocks. In addition, I would add more macroeconomic indicators such as GDP and CPI to increase the accuracy of my support vector machine analysis to match the accuracy of support vector machine analysis in similar studies. Lastly, I would analyze the effects of unemployment in specifically the technology sector and retail sector to eliminate the impact of unemployment in other industries. By selecting a higher quantity of industry specific data, I will come closer to finding a more accurate understanding of how the impact of unemployment on the stock price of retail companies compares to its impact on the stock price of tech companies.

8. Reference

[1] "12 Biggest Industries in the US Heading into 2023." *Yahoo!*, Yahoo!, https://www.yahoo.com/now/12-biggest-industries-us-heading-210111831.html.

[2] Algieri, Bernardina, et al. "Stock Market Volatility, Speculation and Unemployment: A Granger-Causality Analysis." *PSL Quarterly Review*, vol. 73, no. 293, June 2020, pp. 137–160., https://doi.org/10.13133/2037-3643_73.293_3.

[3] "Alphabet Inc. (GOOGL) Stock Historical Prices & Data." *Yahoo! Finance*, Yahoo!, 8 Jan. 2023, https://finance.yahoo.com/quote/GOOGL/history?period1=1092960000&period2=1667260800&interval=1mo&filter=history&frequency=1mo&includeAdjustedClose=true.

[4] "Amazon.com, Inc. (AMZN) Stock Historical Prices & Data." *Yahoo! Finance*, Yahoo!, 8 Jan. 2023, https://finance.yahoo.com/quote/AMZN/history?period1=863654400&period2=1667260800&interval=1mo&filter=history&frequency=1mo&includeAdjustedClose=true.

[5] "Apple Inc. (AAPL) Stock Historical Prices & Data." *Yahoo! Finance*, Yahoo!, 8 Jan. 2023, https://finance.yahoo.com/quote/AAPL/history?period1=345427200&period2=1667260800&interval=1mo&filter=history&frequency=1mo&includeAdjustedClose=true.

[6] Bernanke, Ben, and Kenneth Kuttner. "What Explains the Stock Market's Reaction to Federal Reserve Policy?" *Journal of Finance*, vol. 60, no. 3, 3 May 2005, pp. 1221–1257., https://doi.org/10.1111/j.1540-6261.2005.00760.x.

[7] Bhutta, Neil, et al. "Changes in U.S. Family Finances from 2016 to 2019: Evidence from the Survey of Consumer Finances." *Federal Reserve Bulletin*, vol. 106, no. 5, 2020, pp. 1–42., https://doi.org/10.17016/bulletin.2020.106.

[8] Boyd, John H., et al. "The Stock Market's Reaction to Unemployment News: Why Ad News Is Usually Good for Stocks." *The Journal of Finance*, vol. 60, no. 2, 2005, pp. 649–672., https://doi.org/10.1111/j.1540-6261.2005.00742.x.

[9] "Bureau of Labor Statistics Data." *U.S. Bureau of Labor Statistics*, U.S. Bureau of Labor Statistics, 2023, https://data.bls.gov/timeseries/LNS14000000.

[10] "CBOE Volatility Index: VIX." *FRED*, Federal Reserve Bank of St. Louis, 6 Apr. 2023, https://fred.stlouisfed.org/series/VIXCLS.

[11] Chi, David. Semantic Scholar, 2021, *Unanticipated Unemployment Rate News on the Stock Market*. Accessed 1 Jan. 2023.

[12] "Coincident Economic Activity Index for the United States." *FRED*, Federal Reserve Bank of St. Louis, 4 Apr. 2023, https://fred.stlouisfed.org/series/USPHCI.

[13] "Delinquency Rate on Consumer Loans, All Commercial Banks." *FRED*, Federal Reserve Bank of St. Louis, 21 Feb. 2023, https://fred.stlouisfed.org/series/DRCLACBS.

[14] Esipov, Mikhail. *An Analysis of the S&P500's Overnight Reaction to Unemployment Rate Surprise and an Analysis of the Forecasting Power of Gallup's Unemployment Rate Estimates, New York University*, May 2010, https://www.stern.nyu.edu/sites/default/files/assets/documents/con_043006.pdf. Accessed 1 Apr. 2023.

[15] "Federal Funds Effective Rate." *FRED*, Federal Reserve Bank of St. Louis, 3 Apr. 2023, https://fred.stlouisfed.org/series/FEDFUNDS.

[16] Gonzalo, Jesús, and Abderrahim Taamouti. "The Reaction of Stock Market Returns to Unemployment." *Studies in Nonlinear Dynamics & Econometrics*, vol. 21, no. 4, 2017, https://doi.org/10.1515/snde-2015-0078.

[17] Han, Shuo, and Rung-Ching Chen. "Using SVM with Financial Statement Analysis for Prediction of Stocks." *Communications of the IIMA*, vol. 7, no. 4, 2007, https://doi.org/10.58729/1941-6687.1059.

[18] "International Business Machines Corporation (IBM) Stock Historical Prices & Data." *Yahoo! Finance*, Yahoo!, 8 Jan. 2023, https://finance.yahoo.com/quote/IBM/history?period1=315532800&period2=1667260800&interval=1mo&filter=history&frequency=1mo&includeAdjustedClose=true.

[19] "International Standard Classification of Occupations (ISCO)." *ILOSTAT*, International Labour Organization , https://ilostat.ilo.org/resources/concepts-and-definitions/classification-occupation/.

[20] Italo Zoppis, Giancarlo Mauri, Riccardo Dondi, Kernel Methods: Support Vector Machines, Encyclopedia of Bioinformatics and Computational Biology, Academic Press, 2019, Pages 503-510, https://doi.org/10.1016/B978-0-12-809633-8.20342-7.

[21] Jareño, Francisco, and Loredana Negrut. "US Stock Market And Macroeconomic Factors." *The Journal of Applied Business Research* , vol. 32, no. 1, Jan. 2016, pp. 325–340., https://doi.org/10.19030/jabr.v32i1.9541.

[22] "Kohl's Corporation (KSS) Stock Historical Prices & Data." *Yahoo! Finance*, Yahoo!, 8 Jan. 2023, https://finance.yahoo.com/quote/KSS/history?period1=706320000&period2=1667260800&interval=1mo&filter=history&frequency=1mo&includeAdjustedClose=true.

[23] Khan, M.N., Zaman, S. (2012). Impact of Macroeconomic Variables on Stock Prices: Empirical Evidence from Karachi Stock Exchange, Pakistan. In: Zhu, M. (eds) Business, Economics, Financial Sciences, and Management. Advances in Intelligent and Soft Computing, vol 143. Springer, Berlin, Heidelberg. https://doi.org/10.1007/978-3-642-27966-9_32

[24] "Largest Tech Companies by Market Cap." *CompaniesMarketCap.com - Companies Ranked by Market Capitalization*, https://companiesmarketcap.com/tech/largest-tech-companies-by-market-cap/.

[25] "Market Yield on U.S. Treasury Securities at 10-Year Constant Maturity, Quoted on an Investment Basis." *FRED*, Federal Reserve Bank of St. Louis, 7 Apr. 2023, https://fred.stlouisfed.org/series/DGS10.

[26] "Microsoft Corporation (MSFT) Stock Historical Prices & Data." *Yahoo! Finance*, Yahoo!, 8 Jan. 2023, https://finance.yahoo.com/quote/MSFT/history?period1=511142400&period2=1667260800&interval=1mo&filter=history&frequency=1mo&includeAdjustedClose=true.

[27] "Mobile Fact Sheet." *Pew Research Center: Internet, Science & Tech*, Pew Research Center, 3 Apr. 2023, https://www.pewresearch.org/internet/fact-sheet/mobile/.

[28] Osiemo, John R. "Relationship Between Unemployment and Stock Prices of Retail Companies: Correlational Study." *University of Phoenix* , ProQuest, 2016, pp. 1–132.

[29] Pan, Wei-Fong. "Does the Stock Market Really Cause Unemployment? A Cross-Country Analysis." *The North American Journal of Economics and Finance*, vol. 44, Apr. 2018, pp. 34–43., https://doi.org/10.1016/j.najef.2017.11.002.

[30] "Shares of Gross Domestic Product: Personal Consumption Expenditures." *FRED*, Federal Reserve Bank of St. Louis, 23 Feb. 2023, https://fred.stlouisfed.org/series/DPCERE1Q156NBEA.

[31] "S&P 500 (^GSPC) Historical Data." *Yahoo! Finance*, Yahoo!, 15 Jan. 2023, https://finance.yahoo.com/quote/%5EGSPC/history?period1=315532800&period2=1667260800&interval=1d&filter=history&frequency=1d&includeAdjustedClose=true.

[32] "Target Corporation (TGT) Stock Historical Prices & Data." *Yahoo! Finance*, Yahoo!, 8 Jan. 2023, https://finance.yahoo.com/quote/TGT/history?period1=315619200&period2=1667260800&interval=1mo&filter=history&frequency=1mo&includeAdjustedClose=true.

[33] "Top 100 Retailers 2022 List." *NRF*, National Retail Federation, https://nrf.com/resources/top-retailers/top-100-retailers/top-100-retailers-2022-list.

[34] USAFacts. "What Percentage of Americans Own Stock?" *USAFacts*, USAFacts, 9 Mar. 2021, https://usafacts.org/articles/what-percentage-of-americans-own-stock/.

[35] Vijh, Mehar, et al. "Stock Closing Price Prediction Using Machine Learning Techniques." *Procedia Computer Science*, vol. 167, 2020, pp. 599–606., https://doi.org/https://doi.org/10.1016/j.procs.2020.03.326.

[36] "Walmart Inc. (WMT) Stock Historical Prices & Data." *Yahoo! Finance*, Yahoo!, 8 Jan. 2023, https://finance.yahoo.com/quote/WMT/history?period1=315619200&period2=1667260800&interval=1mo&filter=history&frequency=1mo&includeAdjustedClose=true.

[37] Z. Hu, J. Zhu and K. Tse, "Stocks market prediction using Support Vector Machine," *2013 6th International Conference on Information Management, Innovation Management and Industrial Engineering*, Xi'an, China, 2013, pp. 115-118, doi: 10.1109/ICIII.2013.6703096.

Made in the USA
Monee, IL
02 December 2023